MAJOR GENERAL GEORGE G. MEADE

THE BATTLE OF
GETTYSBURG

A COMPREHENSIVE NARRATIVE

BY

JESSE BOWMAN YOUNG
AN OFFICER IN THE CAMPAIGN

WITH MAPS, PLANS
AND ILLUSTRATIONS

JOHN KALLMANN, PUBLISHERS
701 West North St. • Carlisle, PA 17013

THE GETTYSBURG ORATION

OF

ABRAHAM LINCOLN

Fourscore and seven years ago our fathers brought forth on this continent a new nation, conceived in liberty, and dedicated to the proposition that all men are created equal.

Now we are engaged in a great civil war, testing whether that nation, or any nation so conceived and so dedicated, can long endure. We are met on a great battle-field of that war. We have come to dedicate a portion of that field as a final resting-place for those who here gave their lives that that nation might live. It is altogether fitting and proper that we should do this.

But, in a larger sense, we cannot dedicate, we cannot consecrate, we cannot hallow this ground. The brave men, living and dead, who struggled here have consecrated it far above our poor power to add or detract. The world will little note, nor long remember, what we say here, but it can never forget what they did here. It is for us the living, rather, to be dedicated here to the unfinished work which they who fought here have thus far so nobly advanced. It is rather for us to be here dedicated to the great task remaining before us, that from these honored dead we take increased devotion to that cause for which they gave the last full measure of devotion; that we here highly resolve that these dead shall not have died in vain; that this nation, under God, shall have a new birth of freedom; and that government of the people, by the people, for the people, shall not perish from the earth.

CONTENTS

Part I

PRELIMINARY SURVEY

Part II

THE NARRATIVE OF THE BATTLE

CONTENTS

FIRST DAY

SECOND DAY

THIRD DAY

CONTENTS

Part III

THE OPPOSING ARMIES—EN MASSE AND IN DETAIL

ILLUSTRATIONS

MAPS AND PLANS

ILLUSTRATIONS

PREFACE

About the Author and His Book

Jesse Bowman Young, the son of the Rev. Jared H. Young and Sarah Bowman Young, was born on the day after Independence Day, July 5, 1844, in Berwick, Pennsylvania. In just nineteen years, as a First Lieutenant in the 84th Pennsylvania Volunteers, the youth had experienced the most momentous event in the history of the United States, the Battle of Gettysburg and what is now called the Gettysburg campaign. At the beginning of the campaign, the youthful officer was detached from his regiment and assigned staff duty with General Andrew A. Humphreys. At the time of the battle, Young was acting Assistant Provost Marshal. Of this role, the author wrote modestly in 1913, "In this capacity, I took part in the campaign, my duties on the march and in the battle giving me unusual opportunities, in view of my youth, to be in personal touch with the great movement."

If it were only for his eyewitness observations, the author would be in competition with thousands of others who could make the same claim. Even considering his advantaged position, this alone cannot make the thoroughgoing piece of writing and investigation that is presented in this fine book. The author has read and utilized most available first-hand accounts, official reports and documents. As a post-war resident of the immediate Gettysburg area, "circuit rider" Young was able to criss-cross every road and pass, see every field, orchard, farm, to sense the terrain. The modern army officer candidate today is routinely indoctrinated with a course in "terrain studies," something Young was doing before the discipline had a name.

First-hand eyewitness and a sense of the landscape were certainly valuable elements in writing an authoritative account of Gettysburg. This is indisputable. But what distinguishes this text from the miles of printed pages published before and after Jesse Bowman Young's book?

The special element in Young's writing is his synthesis of primary source information, presented in a clear and succinct way that encourages the reader to delve deeper into the great questions of this historical event, the Gettysburg campaign of June and July of 1863. Although not recognized by the participants at the time, the northern advance of the Army of Northern Virginia was to become a turning point in the war. The author frequently describes this in the text as "pivotal."

There is yet a fourth dimension, if you will. This has to do with what the author has done with the above mentioned sources and personal experiences. We refer to synthesis in our last point. Young takes it a step further. The essence of this extra step was expressed by H. W. Boynton in his front-page *New York Times Book Review* critique:

"The extraordinary thing is that Mr. Young has succeeded in assimilating all his materials, and instead of making a book out of them, has

PREFACE

presented an interpretation which owes something to them, but more to his own constructive insight. The reader will turn from this volume with a clear and consistent impression of a crucial episode in our history as a nation." —Excerpted from *New York Times Book Review,* Sunday June 29, 1913, pp. 377–8.

The author's childhood was quiet and studious, growing up in a household where his father was a Methodist clergyman. The *Dictionary of American Biography* describes the young man as, "A pale, delicate-looking boy, fond of books and averse to outdoor activities. . . ." His parents sent him to do his college preparatory studies at Dickinson Seminary in Williamsport, Pennsylvania where he would follow in his father's footsteps. In the interim came the great rebellion and Young had patriotic feelings, plus he had an uncle, Major Samuel M. Bowman of the 4th Illinois Cavalry, whom he wished to emulate. At first his mother tried to stop the young man, but he eventually enlisted at the tender age of seventeen in his uncle's Illinois unit. A year later, his uncle transferred to the 84th Pennsylvania Volunteers and Jesse Bowman Young followed. Young remained with the regiment, taking the special assignment mentioned above, and served until mustered out as a captain in December 1864 with three years of service.

Returning to Dickinson Seminary, Young completed his preparatory studies and advanced to Dickinson College in Carlisle, Pennsylvania, receiving an A.B. degree in 1868. At commencement, Young was bestowed with one of two medals awarded for distinction in writing. The other medalist was John Franklin Goucher, later an educator, philanthropist and founder of what is now Goucher College near Baltimore.

In keeping with his father's vocation, Young was ordained as a minister in the Central Pennsylvania Conference of the Methodist Episcopal Church, serving as a deacon in 1870 and an elder in 1872 and as a traveling pastor in the south central Pennsylvania region until 1888. It was during this period of "circuit riding" through the Gettysburg approaches that pastor Young relived his soldiering experiences in the area, "the air was then vibrant with reminiscences of the battle; every crossroad and orchard and farmhouse, every man, woman, and child had a story to tell."

For many years, Young lived in the vicinity of Gettysburg and for three years he lived in the town itself. During that period of residence, he explored every acre if not every square foot of the great battlefield and its voluminous literature. Young knew, "almost literally the location of every organization on either side which took part in the engagement."

Young's first published book on the U.S. Civil War was *What a Boy Saw in the Army,* illustrated in pen and ink drawings by the famous artist, Frank Beard (Thomas Francis Beard, 1842–1905), a prolific contributor to the wartime weeklies, *Leslie's Weekly* and *Harper's Weekly.* Beard, born in Cincinnati, served in a Southern Ohio Regiment during the Civil War. Designed for a young reader audience, this popular book was published in 1894, setting a high standard for graphic presentation and adolescent appeal.

PREFACE

A prolific writer, Jesse Bowman Young wrote extensively on religious subjects in numerous books and articles over three decades from the 1880 to 1910, yet the book for which he is best known is this one, *The Battle of Gettysburg,* "A book indeed which will have a permanent value."—A.M. Chase, *Bookman,* July 1913, p. 566. Published in June 1913, on the eve of the 50th Anniversary of the campaign, this book is one of the last links to living participants with scholarly and literary merit.

April 15, 1996   John Kallmann, Publishers

PART ONE

PRELIMINARY SURVEY

THE BATTLE OF
GETTYSBURG

I

INTRODUCTION

THE man who at this remove from the events
in question ventures upon a fresh survey of the
campaign and battle of Gettysburg, particularly in
view of the body of literature already bearing on that
theme, owes to himself and to the public a representation of the sufficing reasons which may be alleged
to justify the enterprise.

Accordingly, my motives in the preparation of this
work, and an intimation of the special features which
distinguish it, may herewith be rehearsed.

(1) Although but a stripling, I was an officer in
the battle. While serving as First Lieutenant,
Company B, Eighty-fourth Pennsylvania Infantry, I
was detached from my regiment, at the opening of
the campaign, two days after we had left our winter
rendezvous at Falmouth, and assigned to duty at the
headquarters of that great soldier, Brig. Gen. Andrew
A. Humphreys, as assistant provost marshal, Second
Division, Third Army Corps. In this capacity I took
part in the campaign, my duties on the march and in

2   3

battle giving me unusual opportunities, in view of my youth, to be in personal touch with the great movement.

(2) For a dozen years after the war I resided almost continuously in the Cumberland Valley, Pennsylvania, and in Adams County adjoining, of which Gettysburg is the county-seat, for three years of that time in Gettysburg itself; my duties as a "circuit-rider" leading me in due time, week by week, over all the roads traversed by the two armies which fought on that field. I thus became in a singular way familiar with every village, thoroughfare, and mountain-pass connected in any way with the campaign, from the Potomac to the Susquehanna and throughout the intervening territory. During those years the different landscapes, along with the incidents and movements in question, wove themselves into panoramic visions in my brain so vividly that they have become an indelible part of my experience. The air was then vibrant with reminiscences of the battle; every crossroad and orchard and farm-house, every man, woman, and child, had a story to tell concerning the marching of the two militant hosts to and from the place of encounter, the tragic phases of the fight, and the later scenes in the hospitals—these, in their cumulative impressions, interfibering with my own experiences and observations, helped to make it imperative that I should in due time organize at least some of the data into a narrative.

(3) During my residence in Gettysburg I came to know by personal contact and daily study every foot of the great battle-field, and almost literally the loca-

tion of every organization on either side which took part in the engagement.

Many circumstances tended to reproduce the shifting scenes and manœuvers of the campaign and battle before my imagination, and to inscribe them in my soul. I knew the veteran guides who had made it their vocation to go over the field every day, gathering up fresh impressions and reminiscences from survivors returning to revisit the place; and I was furthermore advantaged by intimate friendship with the men who organized the Battle-field Memorial Association, out of whose prescient plans came the formation of the National Cemetery, and then the Military Park, famous for its historic associations and its hundreds of monuments, surpassing anything of the kind in the world—who almost from the day the battle ended began to gather up historical material bearing on the campaign — men like David Wills, David McConaughy, David A. Buehler, long-time editor of the *Star and Sentinel*, and his brothers, Col. C. H. Buehler and A. D. Buehler, types of civic worth and patriotic citizenship; John Lawrence Schick; Professor M. Jacobs and his coworkers in the Lutheran Theological Seminary and Pennsylvania College; and the Hon. Edward McPherson, for years the clerk of the House of Representatives at Washington, and famous throughout the world as a statistician, and an authority on current political history.

In the midst of these scenes, and prompted by these unusual associations and stimuli, I prepared a lecture on the engagement, "The Story of a Great

Battle," which was delivered hundreds of times. Some twenty years later, in the early nineties, I went over my material, old and new, and incorporated it afresh in three chapters of my volume, *What a Boy Saw in the Army*. These tasks—although the by-products of a busy life—served to keep Gettysburg constantly in mind, so that from year to year all new data which came to light in the form of reminiscences, personal experiences, and military criticisms from leading officers were instinctively seized upon and assimilated. Hence it can hardly be a matter of wonder that this narrative has been in due time evolved.

(4) A further event which deepened my interest in the battle was the commemoration prepared by Pennsylvania in remembrance of her soldier sons, and embodied in the magnificent memorial erected by that Commonwealth on the field in September, 1910. In advance of that celebration I was attracted to study afresh the record made in the campaign by Pennsylvania officers and men, and to locate and define the work of each individual organization furnished by the Commonwealth, some of the products of that self-imposed task being at the time published in the *Philadelphia Press*, *The Philadelphia Record*, and other journals. These studies proved so fructifying to my own mind, and awakened such interest on the part of some who read them, that I was gradually led to undertake the broader range of inquiry and the comprehensive plans which have at last eventuated in this completed form.

INTRODUCTION

(5) In pursuing this enterprise my recent residence of four years in Jacksonville, Florida, gave me access to a fresh body of information concerning the men and movements of the Army of Northern Virginia, information wholly new to the great mass of the reading public and known only to expert students here and there in the land—such as the *Confederate Military History* compiled a few years ago under the editorial supervision of the late Maj. Gen. Clement A. Evans, of Atlanta, in twelve octavo volumes, which are wonderfully rich in biographical material, and which include the detailed record of every Southern State in the Civil War, with its contribution of regiments and batteries to the armies of the Confederacy; the similar enterprise in half a dozen large volumes pertaining to the troops of North Carolina, and many other works rich in Confederate memorabilia.

Moreover, the volumes of Southern reminiscences, many of them of recent origin, written by Longstreet, Early, Gordon, Hood, Alexander, Sorrel, Mosby, McKim, Oates, Long, Taylor, Robert Stiles, Mrs. Pickett, and others have been carefully read, and from them occasional bits of comment, adventure, and criticism have been with due credit woven into the story. The light thus shed upon the campaign and battle, and the information thus secured as to the leading officers of Lee, and hosts of lesser rank, form, it is believed, an unusual element of value in the work, particularly as the country at large, and even many studious readers, have been able up to this time to secure only a nebulous and wholly inadequate notion of the official personnel of Lee's army.

It has been a grateful service to indicate in this relation the later and larger patriotic work of many surviving ex-Confederates in the service they have rendered in the creation of the New South, the establishment of a reunited nation, and the development of American civic life. For illustrations of new light thrown on the records of noted Confederate leaders reference may be made to the sketches of Armistead, Gordon, Kemper, Barksdale, Pickett, Hilary A. Herbert, and Trimble—to go no farther. In most cases the sketches are of necessity brief— thumb-nail portraits—but they are based on a great mass of vitalizing data freshly gathered from official documents, biographical annals, unusual volumes, private letters, and other memoranda, which for the first time—in many cases, at least—bring out clearly and fully the record of the men thus portrayed.

(6) Necessarily the portions of the *Official Records* dealing with the Gettysburg campaign—namely, Parts I, II, and III, in what is styled Volume XXVII, each "Part" being an octavo volume of more than a thousand pages—have been read and reread again and again. The thesaurus of which they form a part, making in all a library of a hundred and twenty-eight octavo books, issued by the United States Government, is a literary and historical treasure-house the like of which has never been created by any other nation. No student can consult these volumes without feeling afresh the debt he owes to the skil-

ful, alert, and accomplished men who for years carried forward to completion the colossal enterprise.

Much other material has been in hand, particularly those magnificent volumes *New York at Gettysburg* and *Pennsylvania at Gettysburg*, enriched with maps, portraits, biographical sketches, regimental and battery annals, and the pictures of many scores of monuments; and in addition books or booklets of similar scope from other Commonwealths. The papers in the *Century War Book*, various writings from the pens of Humphreys, Walker, Howard, Schurz, Doubleday, and other officers of the Union Army; the critical works produced on the other side of the sea by John Formby and Cecil Battine; the various *Lives* of Lee and of Meade, particularly Pennypacker's biography of the latter; and much other collateral literature, criticism, and memoranda in the *Nation*, and in other journals and magazines— to all this material assiduous attention has been given. The effort has been made to scan, analyze, and organize, so far as possible, all the information in print bearing on the subject in hand; and especially to give heed to critical questions pertaining to the campaign or fight. Occasional citations from experts will be found here and there in this respect, but at the same time the writer has endeavored to form an independent judgment on every disputed point, and to compose a fresh and individual narrative, and not offer to the public a mere compilation of the work of other historians.

It may be taken as a matter of course that no well-informed man would undertake to write elaborately of this battle without having at hand, for at least occasional consultation, the great work of the Comte de Paris, *The History of the Civil War in America*, translated with masterly skill by Col. John P. Nicholson, for many years at the head of the Gettysburg Park Commission, himself an officer in the battle, who was at the end of the war thrice brevetted for gallantry.

(7) The manifold personal sketches throughout the work involve the careers not only of all the general officers in both armies, including many colonels commanding brigades, but also many other gallant officers whose later history indicates them as worthy of special mention. It is a revelation in this respect, as we study the muster-rolls on either side, to group the company of distinguished men whose names appear in the records of this engagement, distinguished not only for what they did at Gettysburg, but for later achievements as Cabinet officers, foreign ministers, Senators, Congressmen, Governors, and judges. Three or four instances pertaining to the Regular Army may be taken as illustrations: the late Maj. Gen. Charles L. Hodges, who completed his half-century of service in the army not long before his recent retirement and later decease, in 1911, was a private soldier at Gettysburg; and three of our retired lieutenant generals did heroic things in the battle: S. B. M. Young as a major in the Fourth Pennsylvania Cavalry; Adna R. Chaffee as a second lieutenant in the Sixth Regular Cavalry; and John C. Bates as captain in the Eleventh Infantry, and aide-de-camp to Maj. Gen. Meade; while two of our most distinguished major-

generals now on the retired list won great credit for their services there, the one being then known as Col. John R. Brooke, of the Fifty-third Pennsylvania Infantry, and the other as First Lieut. James F. Wade, Sixth Regular Cavalry, and aide-de-camp to Pleasanton, winning in the campaign his first brevet, to a captaincy. As a further instance of the gifts and skill represented at Gettysburg it may be worth while to suggest that five officers then under Meade's command afterward rose to the highest post of military efficiency in the Regular Army— that of Chief of Engineers—Generals Humphreys, Wright, and Newton; Capt. John W. Barlow, and Lieut. George L. Gillespie.

Another feature of this work is its compact array of the entire record of all West Point graduates who served in the campaign and battle, including those who were in the Army of Northern Virginia. Wherever possible the effort has also been made to indicate those who had a partial training at West Point. We are aware of no previous effort to show the extent to which the Military Academy has been represented by its alumni in various positions and services in any campaign or battle of the Civil War. Even a casual study of the magnificent record in this regard unfolded in our volume will serve to suggest the incalculable debt which the nation owes to that school for the services rendered by her graduates in the exigent posts of responsibility in which they served the Republic.

In the case of Lee's army it has been possible in most cases also to indicate the scholastic and military training of officers who were not West-Pointers but who had the opportunity of an equipment conferred by other military schools. This record in the aggregate shows that Lee had under him an extraordinary number of officers who were equipped either by previous military experience or by their schooling for posts of command.

(8) The extraordinary record made in later years by subalterns of the Regular Army on duty in the battle, in most cases apart from the list of West Point graduates—young men hardly out of their teens—finds some measure of recognition in an addendum to the Roster in Part Three. The data there, for the first time collated and emphasized, help one to realize the remarkable quality of soldierly material embodied in the broken and depleted regiments and batteries of regulars in the battle.

(9) The death-list of officers on both sides is as complete as careful research can make it. In some cases the Southern records are entirely deficient in this regard. Sometimes the commanders failed to make report after a battle; in other cases the reports were lost or destroyed in the exigencies of war; at Vicksburg, for example, valuable muster-rolls were mislaid, hidden, or thrown away, and records contained therein were never replaced. Data of priceless value to some of the Southern States are accordingly now beyond reach.

(10) Some incidents illustrative of extraordinary valor, deeds performed by private soldiers, color-bearers, non-commissioned or commissioned officers, often in the hour and article of death, are now and

INTRODUCTION

then briefly recited. These incidents, hitherto scattered and hidden in the midst of thousands of pages of Government reports or in hundreds of regimental records, are abundantly worthy of preservation; they deserve to be kept in the foreground of our annals, since they embody in heroic individual achievement what Mr. Lincoln in his speech at Gettysburg so well defined as "the last full measure of devotion," often exhibited by valiant soldiers who for liberty and Union were shedding their blood on that hallowed ground.

It remains only to add that this volume has been prepared in view of the semi-centennial of the battle, the fifty-year period, July 1-3, 1863—July 1-3, 1913, with the hope that it may be found to contain a valuable body of information, a fresh treatment of some phases of the campaign not hitherto fully utilized, and a worthy contribution to the literature of the Great Battle.[1]

[1] For skilful labor in preparing this manuscript for the publishers, in verifying names and other data, and for valuable suggestions in the case, I am indebted to my son, Jared Wilson Young, LL.B., of Chicago. It chanced that he was born at Gettysburg years after the battle, in a parsonage whose shattered upper wall bore an unexploded shell which lodged therein during the cannonade. That fact in after-time may have helped to interest him in the various phases of the battle; or he may have been impressed with the example of his paternal great-grandfather, Maj. John Young, of the Pennsylvania troops in the War of 1812; or he may have had a pardonable filial admiration for my own three years of soldier life; or perhaps his own experience in the Spanish-American conflict as a sergeant of the First Missouri Infantry, or all of these together, may have given him an unusual appreciation of what the Great War really meant for America and for the world—at any rate, he has given me a goodly measure of help in making this book what it is.   J. B. Y.

II

ON what grounds did General Lee make his plans for the invasion of the North in June, 1863? What reasons prompted him to undertake what is now known as the "Gettysburg campaign"? A careful study of the data in the case, and a discerning consideration of the manifold and complex motives which formed the basis of the whole movement, should throw light on this period of the war and aid us in apprehending the progressive phases of the campaign.

(1) One of the distinctive aims of General Lee, as indicated in his first report of the campaign (dated July 31, 1863, *Official Records*, XXVII, 2: 305), was to place, if possible, the Army of the Potomac in such straits by his advance that the authorities at Washington would be led to "draw to its support troops designed to operate against other parts of the country." It is a significant fact that when the Confederate commander revised his report in January, 1864, this phrase is omitted. It would appear that General Lee had himself come to see that the motive might have been discerned at the start to be invalid.

As every student of that period of the war must

at a glance apprehend, the particular point from
which Lee hoped that Union troops might be withdrawn for the defense of the threatened capital and
the imperiled Army of the Potomac, was Vicksburg,
in which besieged city, on the 18th of May, 1863,
General Pemberton had been shut in with thirty-
three thousand men, as the direct result of a series
of extraordinary manœuvers and battles planned by
Grant and executed under his personal leadership—
movements which illustrate in a monumental way
for all time the enterprise, the audacity, the courage,
and the military skill of that commander. That
keen strategist Joseph E. Johnston, foreseeing the
peril, in vain strove to safeguard Pemberton from
the policy by which he was finally forced to occupy
and hold the city of Vicksburg, where he would
inevitably be in a little while at the mercy of his
opponent. Pemberton, however, perverse and blind,
disobeyed the orders of Johnston, and was crowded
into straits which made it imperative, after a certain juncture had been passed, for him to shut himself up within the fortified hills which surrounded
the doomed city. Then Johnston found it impossible with the force at his command to interfere by
any attack on the assailing forces, and the authorities at Richmond were hopeless of affording relief
unless, perchance, Washington might be so straitly
threatened that, in order to relieve it from danger,
the army of Grant in front of Vicksburg might be
depleted by the withdrawal of an army corps or
two for temporary service in the region surrounding
the capital.

GETTYSBURG

As bearing on this point Gen. W. C. Oates, of the Confederate Army, in his volume *The War Between the Union and the Confederacy*, page 189, thus indicates the situation:

Mr. Davis held a conference with his Cabinet, Generals Lee, Longstreet, and others, as to the best way to relieve Vicksburg. Longstreet was in favor of transferring his troops to the West and collecting an army large enough to cope with Grant, draw him away, and relieve Vicksburg in that way. Lee favored the invasion of Pennsylvania, to let the people of that State feel the scourge of war, and imperil the Capital at Washington, which he believed would cause such a withdrawal of troops from Grant's army to send against his and protect Washington as to raise the siege and relieve Vicksburg. Mr. Davis adopted it [this plan] and ordered the campaign.

At this distance from the scene it is clearly evident that this part of the scheme was based on a delusive view of Grant's ability as a general and a mistaken apprehension of the whole situation. In such an emergency as a siege of Washington might possibly have presented the War Department had many other resources near at hand to draw upon, at Fort Monroe; at Suffolk, North Carolina; in General Schenck's department, and elsewhere, so that except in the direst extremity no one could in reason have thought of the possibility of interfering with Grant's campaign against the doomed city of Vicksburg in order to strengthen the Army of the Potomac. The hope that any movement of Lee at that juncture could disturb Grant's plans was clearly little better than a delusion.

(2) The hope of securing by a victorious campaign on Northern soil the recognition of the Confederacy

16

GENERAL ROBERT E. LEE

MOTIVES

by England and France was a distinctive element
in the campaign. John Formby, in a recent volume
—the most carefully wrought out work of the sort
made in compact shape by any foreign military
historian, *The Civil War in America*, Scribners, 1910
—thus defines the situation in this respect after the
Union reverse at Chancellorsville:

> The South was elated, thinking that the war could now be
> finished by another victory, this time on Northern soil. The
> reports of its agents, both abroad and in the Northern States,
> all spoke of a favorable change of opinion, that France was be-
> coming very civil, and England only waiting for some such event
> to recognize or even join them. [Page 194.]

The hope of foreign recognition was from the
beginning the very life-blood, the vitalizing suste-
nance, of the inchoate Confederacy. Skilful diplo-
mats had been sent abroad from time to time to
present the claims of the South to different European
governments and secure action from them, if possible allying them with the new political entity presumably established on Southern soil. The hopes
of these agents had been brightened by the victory
at Chancellorsville, and the spirits of many friends
of the Union in Great Britain had been thereby cor-
respondingly depressed. Meetings pro and con were
held in various parts of England, and the newspapers
were divided as to the propriety of recognition; but
most ardent efforts were being made at this juncture
to organize and establish sentiment in favor of the
South. In June, 1863, the Confederate commercial
agent in London wrote to Secretary of State Benjamin, at Richmond, concerning the prevalent

"people's movement" intended to help the South; and there appeared a "people's champion" in the House of Commons, where, on the 30th of June, the day before the opening gun was heard at Gettysburg, Mr. Roebuck had offered a motion instructing the English Government to "enter into negotiations with the great powers of Europe for the purpose of obtaining their co-operation in the recognition of the Confederacy." In advocating this motion Mr. Roebuck declared that he had recently had an interview with the Emperor of the French, who had declared his intention to act in this regard with England. Moreover, the streets of London had been, some weeks before that incident in the House of Commons, placarded in every available space with the newly adopted flag of the Confederacy, conjoined to the British national ensign, as a "demonstration," so reported the Southern agent in London, "to impress the masses with the vitality of our cause."[1]

Months before this Mr. Gladstone had declared publicly that the Southern States had organized "not only an army and a navy, but also a nation"; but it must be conceded that the English authorities had already, in the spring of 1863, called a halt in the enterprise of fitting out privateers for the Southern States, and a strong sentiment had begun to manifest itself in the country, organized and expressed by men like Goldwin Smith, Bright, Forster, and others, in favor of the principles and policy represented by the National Government in its life-and-death struggle

[1] For other data and a full representation of the status in England at this time, see James Ford Rhodes's *History*, vol. iv., chap. xxiv.

for existence. Yet, as matters then stood, if Lee
had won a decided victory in Pennsylvania, inflicting
an overwhelming disaster upon the Army of the
Potomac, and then marched either on the capital or
on Philadelphia, who can tell what calamities would
have followed? Unless there had been an immediate
rallying of the masses in force and a counter-stroke
had been inflicted upon Lee, the foes of the United
States on the other side of the Atlantic who had been
saying to one another, "Behold! the republican bub-
ble is about to burst," might have been able to secure
recognition of the Confederacy offhand. At any
rate, it was this hope and aim which were foremost
in the thought of the Cabinet at Richmond when it
sanctioned the forward movement.

(3) It was, of course, in Lee's mind by his proposed
campaign to relieve for the time being war-worn
Virginia from the burdens she had been bearing for two
years, and to transfer the scene of hostilities for a
while to regions which thus far had known none of
the horrors of the conflict, such as were evidenced
by the wasted fields, the empty homes, the barren
valleys of those sections of Virginia where both armies
in succession again and again had camped and
marched and fought.

(4) A further reason urging Lee to undertake an
offensive policy is to be found in the scarcity of food
supplies in the South, occasioned by the partial collapse of the whole system of railroad transportation
in that section. The tracks were worn out, the equi-
page was run down, and it was difficult to bring supplies of food, and utterly impossible to haul forage

from distant points to the region where Lee's army was encamped. The meat ration for his troops had been largely reduced; flour was scarce; and in order to guard against scurvy daily details during the winter and spring of 1863 had to be sent out to scour the fields and forests around Fredericksburg to gather edible weeds as a substitute for vegetables. A little over a hundred miles to the north from Fredericksburg were the bountiful harvest-fields of Pennsylvania, her full granaries, her farms with their stock of horses and cattle, and—this was a point to be heeded—her towns and cities with an ample supply of boots and shoes. It is no wonder that the chief commissary at Richmond suggested to the commander of the Army of Northern Virginia, "If General Lee wants rations, let him seek for them in Pennsylvania."

(5) The political and financial situation in the North, in 1863, inspired Lee and his generals, as well as the Confederate authorities, with hope. Dissensions were prevalent in the Union States; and here and there men openly advocated the doctrine that the war was a hopeless enterprise, that the Union could never be restored, and that it would be better to agree upon a treaty of peace with the South and let the Confederacy by common consent be established. In Wall Street, furthermore, gold had gone up with each announcement of Union defeat; the Government authorities were wellnigh distracted at the difficulties which beset them in their efforts to meet the enormous war expenses, notwithstanding the loyalty of the masses and the eagerness of multitudes to buy Government bonds and thus evince their faith in a

practical way in the permanence and credit of the nation. Under these circumstances it was hoped on the part of the South that a crushing defeat administered to the Union forces on Northern soil would send gold still higher, bring about panic and disaster in financial circles, assure the success of the factions which were opposing Mr. Lincoln's administration and advocating peace at any cost, and thus by a combination of all the anti-national elements then in operation secure the triumph of the Confederate cause.

(6) Lee could hardly have cherished much hope of capturing or even endangering Washington or Baltimore with the forces which he had in hand, unless he should first defeat the Army of the Potomac, and yet it is not difficult to credit him, just at that juncture, with aiming even at that project. Gen. A. L. Long, Lee's military secretary, in his *Memoirs of Lee* indicates that one aim in the campaign was to frustrate the Union advance on Richmond, and delay at least for a time the attack on that city (page 267). A little later in this chapter he says that there was in Lee's mind—

no thought of reaching Philadelphia, as was subsequently feared in the North. Yet he was satisfied that the Federal Army, if defeated in a pitched battle, would be seriously disorganized and forced to retreat across the Susquehanna [in case the engagement occurred in the neighborhood of York or Harrisburg or possibly Gettysburg], an event which would give him control of Maryland and western Pennsylvania, and probably of West Virginia, while it would very likely cause the fall of Washington city and the flight of the Federal Government. Moreover, an important diversion would be made in favor of the Western department, where the affairs of the Confederacy were on the decline. These highly important results, which would in all probability follow a successful battle, fully warranted, in his opinion, the hazard of an invasion of the North. [Page 269.]

General Lee's own statement of the case, as found in his report of the Gettysburg campaign, made under date of July 31, 1863 (*Official Records*, Vol. XXVII, 2:305) sums up some of these impelling reasons as follows:

The position occupied by the enemy opposite Fredericksburg being one in which he could not be attacked to advantage, it was determined to draw him from it. The execution of this purpose embraced the relief of the Shenandoah Valley from the troops that had occupied the lower part of it during the winter and spring, and if practicable the transfer of the scene of hostilities north of the Potomac. It was thought that the corresponding movements on the part of the enemy to which those contemplated by us would probably give rise might offer a fair opportunity to strike a blow at the enemy, then commanded by General Hooker, and that in any event that army would be compelled to leave Virginia, and possibly to draw to its support troops designed to operate against other parts of the country. In this way it was supposed that the enemy's plan of campaign for the summer would be broken up, and part of the season of active operations be consumed in the formation of new combinations and the preparations they would require. In addition to these advantages, it was hoped that other valuable results might be attained by military success.

(7) A further element in the case, which, although not hinted at by General Lee in his report, had tremendous weight in the decision to enter upon the campaign, and in deciding certain phases of its policy, both tactical and strategic, deserves consideration just here—namely, the almost contemptuous estimate which the Southern leader and his officers and men

had come to cherish concerning the fighting ability of the Army of the Potomac and the skill of its successive commanders. Since the battle of Fair Oaks, on the Peninsula, May 31, 1862, when Joseph E. Johnston was wounded and Lee was summoned to command the Army of Northern Virginia, the latter general had repeatedly met his opponents in battle. He had measured McClellan, tested him at all points, and taken his true weight. Indeed, one of Lee's most valuable assets—until Gettysburg—was his accurate insight into the methods, character, and skill of his antagonist. He had been taught to respect McClellan's skill in carrying out the retreat from the Peninsula; he had keenly felt the terrific punishment directed against the Southern Army by the Army of the Potomac, standing at bay at Malvern Hill; and he conceded McClellan's scholarship and engineering and organizing powers. But he had quickly come to recognize that general's constitutional defects—his lack of aggressive force, his disposition to manifold in his estimates the numbers against him, and his utter inability to recognize and use exigent opportunities. These qualities were all revealed at Antietam and South Mountain, where the Union commander's incapacity to see his opportunity (when by a singular chance he had secured a lost copy of Lee's order of march and battle, and thereby had it in his immediate power by expeditious action to destroy in detail the then widely separated Confederate army corps) must have awakened Lee's amazement, if not his scorn.

When McClellan passed off the scene Lee played

with Burnside in a tragic way at Fredericksburg, and made him and his great army the laughing-stock of the Confederate forces. Then he measured swords with Hooker at Chancellorsville, and showed so little respect for him and his forces that in full light of day, having not half as many men as his opponent, he divided his little army in two, sent Jackson on his flank movement, breaking to pieces thereby in his audacity all the scientific canons of strategy and tactics as laid down by the masters of war for centuries, to fall on the Union right flank and beat it to fragments; then he united the two wings of his army and forced Hooker back into his entrenchments; and finally he turned to smite the struggling Sixth Corps at Salem, while Hooker, in seeming imbecility, with thousands of men eager to pitch in, was left to occupy the woods and listen to the guns which testified that the chief part of the Army of Northern Virginia was concentrated on Sedgwick. Such utter contempt had he for Hooker that, before Hooker finally withdrew from Chancellorsville Lee had made his plans, with his depleted force, to attack the Army of the Potomac in its strongly fortified position in the woods, with the avowed purpose of driving the Union Army in dismay into the swollen river in its rear.

When one recalls the tragic story of the brave but discomfited, humiliated, mismanaged Army of the Potomac, a splendidly disciplined force, magnificently outfitted with artillery and equipment, well fed, well clad, ably officered, made up of the flower of the Northern States, and then led by incapacity and blundering into multiplied defeats and disasters, one does not marvel that the Army of Northern Virginia and its commander had reached that point of view in which they concluded that, in undertaking the movement into Pennsylvania, their opponent might just as well be left out of the reckoning.

This spirit, pervading Lee and his army, made an element which must be considered in any discerning study of the campaign. Testimonies confirmatory of the view set forth in the foregoing paragraphs abound on every side. Colonel Fremantle, of the British Army, who spent some time with Lee's forces before and during the Gettysburg campaign, says in his *Three Months in the Confederate States* that the "universal feeling in that army was one of profound contempt for an enemy whom they had beaten so constantly and under so many disadvantages." One of Lee's best generals has suggested that in his opinion "Lee's superb equipoise was threatened" by the remarkable successes he had won. Another one of his subordinates, Fitzhugh Lee, declares that his uncle's judgment "was controlled too far by the great confidence he had in the fighting qualities of his troops, who begged only to be turned loose upon the Federals."

Mr. E. A. Pollard in his *Lost Cause* animadverts on this phase of the situation, and says that "the Army of Northern Virginia, flushed with victory, was supposed to be equal to anything short of a miracle."

Capt. Cecil Battine, the masterly English critic, in his *Crisis of the Confederacy*, pages 115 and 118, says:

The horses had rested, the men were eager for action; confidence indeed ran to the dangerous excess of contempt for the foe—a foe by no means to be despised. . . . One thing seems certain: from the soldiers in the ranks to the chief of the Confederate armies a feeling of undue contempt for the adversary engendered a want of that caution which should mingle even in the most audacious enterprises of war.

The Comte de Paris, in his third volume of *The Civil War in America*, in opening the story of this campaign (page 451), after depicting the matured, disciplined, veteran army which had been brought together under Lee's command, specifies this particular feature which we have been dwelling upon: "The extreme confidence which animated it, as we have observed, imparted to it immense strength on the field of battle, but it also inspired it with an imprudent contempt for its adversaries."

Another putting of this aspect of the case is made by Nicolay and Hay, who in opening their account of the invasion of Pennsylvania (*Abraham Lincoln: A History*, vol. VII, p. 202) declare that the "most audacious and ambitious hopes ever entertained by the Confederate Government" were involved in this proposed campaign. "They expected no less than to conquer a triumphant peace in this campaign of General Lee. They looked upon their army as a machine so perfect in composition and in discipline that it could go anywhere and do anything. If the Army of the Potomac stood in its way, they expected to beat it as they had done before."

Other citations putting stress on this spirit of elation and undue self-confidence which marked Lee and his men at this time might be made were it needful to show that it constitutes one of the elemental facts which must be constantly borne in mind if one would interpret the story aright. The Confederate chieftain and his army had come to judge the Army of the Potomac as well as its commanders, in respect to courage, fighting capacity, steadfastness, and enterprise, by the shortcomings and blunders of the Peninsula, the Second Manassas, Antietam, Fredericksburg, and Chancellorsville campaigns, not discerning what the Union Army had understood from the beginning of its woes, that its only weakness was the lack of proper leadership. Never for one moment, in its darkest hours of dismay and depression—after Malvern Hill, and after Chancellorsville, for example—did the Army of the Potomac in its inmost thought question its own strength, courage, or temper; never did it lose faith in itself or in its heroic fighting capacity. It felt always that its only need was a commander able to appreciate its caliber and force and to handle it in battle. And at Gettysburg, with Meade at the head of the Union forces, the habit which Lee and his troops had formed of pluming themselves on their superiority to their opponents became finally a delusion and a snare.

III

PIVOTAL ISSUES DECIDED

The battle of Gettysburg was the most significant battle that has ever been fought. It settled the question whether or not the Government would be of the people, by the people, and for the people.—*Hon. Andrew D. White, in an address at Ithaca, New York, to veterans of the Civil War, September 28, 1910.*

WHAT results, either immediate or far reaching, were determined by this engagement? In what respect did its decisions affect the conduct of later campaigns, and what relation did they sustain to the whole period of struggle? How far were General Lee's motives and aims justified by the fight? What was there of pivotal character and consequence that hinged upon the defeat or victory, of one side or the other, in this battle? These questions bring into view a large horizon, but with more or less clearness they can be definitely answered.

It is, of course, conceded by nearly every one as a general truth that the whole struggle was in some large respects decided at Gettysburg. "This battle," says Gen. John B. Gordon, one of the ablest of the Confederate leaders, "was the turning-point in the South's fortunes." The English military critic, Battine, in the very title of an able and clear-sighted volume, declares Gettysburg to have been "The

PIVOTAL ISSUES DECIDED

Crisis of the Confederacy." Many writers have christened the clump of trees which stood where the advanced line of Pickett's charge indented the Second Corps battle-line, "the high-water mark of the rebellion." Maj. Gen. Slocum, in an address at the dedication of a monument on the field, September 18, 1892, said:

> Upon no other battle ever fought were such great results depending—a battle greater than that of Waterloo; greater in the number of men engaged; greater in the loss of killed and wounded; and far greater in its effects upon the destinies of mankind. It was the turning-point in our Civil War.

The full measure and meaning of this fact may not have been appreciated until long after the battle; but, whatever glimpse of the truth involved may have been half discerned at the time, there can be no question now that Gettysburg marked the culmination of the military power and successes of the Confederates and the beginning of their final downfall. From that time until the end the Confederacy carried a death-wound in its vitals. Many witnesses on the Southern side have testified to this effect, among them General Longstreet, who has left this record:

> For myself, I felt that our last hope was gone, and that it was now only a question of time with us. [*Battles and Leaders*, vol. III, 350.]

The Comte de Paris, in his first sentence when setting out to describe this campaign, lights with his usual insight on this elemental and vital aspect of the movement, and thus indicates the pivotal character of the struggle at Gettysburg:

GETTYSBURG

On the 3rd of June, 1863, Lee put his army in motion. The future of America was about to be decided forever.

For the sake of securing a flood-tide of light to illumine this truth let us cite but two more witnesses—the one a distinguished historian, and the other eminent for services in executive office, as a United States Senator, and as a judge on the bench.

(1) Dr. Benson J. Lossing, in a speech at Gettysburg, when a monument was unveiled, September 17, 1889, said:

We did not know it then, but we do now, that the battle of Gettysburg was the pivotal event in the war, which determined the destiny of our beloved country. Eleven years before that battle Professor Creasy had published his famous *Fifteen Decisive Battles of the World, from Marathon to Waterloo.* To that record a sixteenth should be added—Gettysburg—for it was more decisive, solved a greater, a more momentous problem of human history, than any battle ever fought before or since.

(2) As to the decisive character of the battle, the Hon. Joseph Benson Foraker, when Governor of Ohio, and presiding on the occasion of the dedication of the Ohio monuments at Gettysburg, September 14, 1887, uttered this conviction:

Until the march of time and progress brought us to this field free popular government was indeed but an experiment, menaced by a doubtful as well as an irrepressible conflict. Here was found the beginning of the end. . . . On this field the cause of liberty and Union gained a positive and permanent triumph. When the retreating battalions of Lee marched out of Pennsylvania it was already virtually determined that the American Union was indissoluble; that the Constitution of the United States was the organic law of the people; that no State had the right to defy the National power; that slavery must perish;

that the whole land should be dedicated to human liberty; that we should have but one government, one flag, and one destiny for the whole American people.

Before we develop with some elaboration and detail this fundamental fact of the pivotal character of the battle in its larger aspects, it may be well to inquire what aims of General Lee really were accomplished and which ones proved abortive.

(1) His immediate purpose—to secure food, shoes, and other supplies, and particularly to recruit his stock of horses for cavalry and artillery purposes—was to some extent achieved, but by no means so far as to suffice for the enormous outlay which had to be made in return. The expenditure of ammunition, the havoc in horse-flesh, the depletion of his fighting forces, and the sufferings and death of many thousand brave men, summed up a heavy bill to pay for the movement. The supplies that were taken South during the campaign were comparatively of little worth, even though we reckon that the army managed to live in a sort of way on the country which they occupied for the time being, and that Early contrived to collect from the Cumberland Valley and from the rich county of York a large sum of money.[1]

[1] In the interesting autobiographical volume *General Jubal A. Early*, issued in the fall of 1912, with notes by R. H. Early, the author says (p. 261):

"In compliance with my requisition some twelve or fifteen hundred pairs of shoes, all the hats and socks and rations called for [a thousand hats, a thousand pairs of socks, and three days' rations for the troops], and $28,600 in money were furnished by the town authorities."

On page 286 General Early is able to suggest only two leading results of the campaign worthy of record: "Our army was supplied [with rations] for more than a month, and this gave a breathing-spell

GETTYSBURG

One phase of the loss sustained by Lee's army—hardly alluded to so far as we have noted by any of the writers on Gettysburg—is suggested by the report of Col. R. L. Walker, chief of artillery, Hill's corps (*Official Records*, XXVII, 2:611), who found it impossible to secure horseshoes and nails wherewith to shoe his horses, and accordingly hundreds of them were ruined "because of the lameness incurred in traveling over turnpikes, and especially over the roads from Hagerstown to Gettysburg, without shoes." He estimates the value of the horses abandoned in that one corps "from this single cause during the march at seventy-five thousand dollars, while the injury to others amounted to the same sum." When one estimates the heavy additional loss of horses slain or abandoned on the field at Gettysburg one comes to understand how irreparable this phase of the case was, even granting that many animals were gathered up in Pennsylvania during the march.

A further testimony of this phase of the loss is given in the article by Gen. E. P. Alexander, on the "Artillery Fighting at Gettysburg" (*Battles and Leaders of the Civil War*, vol. III, p. 367), in which he says:

The retreat was a terrible march for the artillery, crippled as we were by the loss of so many horses in battle, and the giving out of many more on the stony roads for the lack of horseshoes. We were compelled to trespass on the reluctant hospitality of the

to our commissary department, which had been put to great straits . . . a change of diet was actually necessary for our men."

The other point he makes is this:

"The campaign into Pennsylvania certainly defeated any further attempt to move against Richmond that summer, and postponed the war over into another year."

neighboring farmers, and send squads in every direction to get horses. Wherever found they were to be bought, whether the owner desired to sell or not.

(2) It goes without saying, in regard to the campaigns in the West, where the Confederate armies were in sore extremities, that the movement into Pennsylvania had no effect whatever, except that when the news of the victory of Meade reached that region there was an added burden of depression and dismay imposed upon those armies, not fully realized in many cases by the mass of the soldiery, but nevertheless keenly felt by the better-informed officers, who could understand even at long range the far-reaching results of the battle from which Lee had to retreat with heavy loss into Virginia again. No forces were withdrawn from the West to help the Army of the Potomac, and no relief was administered to the Confederates under pressure in that section of the vast field of conflict.

(3) It is clear that General Lee and his army were instructed and enlightened as to the fighting and staying qualities of the Army of the Potomac by the struggle at Gettysburg. Foreign experts, in their comments on the battle, generally agree with the critical judgment of Formby that "Meade had proved himself a first-rate handler of large numbers," and that his army "had never before been so smartly handled." He further says of Meade that "when appointed to command the Army of the Potomac, three days before Gettysburg, his grasp of the scattered situation was instant and masterly," and that "he showed both judgment and nerve," and was "a

great army commander" (*The Civil War in America,*
pp. 210, 214, 456).

One of the facts, indeed, proclaimed to the world
on that great Fourth of July, 1863, was that at last,
after two years of waiting, of humiliating reverses
and disappointments, and much unavailing slaughter
and suffering, the Army of the Potomac had found a
commander fit to lead it in battle.   That that army
was brave, well disciplined, and led by many hundreds of skilful and devoted officers, there had been
no doubt—except on the part of the Southern Army
opposed to it, who had often looked on the Northern
soldiers and their successive leaders with derision.
Lee, it is true, had good ground for the estimate he
had made of the generalship of the several commanders in chief of the Union Army.   He had plausible
reasons for reckoning in advance that when he and
Hooker should meet once more on the field the latter
would be assuredly defeated again.   But it would
seem that he might have divined that under fit leadership that magnificent army, which he had faced for
two years again and again in battle, might reveal
hitherto unsuspected qualities of dash, fortitude,
celerity, and staying-power.   It is clear to us now
that the Confederate commander did not take this
into his account, did not at all anticipate that the
Union Army on Northern soil would show a courage,
an enthusiasm, and a devotion hitherto never surpassed, and that a new commander might appear
fully adequate to lead the Union forces to victory.
Had General Lee possessed a correct apprehension
of the spirit, the resources, the desperate courage,

and the magnificent discipline of the Army of the Potomac at this time he never would have attempted certain most venturesome enterprises of the campaign.

This is more than hinted at by General Longstreet in his volume *From Manassas to Appomattox*, where he puts on record some of the disquietude of spirit which he felt when he diagnosed the venturesome and almost reckless condition of the great Virginian's mood. Longstreet tells us substantially that he pleaded with Lee, and apparently secured his assurance that the campaign should be "offensive in its strategy, but defensive in its tactics"; or, in other words, that the Army of Northern Virginia should so manœuver as to secure an advantageous position in which the Union Army would feel forced to attack. Longstreet also testifies to the amazement and alarm which he felt when Lee, contrary to their understanding, announced at the close of the first day at Gettysburg that he intended to assail Meade's strong position on the morrow.

This diagnosis agrees with the analysis also of Gen. E. P. Alexander, who in his *Military Reminiscences of a Confederate* emphasizes the fact that while General Lee was in popular estimation a singularly well-balanced character who held his judgment in constant equipoise, he was in fact "a pattern of audacity, willing to take extraordinary risks," and at times daring to the point of absolute recklessness. This latter element really predominated in the Gettysburg campaign.

(4) The purpose of Lee to arrest and postpone the plans and operation of the Army of the Potomac, at

least for the time being, was accomplished by this campaign. It chanced that this policy fitted in with the purposes of the authorities at Washington to make the West the chief scene of military transactions and activities for the fall and winter of 1863. Accordingly—in part to encourage Hooker, give him a fresh chance, and provide for his restless spirit something to keep it in useful service—the Eleventh and Twelfth Corps were detached from Meade's army after Gettysburg and sent to Grant at Chattanooga, under Hooker's leadership. By this depletion of Meade's army it seemed to be conceded that no important movement was to be expected along the Rappahannock. At any rate, with the exception of the Mine Run advance, in November, 1863, which proved abortive, nothing was done by that force for ten months after the battle of Gettysburg. No forward movement was undertaken until the Wilderness campaign began, early in May, 1864. Whether that long delay was on the whole an advantage or a disadvantage to Lee can hardly be questioned, as it simply postponed the day of his downfall. But a discussion of the problem involved in that phase of the matter does not fall within our aim in this volume.

(5) The intention of General Lee—or one of his aims—was to add to the strength of the peace party in the North, secure enlistments in Maryland for his army, if possible, and by dividing public sentiment and awakening popular discontent with the war and antagonism against the administration force an early compromise with the National Government. In a letter written to Jefferson Davis, June 10, 1863

PIVOTAL ISSUES DECIDED

(*Official Records*, XXVII, 3:881), soon after his movement toward Pennsylvania had opened, Lee says:

> ... our resources in men are constantly diminishing, and the disproportion in this respect between us and our enemies, if they continue united in their efforts to subjugate us, is steadily augmenting. The decrease of the aggregate of this army, as disclosed by the returns, affords an illustration of the fact. Its effective strength varies from time to time, but the falling off in its aggregate shows that its ranks are growing weaker and that its losses are not supplied by recruits. Under these circumstances we should neglect no honorable means of dividing and weakening our enemies, that they may feel some of the difficulties experienced by ourselves. It seems to me that the most effectual mode of accomplishing this object, now within our reach, is to give all the encouragement we can, consistently with truth, to the rising peace party of the North. Nor do I think we should in this connection make nice distinctions between those who declare for peace unconditionally and those who advocate it as a means of restoring the Union, however much we may prefer the former.

This entire purpose was frustrated by his campaign. He had given authority to Bradley T. Johnson and Gen. I. R. Trimble, two able men from Baltimore, to recruit any force which they might be able to secure in Maryland; but it is clear they did not get a single fresh soldier. A similar hope, cherished in the Antietam campaign, had proved baseless. It was found difficult even to reorganize the Maryland troops which had been for a year or two in service and whose time had expired, for their case was different from that of men whose States had joined the Confederacy. Marylanders who became Confederate soldiers doomed themselves to exile from their Commonwealth and alienation from their own homes; besides, Union sentiment had grown at a rapid rate in that State, and the people of Maryland by this time had come to apprehend that the Confederacy was a doomed institution, and they did not wish to set sail in a sinking ship.

So far as the rest of the North was concerned, the invasion of Pennsylvania, instead of adding to the dissensions then prevalent and increasing the power of the peace party, created an unwonted uprising of patriotism, particularly along the border. In a few days fifty thousand militia and emergency men were organized for immediate service at Harrisburg under Governor Andrew G. Curtin and Maj. Gen. D. N. Couch; while from Philadelphia, New York, Boston, and scores of other cities came money, medical supplies, surgeons, nurses, and, better than all else, manifold assurances of patriotic devotion, unquestioned loyalty and united prayers in behalf of the work of the army and the administration. With the Confederate Army in Pennsylvania the voice of carping opposition to the war was for the time hushed, and the people everywhere were united with a new earnestness in the purpose to re-establish the unity and authority of the nation. Instead of strengthening the peace party, therefore, Lee's advance put a muzzle on its lips, and served only to quicken and then to reveal in a magnificent way the love which the people of the loyal States bore for the Union.

(6) One of the ultimately paralyzing blows dealt to the Confederacy by Meade was this: that battle decided that the war policy of the South would be, until the end, inevitably and only defensive in character. Two invasions had now been made wherein

Lee had crossed the border; in each case he met with a reverse. He could not hope for any larger force in the future than that which followed him to Pennsylvania; he had no resources adequate to the task of undertaking another offensive campaign. And a defensive policy meant, without question, ultimate defeat. Let the war go on, let the Union armies continue their aggressive plans and movements, let the territory of the South continue to be divided, as it now was by the other victory of the same date at Vicksburg, let the Mississippi be opened to the Gulf, and let the blockade continue to shut the Confederacy in from access to the outer world—what was there in such a situation except despair and defeat for the Confederates? The clearest-eyed among them saw the situation as we have thus portrayed it in brief; the whole world sees now that by virtue of that situation, and in view of the foredoomed defensive policy made imperative at Gettysburg, the South had already lost its "cause." The resources of the Confederacy were nearing their final limit, while the National Government had ample supplies of men, treasure, and munitions of war. All that was necessary now in order to restore the Union was to keep "pegging away"—to use the expressive phrase of Mr. Lincoln —until the South was absolutely exhausted, or until her leaders were willing to recognize their hopeless plight.

(7) The battle of Gettysburg decided that there would never come to the South any measure of foreign recognition. When Lee retreated the die was cast so far as this hope of recognition from France and

England was concerned. The motion for recognition, made June 30th, in the House of Commons in London, was withdrawn two weeks later. The news of a Confederate defeat on Northern soil turned the tide. From that hour there was not the shadow of a chance that any European power would give encouragement of any sort, or financial help, or any show of recognition to the Confederate States of America. And without such recognition even Mr. Davis, who was the last to succumb and lose hope, knew in his deepest thought that his plans were impossible.

So far as the nations mentioned were then concerned, it was no longer a case of sympathy or sentiment; the whole matter was reduced to a problem in political economy. The Confederate States had no outside resources to depend upon; the blockade shut them out from the markets of the world where clothing, blankets, shoes, guns, and ammunition might be purchased; and even if they could run the blockade they had no money; their finances were in a hopeless plight; their currency was rapidly becoming literally worthless. The rulers of the Old World could clearly see this situation after Gettysburg, and from that hour, therefore, the "cause" was doomed.

On the other hand, the resources of the Union had not been much diminished by the excessive drafts which had been made upon them. The North was rich and prosperous; manufactories were in full blast; "greenbacks" were abundant; and, in spite of the delays and frictions and occasional riots occasioned by the conscription measures, multiplied thousands of men were to be had for the army. These facts speedily became unmistakable to the nations of Europe, and when discerned made anything like interference or recognition impossible.

In view, therefore, of the data we have elaborated, it is worth while, we judge, to keep to the foreground the distinctive qualities which make Gettysburg one of the decisive battles of history. The conflict was large in every sense, but it was largest in this regard, that by its verdict and results it was determined that the authority of the Union was to be finally supreme on American soil, that the attempt to build up a Confederacy on slavery and secession as a part of the foundation would fail, and that the institutions of liberty which had been incorporated in the National Constitution, and which were symbolized by the Stars and Stripes, were destined to survive the war and endure, we may trust, in imperishable splendor for the ages to come.

That Fourth of July, 1863, when the twin victories of Gettysburg and Vicksburg became historic, may well be recalled as the turning-point of our national destinies. From that day the armies of the Confederacy staggered under their death-sentence, carrying on their hopeless struggle for twenty-one added months under the inevitable doom of final overthrow. And now every monument at Gettysburg, every bit of topographical decoration added to the beautiful field, every service held on its hills, helps to repeat to the world the proclamation: Here the verdict was rendered, here the decision was made, that government of the people, by the people, and for the people shall not perish from the earth.

IV

TO the field of Gettysburg the Commonwealth of Pennsylvania possesses a manifold title, along with ample reasons for reckoning it as chief among her patriotic heritages. Not only is the field rich in historic associations, crowded with reminiscences of valor, matchlessly adorned by the hands of a grateful, bereaved people, and marvelously inspiring to the patriot's imagination, but the battle fought thereon was marked throughout by leadership wrought out by sons of the Keystone State.

This point can be maintained without making any invidious distinctions and without discriminating against officers from other States. It was not by any dereliction of theirs—for they all rendered magnificent service—it was not through the fault of other Commonwealths, but by the singular ordination of an overruling Providence, that it came to pass that when Pennsylvania was to be defended from invasion, and when upon her soil the pivotal struggle was to be decided for all time in behalf of Union and liberty, nearly twoscore of her sons were found in the van, directing the plans, ordering the movements, stationing the troops, and occupying foremost places in the operations whereby the victory at last was won.

PENNSYLVANIA OFFICERS

There were eighteen different States represented in the Army of the Potomac in the battle, of which two stood close together in the number of men actually engaged—Pennsylvania and New York— the former with sixty-eight infantry regiments, nine cavalry regiments, and seven batteries of artillery; the latter with sixty-eight regiments of infantry, seven regiments of cavalry, and nineteen batteries; eight of the New York infantry organizations, however, were made up of fragments which, all told, aggregated only some twenty companies.

Other States were represented, the numbers indicating the infantry regiments contributed: Massachusetts, 18; Ohio, 13; New Jersey, 12; Vermont and Maine, each 10; Michigan, 7; Wisconsin, 6; Indiana and Connecticut, each 5; Maryland and New Hampshire, each 3; Delaware, 2; Illinois, Minnesota, Rhode Island, and West Virginia, each 1, with regiments of cavalry and batteries of artillery from several of these States in addition, as well as from the Regular Army, to be detailed later, helping to complete the great muster-roll.

It is not, however, the number of soldiers, but the number of leading and influential officers furnished by Pennsylvania which we here would emphasize. Of course it cannot be claimed at this date as a fresh discovery that Pennsylvania officers were singularly in the lead in this fight; in the main that phase of the case has been known ever since the data were tabulated. The facts were summarized with force and eloquence in a speech made on the battle-field, September 12, 1889, by Gen. James A. Beaver, then

Governor of the State, when he accepted in behalf of the Commonwealth the regimental monuments which had been there erected:

> On every portion of this historic battle-field Pennsylvania acted a prominent part. Her sons, as was meet, were the heroes of the field. Meade commanded the army; Reynolds fell in the forefront of the battle in the first day's fight; and Hancock directed the details of preparation for heroic and stubborn resistance which was made to the determined assaults of the enemy upon the second and third days. . . . Pennsylvania batteries occupied vital points in our defensive line; and Pennsylvania cavalry was conspicuous under a gallant Pennsylvanian in their brilliant operations upon our right flank and rear.

When the data are fully brought out this claim is more than made good. For example, three days before the battle a gifted Pennsylvanian came to the front as the newly appointed commander of the army.

Maj. Gen. George Gordon Meade

When this veteran officer, on Sunday morning, June 28, 1863, not long after midnight, at Frederick, Maryland, was awakened from his sleep by a messenger from the War Department to hear the astounding news that he had been chosen as the successor of Hooker, he was stunned as he faced the sudden and tremendous task. Among the prevailing voices which summoned him to his post of duty and responsibility sounded the summons of his own native State. Surely he heard a message like this:

"Pennsylvania needs your help. Your own State is invaded. Your home city is imperiled. In this critical hour the Keystone State, as well as the nation, needs you as the chief standard-bearer."

At any rate, by a complicated series of events, it resulted that a Pennsylvanian was in command when the greatest of the decisive battles of the century was fought on Pennsylvania soil. It is on record that this fact that Meade was a Pennsylvanian, and that he would therefore be incited to extraordinary efforts to defend his own State, in case the struggle should be fought, as was then probable, north of the Maryland line, was a final and deciding factor which induced the President and the War Department to unite on him as the fit man, above all others, to lead the Army of the Potomac in the crisis then faced. Gen. Francis A. Walker, in an article on "Meade at Gettysburg" (*Battles and Leaders of the Civil War*, vol. III, p. 407), makes an effective use of this aspect of the case. Noting the reasons which moved Meade, for example, to withdraw Slocum's corps from the movement which had been begun by Hooker toward the rear of Lee, and directing that command with other portions of the army in a northward direction, which would lead them across the Maryland line, Walker says:

How far Meade's better choice was a mere matter of military judgment; how far it was due to the accident that he, the new commander, was himself a Pennsylvanian, it is difficult to say. There can, I think, be no doubt that the special instincts of local patriotism had much to do with bringing on and fighting through to a successful conclusion the battle of Gettysburg. It is remarkable that in the one Pennsylvania battle of the war the men of that State should have borne so prominent a part. . . . For one, I entertain no doubt that the military judgment of

General Meade, which dictated his decision on the 28th of June
to adopt the direct and more effective plan of moving straight
northward from Frederick, instead of persisting in the division
of the army which Hooker had initiated, was largely influenced
by that intensity of feeling which actuated him as a Pennsylvanian. At such a crisis stress of feeling drives the intellect to
its highest work. So long as moral forces enter into the conduct of war, can we doubt that it was fortunate for the Union
arms that they so largely were Pennsylvanians who hurried forward the troops in their long and painful marches northward,
and who threw the veteran corps of the Army of the Potomac
upon the invading army?

This principle, luminously stated by General
Walker, will find ample embodiment as we pursue
the story of the battle, which had hardly opened before a second Pennsylvania soldier was placed by his
heroic devotion in the foreground of the fight, pinnacled there for evermore—

Maj. Gen. John Fulton Reynolds,

who had been put the day before the fight in command of the advancing wing of the army, made up of
three army corps. In the attitude of marshaling his
forces, of safeguarding the heights in his rear, of holding the advanced line until other forces should appear, the world still watches him, and will for all
time. Had he been privileged to make choice of the
best investment to be made of himself, his gifts, his
influence, his fame, his life, so as to secure the largest
fruitage and accruing income for all the future, what
better fate could he have asked than to have his
name and record enduringly allied with the destinies
of the battle in which the integrity of the Union was
forever assured?

Later on that fateful first day a third soldier of the Keystone State came into leadership, his name,

Maj. Gen. Winfield Scott Hancock,

betokening in advance his military character, as though he had been dedicated to the mastery of the profession of arms from the time he was christened; and his physique, his personal magnetism, his skill in commanding men in battle, all justify the use of the adjectives "superb" and "magnificent," often employed in depicting him.   To him was awarded the privilege of aiding to rally the troops at the end of the disasters of the opening day, of assigning stations to the reinforcing columns, and securing by personal study of the field such knowledge as might be of service to the commander-in-chief in determining whether or not the battle should be fought at Gettysburg. To him also came the duty of commanding, in face of the assaults of the second and third days, a line of battle which was over a mile in length, and included other portions of the army besides his own Second Corps, in emergencies which required military ability of a high order in order to meet them.

A fourth Pennsylvanian emerges from the tempest of battle as commander of a division, and for a while in charge of a corps,

Maj. Gen. John Gibbon,

an artillerist of high rank, a veteran soldier, born in Pennsylvania, but appointed from North Carolina to West Point, in connection with which his career is outlined in this volume. He was wounded in the very crisis of the battle at the moment when his division was engaged in its death-grapple with Pickett's men.

Another Pennsylvanian noted for courage and skill was a division commander in the fight on the second day in front of Little Round Top, and for a little while in charge of the Third Corps—

Maj. Gen. David B. Birney,

who entered service at the head of a notable Philadelphia regiment, the Twenty-third Infantry, in August, 1861, and who speedily won a brigadier's star and then the post of major general. At Fredericksburg, at Chancellorsville, and at Gettysburg his division under his leadership did service that has become historic. Later under Hancock he commanded a division in the Wilderness campaign, and on July 23, 1864, he became commander of the Tenth Army Corps, in the Army of the James. In barely two months, after skilful services as a corps leader, he was stricken with fever, and upon being taken to his home in Philadelphia he died, October 18, 1864, one of the best types of a volunteer general developed in the whole war.

In this same Third Corps to which Birney was attached in the battle another notable soldier, also a Philadelphian, reflected glory in unusual measure upon the State which had given him birth—

Maj. Gen. Andrew A. Humphreys,

whose final record of skill, of courage, and of great achievements singled him out at last as one of the most eminent of the great soldiers of the Republic. He combined broad and profound technical scholarship, the highest engineering abilities, mastery of logistics—the art of moving and locating troops in large numbers—with a gift of personal leadership on the field of battle, such as only the very greatest' captains have ever revealed. He will never receive the credit which his abilities warranted, since much of his work was swallowed up in the mass, having been rendered when he was chief topographical engineer under McClellan or chief of staff under Meade. His change of front on the second day, under terrific fire, assailed in front and on both flanks, was a manœuver which takes its place as an extraordinary achievement, a movement which some writers on war have listed among the impossible things.

Another division commander from Pennsylvania did some notable things at the close of the fight on the second day—

Maj. Gen. Samuel Wylie Crawford,

who commanded the famous Pennsylvania Reserves, and who, with McCandless, of Philadelphia, led that organization with rousing enthusiasm down the slopes of Little Round Top, and across the deadly Wheatfield, in the successful effort to check the final advance which the Confederates made against that embattled height.[1]

[1] General Crawford had been in the Regular Army for ten years as an assistant surgeon when the war broke out; developing military aptitudes and experience in that time, and becoming widely known because of his service in Forts Moultrie and Sumter, and his gallantry in the crisis pertaining to those strongholds, he was appointed major of the Thirteenth Infantry in May, 1861, and brigadier general less than a year later. These promotions were abundantly justified by his hero-

GETTYSBURG

Maj. Gen. John W. Geary

was another division commander who did effective
service for his own State on his native soil, finding his
work and opportunity at Culp's Hill. He earned
here in part the distinction given to him by his brevet
rank of major general, January 12, 1865, conferred
"for fitness to command and promptness to execute."
He served in the Mexican War, rising from captain
to colonel, and distinguishing himself for bravery and
leadership at the storming of Chapultepec, where
he was wounded. In the fifties he served as Governor
of Kansas during the struggle between desperate
factions in that territory; early in the Civil War he
organized and led to the front the Twenty-eighth
Pennsylvania Infantry, was promoted to be brigadier
general, and later received the higher brevet rank.
He did heroic service at Chickamauga and Lookout
Mountain, and during his service was twice severely
wounded. After the war he served two terms as
Governor of Pennsylvania. (Born, 1819; died, 1873.)

The Third Division, First Army Corps, made up
almost entirely of Pennsylvanians, was in the thick
of the fight the whole of the first day under command
of the gallant

Brig. Gen. Thomas A. Rowley,

of Pittsburg, a veteran of the Mexican War, who entered the Civil War as colonel of the Thirteenth

ism in battle and his skill in command. He was brevetted colonel
U.S.A., for Gettysburg, and other brevets followed up to major
general, in both the Regulars and Volunteers. He was retired from
the Regular Army, in 1875 with the rank of brigadier general, and
died November 3, 1892.

Pennsylvania Infantry in the three months' service, and then organized the noted Pittsburg regiment, the 102d Pennsylvania, winning promotion to the next rank in 1862, and showing himself on many a field a leader of poise and courage. (General Rowley died in 1892.) Doubleday says of him at Gettysburg:

General Rowley himself displayed great bravery. He was several times struck by spent shot and pieces of shell, and on the third day his horse was killed by a cannon-shot while he was holding him by the bridle and conversing with me.

Another division in the army, in the Second Corps, was led by a Pennsylvanian,

Brig. Gen. Alexander Hays,

a graduate of the Military Academy. We cannot summarize here what Hays's division did on the third day, when the final blow, embodied in Pickett's and Pettigrew's charge, fell directly upon their front. When the fight ended that afternoon fifteen colors and over two thousand prisoners fell into their hands. Magnificently were they led by their division commander.

Another Pennsylvanian, also a West Point graduate,

Brig. Gen. David McMurtrie Gregg,

was at the head of the Second Division, Cavalry Corps. He led a Philadelphia regiment, the Eighth Pennsylvania Cavalry, to the front in 1861, and speedily became a brigadier general. He had few peers in the skill and courage which he displayed as a cavalry

leader, and his work in command of the Union horsemen on the Union right on the afternoon of the last
day was a notable feature in the battle, although its
significance was for a long time obscured in view of
the decisive character of the infantry and artillery
operations which occurred at the same time, and
by which its importance was overshadowed.

Pennsylvania Brigade Commanders.

In passing now to enumerate the Pennsylvanians
who commanded brigades in the battle it is worth
while to note a fact which stands in striking contrast
with the policy pursued by the Confederate authorities—namely, that in the Union Army many brigades
were led by colonels, often men of proved ability,
who had demonstrated their capacity to do honor to
the rank of a brigadier general, but who for one reason
and another had not received the recognition which
was due them from the authorities at Washington;
while, on the other hand, in the Army of Northern
Virginia the brigades were in all cases—except when
a sudden necessity made it imperative to assign a
colonel to the position—led by brigadier generals.
When a man showed himself capable of leading a
brigade he was immediately honored with the commission which indicated him in that post. This
prompt recognition had much to do in keeping officers
in fighting trim.

The case was otherwise in the Army of the Potomac.
This writer could indicate offhand a score of instances
in which men of conspicuous ability—like Miles,

Carroll, Strong Vincent, Beaver, Upton, Brooke—
who had been tested in camp, on the march, and in
battle as leaders of brigades, and who had fully
proved their utmost fitness for such leadership by
long months, and even years, of such service, were
kept waiting month after month for the promotion
which they had abundantly won, and which sometimes, as in the case of Vincent, reached them only
when they had been stricken down with fatal wounds
and were at the point of death. Gregg's division
is a case in point, where each brigade was in charge
of a colonel, who had to win his star ten times over
before it came. In this instance each officer was a
Pennsylvania colonel—two of them regular officers
with the training, skill, and courage of veterans.
They all in later months won brevets and full com-
missions which they had earned and should have
received long before this battle. It is worth while
to glance at these tried and fully tested officers and
their records.

The commander of the First Brigade in this division was

Col. John Baillie McIntosh,

who in his youth had the advantage of two years'
service as a midshipman in the navy. He was commissioned a second lieutenant in the Second Cavalry,
June 8, 1861; colonel of the Third Pennsylvania
Cavalry, November 15, 1862; and then had to wait
until July 21, 1864, for his commission as brigadier
general of volunteers. After the war was over came
his brevets one after another, up to major general of

volunteers, and also major general in the Regular Army—the brevet rank of lieutenant colonel being for gallantry and skill at Gettysburg. He entered the list of retired officers, U.S.A., with the rank of brigadier general, July 30, 1870, and died June 29, 1888. His work in the Gettysburg campaign began early in June, and did not cease until nearly two months later, when the two armies had resumed their positions on the Rappahannock.

At the head of the Second Brigade was that intrepid soldier

Col. Pennock Huey,

who, starting in as captain in the Eighth Pennsylvania Cavalry in 1861, reached the colonelcy of his regiment a week before Gettysburg opened; during the campaign he led his brigade, as his commanders testify, with gallantry and devotion, and continued in brigade command until the struggle ended—his reward was a brevet rank of brigadier general at the end of the war.

The leader of the Third Brigade was

Col. John Irvin Gregg,

who rose by gallantry from private to captain in the Mexican War; became captain Sixth Cavalry in 1861, and colonel of the Sixteenth Pennsylvania Cavalry, November, 1862; he rendered magnificent service until the war ended in cavalry commands, at the head of his brigade and in larger fields, but no brigadier's commission reached him in all these toil-ful perilous days; at the end, however, brevets one after another were awarded him up to the rank of brevet brigadier general, U.S.A., and brevet major general of volunteers. He remained in the regular service and was retired as colonel of the Eighth Cavalry in 1879; he died January 2, 1892.

Turning now to the several Infantry Army Corps, let us in brief enumerate the Pennsylvanians who commanded brigades in the battle.

First Army Corps

Second Division, First Brigade: Col. Richard Coulter, who organized the Eleventh Pennsylvania Infantry and led it in many a battle, and was mustered out at its head after nearly four years of notable service, led this brigade after three other leaders had been stricken down on the first day. He was a soldier in the Mexican War, and at the very opening of the Civil War went to the front in a three months' regiment as captain, rising in a few weeks to be lieutenant colonel; on his return from that term of service he took into the army the regiment which became under his leadership a command typical for its discipline and courage. He was brevetted brigadier general for gallantry in the Wilderness, and major general for his services at the very end of the war, in an energetic assault at Five Forks.

Col. Peter Lyle, amid the emergencies of the disastrous first day, was also summoned to the leadership of this brigade; he was colonel of a three months' regiment; and then helped to organize in his patriotic

city of Philadelphia the Ninetieth Pennsylvania Infantry, becoming its colonel and aiding to give it a
reputation for bravery and good conduct which is
now a heritage of the city which sent it to the front.
He was brevetted brigadier general in March, 1865,
"for gallant services in battle"; he died July 17,
1879.

Third Division, First Brigade: This was first under
command of Gen. Thomas A. Rowley, who has already been noticed as in command of the division
when Doubleday took charge of the corps. He was
succeeded by Col. Chapman Biddle, one of the most
eminent citizens of Philadelphia, a representative of
wealth, the finest society, the intelligence and the
patriotic devotion of the city where his ancestors
had lived for more than a century—a man equipped
for leadership in any realm, a lawyer, a financial expert, and a citizen in touch with all the higher interests of the metropolis of Pennsylvania. An in-
incident in connection with his service on the first
day at Gettysburg is given in the official report of
a Confederate annalist in the record he makes of his
own organization and its work that day. He tells
how through the smoke of battle he and his comrades were impressed with the splendid example of
a brigade-leader in their front, in a crisis when the
two lines were near together. They saw this officer,
finely mounted, seize the brigade colors, and ride up
and down his line rallying his men and with enthusiastic intrepidity leading them forward. The spectacle
was so thrilling that no man drew aim on the officer;
his valor won the tribute of his foes. The record goes

on to say that the Confederates, on ascertaining who the officer was—Col. Chapman Biddle, of Philadelphia, and that he had survived the battle—rejoiced in his escape from the perils of that dreadful scene.

The Second Brigade was led first by Col. Roy Stone, of the 149th Pennsylvania, who commenced his service in the spring of 1861 in the Pennsylvania Reserves as captain, and who, after having been promoted to be major in that force, was made colonel of the 149th, winning as its commander, and as the long-tried and gallant leader of a brigade, the brevet of brigadier general, September 7, 1864. In the Spanish-American War he also served as brigadier general from June 3 until December 31, 1898. A single sentence from Doubleday's report may indicate what stuff this officer was made of: "Stone was shot down, battling to the last."

Colonel Stone was followed in command of the brigade by Col. Langhorne Wister, who had been a captain in the Thirteenth Reserves, in the spring of 1861, until he was made colonel of the 150th Pennsylvania, in September, 1862. His brevet in 1865—that of brigadier general—was particularly awarded on the ground of meritorious service at Gettysburg, where he displayed coolness and gallantry at the head of his regiment, and also in leading the brigade in critical hours. It was Wister who met in the midst of the fight the valorous John Burns and advised him how, as a private citizen on danger bent, he might do his work to advantage! Wister was shockingly wounded in battle by a bullet which passed through his cheek and mouth. With characteristic pluck he remained on the field, giving assistance even when his injury kept him from continuing in command.

When Wister was hurt the brigade was led by Col. Edmund L. Dana, organizer and leader of the notable Wilkesbarre regiment, the 143d Pennsylvania. This officer saw service as captain in a regiment from his State in the Mexican War; and his courage and skill were recognized at the end of the Civil War by the brevet rank of brigadier general.

Second Army Corps

First Division, First Brigade: Col. H. Boyd McKeen, Eighty-first Pennsylvania Infantry, followed Col. E. E. Cross, of the Fifth New Hampshire Infantry, in the fight of Thursday, when the latter was mortally wounded in crossing the Wheatfield and advancing to the help of the Third Corps. Colonel McKeen, an "ideal of manly beauty and grace," as well as of soldierly skill and devotion, was killed in command of a brigade at Cold Harbor, June 3, 1864.

Third Brigade: After General Zook was slain, Thursday afternoon, in front of Little Round Top, Lieut. Col. John Fraser, 140th Pennsylvania, led the command. He became colonel of this regiment soon after the battle, and brevet brigadier general at the end of the war.

Fourth Brigade: Col. John R. Brooke, Fifty-third Pennsylvania Infantry, which he had organized and led since 1861, commanded this force. He had to wait until May 12, 1864, for his first star. He was brevetted colonel for his services in this battle, and then brigadier and major general. Remaining in the regular service, he was retired, July 21, 1902, as major general, U.S.A., after a long and brilliant record, the closing portion of which had given him distinction in the Spanish-American War, in which he served first as governor general of Porto Rico and then of Cuba. At this writing (1913) this veteran officer, in his seventy-fifth year, is still living.

Third Army Corps

First Division, First Brigade: When Gen. Charles K. Graham was wounded and captured, Col. Andrew H. Tippin, Sixty-eighth Pennsylvania Infantry, took command. Colonel Tippin was a lieutenant in the regular infantry in the Mexican War, and won a brevet by his gallantry in the battles of Contreras and Churubusco. (Died in 1870.)

Fifth Army Corps

First Division, Second Brigade: Col. Jacob Bowman Sweitzer, who entered service as major of the Sixty-second Pennsylvania Infantry July 4, 1861, and reached the colonelcy in June, 1862, led this brigade. He was brevetted brigadier general March 13, 1865. After the war he resumed practice at the bar in Pittsburg, where in later years he rendered service as prothonotary for the western district of the Supreme Court of Pennsylvania, dying in that office in 1888.

Third Brigade: Col. Strong Vincent, Eighty-third

Pennsylvania, who gave his life at the head of this brigade while leading it in its vital work of saving Little Round Top when the battle opened on the Union left flank on Thursday afternoon, receives notice in another place in this volume. His memory is still green among those who long ago were impressed with the charms of his mind and character.

Third Division, First Brigade: Col. William McCandless, a distinguished Philadelphian, colonel of the Second Reserves, led this brigade. His example and skill were important factors in the work of the command when it made its magnificent charge down the rugged slopes of Little Round Top, near the close of the fight on Thursday evening. In July, 1864, when mustered out with his regiment, Colonel McCandless was proffered a brigadier's commission, but declined it.

Third Brigade: Col. Joseph W. Fisher, of the Fifth Reserves, was in command; he aided in getting hold of Big Round Top and making it secure against the foe, Thursday night. His gallantry was rewarded in 1865 by the brevet rank of brigadier general.

Sixth Army Corps

Second Division, Third Brigade: Brig. Gen. Thomas H. Neill, a West Point graduate, class of 1847, has due notice elsewhere. He followed David B. Birney in the colonelcy of the famous Philadelphia regiment, the Twenty-third Pennsylvania Infantry, when the former was promoted.

PENNSYLVANIA OFFICERS

Eleventh Army Corps

Third Division, First Brigade: Alexander Schimmelfennig, a trained Prussian officer, full of ardor for the Republic which had welcomed him from persecution abroad, led the Seventy-fourth Pennsylvania Infantry from September 30, 1861, until his promotion to the rank of brigadier general came to him, November 29, 1862. He died September 7, 1865, leaving a noble record of service performed for the State he loved and the nation he served.

Twelfth Army Corps

Second Division, Second Brigade: Brig. Gen. Thomas L. Kane entered service June 21, 1862, as lieutenant colonel Thirteenth Reserves; he was made brigadier general Sept. 7, 1862, and was brevetted major general for gallant and distinguished service at Gettysburg. Although prostrated with severe illness and unable to keep command of the brigade all the time, he would not leave the field. General Kane found himself physically disabled for active service after Gettysburg and resigned the following November. He died in 1883.

Col. George A. Cobham, Jr., of the 111th Pennsylvania Infantry, alternated with General Kane in the command of the brigade during and after the battle. For Gettysburg and other battles he was brevetted brigadier general, to date from July 19, 1864—the day before he was killed in the battle of Peach Tree Creek, Georgia, in Sherman's campaign. He had taken a gallant part in the battles which preceded that engagement.

It will be seen by running over this list that of the men who commanded for a longer or shorter time an army corps at Gettysburg four were Pennsylvanians; that eight divisions out of twenty-two, and twenty-two brigades out of fifty-nine, were led by officers from the Keystone State.

This full exhibit, not heretofore made in all its details, may help to emphasize the enduring interest which Pennsylvania possesses in the campaign, the battle, and the field of Gettysburg, and to suggest at least one of the reasons why it behooved the Commonwealth to erect and dedicate in September, 1910, its magnificent memorial, containing on tablets of bronze the name of every officer and soldier from the State who was present in the struggle on the three opening days of July, 1863.

V

THE EMPIRE STATE IN THE BATTLE

THE United States will never cease to recognize the services rendered during the season of stress and danger in the early sixties by those two massive strongholds of Union sentiment and patriotic devotion, the Commonwealths of Pennsylvania and New York. These services are in part commemorated at Gettysburg by hundreds of bronze and marble monuments designating in the aggregate the work done on that field by thousands of officers and men from those States, a work so vast and valuable that one is puzzled to declare which one is foremost in its claim upon the people's patriotic regards. This truth is so self-evident that it would be unfair to withhold from New York, after having given detailed treatment to the sister Commonwealth, its full measure of appreciation and praise.

There is one phase of service which these two States rendered which is not usually considered to rank very high, and yet which deserves emphasis— the immediate and generous response which both of them gave in June and July, 1863, before, during, and after the battle, in the form of a vast outpouring of emergency men and militia regiments organized at Harrisburg, and made ready to afford help to the

63

interests which were then so gravely menaced. New York, for example, within three days of the time when the call was issued announcing the critical situation, sent to Harrisburg thousands of her organized militia force, well drilled and well disciplined, prepared at once for the field. Maj. Gen. D. N. Couch, commanding the Department of the Susquehanna during the exigent period in question, pays this tribute to Horatio Seymour, then Chief Executive:

> The Governor of New York pushed forward his regiments with alacrity. They were generally armed and equipped ready for field service, and their arrival brought confidence.

Nearly sixteen thousand men during the time of danger were sent by that Commonwealth to serve the nation's needs; and, in addition, when a few days after the battle a draft riot broke out in New York City, other thousands were furnished by the State to suppress disorder there, and to supplement the work of veteran soldiers from the Army of the Potomac.

Col. William F. Fox, the author of the story of the battle published in the great three-volume work *New York at Gettysburg*, in summarizing the services of his State in the engagement, says:

> This Commonwealth furnished one-third or more of the corps, division, and brigade commanders; she furnished the most men and filled the most graves. More than one-fourth of the Union army marched there under the flags of the State of New York; more than one-fourth of those who fell there followed those colors to their graves.

We have already indicated, in comparison with Pennsylvania's share in the conflict, that New York's organizations were as follows: sixty-eight regiments of infantry (fragmentary detachments amounting to some twenty companies making up eight of these), seven regiments of cavalry, and nineteen batteries.

In the Roster the individual organizations will find their distinctive places. In this chapter it remains for us to indicate the rank and service of the leading officers from New York who served as commanders in the fight.

At General Headquarters, in close and confidential relations with Meade, was his West Point classmate, the provost marshal general of the army, Marsena R. Patrick, who for years before the war was indentified with his native Commonwealth in civic services and as a leading educator.

Another leading officer from this State was Maj. Gen. Daniel Butterfield (1831–1891), chief of staff to General Hooker, who remained in the same relation with Meade, at the latter's request, for a few days during and after the battle. Butterfield had reached the station of colonel in the militia service in New York when the war began, and was appointed brigadier general of Volunteers and lieutenant colonel of infantry in the Regular Army in 1861; later he became a major general, commanding the Fifth Corps at Fredericksburg. He was awarded a medal of honor for gallantry at Gaines' Mill. For some years after the war he was sub-treasurer of the United States in New York City. He was slightly wounded at Gettysburg.

The Chief Engineer, Brig. Gen. Gouverneur K. Warren, to whom was due the salvation of Round Top on the second day, and the veteran Inspector General of the Army of the Potomac, Colonel, afterward Brvt. Maj. Gen. Edmund Schriver, both of them distinguished Academy graduates, are in this list.

Three generals from this State held command of army corps at Gettysburg; two were Academy graduates: Maj. Gen. H. W. Slocum, who led the Twelfth Corps, and who by fortifying that part of the line at Culp's Hill, where he had charge, contributed largely to the success achieved in repelling the various terrific assaults made on the Union right wing; and Maj. Gen. Abner Doubleday, who during the first day commanded the First Corps in its position along Seminary Ridge, making there a record for skill, courage, and leadership which is now a part of the annals of the battle.

The Third Corps was commanded by Maj. Gen. Daniel Edgar Sickles. This notable man was a New-Yorker born and bred, his birth occurring in that city, October 20, 1825. Before the war broke out he had come to the front as a lawyer and party leader, and had reached a place of influence in national politics. He had also been a member of the Legislature, State Senator, Secretary of Legation in London, and member of Congress. He was at the outbreak of hostilities a Democrat with intense patriotic convictions in behalf of the Union, and it was largely through his influence that the New York City Board of Aldermen and other branches of the municipal government were strongly committed to the defense of the new national administration. President Lincoln was sincerely grateful for Sickles's valuable support, and recognized his military abilities by a commission as brigadier general after Sickles had organized the Excelsior Brigade, in which for the opening months of the war he was colonel of the Seventieth New York. He won the rank of major general on the Peninsula and at Antietam, and in the struggle at Chancellorsville did fine service as a corps commander. At Gettysburg he was severely wounded, losing his leg; he was brevetted twice for gallantry, and was awarded the Congressional Medal of Honor for his bravery in this battle. He served as United States minister to Spain, 1869 to 1873, and in Congress, 1892–94, and has occupied other high offices. He was put on the retired list of the United States Army with the rank of major general in 1869. At this writing (1913) General Sickles is still living in New York.

New York furnished five division commanders; four of them were in the opening day's desperate conflict. In the First Corps at the head of the First Division was Brig. Gen. James S. Wadsworth, a great citizen and a notable patriot. Born in 1807, he was graduated from Harvard, and then settled down, after taking a course in law, to manage the affairs of his large estate, and to administer the tasks which came to him as a philanthropist. In August, 1861, when there was fear that the National Government might run short of supplies, he bought and forwarded to Annapolis two vessels loaded with provisions. He served as a volunteer aide to McDowell at Bull Run, became brigadier general in August following, and for more than a year occupied the important post of military governor of the District of Columbia. In

December, 1862, eager for active service, he was made the head of the division which he led with brave devotion for many months. He did faithful service at Gettysburg in the face of overpowering opposition. He was killed in the Wilderness, May 6, 1864, the brevet of major general, dating from that day, proving a posthumous honor.

The Second Division in this First Corps was led by Brig. Gen. John Cleveland Robinson (1817–1897), appointed from his native State of New York to West Point, where he was a cadet from July 1, 1835, until March 14, 1838, when he resigned to study law. A soldier's life, however, re-allured him, and he secured a commission as second lieutenant, Fifth Infantry, in October, 1839. A captain when the war broke out, he was made colonel First Michigan, July, 1861, and promoted to be brigadier general, April 28, 1862. He was brevetted colonel for Gettysburg, where he led his forces with distinguished ability. Brevets up to major general followed, and also a medal of honor for gallantry in leading a charge on the breastworks at Laurel Hill, May, 1864, where he lost a leg. He was retired as major general in 1869. He was elected Lieutenant Governor of New York in 1872, and served as commander in chief of the G. A. R., in 1877 and 1878, and in 1887 as president of the Society of the Army of the Potomac.

Two division commanders were in the Eleventh Corps:

Brig. Gen. Francis C. Barlow (1834–1896), commander First Division, and severely wounded in the battle, was born in Brooklyn and educated at Harvard; studied law, and served for a time as editorial writer on the *New York Tribune*. In the three months' service he was a private; from the lieutenant colonelcy of the Sixty-first New York Vols. he rose to be major general, developing superb qualities of leadership, in spite of his youth and boyish appearance; he was several times dangerously wounded. After the war Barlow served as Secretary of State of New York, United States marshal, and Attorney General of New York.

Brig. Gen. Adolph von Steinwehr, commanding the Second Division (1822–1877), was a thoroughly trained German officer, with distinctive gifts as an architect and engineer, who revealed years after the war high accomplishments in cartography and in the preparation of school-books in geography. He came to this country to reside in 1854; at the outbreak of the war was made colonel of the Twenty-ninth New York Vols., and later a brigadier general. He did fine service at Gettysburg on the first day in fortifying the northern front of Cemetery Hill at Howard's suggestion. He will be remembered as one of the notable contributions made by Germany to the service of the Union.

Brig. Gen. Romeyn B. Ayres, who commanded the "Regular Division" in the Fifth Corps, which did such heroic service near Round Top on the second day, was appointed to West Point from New York.

Among the COMMANDERS OF BRIGADES belonging in this enumeration are the following who were graduates of West Point:

Brig. Gen. George S. Greene, Third Brigade, Second Division, Twelfth Corps, the great engineer who in person superintended the fortification of Culp's Hill; Brig. Gen. Alexander S. Webb, Second Brigade, Second Division, Second Corps, in command at the exact point where on the last day the final charge of the Confederates culminated; Brig. Gen. David A. Russell, Third Brigade, First Division, Sixth Corps, his force being chiefly held in reserve on the extreme left, not far from Round Top; and Brig. Gen. Stephen H. Weed, who gallantly fell on Round Top, Thursday evening, at the head of the Third Brigade, Second Division, Fifth Corps, an artillerist of unusual capacity, and a fine specimen of soldierly manhood.

Among the others who held brigade commands Col. Charles S. Wainwright, First New York Light Artillery, commanding the artillery brigade of the First Corps, deserves generous recognition. He was brevetted brigadier general in 1864 "for brave, constant, and efficient service" in the campaigns of that year.

Each of the three brigades in the First Division, Third Corps, was led by a New York commander. The First Brigade had at its head Brig. Gen. Charles K. Graham. Born in New York City in 1824, he died there in 1889. He had the advantage of some years of training and experience in the United States Navy in his youth; at the outbreak of the war he was a civil engineer employed in the Brooklyn navy-yard. He organized and was made colonel of the Seventy-fourth New York in the Excelsior Brigade, and was promoted to be brigadier general November 29, 1862; he led his brigade gallantly at Chancellorsville, and at Gettysburg he was a conspicuous figure in the Peach Orchard struggle, where he was wounded and captured. At the end of the war he was brevetted major general. In later years, from 1873 till his death, he held prominent Government posts in New York, including that of surveyor and also naval officer of the port.

Brig. Gen. John H. H. Ward (1823–1903), commanding the Second Brigade, born in New York City, served in the United States Army from 1842 to 1847, gaining valuable experience as a first sergeant in the Mexican War. For nearly a decade he served, after leaving the army, as assistant and then as full commissary general of the State of New York. At the outbreak of the war he became colonel of the Thirty - eighth New York, which he had recruited; at the head of this organization he fought in the first Bull Run battle and on the Peninsula; he was made brigadier general in November, 1862, and was a leading figure in his corps from that time. At Gettysburg his command was posted at the Devil's Den, where some terrific fighting was done on both sides. For years after the war General Ward was deputy county clerk of New York county.

Col. Philip Regis de Trobriand, an accomplished French officer, commanded the Third Brigade; his men, near the Wheat-field and the Peach Orchard on the second day, did some sharp fighting and suffered greatly. At the end of the war he was brevetted brigadier and major general. Continuing in service, he was retired as colonel of the Thirteenth Infantry in 1879, and died July, 1897.[1]

At the head of a brigade which served throughout the campaign, and which did work that was invaluable the day and night before the battle and during the opening hours of the fight in Buford's cavalry division, was Col. Thomas C. Devin, who became a brigadier general later in the war, and was brevetted major general, besides winning other brevets for special acts of gallantry. Entering the Regular Army after the Civil War, he died, colonel of the Third Cavalry, April 4, 1878.

In the Second Division, Third Corps, Brig. Gen. Joseph B. Carr (1828–1895) was at the head of the First Brigade. He had been advantaged by skilful militia service in his State for a dozen years before the outbreak of the war, when he began his career as the colonel of the Second New York; he became brigadier general September 7, 1862, and was brevetted one degree higher in 1865. He served as Secretary of State in New York from 1879 to 1885.

Col. Wladimir Krzyzanowski, Fifty-eighth New York, commanding the Second Brigade, Third Division, Eleventh Corps, was born in Poland, and before coming to this country served as an officer in the army of his native land. For a while he was a

[1] General de Trobriand, in 1867, wrote for his French countrymen an interesting volume making clear to them the issues involved in the Civil War, and recounting with vividness his own observations and experiences, *Four Years with the Army of the Potomac.* It was translated into English by George K. Dauchy, and issued on this side of the water by Ticknor and Company in 1889. The work is reminiscential, gossipy, critical, and descriptive by turns.

brigadier general of Volunteers in our struggle. He died January 31, 1887.

Brig. Gen. Alexander Shaler (1827–1911), commanding First Brigade, Third Division, Sixth Corps, united with the New York militia service at the age of eighteen — in 1845; when, the war broke out he was major of the famous "Seventh Regiment"; he served as lieutenant colonel and then as colonel of the Sixty-fifth, winning a brigadier's commission in May, 1863, and one as brevet major general in 1865, as well as a Congressional medal for gallantry at Marye's Heights; and was three months a prisoner of war. After the war he was a mighty force in reorganizing the fire department of New York City; he gave similar help also to Chicago after its great fire in 1871. In other respects he achieved a most creditable civic career.

Brig. Gen. Joseph J. Bartlett (1820–1893), leader of the Second Brigade, First Division, Sixth Corps, and in combination with that also in charge of the Third Division for a time, his command being chiefly held in reserve, and later being occupied in the task of following up the retreating army of Lee, entered service as major of the Twenty - seventh New York in May, 1861, and after winning the rank of brigadier general and the brevet rank of major general was mustered out with honor, January 15, 1866. In every battle from Bull Run to Appomattox he and his regiment, brigade, or division made a heroic record. He served after the war as United States minister to Norway and Sweden, and later as Deputy Commissioner of Pensions.

73

GETTYSBURG

Brig. Gen. Samuel K. Zook (1821 – 1863) led the Third Brigade, First Division, Second Corps, with credit at Fredericksburg, Chancellorsville, and in the campaign of Gettysburg up to the afternoon of the second day, when he fell at the head of his command in the bloody Wheat-field in front of Little Round Top, and died the next day. The War Department dated his commission as brevet major general, so as to recognize his crowning services, July 2, 1863. He had served in the New York militia for a decade before the war, in which he entered the three months' service as lieutenant colonel of the Sixth New York. Soon after his return from that service he recruited the Fifty-seventh, and became its commander, winning a commission as brigadier general in November, 1862.

The following officers served as commanders of brigades in the battle, in addition to those who had won the rank of brigadier general:

Col. William R. Brewster, Seventy-third New York (later brevet brigadier general), led the Excelsior Brigade, Second Division, Third Corps.

Col. Patrick Kelly, Eighty-eighth New York, was in charge of the "Irish Brigade," First Division, Second Corps.

Col. Kenner Garrard (see West Point list), One Hundred and Forty - sixth New York, took Weed's brigade, Fifth Corps, after the death of that soldier.

Col. James C. Rice (brigadier general, August 17, 1863; killed in battle, near Spottsylvania, May 10, 1864), Forty-fourth New York, succeeded Strong Vincent after that leader had fallen on Little Round Top, Third Brigade, First Division, Fifth Corps.

THE EMPIRE STATE

In the Second Corps, Third Division, Third Brigade, three New York officers commanded in succession in the battle.

Col. George L. Willard (a regular-army officer, with sixteen years of service to his credit, in which time he had risen from private to major Nineteenth Infantry), 125th New York, and brevetted colonel for his services at Gettysburg, was killed in the effort to stay the progress of the Confederate attack on the left of the Second Corps, late Thursday afternoon.

When Willard fell Col. Eliakim Sherrill, 126th New York, assumed command of the brigade. He was killed next day in the midst of the battle when Pickett's charge was broken, that attack falling in part upon the portion of the line where this command was posted. Colonel Sherrill was an eminent citizen and a fine type of soldierly excellence; he had served in the State Senate and as a Congressman, and in many ways stood high in the Commonwealth.

When Sherrill was killed Lieut. Col. James M. Bull, of the same regiment, took charge of the brigade.

Col. Charles R. Coster, 134th New York, commanded the First Brigade, Second Division, Eleventh Corps.

Col. George Van Amsberg, Forty-fifth New York, commanded the First Brigade, Third Division, Eleventh Corps, for a time during the battle.

Col. Archibald L. McDougall, 123d New York, was at the head of the First Brigade, First Division, Twelfth Corps.

Col. David J. Nevin, Sixty-second New York, was

for a time commander of the Third Brigade, Third Division, Sixth Corps.

Colonel Fox, in the work already referred to, *New York at Gettysburg*, sums up, after careful examination of all the data, the total strength of New York organizations in the battle at 27,692, and the total losses, 989 killed, 4,023 wounded, and 1,761 captured or missing—a total of 6,773.

VI

THE detailed narrative of the Gettysburg campaign is long and complicated. Only historical specialists and military experts can be expected to apprehend all the chapters of the history in their interrelations and completeness, embracing an elaborate account of marches and countermarches, skirmishes by the score, advances and retreats, and cavalry encounters, extending from the third of June until the third of August, 1863—movements participated in by more than two hundred thousand men (including the forces concentrated at Harrisburg, Pennsylvania), and which reached their climax in one of the bloodiest, most desperate, and most decisive of all the battles of the century, July 1–3, in and around the village which has been made famous forever by the struggle which culminated there.

While the ordinary reader, then, finds it impossible to hold in mind the thousands of details which make up the operations of this vast and elaborate campaign, nevertheless he may easily get a bird's-eye view of the chief features of the great movement, a panoramic glimpse of the essential features of the work of the two armies, from the time they left the Rappahannock until they faced each other, after Gettysburg, at Falling Waters, on the Potomac, and found there that the campaign was substantially at an end.

In advance, therefore, of an attempt to elaborate the details of the battle, it may be helpful to give a simple outline to serve as a flash-light illumination of the landscape, stretching from Fredericksburg, Virginia, to Gettysburg, Pennsylvania, across which the armies moved to their place of encounter.

(a) *The Situation on the Rappahannock.*—The battle of Chancellorsville, fought May 1-4, between Hooker and Lee, had brought humiliation and defeat to the Army of the Potomac, which in addition to its losses in that conflict was immediately depleted by the muster-out of a score or more of short-term regiments. Nevertheless, the army was not in any large sense either disheartened or demoralized; but it was heartsick and sorely disappointed in view of Hooker's lack of adequate leadership. Still, as reinforcements were received and officers and men gathered themselves together for a fresh effort in case a movement should develop, within a month the Army of the Potomac was itself again. Its commander had not, apparently, any immediate plan for an aggressive movement, but was alert in watching his adversary. Lee, on the other hand, for reasons which we have already given in detail, accepting in addition the counsels of the authorities at Richmond, had determined to march into Pennsylvania. With regard to his plans at this juncture a criticism has been urged by a British military expert which may aptly be dealt with just here.

A FLASH-LIGHT VIEW

One of Battine's critical suggestions, repeated in one form or another in his valuable book, *The Crisis of the Confederacy*, is to the effect that Lee should have made his advance into the North immediately after Chancellorsville; and he argues in support of this criticism that the Army of the Potomac was at that time so demoralized by its recent defeat, and the North was so depressed by the successive reverses which had overtaken the Union Army, that an aggressive campaign in May instead of June would have given Lee assurance of victory.

This suggestion, like some others made at long range on the other side of the sea, with incomplete grasp of the local situation, is not warranted by the facts in the case. The losses in the Army of the Potomac, as well as the fighting, had been confined to less than half of that army, and even the three corps which suffered the most were not by any means demoralized. They quickly recovered their tone and temper, and in a fortnight would have eagerly taken the field once more. As to the requirement that Lee should have moved earlier in the season, let Longstreet's testimony suffice. He says in his book *From Manassas to Appomattox*: "General Lee was actually so crippled by his victory [at Chancellorsville] that he was a full month restoring his army to a condition to take the field." By the early part of June, however, his army was in eager and enthusiastic mood, and recouped for its work, so that now he was ready for the forward movement.

(b) *The Plan.*—General Lee set out to march into the North by way of the Shenandoah and Cumberland valleys, which are continuous thoroughfares, his aim being to strike at the Susquehanna in the neighborhood of Harrisburg, to reach York with one of his columns, and possibly to cross the river and threaten other Northern cities, meanwhile menacing Baltimore and Washington, and, if the opportunity opened, make an advance upon them. He had a clear understanding, however, of the fact that Washington was thoroughly protected by its fortifications, and that it would be idle to dream of assaulting an army ensconced behind them. If the reader will examine the map and trace the path of Lee's army by the route indicated, and then draw a line almost due north from Fredericksburg through Frederick, Maryland, to Gettysburg, he will see the advantage possessed by the Union forces in pursuing this latter inside line to the place of encounter.

(c) *The Opening Moves.*—Lee left Hill's corps at Fredericksburg to observe Hooker's manœuvers, and concentrated the rest of his army, for the time being, at Culpeper, June 3–10, whence, after the cavalry fight to be noted below, a forward movement was begun on the 11th, Ewell's corps leading into the Shenandoah Valley, where it captured Winchester, June 13–15, the delay thus occasioned giving Hooker opportune time for his movements to interpose between Lee and Washington. The Confederate Army crossed the Potomac at Williamsport, Maryland, June 23–25, and halted at Chambersburg, Pennsylvania, June 27–28, with portions of Ewell's corps advanced to Carlisle and York, threatening the region of the Susquehanna, and aiming finally at Harrisburg.

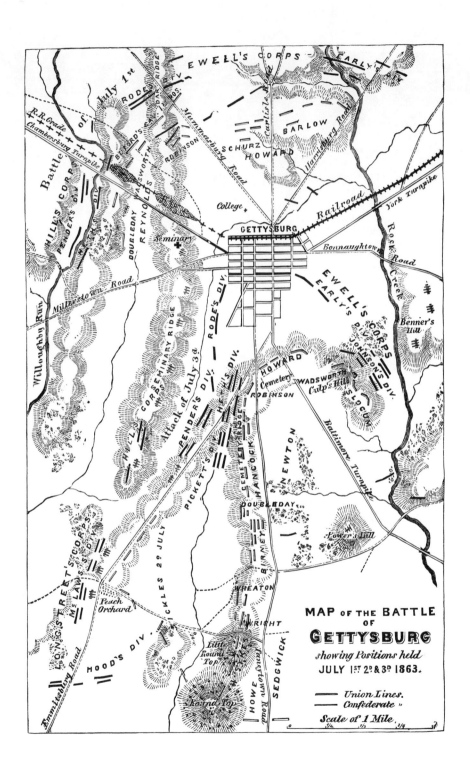

MAP OF THE BATTLE
OF
GETTYSBURG
showing Positions held
JULY 1ST 2D & 3D 1863.

───── Union Lines.
──── Confederate "

Scale of 1 Mile

(*d*) Hooker, at the head of the Army of the Potomac, discovered, June 4–8, through his scouts and cavalry, that threatening movements were going on in Lee's army; he was assured of Confederate plans looking toward an invasion of the border States by a fight on June 9th, extending from Beverly Ford to Brandy Station, between the cavalry forces of the two armies, headed respectively by Stuart and Pleasanton, the latter making the attack for the purpose of ascertaining the meaning of the fresh activity of Lee's forces. This engagement revealed to the Union cavalry the presence of the Confederate cavalry corps and also infantry forces at Culpeper, close by, centered there for a forward movement. On June 11th Hooker, in order to protect his own right flank and also to guard Washington, started his army northward, keeping between Lee and the Capital.

When Lee's movement was developed, Hooker also crossed the Potomac at Edwards Ferry on pontoons, June 25–26, focusing his army at Frederick City, Maryland, at which point—deeming himself hindered and aggrieved by the treatment he was receiving from the general in chief, Halleck—on June 28th he asked to be relieved. His request was at once granted, and Maj. Gen. George G. Meade was put in command of the army.

(*e*) Both Meade and Lee foresaw the bare possibility of an encounter at Gettysburg, because of its strategic value as a point where ten roads centered, but neither of them, until the fight was on, really expected the engagement to take place there. Meade was feeling his way northward and trying to find out what Lee was planning; Lee, learning that the Union Army had crossed into Maryland, wisely determined to withdraw his advance divisions and concentrate his forces at Cashtown, Pennsylvania, on the eastern flank of the South Mountain Range, as the most convenient point of meeting for his scattered troops. It happened, however, that the heads of columns, marching on roads that centered in Gettysburg, had a collision, and became so entangled in a fight that neither side could withdraw.

(*f*) Buford's Union cavalry early on the morning of Wednesday, July 1, uncovered the Confederate advance, which had not intended to be drawn into a fight, but was simply trying to locate the Union forces. The fight began two miles from Gettysburg, on the Chambersburg Pike, skirmishing going on all the morning, the cavalry, dismounted, keeping the Confederates at bay until Major General Reynolds, commanding the left wing, could come up with his troops. This officer had hardly formed a division of his own First Army Corps into line facing westward and ordered them forward when he was killed. The fight of the corps, including intervals, lasted six hours or more, under Doubleday, the troops of the enemy being under Hill. When at noon the Eleventh Corps arrived it was sent by Major General Howard to occupy the region north of the town, where portions of Ewell's corps were beginning to arrive from York and Carlisle. After two hours of hard fighting here the Eleventh Corps was flanked and overmatched, and had to withdraw, leaving their wounded, and losing hundreds of prisoners as it crowded through the town toward Cemetery Hill, where Howard, in command, with other troops arrived or arriving, was ready to encourage them; while Hancock, sent by Meade to study the situation, gave new strength to the fugitives. Meanwhile the First Corps, which had been fighting for six hours, was also flanked and forced back to Cemetery Hill, which had been fortified, and with batteries in place was made strong enough to be held in case of further pursuit. The Confederates, on noting the strength of the hill and apprehending that the forces thereon were sufficient to resist any attack that might be made just then, concluded to be satisfied with the successes already won that day.

(g) The morning of the second day was occupied by both Meade and Lee in locating troops and getting ready for further activities. At 3.30 P.M. Longstreet's corps opened an almost overwhelming attack on the Union left flank, commanded by Sickles, in front of the Round Tops. The fight lasted until dark, and although the Third Corps was heavily reinforced, it could not maintain the advanced ground which Sickles had occupied at the Peach Orchard. Round Top, however, was held and fortified, and the line from that point north as first indicated as the line of battle was securely held.[1]

The assault against the Union line, undertaken at Round Top and pushed with success at the Peach Orchard, was taken up by other parts of the Confederate line along Seminary Ridge toward the north, the

[1] There are two Round Tops, with a defile between them. It is "Little" Round Top which is the important point, and henceforth in the story the adjective may be at times omitted when the reference is clear.

assault of Wright's brigade on Hancock's line being one of fury and peril. It was not, however, supported by other brigades, and with that assault the attack on the line at that point ceased at dark.

(*h*) At 7.30 P.M. two Confederate brigades, led by Hays and Avery, made a charge against the Cemetery Hill position, driving back the thin line of infantry that had been left to hold it and reaching the batteries on the hilltop. This charge, after considerable fighting, was repulsed.

(*i*) Johnson's division at Culp's Hill made an advance after dark and secured a foothold in a line of entrenchments near the top of the hill which had been in part left vacant by the withdrawal of the Union forces in order to strengthen the imperiled left in the afternoon. The Confederates held this position until eleven o'clock Friday morning, when, after seven hours of fighting, commencing at dawn, they were at last driven back.

(*j*) The final features of the battle were the cannonade, from one to three on Friday afternoon, July 3d, intended to break in the Union left center; and the charge of Pickett's and Pettigrew's divisions against Hancock's line, a charge which resulted in disaster to the Confederate attacking force and gave the victory to the Union cause.

(*k*) At about the time this charge was made a cavalry action took place between Stuart's forces on the one hand and the Union horsemen on the other, two miles east of Culp's Hill, where Stuart had hoped to break through and get into the Union rear and bring panic and disaster to the trains. The Confederate cavalry were checkmated in their effort, and late in the evening withdrew from the field.

(*l*) The Fourth of July was passed in quiet, Lee having drawn in his troops from Culp's Hill and abandoned the town during the previous night. He began on the night of the Fourth to retreat. Ten days later, after great suffering on the part of his wounded, taken with great difficulty by the thousand with him in the withdrawal, he and his army made their escape across the Potomac at Williamsport and Falling Waters on the morning when the Union forces, confronting the Confederate position, one of great strength, were under orders to attack.

Here we have an outline view of the events of the campaign, which will serve as a mental guide for further exploitation of the incidents of that moment-ous period, June and July, 1863.

We are now ready to undertake such an elaboration of this outline view as will bring into prominence its strategic points, and lay stress on the chief manœuvers and movements, the critical and essential data of the story. This method, in brief, is a preliminary requisite for the reader who would grasp the signifi-cance of the engagement and apprehend the relative value and bearings of the shifting phases of the campaign and battle.

VII

(1) *Artillery Reorganized.*—In the month of May, after the battle of Chancellorsville, General Lee, in reorganizing his army for the forthcoming invasion, made some important changes. His ablest leader, Stonewall Jackson, was dead, and thus far no man had appeared in sight evidently able to handle the large force which that officer had been accustomed to marshal with matchless swiftness and skill under his own individual command in a single compact organization. It seemed necessary, therefore, for Lee to redistribute his troops, after he had managed to secure additional forces from other parts of the South, so as to be sure that they were arrayed under leaders who could ably manœuver them. He finally concluded, while retaining Longstreet, tested on many fields, at the head of the First Corps, to divide the remaining infantry into two additional army corps, to be led by Ewell and A. P. Hill, each a man of skill and reliability, who had acquired experience and developed capacity under the immediate eye and command of the great Confederate leader since he had been at the head of the Army of Northern Virginia. These two officers were accordingly promoted to be lieutenant generals and assigned respectively to the Second and the Third Army Corps.

86

SOME PRELIMINARY STEPS

In connection with this assignment it may be well for us to keep in mind that a corps in Lee's army was about twice as large as one in the Union Army, while the divisions also were of correlative size. The entire infantry force, thus recruited and organized, made up an aggregate of 68,000, while in J. E. B. Stuart's cavalry division there were in the neighborhood of 12,000 horsemen.

The artillery also underwent an important redistribution, with Pendleton, who had been in command of the reserve of that arm of the service, now assigned as chief, the batteries which had been under him being now scattered throughout the army. Four batteries were united to form a battalion of artillery, with a chief at its head; a battalion was assigned to each division of infantry, and in addition two battalions served as reserves for each corps, with a corps chief of artillery in command of all the batteries in his organization. Each one of these chiefs was chosen because of his skill in that particular arm of the service; besides this weaponry six batteries of horse artillery, thirty pieces in all, were attached to Stuart's cavalry division, under a gifted young West-Pointer, Maj. Robert F. Beckham. The entire artillery force, therefore, amounted to about 270 guns, and as now reorganized under expert corps and battalion chiefs they promised to develop new and terrible effectiveness, in spite of some inferior armament, occasional quantities of defective ammunition, and many unshod and badly nourished horses.

A similar but more far-reaching reorganization of the artillery in the Army of the Potomac—begun be-

fore Chancellorsville under that matchless chief of
his branch of the service, Henry J. Hunt—was now
perfected in advance of the Gettysburg campaign.
Clusters of five batteries were massed into brigades—
corresponding fairly well to the organizations called
battalions in the opposing army; a brigade of artillery
was assigned to each army corps, under a well-chosen
chief; while in addition an exceedingly strong artillery
reserve was accumulated, five brigades of four batteries apiece — a battery usually being a six-gun
affair—serving in that command. This tremendous
reserve was a vital factor in the fight at Gettysburg.
It made possible a development of strength which
Longstreet noted during the climax of the fight, and
which he recorded in his official report when he said
that in watching the effect of the cannonade which
preceded Pickett's charge it appeared to him, as he
was observing the effects of the Confederate fire upon
the Federal lines, "that the enemy put in fresh batteries about as rapidly as others were driven off."
A glance at Hunt's report will show that this impression made on Longstreet in the crisis of the fight
was based on fact, and that this procedure was made
possible because of the prevision and skill which had
brought together an immense reserve supply of guns
and ammunition for use in just such a crisis as that
which then confronted the Army of the Potomac.

When we reckon up the artillery just noted as connected with the seven corps of the Army of the
Potomac, and then add the forty-four pieces of horse
artillery—nine batteries, formed into two brigades—
which accompanied Pleasanton's cavalry corps, we

have an aggregate of 364 guns of various sizes, makes, and patterns, each one of them at one time or another in use in the battle; thus presenting a larger, stronger, and better-equipped organization of cannon than that which General Lee had been able to secure.

The wisdom of the policy whereby artillery adepts, as we have just shown, were chosen for special service in the two armies, in command of clusters of batteries called in the one case "brigades" and in the other "battalions," may be dwelt upon briefly for the sake of the untechnical reader. It had been found in due time in both armies that there were occasional brigade and division commanders who could skilfully handle their infantry in battle, but who were not versed in artillery tactics nor trained in the effective use of cannon on the field. Consequently, unless the battery commander was unusually skilful, or a staff-officer was at hand to give advice or spring into the breach when the guns were to be used to advantage, a valuable opportunity might be lost or a blunder might be made. After months of experiments the leaders on both sides concluded that the right policy would be to mass the batteries, and place them in properly sized units of organization under division or corps chiefs, each of these being a picked man, recognized as versed in that arm of the service, fit in all respects to post the batteries, direct their fire, and co-operate with the infantry, and needing but a word from his command-ing officer in order to act with vigilance, promptitude, and skill in supplementing and making effective the work of the other arms of the service. This policy as finally determined upon was never reversed, and when fully embodied in the conduct of many battles finally approved itself to the military circles of the world.

(2) *A Tentative Start.*—With preparations duly completed, the Confederate commander, using all precautions to keep his adversary in ignorance of his plans and movements, started Longstreet's corps from Fredericksburg, June 3d, toward the Shenandoah Valley, which had been chosen as the route into the North, the first rendezvous being indicated as Culpeper Court-house, about fifty miles a little north of west from the camps they had occupied all winter. Ewell's corps closely followed Longstreet on the 4th and 5th of June, and by the 7th these forces were bivouacked at Culpeper, while Hill's corps was left temporarily at Fredericksburg to mask the movement, its lines being so deployed as to cover substantially, but of necessity meagerly, the front hitherto occupied by the entire three corps. Lee himself, with his headquarters and the officers of his staff, remained until noon on the 6th at Fredericksburg to watch developments there.

Hooker, however, was on his guard; indeed, his alertness and prevision must have surprised and disappointed his great opponent. The scouts and balloon observers of the Union Army had discovered, within a day after Lee's movement began, signs of unusual activity in the camps on the other side of the Rappahannock—troops in motion, dust rising from roads in the rear of Lee's encampments, and other tokens which suggested a forward movement, which on various grounds Hooker had surmised might at any hour be undertaken, and accordingly he was not even for a day nonplussed.

The flanks of the Army of the Potomac were so well guarded by the Rappahannock that Lee could not assail them without endangering his own communications with the South, but Hooker had for some time apprehended a Confederate advance into the North, or, if a favorable opportunity justified it, an effort once more to threaten Washington. In either contingency he had in mind a possible movement against the enemy's rear, which on the morning of June 5th, while Lee's first ventures were going forward, he suggested to President Lincoln. (*Official Records*, XXVII, 1:30.) Hooker in his despatch makes known the situation then confronting him, and in view of the evident activity in Lee's army discerningly and presciently says:

> He must either have it in mind to cross the Upper Potomac or to throw his army between mine and Washington, in case I am correct in my conjecture. . . . The head of his column will probably be headed toward the Potomac, *via* Gordonsville or Culpeper, while the rear will rest on Fredericksburg. After giving the subject my best reflection I am of the opinion that it is my duty to pitch into the rear, although in so doing the head of his column may reach Warrenton before I can return.

These utterances are so creditable to Hooker's military insight in that particular juncture that they deserve emphasis, showing as they do, when taken in connection with the emergent movement then going on in his army under his immediate eye, that he was forecasting with literal accuracy the plans and purposes of Lee, and was projecting without a moment of delay a manœuver to checkmate him by crossing at Fredericksburg and attacking the troops posted there. In order, however, to be sure of his ground in case of a fight, he inquires in the same despatch to the President whether his standing instructions to keep Washington and Harper's Ferry covered in any event by the Army of the Potomac will allow him to attempt a movement upon the rear of Lee. The very suggestion of such a manœuver was startling to both Mr. Lincoln and General Halleck, to whom the safety of Washington was a fundamental condition in any campaign, and the decision of the War Department must have been a foregone conclusion to Hooker; but the latter, without waiting for a formal reply to his inquiry, proceeded at least to exploit the region on the Confederate side of the Rappahannock in order to satisfy himself what force was there arrayed before him. This procedure was in any event incumbent upon him, no matter what decision might be announced from Washington. Therefore, as a precautionary measure and to ascertain the facts in the case, pontoon bridges were thrown across the river at the point below Fredericksburg known since the preceding December as Franklin's Crossing—a process which was attended with delay and danger on account of the resistance made by Confederate sharpshooters sheltered behind extemporized rifle-pits.

A serious loss occurred in the effort of the engineers to launch the pontoons and project the bridge, their gallant commander, Capt. Charles E. Cross, of the Engineer Corps, a graduate of West Point, being shot and instantly killed—the first alumnus of the Military

Academy to fall in the Gettysburg campaign. Although but twenty-six years of age, he had shown himself for half a dozen years increasingly resourceful in his profession, helping to plan and build the magnificent fortifications around the nation's Capital, commending himself to McClellan by his splendid work on the Peninsula, and winning by his gallantry several brevets.

The Sixth Corps, whose camps were not far away from the proposed place of crossing, furnished troops for the venture, the Second Brigade.[1] of Howe's division leading the way, commanded by Col. Lewis A. Grant, who at this writing (January, 1913) still lives at his home in Minneapolis, to enjoy the fame and honors which his military and civic services have assured him.

This brigade, about the middle of the afternoon of June 5th, arrived at the place where the engineers were struggling to launch their pontoons, hindered and baffled for the time by the murderous fire from the rifle-pits on the other bank. Efforts had been going on for an hour or more to silence this fire by a battery or two of artillery, but the Confederate shelter was effective nevertheless. Colonel Grant, consulting with the engineers, combined with them in a dash across the river in the pontoons, the Fifth Vermont and the New Jersey regiment uniting in the exploit, which was a splendid piece of successful enterprise. The soldiers lost but few men in their work, landed with expedition, dashed up the bank,

[1] Second, Third, Fourth, Fifth, and Sixth Vermont, and Twenty-sixth New Jersey.

captured over a hundred Confederates, dispersed the
rest, and thus opened the way for their comrades to
follow and occupy a strong position on the enemy's
side of the river. With this lodgment assured the
bridges were soon built, and other forces a little later
made their way over the river.

(3) *Hooker's First Plan.*—For a full week (June
4–10) Hooker cherished the plan of endeavoring to
checkmate Lee by crossing in force at Fredericksburg, defeating and dispersing Hill's corps, and then
—disregarding the other portions of Lee's army, which
were on their way north—pressing on toward Richmond. We have indicated some data bearing on his
purpose in this direction; other phases of the case
may be summarized without elaboration at this point.

Lee tarried at Fredericksburg until noon on June
6th, carefully studying the attitude of his opponent's
troops; and finding no sign that Hooker intended to
advance across the river with a large force, and
rightly concluding that no serious attack would be
made upon Hill, and trusting that in any event the
situation would be safe in the hands of that general,
the commander in chief took his departure, joining
the other two corps of his army at Culpeper next
day.

Turning once more to Hooker and his situation, we
find him for some days at Falmouth watching closely
the situation, holding his army in hand, maintaining
his equipoise, notwithstanding the critical condition
of affairs, keeping track by despatches from Washington and through the reports of his scouts and balloon
corps and his spies concerning the whereabouts of

Lee's advancing troops, but hindered by order of the War Department from making any attack upon the corps of Hill, in his front. This last-named officer, obeying instructions given in advance by Lee, kept up his show of force along the river until June 14th, and then made a hurried march to join the other portions of the Army of Northern Virginia, the advancing corps of which, under Ewell, on the evening of that day captured Winchester and Martinsburg, although news of the victory had not of course reached Hill.

Meanwhile, on June 10th and 11th Hooker's army had hurriedly undertaken their withdrawal from their winter quarters at Falmouth; the stores at Acquia Creek, where the main depots of supplies for months had been located, were removed by steamer to Washington; and by June 14th the entire Army of the Potomac was skilfully spread out in strategic locations between the Shenandoah Valley and the outer line of fortifications which protected Washington. We have thus anticipated some of the subordinate movements which led to this result, and they must now be briefly rehearsed, but not until we have given some attention to the general policy which Hooker proposed, as contrasted with that which the War Department urged.

In reply to Hooker's inquiries as to his proposed attack on the rear of Lee, word came promptly from Washington, both the President and General Halleck uniting in their judgment that no movement on the force at Fredericksburg would be feasible or wise. Mr. Lincoln's telegram contains the following characteristic counsels (dated June 5th, at four in the afternoon—the very hour, we may recall, when Colonel Grant's brigade forementioned was affording help to get the pontoon bridge laid across the river below Fredericksburg):

> In case you find Lee coming to the north of the Rappahannock, I would by no means cross to the south of it. If he should leave a force at Fredericksburg, tempting you to fall upon it, it would fight in intrenchments and have you at disadvantage, and so, man for man, worst you at that point, while his main force would in some way be getting the advantage of you northward. In one word, I would not take any risk of being entangled upon the river like an ox jumped over a fence, and liable to be torn by dogs, front and rear, without a fair chance to gore one way or kick the other. If Lee would come to my side of the river, I would keep on the same side, and fight him or act on the defense, according as might be my estimate of his strength relatively to my own.

Halleck chimes in with the President in cautioning Hooker against any movement upon Fredericksburg, but suggests that if Lee continues to spread out his forces, leaving troops behind at that point and prolonging his line toward the Potomac, such an operation would give the Union commander great advantages upon the Confederate flank to cut Lee's army in two and fight his divided army. Five days later Hooker urged once more his reasons for crossing at Fredericksburg, and after worsting the troops that had been left there, advancing on Richmond from that point, leaving the Union forces around Washington to deal with the advancing troops of Lee. Of course, this plan was forbidden, Mr. Lincoln quaintly saying in response:

> I think Lee's army, and not Richmond, is your true objective point. If he comes toward the upper Potomac, follow on his

flank and on his inside track, shortening your lines while he lengthens his. Fight him, too, when opportunity offers. If he stays where he is, fret him and fret him.

When Hooker came finally to move his army his policy agreed with that of Mr. Lincoln as thus oddly given. But a little later, June 14th, the President made another suggestion bearing on the campaign, showing how closely his penetrating mind was engaged with the various problems then complicating the case:

> If the head of Lee's army is at Martinsburg, and the tail of it on the Plank Road [a hundred miles away] between Fredericksburg and Chancellorsville, the animal must be very thin somewhere. Could you not break him?

The leading military critic to urge that Hooker should have been permitted to carry out his proposed plan—"to pitch into the rear of Lee" at Fredericksburg, and then, after beating Hill's force at that point, press on to Richmond, allowing Lee either to march against Washington or to invade the North, just as he pleased—is the Comte de Paris (*Civil War in America*, vol. iii, p. 469–472), who takes the ground that the commander of the Army of the Potomac could have afforded to disregard the plans of Lee and his invasion of the North, or any possible movement that was made against Washington, for the sake of capturing Richmond. But when we recall the inroads which Lee made, notwithstanding the work of the Army of the Potomac, the narrow margin by which the victory at Gettysburg was won, and the panic and horror which smote the entire North in view of

Lee's advance and temporary success, it would seem self-evident at this far remove from the time of the invasion, and in view of all the data which are now historic, that Lincoln was correct in his suggestion to Hooker that "Lee's army, and not Richmond, was the true goal" at which he must aim. It may be further borne in mind that even when Hooker's plans to attack Lee in the rear were kept in abeyance, in view of orders from headquarters, the commander of the Army of the Potomac, by his alertness, his vigilant and rapid movements, and his ready insight into every phase of the situation, changing every hour, made a record wholly creditable to his intelligence, his military judgment, and his fidelity. What he might have done at the head of his army, had he been continued in that post until the two belligerent hosts collided, is not a question for surmise here, but it is certain that the Joseph Hooker of June, 1863, was an altogether different man from the Joseph Hooker of May 3d and 4th of that year, in the critical hours during which the issues of Chancellorsville were decided.

(4) *Cavalry Fight near Beverly Ford.*—On the 9th of June an all-day struggle took place in an extended arena, stretching from the Rappahannock River on the one flank in the direction of Culpeper Court-house on the other, between the cavalry forces of the two armies, led respectively by J. E. B. Stuart and Pleasanton, both officers having been summoned to their respective posts of leadership on account of their services at Chancellorsville in the early part of May.

The whole field was quadrangular in shape, one side extending along the river from Kelly's Ford to Beverly Ford, about seven miles, and the opposite side stretching from Stevensburg on the south to Brandy Station and Fleetwood on the north, the intervening territory, here and there hilly and well wooded, and in part open farm land, making more than seventy square miles through which the fighting forces were scattered in fierce and occasionally close array.

The fight was notable for several reasons: it was the first hand-to-hand encounter that had taken place between the entire cavalry force of the two armies; it assured both parties that they had on the "other side" foemen worthy of their steel; and it revealed to Hooker, when the day was done, certain facts which had a vital bearing on his immediate plans and movements. Indeed, it was to ascertain these facts, if possible, that the advance and attack were ordered by Hooker, who had for days been kept in perplexity by the rumors which had come to him with regard to the presence and movements of Lee's forces at Culpeper. Was the Confederate leader preparing for a raid against the Union right flank? Was he concentrating his army for the purpose of an advance down the Shenandoah Valley? Was he proposing a campaign against Washington and Baltimore? Was there at Culpeper a body of infantry as well as a cavalry force? Was Lee collecting at that point the troops which had evidently been abandoning their winter quarters at Fredericksburg?

These, in brief, were some of the questions which Hooker had to solve. He had been, as we have seen, exploiting the situation along his left flank at Franklin's Crossing; but the safety of his right flank seemed now to be menaced in the neighborhood of Rappahannock Station, where the Orange and Alexandria Railroad crosses the river, a point of importance from which the track leads in one direction to Washington and in the other "on to Richmond." Kelly's Ford, by the way, is about six miles from this bridge, and Beverly Ford in the opposite direction about two miles away. These topographical data may help us to apprehend the significance of the movement under consideration in connection with the appended map, on a later page.

It chanced that on the 8th of June, the day before the Union forces crossed the river, and while they were heading in the direction of their fording-places, Stuart had arranged a cavalry review to show the commander in chief what a body of horsemen he had organized. When all was ready and Lee with a large retinue of generals and staff-officers had taken their posts, an imposing display aggregating over nine thousand cavalry was arrayed before them, the brigades of Wade Hampton, B. H. Robertson, A. G. Jenkins, William E. Jones, Fitzhugh Lee, and W. H. F. Lee, with Imboden's Partisan Rangers, for the time assigned to Stuart, and the mounted batteries under Beckham, taking part in the pageant, led with pride by Stuart—a ceremonial which was not merely a review according to the tactics, but a magnificent exhibit of skilled horsemanship, charges, repulses, flank movements, mock battles, feats with the saber and pistol, with artillery salutes thrown in for good measure.

SOME PRELIMINARY STEPS

Meanwhile the forces under Pleasanton, marching from various rendezvous for the designated fords on the river, heard with amazement the noise of cannon in the direction of Culpeper, and marveled what had occasioned the thunder of artillery in that region.

Pleasanton divided his forces into two wings: the right wing, which he accompanied at the start, under Buford, made up of three brigades, led by Davis, Devin, and Whiting, was directed to cross and attack at Beverly Ford, supported by a detachment of infantry under command of Brig. Gen. Adelbert Ames.[1]

The left wing, commanded by D. M. Gregg, made up of his own brigades, led by Kilpatrick and Wyndham, and Duffié's division, with Colonels Di Cesnola and J. Irvin Gregg as brigade commanders, was instructed to cross at Kelly's Ford, three infantry regiments under Brig. Gen. D. A. Russell accompanying them.[2]

These two wings had orders to push at once from their crossing-places on the river back to Brandy Station, five or six miles away, almost equidistant from the two fords, and understood to be the depot of supplies and possibly the chief rendezvous of the Confederate cavalry. At this point the two wings were to unite with Pleasanton in charge of them both, and serve the cause as opportunity might then develop.

The Confederates at neither place were expecting an attack. At dawn Buford's force made the cross-

---

[1] Second and Thirty-third Massachusetts, Eighty-sixth and 124th New York, Third Wisconsin.

[2] Second and Seventh Wisconsin, Fifty-sixth Pennsylvania.

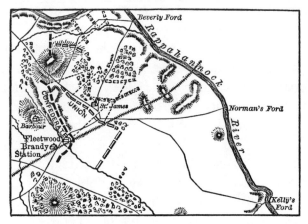

CAVALRY FIGHT AT BRANDY STATION

ing at Beverly, Stuart's cavalry pickets being taken by surprise and some of them captured. The skirmishing at the river, however, alarmed the grand guard, and W. E. Jones, the brigade commander, one of the best outpost officers in Stuart's cavalry, was quickly alert, although at some distance from the scene. Word was speedily sent to Stuart at Fleetwood Hill, his headquarters, not far from Brandy Station, and he in turn summoned the brigades of Hampton, Robertson, and W. H. F. Lee to his aid. These operations consumed a couple of hours, and meanwhile a fierce fight was going on in the neighborhood of the crossing at Beverly.

Turning to that point, we find Col. Benjamin F. Davis, in command of Buford's leading brigade, at the head of his men—his own regiment, the Eighth New York Cavalry, together with the Sixth New York and the Eighth Illinois Cavalry, in the lead. He had crossed the river, and after forming his lines—the pickets being driven back or captured—was pressing forward through the woods to attack the camp of Stuart's horse artillery, four batteries of which had been located the night before a mile and a half from the river, without any protection except the picket line in their distant front. Major Beckham, the artillery battalion commander, in his report (*Official Records*, XXVII, 2:772) shows how narrow the margin of safety was in that hour:

> The enemy approached rapidly and boldly, and had it not been for the delay of a few minutes caused him by the arrival of a regiment under General Jones, it is more than probable we would have been compelled to abandon the pieces. As it was, several of the horses were wounded before we could move from camp.

General Jones, who understood the dangerous situation of the artillery, says in his report: "The batteries being neither ready for action nor movement, it was a matter of the utmost importance to gain time."

It was at this juncture that the assailing force met with a grievous loss. Their line, advancing from the river, eager to meet and overthrow the enemy, and urged on by the example and words of the brigade commander, Col. Benjamin F. Davis, had hardly gone half-way to the artillery camp when they were met by the Sixth Virginia Cavalry, under Major Flournoy, galloping down the road in a desperate charge. The Union forces were for a moment checked and confused, and Colonel Davis with characteristic skill and courage strove to rally them and lead them forward against the foe. It was while in this act of intrepid leadership that he was shot through the head and instantly killed. The check administered to the head of the brigade by the charge of the Confederates and the death of its leader lasted but a little while; it was quickly rallied and, reinforced by the troops behind them, crowding forward from the ford, the entire body at once pressed forward, driving their assailants in turn back toward Fleetwood.

By the death of Colonel Davis the Army of the Potomac lost one of its most gifted and gallant cavalry leaders, for whom his comrades and superior officers had foretold a brilliant career. Born in Alabama, appointed to the Academy from Mississippi, and graduating thence in 1854, he had attained a captaincy in the First Cavalry in 1861; in June, 1862, he was made colonel of the Eighth New York Cavalry; and in September following he had won the brevet of major by a feat of extraordinary gallantry, when, at the head of his regiment, he cut his way through the enemies' lines at Harper's Ferry just before that point was surrendered to the Confederates. And now we see him at the age of thirty-one crowning his all too brief career by a heroic death while leading his command at Beverly Ford.

(5) *Cavalry Fight: Kelly's Ford to Fleetwood.*—The fight in front of Beverly Ford for three hours after the death of Colonel Davis was a broken one, the commanders on either side being moved to caution in view of the exigencies involved in the situation. By nine o'clock the brigades of Jones, Hampton, and W. H. F. Lee were in Stuart's hands for service, and there had been charges and countercharges and skirmishing between dismounted troopers on both

BATTLE AT BRANDY STATION
(From a print of the time)

sides, while the infantry accompanying Buford had, on the flanks, also taken some part in the strife. Stuart indicates in his account of the affair that he was hesitant because he was not certain how much force there was in his front, and he was also evidently desirous of finding out whether this movement betokened a general advance of the Army of the Potomac. In addition, he had been warned by his signal-station men and by scouts that a Union column was making its way from Kelly's Ford, and that Stevensburg had been threatened. Sending Hampton in that direction with two or three regiments, and summoning Robertson to join him from the upper fords of the river, he kept up a warm fight against the force of Buford.

Meanwhile Pleasanton, holding his main attack in abeyance until he could unite his force with that of Gregg, waited anxiously for the sounds of battle which should indicate that the left wing under Gregg had reached the vicinity of Brandy Station.

Gregg's command, delayed in crossing at Kelly's Ford by the tardiness of one of its components, took by surprise the Confederate pickets, and in due time made its presence known as it approached Brandy Station. Half-way to that point Colonel Duffié, with his detachment of cavalry, branched off to his left to Stevensburg, and there caught two or three regiments napping—at least he came upon them so unexpectedly that, according to Stuart's report, there was an "unaccountable stampede."

Stuart, about noon, holding his ground between Fleetwood and St. James Church, in Buford's front,

heard the sounds of an attack in his rear toward
Brandy Station, and also found his flanks threatened.
Gregg had arrived, and, notwithstanding the gallant
resistance made by Stuart's forces, had captured that
officer's headquarters tent and baggage at Fleetwood,
and in part destroyed cars laden with supplies at
Brandy Station. The Union leader, however, then
found himself attacked front and rear in turn by a
large part of Stuart's division in a terrific engagement
which lasted over an hour.

At the same time Pleasanton, thus informed that
Gregg was at work, made his advance with Buford's
troopers, and the combined fight made the most
strenuous and terrific cavalry engagement up to that
time ever witnessed on the continent. Sabers, pistols,
and carbines were used; charges were made back and
forth through the woods and across the open fields,
which made a fine arena for such a combat; field-guns
were captured and recaptured, and personal encounters took place many times, each side suffering
confusion and incurring considerable loss.

Both Pleasanton and Gregg, who met before the
conflict was wholly over, after hearing that a body
of infantry from Culpeper was arriving at Brandy
Station to reinforce Stuart, and finding that the Confederate cavalry when united would likely be more
than a match for their forces, and furthermore ascertaining from the letters and orders captured in Stuart's
headquarters baggage that they had secured the information which they had sought, concluded to withdraw. Stuart did not attempt to interfere with their
plan, except that he shelled the Union cavalry at a

distance as they pursued their way to the Rappahannock and Beverly Fords, where they crossed at
five o'clock.

Upon this affair Gregg makes a brief comment in
his booklet [1] as follows:

In our camp, after a day of intense excitement, there prevailed
a feeling of great satisfaction. The enemy had been met on a
fair field with the odds in his favor, and yet we had maintained
our own against him, and conscious of our strength were eager for
further trials with him.

The loss of Pleasanton's force was 844, which included 369 missing — presumably captured; while
Stuart lost in all about 600.

Some notable casualties occurred among leading
officers. Brig. Gen. W. H. F. Lee, son of Robert E.
Lee, was wounded and captured.

Solomon Williams,[2] a West Point graduate, was
killed, as well as Frank Hampton [3] (a kinsman of Wade
Hampton), both men of unusual skill and promise;
while Matthew C. Butler [4] received a wound which
cost him his leg, but which did not keep him from
returning to the field when his hurt had healed.
Colonel Butler rose to be a major general, and achieved
a worthy military record. After the war he vigorously
opposed the current reconstruction anarchy in his
Commonwealth by service in the legislature and by
help given to the successful effort to put Wade Hampton into the governorship. In 1876 he was elected
to the United States Senate, where he gave twelve

[1] *The Second Division in the Gettysburg Campaign.*
[2] Colonel Second North Carolina Cavalry.
[3] Lieut. Col. Second South Carolina Cavalry.
[4] Colonel Second South Carolina Cavalry.

years of service to the country by his advocacy of civil-service reform, a strong navy, and other measures of a national scope. In 1898 Senator Butler was a major general in the war with Spain, and he served also as a member of the commission for the removal of the Spanish forces from Cuba. He died at the age of 73 in 1909.

It is an interesting fact that Colonel Lomax, of the Eleventh Virginia Cavalry, a West Point graduate, a leading figure in the fight that day, and a conspicuous leader of cavalry until the end, rising to be a major general, has been for some years a member of the Gettysburg Battle-field Commission. At this writing (January, 1913) Major Generals Lomax and Gregg are the only survivors among the leading officers of the fierce cavalry battle which opened the Gettysburg campaign.

(6) *Some Fruits of the Cavalry Fight.*—This all-day struggle between the forces of Stuart and Pleasanton was fruitful in both immediate and later results. One permanent effect of the fight was that it inspired each side with a prudent respect for the ability and prowess of its antagonist. Probably the Union leaders did not need any addition to the stock of that material which they already possessed, for thus far the Southern mounted service had made a remarkable record; but after this fight the cavalry forces of the Army of the Potomac knew that they need not fear for the outcome whenever and wherever they might engage the Confederate horsemen on fairly equal terms. They had now learned what they were capable of achieving in close encounters and in impetuous

charges; indeed, one of Stuart's staff, Major McClellan, in a sketch of the conflict, declared that the experience gained at Brandy Station had really "made the Federal cavalry."

Valuable military data were secured by the affair. In Stuart's baggage were found letters and orders bearing on the then inchoate campaign, showing that an incursion into the North was proposed, and that Stuart was at the moment when the fight opened preparing for an advance, possibly a raid around the right flank of the Army of the Potomac, perhaps an advance into Maryland. This information, nebulous as it was, served to confirm the premonitions already avowed on Hooker's part to the authorities at Washington.

An important addendum to this information was the fact that infantry forces as well as cavalry were at Culpeper. Unfortunately for Hooker's plans, he did not learn in this way how far the concentration of Lee's army had proceeded, and he was still left under the impression that Longstreet was close at hand—within supporting-distance of Hill at Fredericksburg—when the truth was that Longstreet's whole corps was at Culpeper, waiting for orders to start northward, while Ewell, on the very morning, June 10th, when Hooker's information gained at Brandy Station reached him, had just set out on his way to the Shenandoah Valley. It was evident, however, that Hooker's right flank at Rappahannock Station, and from that point back toward the defenses of Washington, was in danger, and that Lee was not only proposing but already undertaking some sort of an advance movement. As Halleck, Stanton, and President Lincoln had finally disfavored Hooker's proposition to cross at Fredericksburg, overwhelm Hill, and then, entirely neglecting Lee's movements, move on to Richmond, the Union Army commander found himself compelled, in view of the new developments, to turn his whole attention in the direction of protecting the Capital and checkmating the Confederate leader. To this end his plans and movements were at once directed.

We may anticipate the brief summary which remains to be given concerning the task of placing the Army of the Potomac in strategic relations on the one hand with the menaced cities of Washington and Baltimore, and on the other hand with the marching forces of Lee just now debouching into the Shenandoah Valley. Hooker was hampered by many elements in the situation—his partial knowledge of Lee's movements, his orders from Washington, the friction that had arisen between him and Halleck, and the division of authority in the region threatened by Lee, the territory being unfortunately divided up as to military jurisdiction between Heintzelman and Lew Wallace and Hooker. In spite of this situation Hooker's movements evinced insight, energy, and skill. By his rapid and vigilant marches Lee was shut off from any chance of assailing the Army of the Potomac on its way or of menacing the city of Washington. Every highway and mountain-pass looking in that direction was forefended with swiftness and sagacity against any movement which Lee might think of venturing upon, leading toward the Capital.

SOME PRELIMINARY STEPS

(7) *Hooker Sets His Army in Motion.*—The opening movement of the campaign, immediately incited by the information gained at Brandy Station, was made by the Third Army Corps, which was ordered at noon, on June 11th, to break up its winter-quarters camp at Boscobel, near Falmouth, and start two hours later up the Rappahannock.

Some who read these pages will recall the tremendous pressure which was thus brought suddenly to bear upon commanding officers and soldiers in the ranks, and upon the various departments which had to do with the feeding and moving of troops, by the orders to abandon winter quarters and start out upon a summer campaign. Accommodations for the transportation of baggage for generals and headquarters officers, as well as field, staff, and line officers of regiments, were ruthlessly cut down to a very small number of wagons; extra luggage, tent furniture, and all the "stuff" which had been used to make camp life comfortable during the previous six months had to be destroyed, abandoned, or shipped, if possible, to Acquia Creek; these and all other preparations for light marching order had to be accomplished inside of two startling hurried hours on one of the hottest days in June! The echoes of the message which flew from camp to camp on that sultry noon still bring a thrill: "Hurry up, men! Pack up or throw away everything you can't carry; every man must have three days' cooked rations in his haversack, his knapsack in order, and sixty rounds of ammunition on his person, and be in line ready to move at two o'clock. Hurry up!"

Accordingly, at two o'clock the bugles sounded the assembly, the command resounded far and wide, "Fall in," and the division fared forth upon its long journey. That was the experience of one division, and the other chapters of adventure for that afternoon and for the ensuing three days read likewise.

Humphrey's division, on the evening of the 13th, after a strenuous march of a day and a half, was distributed along the Rappahannock (in the neighborhood of the Orange and Alexandria Railroad bridge) guarding the fords, and ready to prevent any attempt of the Confederates to advance.

The Second Army Corps took position at Acquia Creek, remaining there until the stores were removed and army property had been safeguarded; then it marched toward the rendezvous assigned for the other corps, which within a few days were located at such points as Dumfries, Catlett's Station, Manassas Junction, Centerville, Aldie, Gum Springs, and Fairfax Station, from which points they could immediately be directed across the Potomac or over the Bull Run Range toward the passes into the Shenandoah Valley. The mere presence of the Army of the Potomac at these strategic locations was sufficient to afford immunity to Washington, so far as any movement from the valley on the part of Lee was concerned.

The marching done during those early days of the campaign was accompanied with heroic exertions, never surpassed in the history of that army. A single bit of experience from those strenuous days and nights may serve as a type of the burdens of toil and heat and prostration borne by the marching host in order to make sure that no possibility of advantage should be allowed to Lee in the campaign.

Our division—Humphreys's—of the Third Corps, after three days and nights of marching and counter-marching, digging rifle-pits, and doing picket duty along the Rappahannock, started on the evening of June 14th to march to Manassas Junction, following the course of the railroad. We marched all night, rested for a few hours in the morning, began again at noon, the heat being dreadful in its intensity and sultriness, and continued our journey until midnight of the 15th. General Humphreys in his report says of this task:

> The march was painful in the extreme, for, owing to the long-continued drought, streams usually of considerable magnitude were dried up; the dust lay some inches thick on the roadway, and the fields were equally uncomfortable. The suffering from heat, dust, thirst, fatigue, and exhaustion was very great.

The writer of this narrative had command that day over the rear guard of the division, and strove with his non-commissioned officers and provost guard in vain to keep the ranks closed up. Hundreds were smitten with exhaustion and sunstroke; the ambulances in the rear were crowded with soldiers taken desperately ill or stricken into insensibility, while many who at midnight contrived to get to Manassas Junction fell to the ground in their bivouac more dead than alive.

These side-lights on the preliminary movements of the campaign may help to make vivid the endurance and fortitude of the Union Army on the march.

(8) *Lee's Army Heads Northward.*—The real beginning of Lee's movement toward Pennsylvania, after his partial concentration at Culpeper, where two of his corps had tarried for a few days, occurred on June 10th, the morning after the fight at Brandy Station, when Ewell's corps started for the Shenandoah Valley. A day or two later on the march the cavalry brigade of Jenkins joined Ewell, and with Rodes's division was despatched ahead to clear the way to the Potomac, their first mission being to scatter or capture the Union detachments at Berryville and Martinsburg, and thus cut off Milroy's forces at Winchester from Harper's Ferry and Washington. This work was done so expeditiously that on the 15th of June Jenkins crossed the Potomac at Williamsport, and at once pressed on into the Cumberland Valley—which is simply the prolongation of the Shenandoah Valley across Maryland and into Pennsylvania, debouching upon the Susquehanna River at Harrisburg—his raid spreading dismay and panic throughout the State. Meanwhile, he collected industriously great quantities of supplies of different kinds for the army that was following close behind him.

Longstreet's corps remained at Culpeper until June 15th, when it fared forth into the Shenandoah Valley; after guarding the mountain-passes, in support of Stuart's cavalry, it reached Williamsport, Maryland, on the Potomac, June 24th, ready to cross the river the next day.

Hill's corps, it will be remembered, was left at Fredericksburg, where it remained watching the movements of the Army of the Potomac until June

15th, when, having seen the last of Hooker's troops disappear from their winter-quarters camps at Falmouth, it hurried after the preceding portions of Lee's army, following the Shenandoah route, and reaching Shepherdstown, on the Potomac, on the 23d of June.

We have thus in this summary of events brought all of Lee's army, with the exception of two divisions of Ewell's corps, to the crossing of the Potomac, a portion of it, with cavalry, having advanced into Pennsylvania. The two divisions noted just now, led by Early and Edward Johnson, were halted at Winchester by the effort to defeat or capture the Union commander at that point, Maj. Gen. Robert H. Milroy, and the forces under him. This incident of the campaign now demands attention.

(9) *The Capture of Winchester.* — Robert H. Milroy, an Indiana soldier, had been a captain in the war with Mexico; entering the Civil War as a captain in the Ninth Indiana, he rose step by step to be a major general in November, 1862; moreover proving himself to be a man of conviction, courage, and patriotism. In January, 1863, he was put in charge of Winchester and adjacent posts, that town with its strong fortifications, which Milroy made stronger, being held as an advanced outpost to watch the Confederate forces in the Shenandoah Valley, and to guard the Baltimore and Ohio Railroad, which skirts the Potomac River twenty-five miles away. In Winchester and neighboring points this commander had under him nine thousand men, and with some heavy guns and a good supply of light artillery he contrived to maintain his ground without serious trouble for

9   115

six months, keeping his scouting expeditions at work up the valley, and believing himself and his garrison safe against even an extraordinary raid, being confident in his assurance that he would be warned from Washington in ample time should he be threatened by the advance of Lee's army. It had been intimated to Milroy in previous instructions that Winchester was not a fit place to fight a defensive battle against a large force, but no definite order was given to him to withdraw his troops to Harper's Ferry until midnight of June 11th, and that order was annulled within a few hours on the morning of Friday, June 12th. Up to that time Milroy, it must be remarked in addition, had no information either from Washington or from his department headquarters at Baltimore suggesting that any part of Lee's army was advancing down the valley, although Hooker had given note to Halleck again and again of his apprehensions of danger threatening that region.

On the 12th Milroy sent out reconnoitering parties; one of these returning from an expedition on the Front Royal road brought word that Confederate forces of cavalry, infantry, and artillery had been encountered twelve miles up the valley from Winchester at Cedarville, but the commanding general could not believe that this force belonged to Lee's army, and that he, in command at Winchester, had been left without warning from Washington concerning such approach. That night, Friday, June 12th, at ten o'clock, he informed by wire his department commander, Schenck, at Baltimore, concerning the approach of a considerable Confederate force, and asked for a definite order

SOME PRELIMINARY STEPS

either to hold the place or abandon it. Almost at
once a telegram was prepared directing Milroy to
withdraw immediately, but before the operator could
transmit the message the wires were cut between
Harper's Ferry and Winchester by Jenkins's troopers,
and Milroy got no word. Concluding, therefore,
from all the information he had received that it was
his duty to hold Winchester, he disposed his force
so as to defend the town, learning late on Saturday
for the first time that the troops in his front were two
divisions of Ewell's corps, possibly over twenty thousand in number; accordingly, he became convinced
that evening that unless relieved it would be necessary for him to cut his way through the environing
Confederate lines and make his way, if he could,
back to Harper's Ferry.

It does not cohere with our main purpose just at
this point to detail the fight at Winchester. Suffice
it to say that eligible positions were chosen and occupied by the two divisions of Ewell's corps, commanding the most important earthworks of Milroy, and
that for hours severe skirmishing took place with the
enemy on Sunday, and that in the late afternoon,
under cover of a heavy artillery fire, a main outwork
was assailed by infantry and carried. Colonel Mc-
Reynolds, who was in command of the troops at Berryville, had contrived to elude the columns of Jenkins
and Rodes (who had aimed at capturing him and his
command), and after a hard march had reached Winchester with his forces, bringing the news that retreat
was impossible in that direction.

That night it was determined, in view of all the

circumstances, to abandon the town and make an effort to cut through the surrounding troops and reach, if possible, Harper's Ferry. The endeavor was gallantly made; the retreating forces attacked the Confederates who tried to block the road, and a a hard fight took place, the outcome of which finally was that two columns, by different roads, in part escaped in some confusion and in fragments. Out of the whole number in Milroy's command Ewell captured 4,000, including in that number 700 sick and wounded; a score of guns, 700 wagons, and some stores. Three or four thousand eluded pursuit, and with Milroy and other officers found refuge in part at Harper's Ferry and in part on the southern boundary of Pennsylvania.

A court of inquiry, in session from August 4 to September 7, 1863, made careful investigation into the circumstances of the whole Winchester affair. The relations of Generals Halleck, Schenck, and Milroy to all the varying phases of the case were scrutinized, and finally Mr. Lincoln made his indorsement upon Judge Advocate General Holt's "review" of the proceedings of the court, declaring that it was clear that Milroy never received an order to withdraw, and that no one of the officers in question was deserving of serious blame. It appears to us a fair deduction, drawn from the entire story, that Milroy's claim found in his report is fully warranted. He says:

> After all, it may well be doubted whether the three days' delay, and the loss which my presence at Winchester occasioned the rebel army, were not worth to the country the sacrifice which they cost it. (See *Official Records*, XXVII, 2: 41–197.)

SOME PRELIMINARY STEPS

It is in view of this delay, impeding for that length of time the movements of Ewell's two divisions and also Longstreet's corps, which was of necessity kept in the background until the way was cleared to the Potomac, and in view also of the additional time afforded thereby for Hooker to bring his army from Falmouth and station it in front of Washington, at points where it would be immediately serviceable either for the defense of the Capital or for an advance into the North in the march against Lee—a feature of the campaign which is of very great importance—that we have given this space to the movements in question.

After the obstacle at Winchester had been removed, Edward Johnson's division of Ewell's corps advanced to Shepherdstown on the Potomac, crossing near there on June 18th, after one of his brigades had cut the Chesapeake and Ohio Canal and destroyed some canal-boats and stores located at near-by points. Early's division crossed at the same point on June 22d.

We have thus brought in this preliminary treatment all of Lee's army except the cavalry north of the Potomac. The movements and locations of the several corps after their crossing will be indicated a little later in the story. The preliminary cavalry operations now require at least a brief treatment.

(10) *Pleasanton and Stuart: Check and Counter-check.*—From June 11th until June 25th the work of the cavalry on both sides was an important element in the campaign. The mission of Stuart, on the one side, was to guard the passes in the mountain ranges separating the two armies and prevent the Union forces

from observing the movements of Lee's army, then passing down the Shenandoah Valley toward the crossing-places leading into Maryland. The operations of Pleasanton with the Union cavalry, on the other hand, were to watch the same passes, foil any attempt on the part of Stuart to raid about the flanks of Hooker's troops or advance toward Washington,

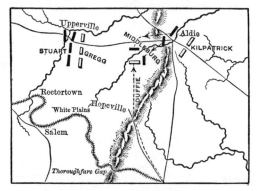

CAVALRY ENGAGEMENT AT ALDIE AND UPPERVILLE
(Federal, ▭   Confederate, ▬)

and meanwhile secure information in all possible ways concerning the whereabouts and manœuvers of Lee's infantry corps.

It will help the reader to note on a map the topography of the region now occupied by the marching armies. Immediately in front of Hooker's army, as now located so as to cover the approaches to Washington from the west, was the Bull Run range of mountains, with three principal passes leading through them into an intervening valley—namely, near Leesburg, on the north; at Aldie, in the center; and the Thoroughfare Gap, not far from the southern end of the ridge. The chief points of importance in the valley itself are Salem, Rectortown, Middleburg, and Upperville, and this was the arena of conflict for some days. This valley has as its western limit the Blue Ridge, with Thornton's, Chester, and Ashby's Gaps opening into the Shenandoah Valley beyond, in which large portions of Lee's army were now operating in their movements toward the north, shielded by the two mountain barriers and by the swift and watchful movements of Stuart's cavalry. The vital importance, therefore, of the work done by this officer, and on the other side by Pleasanton, may be seen at a glance.

On the 17th of June a series of encounters opened in the valley between the two mountain ranges, extending from day to day until nearly a week had been spent in strenuous cavalry engagements. On the opening day Pleasanton fought a spirited contest with Fitzhugh Lee's brigade, pressing him back from the neighborhood of Aldie toward Middleburg. At this point Colonel Duffié, who had been on a reconnoitering expedition since early morning with his First Rhode Island Cavalry, was encountered and a sharp fight ensued which continued until after dark. Next day Stuart's brigades contrived to surround and almost destroy Duffié's command, that officer by dint of desperate fighting and hard riding managing to escape with thirty comrades, his colors having been destroyed to keep them from capture, and 214 officers and men having been killed, wounded, or made prisoners—a disaster which debarred the regiment from any further share in the Gettysburg campaign.

In Kilpatrick's direct command that day the First

Massachusetts Cavalry, among other troops, suffered severely, and did some fine fighting; several of its squadrons were cut off from the main body, assailed on the flanks by sharp-shooters, and in part captured.

On June 18th Pleasanton attacked Stuart's whole force at Middleburg, and pressed the Confederates back for some miles, through Upperville into Ashby's Gap, each side suffering loss, the outcome being that nearly the entire valley between the two ranges of mountains was cleared of Confederate cavalry, while at the same time it was disclosed by scouts and the testimony of captured prisoners that the Shenandoah Valley was occupied by the infantry of Lee hurrying down to the Potomac fords on their way northward. As this was the important information which Pleasanton had been trying to secure, and as it now appeared that the Confederate commander was not planning to make his way, as had been done in two former campaigns, down into the Manassas plains and assail Washington from that direction, it was not deemed worth while to urge Pleasanton's cavalry into any further activity. That force had won additional distinction by its brief campaign, gaining information of the movements of its opponents, venturing in every case upon an aggressive policy, and, without grave losses, forcing Stuart to vacate the ground he had been endeavoring to hold. At the same time the honors were about even, for Stuart had guarded well the passes leading into the Shenandoah Valley, and by his stubborn and skilful resistance had prevented Pleasanton from penetrating far enough into the disputed territory to gain full information concerning Lee's whereabouts. The knowledge gained, however, sufficed to warrant Hooker in making further plans and movements when it was supplemented by the news, which was speedily available from the region along the Potomac, as to the advance of cavalry and infantry across Maryland and into Pennsylvania.

So far as Stuart's movements and plans are concerned up to the time when he started on his notable raid, it remains only to be remarked that he assigned to the brigades of B. H. Robertson and W. E. Jones the task of covering the rear of Lee's army as it should proceed northward, Robertson to command both forces. In fulfilling this mission—Jenkins and Imboden having been sent on ahead to serve in the advance—Robertson was kept south of the Potomac for days, and in following up the rear he did not arrive in the neighborhood of the field of battle until July 3d, when his cavalry reached Cashtown in time to be of service in guarding the rear of the retreating army. By this distribution of force Stuart was left with three brigades—those of Hampton, Fitzhugh Lee, and Chambliss — for his raiding expedition, which will be described a little later.

The preliminaries in this narrative being now all cleared away, we deem the line of the Potomac, immediately to be crossed by Hooker's army, as a good demarcation boundary at which to commence the narrative of the battle proper. To that task we shall therefore at once give heed.

PART TWO
THE NARRATIVE OF THE BATTLE

I

THE Army of the Potomac, in the preceding portion of this story, had been brought to the eve of its crossing into Maryland; it may be well, therefore, as we resume the narration, to afford the reader a brief sketch of its commander before he drops out of his post as leader in the campaign.

Joseph Hooker (1814–1879), a native of Massachusetts, was graduated from West Point in 1837; Jubal A. Early, commanding a division in the Confederate Army at Gettysburg; Chilton, Lee's chief of staff; and Sedgwick, a corps commander in the Army of the Potomac, with forty-six others, being in his class. Hooker served first as an artillery officer and then on staff duty in the Mexican War, winning three brevets for gallantry. In 1853, while stationed in California, he resigned to enter civil life, being then a brevet lieutenant colonel in the assistant adjutant general's department. At the outbreak of the Civil War he proffered his services to the National Government, and was appointed a brigadier general of Volunteers in May, 1861; a year later he was promoted to major general in view of his skill and gallantry on the Peninsula, under McClellan, where he commanded a division; he was conspicuous for his services also in the Second Manassas campaign under Pope; and he led an army corps at Antietam, where he was severely wounded, and where his gallantry received recognition by a commission as brigadier general in the Regular Army. When he recovered from his injury he was assigned to the head of the Fifth Corps; in the battle of Fredericksburg he had charge of the Center Grand Division.

On the 26th of January, 1863, he was made commander of the Army of the Potomac, succeeding Burnside. In administering this task he revealed himself as a skilful administrator and organizer, putting into the army a spirit of zeal, energy, and enthusiasm worthy of note, and arresting at once a spell of demoralization and sullenness which Burnside's unfortunate régime had brought about. In the closing days of April and the early days of May, 1863, he undertook with skill and promise the Chancellorsville campaign, in which at first his shrewd and swift manœuvers secured for his army a position of advantage which made it necessary for Lee to leave his stronghold behind Fredericksburg, in order to assail Hooker, and which gave the Confederate leader occasion for deep concern. Then, when victory was in his grasp, and when he had at hand twice the force of his great antagonist, Hooker's wits, in some still unexplained way, utterly forsook him. He withdrew his advanced troops, in spite of the protests of his best officers, from the lines which they had occupied, and thus placed his forces in a position of disadvantage; furthermore, by his blindness and inertness he permitted Stonewall Jackson to pass nearly all day long across his front, and then in the closing afternoon

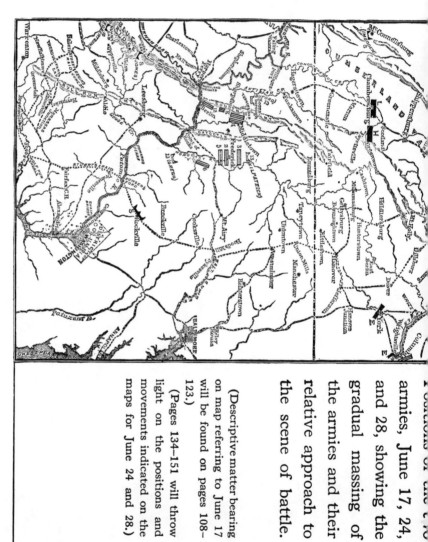

armies, June 17, 24, and 28, showing the gradual massing of the armies and their relative approach to the scene of battle.

(Descriptive matter bearing on map referring to June 17 will be found on pages 108–123.)

(Pages 134–151 will throw light on the positions and movements indicated on the maps for June 24 and 28.)

Positions June 17th.

REFERENCES.

Confederate,   Union,

Infantry,   Infantry,

Cavalry,   Cavalry.

Longstreet's Cps..L.   1st Corps.......1
Ewell's Corps....E.   2d Corps.......2
A. P. Hill's Cps..H.   3d Corps.......3
Stuart's Cavalry.   5th Corps.......5
                        6th Corps.......6
                        11th Corps......11
                        12th Corps......12
                        Cavalry.......13

SCALE OF MILES

Positions June 24th.

assail and break to pieces his right flank—the Eleventh Corps; and finally on the next day he suffered himself to be driven back into his extemporized fortifications, where he held himself under cover while Sedgwick and the Sixth Corps were making a tremendous battle to hold fast to Fredericksburg, which they had taken; in the struggle which followed he permitted Lee to concentrate his whole force on Sedgwick, who was left to shift for himself in a finally successful effort to withdraw his force to the northern side of the Rappahannock.

It was first supposed that Hooker, who had been at times accustomed to convivial habits, was not quite himself in this campaign; but those who knew him best denied this and declared that it was the sudden stoppage of his drink supply—done of his own choice for purposes of prudence—that occasioned a reaction, in connection with the shock occasioned by a wooden pillar which fell upon him in the midst of the cannonade, on Sunday, against the Chancellorsville House, his headquarters in the battle. Whatever was the cause, the condition of Hooker in that engagement still remains an insoluble enigma, and his failure, in view of his overwhelming force in comparison with that which Lee commanded, and in view of the splendid plans which preluded the battle, and the distrust and indignation which the leading officers of his army cherished in regard to the outcome, awakened on the part of Mr. Lincoln, Secretary Stanton, and General Halleck the deep conviction that he was not fit to be intrusted with the command of the Army of the Potomac. This recital will serve to explain his removal on June 28th—later to be noted.

GETTYSBURG

General Hooker, on the 23d of September, 1863, took the Eleventh and Twelfth Army Corps west, and served with Grant and Sherman in the campaigns which led to the capture of Chattanooga, capturing Lookout Mountain in a brilliant achievement known as the "Battle among the Clouds," and did brave service with Sherman up to and including the siege of Atlanta. He proved, however, to be a restless and turbulent subordinate, and Sherman finally grew impatient with his ways, and he was removed from command, July 30, 1864, and that removal ended his activity at the front. Nevertheless, he received the thanks of Congress, along with Meade, Hancock, and Howard, for his services in the Gettysburg campaign, and was brevetted major general, U.S.A., for his gallantry in the battle of Chattanooga.

Hooker, on his white horse, was a commanding figure at the head of his army; no man could have been more brave, alert, and inspiring as the leader of a division or corps; but his temperamental defects— a disposition to criticize his superior officers, a spirit of insubordination, an occasional display of arrogant self-conceit, and sometimes the lack of judicial balance — counterpoised, unfortunately, his higher and nobler qualities and his unquestioned military gifts. Lincoln loved and trusted him as long as it was possible; one of the proofs of this is a letter from the President to Hooker, written when the latter was appointed to command the Army of the Potomac—a notable and characteristic document, full of candor, kindness, insight, and cordial affection. (*Official Records*, XXV, 2:4.)

II

THE UNION ARMY CROSSES INTO MARYLAND

ALTHOUGH the exact whereabouts of the Army of Northern Virginia were still involved in uncertainty, and no one could surmise what Lee's immediate intentions might be, yet it was at least certain that that army was in Pennsylvania. Hooker, therefore, without losing time, concluded that he must at once march northward, having two coincident aims in mind: first, to keep his forces between Washington and the hosts of the invader; and, secondly, to uncover as rapidly as possible the location and movements of Lee, and be prepared to foil his plans and defeat him in battle. Accordingly, on the 25th of June, the pontoon bridges at Edwards Ferry, the chosen place for the transfer of the troops into Maryland, having been swiftly and skilfully built by Benham's engineer corps, Hooker's army began its crossing.

On that day the Confederate forces were distributed as follows north of the Potomac, the cavalry force of Robertson and W. E. Jones remaining in Virginia, as we have already intimated, to guard and follow up the rear:

Imboden's cavalry, which had made an advance raid, destroying the railroad bridges and canal embankment at intervals between Cumberland and

Martinsburg, and then guarded the left flank of the invading force by a roundabout foraging expedition, was in the neighborhood of McConnellsburg, Pennsylvania, aiming to arrive at Chambersburg, bringing up the rear a little later.

Ewell's corps: the divisions of Johnson and Rodes, under the immediate direction of Ewell himself, along with Jenkins's cavalry, were at Carlisle, threatening Harrisburg; the other division, Early's, being at Greenwood, some miles east of Chambersburg, on its way through Gettysburg, to York and Wrightsville, on the Susquehanna, accompanied by two detachments of Virginia cavalry,[1] detached temporarily from Jenkins's brigade.

Longstreet's corps and Hill's corps had just forded the Potomac, and were marching to Chambersburg as a place of rendezvous; at this point Lee had established headquarters, his immediate purpose being to advance against Harrisburg or York, as circumstances might later determine, confident in his belief that Hooker was still south of the Potomac, and not dreaming that on that very day the Union Army was crossing over the pontoons at Edwards Ferry into Maryland.

On the other hand, Hooker could not ascertain the whereabouts of the Confederate forces, except that he knew that a portion of them had threatened or were occupying Chambersburg and Carlisle, and that Harrisburg, the capital of Pennsylvania, where Couch and Curtin were organizing a militia force, was

[1] Seventeenth Regiment, Col. W. H. French; Thirty-fifth Battalion, Lieut. Col. Elijah V. White.

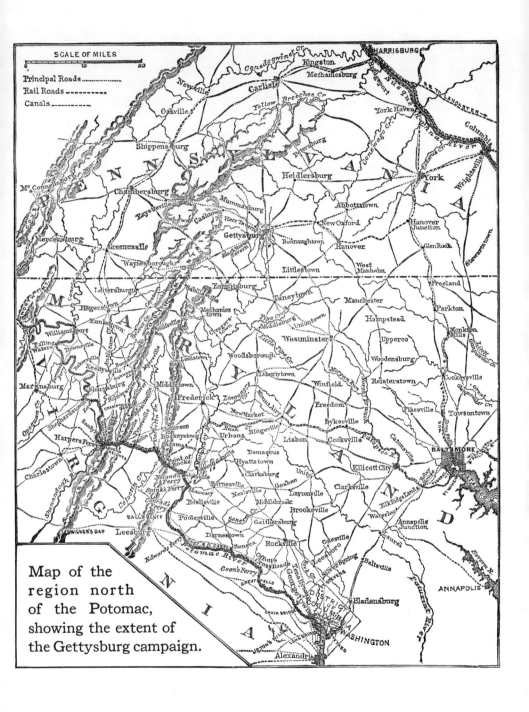

Map of the region north of the Potomac, showing the extent of the Gettysburg campaign.

gravely menaced, while the whole of the State was smitten with panic and forebodings.

Hooker's crossing occupied a little over two days; his army was chiefly directed toward Frederick, Maryland, and nearly all of it was in that neighborhood on the night of the 27th, Crawford's Pennsylvania Reserves to be added to the Fifth Corps, and Stannard's Vermont brigade to join the First Corps, having both been started from the defenses of Washington to recruit Hooker's forces.

III

A NOTABLE feature of the Gettysburg campaign was the adventurous expedition of Stuart, the commander of the cavalry division of the Army of Northern Virginia. It is evident that Lee did not apprehend fully the plans of his cavalry leader when he assented to the undertaking—namely, a raid around the Union forces. It is clearly discernible, even upon a slight examination of the reports, that the commander in chief did not dream that Stuart would separate himself for almost a week from the rest of the army; and in order apparently to avoid any such emergency Lee gave command that Stuart should "after crossing proceed with all despatch to join the right (Early) of the army in Pennsylvania." That word (Early) is inserted in Stuart's report, but it was clearly an afterthought, for when Stuart started out Early had just been ordered to the extreme right of the army,[1] and Lee's unmistakable intention, to use his own language, was that Stuart should "harass

---

[1] Early tells us in his *Autobiographical Sketch*, p. 255, that at Chambersburg, on the afternoon of June 25th, Ewell gave him his orders to cut across the country from Greenwood, where the division was in bivouac, through Gettysburg to York, and that he started next morning. There was no possible way for this news to reach Stuart at that juncture before he started on his raid a day or two later. He learned en route in Maryland that Early was near York.

and impede as much as possible" the Union forces, should they attempt to cross the Potomac. In that event Stuart was directed "to move into Maryland, east or west of the Blue Ridge, as in his judgment should be best, and take position on the right of the [Confederate] column as it advanced."

Possibly Stuart, after getting his command into Maryland, found it out of the question to get into touch with Lee again except by making a long and roundabout course outside of the Army of the Potomac. At any rate, he construed his instructions so as to allow this enterprise, and on the night of June 27th, with much difficulty, guided and helped by Maj. John S. Mosby, who served during the raid as voluntary aid, the entire force crossed at Rowser's Ford, fifteen miles west of Washington, and speedily ascertained that an insuperable obstacle was interposed between it and the rest of Lee's army—namely, the Army of the Potomac.

Nevertheless, Stuart burned bridges, tore up railroad tracks, captured a wagon-train loaded with supplies, foolishly taking his captures with him, thereby greatly delaying and hindering his movements; and at Hanover, Pennsylvania, on the morning of June 30th, he ran into Farnsworth's brigade of Kilpatrick's division of cavalry. Colonel Chambliss, commanding the foremost brigade, made an assault upon the Union forces, which were resting in the streets of the town, and were, as it chanced, in the midst of an ambulance train, the drivers of which became frightened and drove their teams furiously to escape. There were charges and countercharges and much confusion on

both sides. At last the Confederates were forced
out of the town, Stuart in his report declaring that
his two other brigades were away in the rear detained and hindered by "the elongation of the column
by reason of the two hundred wagons and hilly roads."
There was other skirmishing on the way north, each
side taking prisoners and meeting with losses; after a
fruitless and exhausting roundabout raid Stuart, per-
plexed and ignorant of the situation, arrived at
Carlisle, Pennsylvania, on the afternoon of July 1st
—when the first day's struggle at Gettysburg was over.
That night he received word from Lee summoning
him at once to the field, which he reached in the afternoon of the second day, too late to be of any real
service to his commander.

Meanwhile Lee had no cavalry to accompany the
main body of his army, and not even scouts, being left
to grope along in his plans without intelligence as to
the movements of the Union forces until the night of
the 28th of June, when, as we shall soon relate, he
first received word that the army of Hooker had
crossed the Potomac. It is evident that Lee never
surmised that Stuart would possibly cut loose entirely
from all communication with the other portions of
the Confederate Army; indeed, for days the Southern
commander in chief had two leading grounds of
anxiety and perplexity: "Where is Hooker?" "Where
is Stuart?" Not only at the time but ever afterward
Lee apprehended that the absence of his cavalry
under Stuart was an element of weakness in his campaign for which there were no compensations.

Stuart, understanding that he was to unite as

speedily as possible with the right wing of the Confederate Army, which had been reported to him as at York, Pennsylvania, had directed his movements from Westminster, Maryland (through Hanover, where he encountered the Union cavalry, as we have just intimated), toward that point. At daylight of July 1st, some miles west of York, at Dover, Pennsylvania, he crossed the road on which Early and his division twelve hours before had marched on the way to Gettysburg. Either Stuart was remiss in finding out the direction in which the Confederate forces had gone—hearing only that they had left for "Shippensburg in the Cumberland Valley"—or the people were cautious in giving out definite information in the case; for Stuart at that very juncture just missed a great opportunity. Had he turned to the west instead of keeping on his way northward to Carlisle, thirty miles distant, he would have arrived at Gettysburg by two in the afternoon of that momentous day; coming in upon the broken right flank of the Union forces and co-operating with the Confederate troops then on the field, he could have assured a decisive victory for Lee that evening. But it was not so to be. General Lee never pronounced judgment officially on Stuart for his absence, although privately he lamented it again and again. Gen. A. L. Long (*Memoirs of Robert E. Lee*, page 277) recurs thus to this phase of the campaign:

This battle [Gettysburg] was precipitated by the absence of information which could be obtained by an active cavalry force. General Lee had previously considered the possibility of engaging the enemy in the vicinity of Gettysburg, but the time and position were to have been of his own selection. This could have been easily effected had not the cavalry [of Stuart] been severed from its proper place with the army.

Col. Walter Herron Taylor, adjutant general of the Army of Northern Virginia, in his volume *Four Years with General Lee*, pages 92–93, makes a similar comment as to the situation:

> The absence of the cavalry was most seriously felt by General Lee. He had directed General Stuart to use his discretion as to where and when to cross the river—that is, he was to cross east of the mountains, or retire through the mountain-passes into the valley and cross in the immediate rear of the infantry, as the movements of the enemy and his own judgment should determine; but he was expected to maintain communication with the main column, and especially directed to keep the commanding general informed of the movements of the Federal Army.

Colonel Taylor further says that on the 1st of July, when the battle opened:

> No tidings whatever had been received from or of our cavalry under General Stuart since crossing the river; and General Lee was consequently without accurate information of the movements or position of the main Federal Army. An army without cavalry in a strange and hostile country is as a man deprived of his eyesight and beset by enemies.

General Stuart in his report (*Official Records*, XXVII, 2:708) tries to justify his policy and relieve himself from blame by alleging that Jenkins's brigade of cavalry, which had been left in Virginia to follow up the rear, and which had been kept on scouting duty in the Cumberland Valley, where it had no chance to uncover the whereabouts or plans of the Union Army, "was not as efficient as it ought to have been," and declaring in addition that such a command "properly handled should have done everything requisite." The one answer to this statement of the case is that Jenkins was not assigned to the duty of protecting the right flank of Lee's advancing army; and that, so far as is known, General Lee did not charge that force with any dereliction; while, on the other hand, all the Confederate officers who have written on the subject, with one exception, express the conviction that Stuart's movements—attributed by one of them to "a youthful cavalryman's wish for a nomadic ride"—irremediably hampered General Lee in his plans. It might not be necessary to elaborate this part of the campaign at this remove from the battle, but for the attempt which was made in 1908 by the dashing leader, Col. John S. Mosby, to justify Stuart in a volume which we shall notice a little later in the story.

IV

HOOKER DISPLACED—MEADE APPOINTED

THE friction which had been in vogue between Halleck, the general in chief at Washington, and Hooker, at the head of the Army of the Potomac, did not diminish as the situation of that army became more critical after crossing into Maryland. Although Hooker had been assured that in view of his double duty—to defend the Capital, and to relieve Pennsylvania from invasion by defeating Lee's army—he should have command of the troops within reach of the menaced district, yet he found it impossible to secure quick response to his orders, or even to ascertain what troops were within his enlarged jurisdiction. Harper's Ferry turned out to be the particular bone of contention in the case. Directly upon crossing the Potomac Hooker spent a few hours at that point, his inspection confirming his wise judgment already expressed that the troops there were of no account in the campaign, and that Maryland Heights, close by, also should be abandoned. It seems to us that Hooker's judgment was sane in this case, and that he was right in asking that he should be recognized as having within his jurisdiction those two disputed points. Halleck, however, replied:

HOOKER DISPLACED

Maryland Heights have always been regarded as an important point to be held by us, and much expense and labor [have been] incurred in fortifying them. I cannot approve their abandonment except in case of absolute necessity.

Hooker's reply, after his visit of inspection, puts the case with vigor:

MAJOR GENERAL HALLECK,—I have received your telegram in regard to Harper's Ferry. I find ten thousand men here, in condition to take the field. Here they are of no earthly account. They cannot defend a ford of the river, and so far as Harper's Ferry is concerned, there is nothing of it. As for the fortifications, the work of the troops, they remain when the troops are withdrawn. No enemy will ever take possession of them for them. This is my opinion. All the public property could have been secured to-night, and the troops marched to where they could have been of some service. Now they are but a bait for the rebels, should they return.

I beg that this may be presented to the Secretary of War and his Excellency the President.

Hooker was evidently in a petulant and indignant mood when he wrote the preceding telegram, and hampered with a sense of the unreasonable restrictions that had been placed upon him in a difficult situation. Without waiting for an answer to his despatch he "fired" another at Halleck, there being but five minutes' interval at Washington between the two:

My original instructions require me to cover Harper's Ferry and Washington. I have now imposed upon me, in addition, an enemy in my front of more than my number. I beg to be understood, respectfully but firmly, that I am unable to comply with this condition with the means at my disposal, and earnestly request that I may be at once relieved from the position I occupy.

Halleck received this message at three o'clock in

the afternoon of Saturday, June 27th. That evening
at eight his reply was sent:

MAJOR GENERAL HOOKER,—Your application to be relieved
from your present command is received. As you were appointed
to this command by the President, I have no power to relieve you.
Your despatch has been duly referred for Executive action.

When this telegram was sent action, indeed, had
been already taken, and the messenger was on his
way by train to Frederick to notify Hooker in person
what had been done. The latter in his impatient
mood hardly expected to be taken at his word without
any argument, persuasion, or protest; but the War
Department had had its mind made up for weeks
that Hooker could not be trusted to command the
Army of the Potomac in another battle—this conclusion being based in part upon that general's relations with Halleck, and upon his defects of temper,
but chiefly on the failure at Chancellorsville. Accordingly, President Lincoln, General Halleck, and
Secretary Stanton were ready at once to name a
successor, hazardous though the experiment might
be to change commanders on the eve of a great and
decisive engagement such as was now impending.
Three men had been possibilities in the case, should
a vacancy occur; one was Maj. Gen. D. N. Couch, a
man of great ability, whose impaired health forbade
him to consider it. Maj. Gen. John F. Reynolds was
also in mind, and had indeed been "sounded" in advance, but he had expressed unwillingness to serve
unless a greater freedom of action was permitted to
him than at that juncture seemed a probability. The

third man under consideration, and upon whom the lot fell, happily proved to be the man of the hour.

Maj. Gen. George Gordon Meade, commander of the Fifth Army Corps, an engineer officer of distinction and a Pennsylvanian, at two in the morning of Sunday, June 28th, in his headquarters' tent near Frederick, was awakened from sleep and notified by Lieutenant Colonel Hardie, of the War Department, that he had been assigned to command the Army of the Potomac. The order was imperative, and notwithstanding Meade's plea for release and his request that Reynolds might be chosen, the change took immediate effect. No greater military responsibility ever before in the history of this country rested upon a servant of the Republic. Halleck, general in chief at Washington, to encourage the new commander sent him a letter conferring on him extraordinary powers—all possible prerogatives that the President, the Secretary of War, and the general in chief together could grant. Moreover, Harper's Ferry and its garrison—concerning which the trouble had occurred between Hooker and the War authorities—were now placed under Meade's direct orders.

Hooker [1] had no plans which were of avail to the new chief, who in his letter of acceptance to General Halleck said:

As a soldier I obey [this order], and to the utmost of my ability will execute it. Totally unexpected as it has been, and in ignorance of the exact condition of the troops and the position of the enemy, I can now only say that it appears to me I must move

[1] For the correspondence in the case with Hooker and Meade, see *Official Records*, XXVII, 1 : 59–62.

143

toward the Susquehanna, keeping Baltimore and Washington well covered, and if the enemy is checked in his attempt to cross the Susquehanna, or if he turns toward Baltimore, to give him battle.

Only one phase of Hooker's plans had to be revoked; he had directed Slocum, with the Twelfth Army Corps, to march toward Harper's Ferry, and uniting with the troops at that point to enter the Cumberland Valley and watch for an opportunity to attack the rear of the Army of Northern Virginia. Upon considering this policy Meade concluded that it would not be wise to divide his forces, and accordingly he recalled Slocum, thereby keeping all his forces in hand, ready to be concentrated according to the developments of the campaign then opening up.

V

THE PIPE CREEK LINE

ONE of General Meade's first acts was to choose, tentatively, a defensive line of battle on which he might locate his troops in case he had to meet Lee, turning to threaten the Capital. This position, hurriedly but skilfully outlined by Meade, aided by personal examination of the ground made by Maj. Gen. G. K. Warren, the chief engineer of the army, and Maj. Gen. Henry J. Hunt, chief of artillery, June 29–30, followed substantially the line of Pipe Creek, between Middleburg and Manchester, Maryland, covering Westminster as the depot of supplies in the rear, and was chosen for its strategic advantages. It afforded a magnificent defensive location for the army, and gave opportunity also to protect Baltimore and Washington, while at the same time it gave Meade a notable chance to strike at the flank of Lee and endanger his communications, should the Confederate leader turn southward or try to threaten the Capital in his movements.

General Meade in his preliminary orders went so far as to direct the concentration of his several army corps upon this line before Lee's whereabouts and the direction of his marching columns were made clear. Then, late in the afternoon of July 1st, he saw that the conflict would be fought, not on the northern border of Maryland, but on the southern border of Pennsylvania, to which at once he directed all his forces. These details are to be kept in mind, for the selection of the Pipe Creek Line — a wise and prescient piece of work, intended to guard against all possible emergencies — has been made the basis of malicious attacks on Meade, on the alleged ground that he intended to retreat thereto from Gettysburg in the very midst of the battle (*Official Records*, XXVII, 3:458).

VI

UP to the night of Sunday, June 28th, Lee did not know that Hooker's forces had crossed the Potomac. Late that night Harrison, a scout, sent north by General Longstreet at the opening of the campaign to seek and bring back to him tidings of the enemy, arrived at Chambersburg, Pennsylvania, where Lee had his headquarters, with word that the Union forces, now under Meade—the change having been made early that morning—were in the neighborhood of Frederick, Maryland.

As this incident which we have just summarized has been challenged within the past decade, it may be worth while to furnish the data on which the above summary appears to be unmistakably established.

First, let it be noted that General Lee, in his earlier report, dated July 31, 1863 (*Official Records*, XXVII, 2:307), declares:

> Preparations were now made to advance upon Harrisburg; but on the night of the 28th information was received from a scout that the Federal Army, having crossed the Potomac, was advancing northward, and that the head of the column had reached the South Mountain.

This brief statement is amplified by General Longstreet in his *From Manassas to Appomattox*, where he gives the details of the case, the name of the scout, Harrison, and other data. Gen. E. P. Alexander, in his *Reminiscences*, and other leading officers refer also to the matter as within their personal knowledge. And now comes a singular development. Colonel Mosby, in a volume, *Stuart's Cavalry in the Gettysburg Campaign* (1908), whose aim is to relieve Stuart from any blame in the campaign so far as his raid was concerned, undertakes to discredit the whole narrative and to deny that there was any scout who, on June 28th, brought the news of the crossing of the Potomac by the Union Army. This attempt to undermine the testimony of Lee and Longstreet and other officers with regard to this matter is in part based on a letter from Lee to Ewell, purporting to bear the date of June 28th, at 7 A.M., and saying: "I wrote you *last night* that Hooker was reported to have crossed the Potomac," etc. The matter would hardly be worth refutation here were it not for the fact that some critical writers have already been misled. For example, an able book-reviewer in the *Nation*, an expert critic as to Gettysburg data, has declared on the basis of Mosby's volume that this story of Harrison, the scout, was "a fiction" that had been "exposed on Confederate authority." It is worth while then to indicate here that Mosby's work in this regard can hardly be taken as "authority." The letter referred to was copied by Colonel Venable, of Lee's staff, "from memory," and bears on its face the words "sketch of a letter," and thus is entered by Venable in Lee's letter-book. Rev. Dr. R. H. McKim, a staff-officer of George H. Steuart, in the

Army of Northern Virginia in the battle of Gettysburg, has dealt with the whole transaction in a lecture delivered in Richmond, January 21, 1910, in which he shows beyond a doubt that the correct date of the letter in question is "June 29th," and not June 28th, and that with this correction the data in the case become reasonable, intelligible, and coherent. (*A Soldier's Recollections*, pages 337–362.)

Hood, in his *Advance and Retreat*, page 55, testifies also that it was at "Chambersburg where intelligence was received of General Meade's assignment to the command of the Federal Army."

Moreover, Longstreet's assistant adjutant general in the campaign, Lieut. Col. G. Moxley Sorrel, in his recent posthumous volume *Recollections of a Confederate Staff Officer*, relates the circumstances concerning the arrival of Harrison in detail.[1] His reference to this matter was written and published before Colonel Mosby had cast any doubt on the matter, and is all the stronger on that account. Writing of the stay at Chambersburg and of the events of Sunday, June 28th, he says:

> At night I was roused by a detail of the provost-guard bringing up a suspicious prisoner. I knew him instantly; it was Harrison, the scout. His report was long and valuable . . . and was afterward fully confirmed by events and facts. . . . He also informed us of the removal of Hooker and the appointment of Meade to command the Army of the Potomac.

Mosby in his argument makes much of his theory that a scout bringing news from Frederick, Mary-

[1] Colonel Sorrel, a native Georgian, served on Longstreet's staff almost from the opening of the war. He became a brigadier general October 31, 1864, and later led a brigade in A. P. Hill's corps till the end. For years after the strife he resided as a merchant in Savannah.

land, *both* of the crossing of the Potomac and the change of commanders, could not have arrived on the night of the 28th, since it would have been practically impossible for him to have acquired the latter information and made the journey in the time at his disposal. But an examination of the available testimony shows all witnesses agreed on the item of paramount importance—the crossing of the Potomac.

As to the possibility of the scout having been able to secure the information in the time available, it may be noted that, so far as the journey from Frederick was concerned, the interview between Meade and the officer from the War Department took place at two o'clock in the morning of June 28th, and within two hours Hooker was notified. The fact was known at headquarters that morning, long before the official circular was sent out in the afternoon. The spy had been inside the lines during the preceding night of the 27th gathering information. It is not improbable that he got the information before noon, June 28th, and started with it to get through the Union lines toward the west, then in the neighborhood of Boonsboro' and Hagerstown, along the valley, where Buford's men were ranging, June 28-29. After the spy had passed over the mountains into the valley toward Hagerstown—a tramp of sixteen to twenty miles, which he should have done in five or six hours—at dark he could have secured a horse and finished the journey without danger of molestation in five hours of hard riding (thirty-five to forty miles), arriving at Chambersburg before midnight. Captain McKim in his book says that *he* rode the distance of fifty-five miles in the same valley without trouble in a few hours that same week.

Furthermore, Stephen W. Pomeroy, a young man who took the news of Lee's plans from Chambersburg to the nearest point on the Pennsylvania Railroad, and thence telegraphed it to Governor Curtin at Harrisburg, thereby giving first definite news that the Confederates had turned their faces toward Gettysburg, left Chambersburg June 30th, in the morning, walked seventeen miles over the mountains, and then rode horseback to Port Royal, the telegraph station, getting there at midnight, a more difficult task than Harrison's was, for the roads were by-roads and there were two or three ranges to cross. The distance was a little greater in Pomeroy's case, and the parallel is very striking.

In view of this array of concurrent testimony, and in the absence of a motive on the part of any one to conceal or to twist the facts in the case, he will be a bold man indeed who will hereafter attempt with any show of reason to make it appear that this incident pertaining to Harrison is merely an exploded fiction.

VII

LEE CONCENTRATES HIS FORCES

GENERAL LEE'S comment on the information which he had just received, as related in the foregoing section, throws light on his plans:

As our communications with the Potomac were thus menaced, it was resolved to prevent [the enemy's] further progress in that direction by concentrating our army on the east side of the mountains.

The news, indeed, was momentous, and in other regards than that indicated by the Southern commander's statement of the situation. He did not fear Hooker; but he knew Meade to be a brave, accomplished, and wary leader; it should, therefore, have behooved him and his army to be on their guard; yet, Lee himself appears to have been but slightly concerned in view of the new developments. General Long, his military secretary, says:

He was surprised to hear of such a change of commanders being made at that critical stage of affairs. The change itself he considered advantageous to the Federal cause, as he had always held Meade in much higher estimation as a commander than Hooker. But he was of the opinion that the difficulties which would beset Meade in taking command of an army in the midst of a campaign would more than counterbalance his superiority as a general over the previous commander. He was, therefore, rather satisfied than otherwise by the change. The army at large was in no sense discomposed. . . . They had little fear that any of the generals of the Army of the Potomac would prove a match for their own admired and almost worshiped leader. (*Memoirs of Robert E. Lee*, p. 274.)

Although General Lee in his elated mood gave slight heed to the change of commanders and its bearing on the coming battle, he was concerned with regard to the position held by the Army of the Potomac at Frederick, Maryland, where it constituted a serious menace to his communication with the South, which must be maintained at all hazards. In order to safeguard his communications ordinary prudence demanded that he should at once bring his scattered forces together. Stuart was still lost to sight on his nomadic raid; Early's division was at York and Wrightsville; Rodes's was at Carlisle, his advanced skirmish-line being almost at the river at Harrisburg, eighteen miles away; while Lee,· with Hill and Longstreet and their forces, were at Cham-

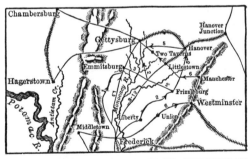

MOVEMENT OF UNION ARMY TO GETTYSBURG

bersburg. Until the news came as to the change of commanders and the location of the Union Army at Frederick the Confederate leader had it in mind to keep right on his course to the Susquehanna. Under the new circumstances presented by the changed situation it was at once imperative that he should get his forces all in hand and be ready with a united army to attack the Union Army or, on the other hand, meet its assault in battle.

Lee had already indicated to himself (Long's *Memoirs*, page 268), and in confidence to his military

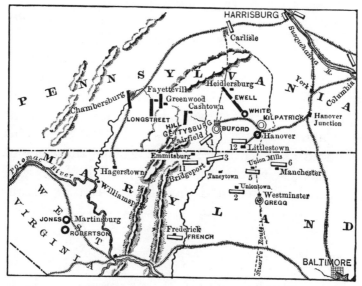

POSITION OF FEDERAL AND CONFEDERATE ARMIES, JUNE 30, 1863

(Federal, ▭   Confederate, ▬)

secretary, on the map, before the campaign began, three possible points in Pennsylvania where an encounter with the Federal forces might with advantage to himself take place—Chambersburg, York, and Gettysburg. A glance at the map shows that at this time there was no other place where Lee's troops

could be so easily and rapidly concentrated as at
Gettysburg. Ten roads center in that town and
radiate from it like spokes from the hub of a wheel.
The Confederate commander at once sent couriers
forth to turn his columns in that direction, and on
the 30th of June, from the west, from the north, and
from the east his troops were hurrying toward the
"hub of the wheel," the advanced division, however,
being ordered first to head for Cashtown, eight miles
west of Gettysburg. On that day Meade's forces
were also marching on the roads that center in Gettysburg, facing toward that town, at distances from ten
to thirty-two miles away.

As the two armies, therefore, were marching toward
a common center on these converging radii, it was
inevitable that the heads of the hostile columns must
soon collide and the desperate struggle begin, although
neither one of the commanders at this time expected
or planned to bring about an encounter there. Lee
was aiming simply to bring his forces quickly together;
and Meade was at the same time feeling his way,
trying to locate his adversary and endeavoring to
secure an advantageous position from which to attack
him or to defend himself if assaulted.

VIII

ON the night of June 30th General Meade's head-quarters were at Taneytown; General Reynolds in command of the left wing—the First, Third, and Eleventh Corps—was at Marsh Run, six miles south of Gettysburg, his troops being between that point and Bridgeport, in the neighborhood of Emmitsburg; the Fifth Corps was at Union Mills, a little to the east of Taneytown, Maryland; the Second Corps was at Uniontown, south of Taneytown; the Sixth was at the farthest remove, away off at Manchester, Maryland; while the Twelfth was at Littlestown, ten miles southeast of Gettysburg. The cavalry was posted at different points on the outer flanks, except that Buford, after days of scouting, was in Gettysburg, having located the advancing columns of the enemy, and being in touch with Reynolds, close at hand. The Confederates were disposed as follows: Stuart's cavalry, after being delayed by its heavy wagon-train, and by a sharp battle with Kilpatrick at Hanover, Pennsylvania, June 30th, made a night march northward, seeking Early in the vicinity of York, and next morning, as already indicated, their leader, by keeping his columns headed toward Carlisle instead of turning west to Gettysburg, just missed the chance of his life to do a great service for the cause he loved. Early spent the 30th on the road from York to a point near Heidlersburg, where Ewell and Rodes's division of his corps, in the evening, were found on their way from Carlisle to Cashtown (the point of concentration indicated by Lee), where Hill's corps was already in bivouac. West of that place, toward Chambersburg—the South Mountain Range intervening—were massed Longstreet's troops and Johnson's division of Ewell's command; and in that region, at Greenwood, Lee himself had established headquarters.

Up to this time he had in mind Cashtown as an opportune place in which to await the advance of the opposing forces. He could have fought here in a very strong position not easily flanked, with his back against the mountains, and with a clear road of retreat open in his rear leading directly to Chambersburg. This road is, indeed, the only highway for miles in either direction which commands a pass through the range into the Cumberland Valley; and had Lee simply planted himself here and waited a few hours, Meade would have been bound to attack him in that position.[1]

Gen. W. C. Oates, in his book *The War Between the Union and the Confederacy*, page 201, says con-

---

[1] To say nothing of the change in the fortunes of the hour which such a situation might have involved, what a narrow margin the country had in regard to the place just mentioned—a decisive battle fought to decide the liberties, the financial integrity, the prosperity, and safety of the nation, and lost by the Union Army at a place with that name—Cashtown! On that term, along with the proverbial phrase, the Almighty Dollar, the jeering foes of the Republic might have rung the changes for the years to come.

cerning Lee's campaign plans at this exact juncture:

> Major General Trimble told the writer after the war that Lee told him on the 28th that his plan of operations was to fall upon the advance of the Union Army, when and wherever he found it, crush and hurl it back on the main body, press forward and beat that before its commander could have time to concentrate his whole force, and that in the event of his success he intended to march on Philadelphia.

This was probably Lee's purpose on the 28th of June, and it was but slightly modified by the news which reached him that night at Chambersburg, that the Union Army was concentrated at Frederick. A further side-light is thrown by General Oates in his book on the reason why the fight occurred at Gettysburg:

> Lee did not intend to fight at Gettysburg, but at Cashtown, and ordered Ewell there at first, where Lee, with his back to the mountains, could have protected his communications and acted on the defensive; but General Hill inconsiderately blundered into the fight [of the first day], and hence Ewell had to leave the road to Cashtown and go to his assistance, and after that day's terrible battle Lee thought it inexpedient to withdraw to Cashtown.

For the sake of accuracy in our impressions of the case it is worth while to recollect that Ewell's forces were on their way to Cashtown from York and Carlisle, and turned toward Gettysburg at a point ten miles or more east of that mountain stronghold in which Lee could have established a defensive position of tremendous strength. The writer of this volume has frequently studied in person the locality indicated— has crossed the South Mountain Range at various points to the north and to the south of Cashtown, and he can hardly overstress the obvious advantage which Lee would have possessed had this original thought been embodied in action, and his forces been permitted to array themselves amid the woods and rolling fields and rocky heights which make up the immediate territory of which Cashtown would have been in that case the center, Lee's line fronting toward the east and forming a semicircle susceptible of being fortified with but little work into an impregnable position, backed by the South Mountain in the rear.

IX

BUFORD UNCOVERS THE ADVANCING CONFEDERATES

THE three divisions of Pleasanton's cavalry corps were thus distributed the day after Meade took command of the army: Gregg covered the rear and right of the army—Frederick, Westminster, and the region north of those points; Kilpatrick marched through Littlestown to Hanover, fighting there, as we have related, with Stuart, and then advancing toward the district west of York; Buford's command was assigned to cover the left of the army, and it is with this force that we have now to deal. The services rendered by this division should never be forgotten, although recent criticism, as we shall indicate later, would have us consider Buford as a brave but foolishly headlong cavalryman who by his fight to keep the Confederate forces back that morning made himself chiefly responsible for the disasters that followed later in the day—a judgment which seems to us wholly unjust.

On June 29th Buford's force—Gamble's First Brigade and Devin's Second Brigade—made a long and circuitous tour of observation from Middletown, Maryland (where they had recouped their men and their horses after many days of scouting and fighting on their way up from the Rappahannock), through

BUFORD UNCOVERS CONFEDERATES

Hagerstown (but recently occupied by Lee, now at Chambersburg, twenty miles farther on in the Cumberland Valley), and thence by the Monterey Gap in the South Mountain Range to Fairfield, Pennsylvania, where they camped for the night—about eight miles south of Cashtown. Between the two places J. R. Davis's Mississippi brigade, of Hill's corps, had located two regiments. People of the neighborhood knew this, but, being terrified by the proximity of the Confederate force, they did not inform Buford, who was allowed to make the discovery for himself in the morning. He might have shelled and scattered the force, but on reflection concluded not to use artillery, lest it might create an impression on Union commanders some miles away that a battle had begun; accordingly, he rode on to Emmitsburg, to report to Reynolds at that point the results of his scouting expedition. Both Buford and Reynolds, the latter being in command of the left wing of the army, had been directed to occupy Gettysburg and uncover the Confederate forces which were reported as heading toward the South Mountain Range from York and Carlisle, as well as from Chambersburg—Cashtown being supposed to be their prospective rendezvous. Buford, therefore, having consulted with Reynolds and given him all the news he had gathered, marched on to Gettysburg, reaching there early in the afternoon of that day, June 30th, just in time to discover Pettigrew's North Carolina brigade about to enter the town in search of supplies — especially shoes for the barefooted soldiers, as it was learned later.

GETTYSBURG

The Confederates were not inclined just at that juncture to be drawn into an encounter—nor was Buford; accordingly, without entering the town Pettigrew's men marched back to their bivouac near Cashtown, leaving midway between Gettysburg and that point a detachment of infantry and some cavalry scouts to watch the situation. Pettigrew that night reported to his division commander, and through him to his corps leader, Hill, what had occurred during the day, his discovery of Federal troops at Gettysburg being the emergent fact in the case which determined Hill upon his course—which it seems he undertook without consulting Lee, who just then was on the western side of the range toward Chambersburg —namely, to march with his corps to Gettysburg and ascertain in person what Union force was there. It was this decision and action which precipitated the battle. Had Hill waited till Lee arrived on the scene, Cashtown, instead of Gettysburg, would have been the point of concentration, since the Confederate forces that night were all on their way thither.

The most recent testimony in regard to this phase of the campaign is found in Early's *Autobiography*, issued while these lines (November, 1912) are being written, page 264, where he tells us that on the night of June 30th, after his march from York to his bivouac near Heidlersburg on his way to the point of assemblage somewhere "on the west side of the South Mountain," he found Ewell, his corps commander, who directed him to march next morning to Cashtown, where Lee's forces were all to meet. That morning, while on his way, his route to Cashtown from Heidlersburg being for a few miles the straight path to Gettysburg, he received a despatch from Ewell to keep on to the latter point inasmuch as Hill had just informed him that "the enemy" had appeared there, and the troops of Hill were marching thither to ascertain what force was present. At the same time Early was informed that Rodes's division, which on the way south from Carlisle had also camped near Heidlersburg, had been diverted from Cashtown to Gettsyburg. Thus, by two almost parallel roads leading in from the north to the latter point the divisions of Early and Rodes, with Ewell himself, the corps commander, guiding the movement, were en route to the place where in the middle of the forenoon of that day, July 1st, two of Hill's divisions were encountering the First Corps of the Union Army.

We have been thus explicit in detailing this incident, in order, first, to make clear that Lee's intention was to mass his troops at Cashtown; and, secondly, to show that the movement of Ewell, which brought his forces to Gettysburg opportunely for the aid of Hill, was made without the knowledge or order of Lee, for that leader got his first notification that a battle was in progress at Gettysburg from the sound of the distant cannon which reached his ears Wednesday at noon, after his arrival at Cashtown, and after he had started down the pike toward Gettysburg, having learned that Hill's forces had gone thitherward. Thus unforeseen circumstances had strangely molded the situation on both sides, and had taken the control of things for the time being out of the hands of both Meade and Lee.

GETTYSBURG

Turning now again to the situation on the Union side, let us look at the movements of the cavalry in the region about Gettysburg during the hours which preceded the outbreak of the battle on the morning of Wednesday, July 1st.

FIRST DAY

X

BUFORD KEEPS THE TROOPS OF HILL AT BAY

DURING the night of June 30th Buford scattered his scouting parties so as to cover the region west, north, and east of the town, the Confederates, as his explorations and reports all now assured him, being headed from Cashtown, Carlisle, and York toward the point where all the roads met—Gettysburg. The information he had secured concerning the locations and movements of Lee's troops was of immeasurable import, and when that night he hastened to send it to Reynolds at Marsh Creek, and through him to Meade at Taneytown, it gave those officers their first definite and reliable data with regard to the situation.

Buford, it is evident, had a critical situation to face with his 3,500 cavalry, having to cover six roads which united in Gettysburg, from various points of the compass, on all of which it was certain that Confederate infantry forces were pressing forward, while it was his bounden duty to hold them in check until Reynolds with his three army corps could arrive on the scene.

In anticipation of this task Buford covered his left front, from the Fairfield road to the Cashtown pike,[1]

[1] Gamble's Cavalry: Eighth Illinois, Major Beveridge; Twelfth Illinois and Third Indiana, Colonel Chapman; Eighth New York, Lieutenant Colonel Markell; Calef's Horse Battery A, Second United States Artillery.

with the First Brigade, and the region extending from the last-mentioned road around the northern and eastern outskirts of the town to the York road with the Second Brigade, with flankers and videttes and smaller detachments on duty for miles on every road above indicated.

Gamble's [1] (First) Brigade occupied a strong picket line in front of Seminary Ridge, with scouts three miles in front toward the west keeping watch of the Confederates through the night as they made preparations for advancing in the early dawn toward the town.

Skirmishing began along the front at about five in the morning of July 1st; at about that hour the first shot was fired from the Union side, three miles out on the Cashtown road—which, it must be remembered, is also called the Chambersburg pike—by Corpl. Alpheus Hodges, of the Ninth N. Y. Cavalry, in charge of the picket outpost. At that early hour he saw threatening signs on the part of the detachment of troops some distance out the road, and to give alarm his carbine was fired.

The skirmishing was at first sporadic and tentative, but two hours later thin lines of pickets began to

---

[1] William Gamble, Colonel Eighth Illinois Cavalry, for months commander of this brigade, was a brave Irishman who had risen from private to sergeant major in the United States Dragoons, 1839 to 1843; he was brevetted brigadier general in 1864, and won the full rank in 1865; after the war he continued in service as major Eighth United States Cavalry, but his career was cut short by death December 20, 1866.

An interesting fact also to be noted here is that the late Louis Henry Rucker, who after forty-two years of active military service, thirty-seven of them in the Regular Army, was retired with the rank of brigadier general, April 19, 1903, was first sergeant of Company G in this regiment, the Eighth Illinois Cavalry, at Gettysburg. General Rucker died in 1906.

press forward cautiously, their apparent aim being at first not so much to make an attack as to ascertain what force confronted them. At Buford's direction, Gamble moved out to meet them, his purpose being to keep them in check until Reynolds could arrive and in person determine the situation, his troops, as Buford knew, being already under orders to advance toward Gettysburg, and some of them by that hour hurrying to the spot. Under these circumstances Buford could not afford to present any other than a bold front, the supposition, reiterated in recent criticism, that he chiefly desired to keep "the town" out of the clutches of the Confederates being based on a mistaken view of the situation. The great cavalryman had two simple things to do: maintain his ground till Reynolds, his chief, should appear and decide what to do; and, moreover, hold fast to a situation which held in reserve for the use of the Union Army when it should arrive its prospective defensive position, just south of Gettysburg, crowned by Cemetery Hill, which for many hours he had had time and opportunity to study.

A hot engagement developed by eight o'clock between the advanced line of the Confederates and the dismounted cavalrymen; for two hours in advance of

OPENING OF BATTLE AT GETTYSBURG, 8 A.M., JULY 1, 1863

the opening of the conflict between these colliding forces the scouts of Buford had kept track of the troops of Hill, marching down the pike from their camps at Cashtown, and the information as it developed was sent to Reynolds, who in turn kept hastening his command—Doubleday at Marsh Creek, in temporary charge of the First Corps, and Howard, with the Eleventh near Emmitsburg—toward Gettysburg. Meanwhile the dismounted cavalrymen contrived by the terrific fire of their breech-loaders, and by their skilful and plucky show of force, to keep the advancing force at bay.

Under Col. George H. Chapman—afterward brigadier general and brevet major general—six companies of his own Third Indiana and four companies of the Twelfth Illinois, did effective service, some of his men finding horse-holders and borrowing muskets and joining in with the Wisconsin Infantry when they came to relieve them at the front. In this struggle Maj. Charles Lemmon, of the Indiana detachment, was killed.

Devin's[1] Second Brigade, on the night of June 30th and the next forenoon, covered the region to the northwest, the north, and the northeast of Gettysburg, from the Chambersburg pike to the York road, its scouts venturing in the direction of Mummasburg, Middletown, Heidlersburg, and Hunterstown, and thus keeping in touch with the Confederate forces which had been at Carlisle and York, and which were known to be headed toward either Cashtown or Gettysburg. Late in the morning a squadron from

---

[1] Devin's Cavalry: Sixth New York, Major Beardsley; Ninth New York, Colonel Sackett; First Pennsylvania, Colonel Kellogg; Third West Virginia, two companies, Captain Conger.

the Seventeenth Pennsylvania, under Major Anderson, received the opening volley from Ewell's advance on the Carlisle road, north of the town, the Ninth New York supporting the detachment and helping to hold in check the Confederates until the Eleventh Corps should arrive. Then, to anticipate the struggle of the afternoon, dismounted cavalrymen from Devin's brigade co-operated with their breech-loading carbines in the struggle that ensued, until at last the Union forces were all pressed back to Cemetery Hill.

Calef's Horse Battery A, Second U. S. Artillery, on duty with the cavalry throughout the campaign, did remarkable service that morning. One of its guns, fired by Lieut. John William Roder, one of Calef's faithful helpers, at the venturesome advancing cavalry skirmish - line which preluded the coming of Archer's infantry on the Cashtown road, at eight o'clock, bore the first artillery shot of the battle. Later in the morning it won this praise from Buford, found in his report:

> This battery, commanded by Lieutenant Calef, fought on this occasion as is seldom witnessed. At one time the enemy had a concentric fire upon this battery from twelve guns, all at short range; Calef held his own gloriously, worked his guns deliberately with great judgment and skill, and with wonderful effect on the enemy.

The service that Buford rendered in keeping the Confederates in check for three hours, from seven in the morning until ten, when Reynolds arrived at the head of a division of infantry, was invaluable in

securing for the Union Army the impregnable position which it occupied during the battle of the two
following days. We shall a little later deal with the
criticism recently made in view of the policy pursued by both officers that morning.

XI

STRENGTH OF THE OPPOSING ARMIES

ON account of varying data and conflicting methods of computation it is not possible to state finally and with perfect accuracy the actual number of men in the two armies, present and ready for battle at Gettysburg, when at last they were all on the field. The full organization and roster of each army will be given later in this volume; it may suffice for our present purposes and for the reader's comprehension of the matter at this point, when the two forces are about to collide, to give this summary and numerical statement.

The Army of the Potomac, under Meade, was composed of seven infantry corps:

First Corps: led successively by Reynolds, Doubleday, and Newton; with the following division commanders: Wadsworth, Robinson, and Rowley; Colonel Wainwright being in charge of the artillery brigade.

Second Corps: led by Hancock, and after he was wounded by Gibbon, and then by William Hays. Division commanders: Caldwell, Gibbon (followed by Harrow), Alexander Hays; artillery brigade, Captain Hazard.

Third Corps: led first by Sickles, and then, when

he was wounded, by Birney. Division commanders: Birney (followed by Ward), Humphreys; artillery, Captain Randolph, and then Capt. A. J. Clark.

Fifth Corps: Sykes. Divisions: Barnes (followed by Griffin), Ayres, Crawford; artillery, Martin.

Sixth Corps: Sedgwick. Divisions: Wright, Howe, Newton (followed by Wheaton); artillery, Colonel Tompkins.

Eleventh Corps: Howard. Divisions: Barlow (followed by Ames), Steinwehr, Schurz; artillery, Major Osborn.

Twelfth Corps: Slocum, and for a time Williams. Divisions: Williams (for a time Ruger), Geary; artillery, Muhlenburg.

Besides this body of infantry and corps artillery, the Cavalry Corps was led by Pleasanton, with Buford, D. M. Gregg, and Kilpatrick in charge of divisions, and Robertson and Tidball commanded the two brigades of horse artillery.

The great array of reserve artillery was in charge of Gen. R. O. Tyler, followed for a time by Capt. J. M. Robertson.

The Army of Northern Virginia, under Lee, was composed as follows:

First Corps: Longstreet. Divisions: McLaws, Pickett, Hood; artillery, Walton.

Second Corps: Ewell. Divisions: Early, Edward Johnson, Rodes; artillery, Brown.

Third Corps: Hill. Divisions: Anderson, Heth, Pender; artillery, Walker.

Cavalry Division: Stuart. Brigades: Fitzhugh Lee,

STRENGTH OF OPPOSING ARMIES

Wade Hampton, Chambliss, Jenkins, Robertson, W. E. Jones, Imboden.

It may be well in glancing at this array of forces to keep in mind what we have already noted, that an army corps in the Confederate organization was fully twice as large as one in the Union Army, and that the brigades and divisions were hence of corresponding size.

Different estimates have been made by expert judges, who have with painstaking care canvassed the returns and endeavored to make an honest count of the two armies. We shall not attempt to do more at this point than to set down the varying results of these computations. The estimate given by the editors of the great work known as *Battles and Leaders of the Civil War* we give under the heading, "Century War Book."

AUTHORITY	MEADE	LEE
Longstreet		75,568
Century War Book........................	93,500	70,000
John Formby, *Civil War in America*......	82,000	73,000
The Comte de Paris, *The Civil War*........	84,000	69,000
Livermore, *Numbers and Losses*...........	83,289	75,054
Col. W. F. Fox, *New York at Gettysburg*.....	85,674	71,675

XII

MAJOR GENERAL REYNOLDS'S left wing was thus disposed on the morning of Wednesday, July 1st: Howard's Eleventh Corps was at Emmitsburg, under orders to follow in the wake of the First Corps with a "marching interval" of perhaps three miles between the two bodies, on the road to Gettysburg; the Third Corps, under Sickles, was directed to hold the region around Emmitsburg, in view of the possible advance of the Confederates at Fairfield and Cashtown in that direction; and the three divisions of Reynolds's own First Corps, commanded by Doubleday, were directed to start at once for Gettysburg, where, it was understood, Buford's cavalry were under pressure in the effort to stay the progress of the advancing Confederate troops. With these arrangements made, Reynolds, going in advance of his leading division, Wadsworth's, and accompanied by his staff, hastened to Gettysburg. As he neared the town the sounds of battle, along with occasional couriers from Buford telling of the increasing peril, quickened his pace as he rode on to observe the situation, locate his troops on arrival, and consult with the cavalry leader.

It will be recalled that Reynolds had no orders to

bring about an engagement at Gettysburg; he was simply to uncover the whereabouts of the Confederates, hold Gettysburg if it could be done without getting entangled with an overwhelming force, and at the same time mask the concentration which was to have been started that day—of the other portions of Meade's army on the Pipe Creek Line, along the northern border of Maryland. But when Reynolds learned that a single worn and weak force of cavalry was trying to head off the whole Confederate Army on the roads leading into Gettysburg from the east, and north, and west, what alternative had he, as a man, a patriot, a Pennsylvanian, and a soldier, other than to direct his men toward the sound of the cannon?

What his policy might have been that day had he been spared to direct the battle we cannot tell. In a brief consultation which he had with Wadsworth, and also with Buford, he indicated that he had considered (en route, and after he had noted the strength of the position at Cemetery Hill) the possibility of withdrawing and occupying the latter point, and also the reasons for holding the town—where the roads centered on which the troops of Lee were advancing—but had concluded that he was bound to maintain the lines already established, at least until further developments should reveal another course of duty. It must be considered in forming a judgment on the decisions he made and the policy he pursued that morning that his conclusions had to be formed offhand, in the midst of confusion and danger. He had only opportunity to consult hurriedly with Buford, to go with that officer to the belfry of the Lutheran Theological Seminary building and survey the field, getting at a glance a striking impression of the strength of the position to be occupied within the hour by the advancing troops of the Eleventh Corps under Howard on Cemetery Hill, and then give personal directions for the formation of his line of battle along Seminary Ridge, facing westward and arrayed to meet the advancing enemy. With quick discernment he recognized the situation—the Confederate Army was massing in front; his one duty was to hold its advance in check until word could be sent to Meade, until additional forces should arrive, until the magnificent line, reaching from Round Top to Cemetery Hill, which he had swiftly surveyed as he rode along the Emmitsburg road a few minutes before, could be manned and strengthened!

Some critics have blamed Reynolds for "bringing on a fight" that morning; but it now seems clear that to parley and retreat at that juncture, to fall back to Cemetery Hill without making a stand on Seminary Ridge, would have resulted in disaster. Severe censure is passed upon both Buford and Reynolds in the most recent volume dealing critically with the battle—*The Campaign of Gettysburg* (Boston, 1912)—written by an anonymous author who entitles himself "Miles," which we take to be the Latin synonym for "A Professional Soldier," and who shows himself a technical student, probably a teacher, of strategy and military engineering. While the work is a valuable one and abounds in critical comments and suggestions, yet the treatment accorded to these

two officers seems to us unjust and unwarranted.
For example:

> At daylight on July 1st the Confederate troops were under arms
> and marching toward Gettysburg. Buford was aware of their
> approach, but instead of falling back upon the First Corps he
> determined to hold the town with his cavalry until the Federal
> infantry could come up to his support. . . . Of Buford's courage
> and energy there can be no question, but he cannot be acquitted
> of an error of judgment which proved most disastrous to the
> Union arms. The movement [under Reynolds to Gettysburg],
> in fact, was strategically unsound, and it was destined to lead to
> a terrible disaster to the Union arms. . . . It is possible that the
> impetuosity of General Reynolds was the cause of this false
> move. Reynolds was a Pennsylvanian. As such he was eager
> to prevent the further invasion of his native State, and his ardor
> may well have overcome his prudence. On the other hand, it is
> definitely stated in Meade's report that he himself ordered the
> forward movement to Gettysburg. . . . So fell Reynolds . . . a victim
> to his own impetuous rashness. . . . It is inconceivable why Buford,
> at Heth's approach, did not evacuate the town and fall back on
> Cemetery Hill [premising that Buford really appreciated the im-
> portance of that position]. [See pages 67, 68, 69, 147 in the volume
> just cited.]

So far as the general movement to Gettysburg by
the left wing is concerned, it was ordered by Meade,
who gave instructions to Reynolds to study the
region and judge of its fitness both for offensive and
defensive purposes; the correspondence makes it clear
that Meade intended to occupy Gettysburg, even after
he knew that the Confederates were headed for that
point. Reynolds was ordered to "hold the enemy in
check and fall back slowly" only in case he found himself in the presence of a superior force. (*Official Records*, XXVII, 3:462–472.) Buford's every movement
was taken when in close touch with Reynolds, and his
orders, in the midst of the turmoil and peril of July

1st, were "to dispute every inch of ground, and only in case of great necessity"—should the enemy "advance in force and press him hard"—to fall back "very slowly to Taneytown." Under these circumstances Buford acted the part of an intelligent, faithful, and heroic officer, obeying the orders given him by Pleasanton, his corps commander, Reynolds, his direct superior, and Meade, the commander in chief.

With regard to the movements suggested by "Miles" in his critical volume, hardly a word is needed to those who know the ground. That Buford should fall back on Cemetery Hill with his cavalry and one battery and try to defend that point from the oncoming forces of Hill early on Wednesday morning, or that he should retreat still farther without any fighting and "fall back on the First Corps" at that time, when he had been commanded by Reynolds to hold his place until the infantry of that corps should arrive—it hardly seems possible that such "moves" at this distance from the scene could be soberly proposed.

We must remember, furthermore, that a campaign and a battle are to be finally judged by the outcome. When we consider the entire case, is it not clear that the field and line of battle as finally occupied by Meade, on July 2d and 3d, were singularly fit and propitious? Those who see a divine hand occasionally revealed in national history might say that that great field was providentially assigned, in view of all preceding movements that led to its use, as the place where the Army of the Potomac might win its pivotal victory.

As we review the events which preceded and followed that opening day of the battle our conviction becomes invincible that the forlorn and hopeless fight waged all day by the First Corps, and the disastrous stand made for the time in the afternoon by the heroic but unfortunate forces of the Eleventh Corps, did a notable service for the Union arms, detaining the advancing Confederates, using up their strength, bidding them pause in their desperate attacks, and thereby gaining time to allow the position to be studied by Meade, the troops to be massed, their commanders to reach a definite conclusion, and the great Cemetery Hill, the center of that splendid Union line of battle, to be occupied with batteries, manned by the arriving regiments, fortified by rifle-pits and lunettes for the cannoneers, and thus to become finally one of the monumental citadels of freedom for all the ages to come! That this was actually the result secured by the work of the first day it may not be necessary to argue further, and yet a single citation from the report of Lieut. Gen. A. P. Hill, commanding the Confederate Third Army Corps, may be made confirming the position we have taken. Summing up the work of the day and bringing the story of his part in the fight down to the time when the Union Army was driven through the streets of Gettysburg, he says:

Under the impression that the enemy was entirely routed, my own two divisions exhausted by some six hours' hard fighting, prudence led me to be content with what had been gained, and not push forward troops exhausted and necessarily disordered, probably to encounter fresh troops of the enemy. [*Official Records*, XXVII, 2: 607.]

Summing up the case, we may say that a fresh

examination of the official reports reveals the fact that the encounter at Gettysburg was brought about on both sides without "malice aforethought." Both forces, Union and Confederate, were reaching out in various directions, trying to determine the plans and whereabouts of each other, and striving to occupy each for itself an advantageous position. And on both sides the forces became engaged with vehement energy and eagerness before their commanders really understood how serious the situation was. On the Union side this fact has already been made abundantly clear, and perhaps it is fully understood also that Lee did not desire a battle to begin except upon grounds of his own selection. Ewell, for instance, in his report (*Official Records*, XXVII, 2:444) tells us instructions from Lee reached him on the way from Heidlersburg to Gettysburg, on the morning of July 1st, ordering that in case the enemy's force was found to be very large "he did not want a general engagement brought on until the rest of the army came up." When, however, these two eager and desperately roused antagonists, the Army of Northern Virginia and the Army of the Potomac, once clinched in the death-grapple that morning, nothing could separate them until they had fought it out.

XIII

DOUBLEDAY'S FIGHT WITH HILL

LIEUT. GEN. AMBROSE P. HILL, commanding the Third Army Corps of Lee's army, at five in the morning of Wednesday, July 1st (anxious to discover what was in his front at Gettysburg, where Pettigrew's brigade had on the preceding afternoon found some Union cavalry disputing its way into the town), started two divisions of his command from Cashtown down the pike for that place, not expecting to find anything more there than a scouting detachment, which he could easily brush aside with the force which he had in hand. He had sent word to the commander in chief, ten miles away in the other direction across the mountains toward Chambersburg, that he was making this movement, and given orders to the courier to hasten the other division, Anderson's, in its journey over the mountains to Cashtown, and thence onward toward Gettysburg to join the preceding portions of the corps. Archer's[1] brigade of Heth's division led the way down the pike, the march being impeded only by the sharp stones of the roadway, which cut the feet of the ill-shod

---

[1] Archer's brigade: Thirteenth Alabama, Colonel Fry; Fifth Alabama Battalion, Major Van de Graaff; First Tennessee, Major Buchanan; Seventh Tennessee, Colonel Shepherd; Fourteenth Tennessee, Captain Phillips.

infantry as well as lamed the unshod horses of the artillery. Between the lameness thus induced and the broiling heat of the July morning, the march was an exhausting one, while the prevalent prospect of a fight perhaps did not tend to cheer up the rank and file on their way, although they looked for a quick and easy victory.

General Hill, that morning, when he gave signal for his men to start down the pike—without waiting to consult Lee—did not even faintly surmise that he was taking the immediate step which would bring on one of the greatest and most decisive battles of history; one of his division commanders, Maj. Gen. Henry Heth, who led the column, says in his report that at the time he found Federal troops in his front three miles west of Gettysburg, at nine o'clock, he was ignorant what force was there, "and supposed it consisted of cavalry, most probably supported by a brigade or two of infantry."

While this was going on, to the west and northwest of Gettysburg, on the Cashtown pike, another scene of momentous meaning was occurring on the Emmitsburg road, from seven to ten miles south of Gettysburg, where Doubleday, now for the time in charge of the First Army Corps of the Army of the Potomac, following the directions of his chief, Reynolds, was gathering his troops in from the picket lines and starting them for Gettysburg, alert and quickened by the reports that had come in the day before and during the night from Buford, indicating the approach of Confederate forces from Cashtown, and also from Carlisle and York.

DOUBLEDAY'S FIGHT WITH HILL

As the roads on which these two combative bodies —one representative of the Army of Northern Virginia, and the other the emerging forces of the Army of the Potomac, each regiment followed in turn by others close behind—formed a right angle at Gettysburg, where they came together, it was inevitable that the eager columns should swiftly collide, and that in their first collision a desperate struggle should begin. Each colossal antagonist for three weeks had been groping in the darkness to find the other, and had been saying, even in his dreams: "Where is he? Let me get at him!" Now that the distance between them was but a few miles, and the question of time had been reduced to a couple of hours, the tragic death-clutch was close at hand.

Half a mile west of Gettysburg Seminary Ridge— on which has stood for many years the Theological Seminary of the Lutheran Church—runs north and south; and beyond that point are parallel ridges of partly wooded and partly cultivated land. On these ridges the first lines of battle were formed, the Cashtown pike and an old railroad cutting crossing them diagonally in a northwest direction. In the Confederate advance Archer's brigade formed line, facing eastward, toward the town, perhaps three miles up the pike, to the right of that thoroughfare; and the brigade of Gen. J. R. Davis[1] connected with it on the left of the pike, a battery first opening fire upon the distant Federal force, just appearing in sight on Seminary Ridge. It was about ten o'clock when Reynolds

[1] Davis's brigade: Second, Eleventh, and Forty-second Mississippi, Colonels Stone, Green, and Miller; Fifty-fifth North Carolina, Colonel Connally.

in person established his first—and, as it chanced, his last—line of battle along Seminary Ridge, hurrying a portion of Cutler's brigade,[1] Wadsworth's division, to the right of the line, northward of the pike, the men having hardly time to deploy before they found themselves engaged in a terrific fight with the emerging foe.

To a Pennsylvania regiment came the chance of firing the first infantry volley — the Fifty-sixth, under Colonel Hoffman — followed at once by the Seventy-sixth New York; while Buford's cavalry, not yet withdrawn to the north on the Ridge, helped the infantry by a flanking fire on the advancing brigade of Davis, while Hall's Second Maine Battery, to distinguish itself, at a heavy cost during the day, opened fire, relieving for a time the worn and weary cannoneers of Calef, on duty for days before the fight opened. The two regiments just mentioned, with

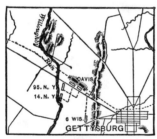

PLACE OF CAPTURE OF CON-
FEDERATES IN THE RAIL-
ROAD AT GETTSYBURG

the 147th New York, found themselves assailed front and flank by the troops of Davis, and in a half-hour had lost heavily, and would have been in part captured but for the order of Cutler to withdraw; then Davis's men pressed too far and were caught in the railroad cutting, where three hundred were taken prisoners, and

---

[1] Cutler's brigade: Seventy-sixth, Eighty-fourth (otherwise called the "Fourteenth Militia"), Ninety-fifth, and 147th New York; Fifty-sixth Pennsylvania. The Seventh Indiana, of this brigade, did not reach the field from special duty at Emmitsburg till late that afternoon, on Cemetery Hill.

the brigade was so badly damaged that the division commander feared to bring them into battle again that day; but later in the afternoon they took a gallant part again.

While this fight was going on along the right of the line north of the pike, a sharp encounter was taking place to the left of the pike in and about McPherson's Woods, overlooking Willoughby Run, which Archer's brigade had crossed in their effort to capture the ridge which was in part covered by the forementioned patch of woodland. To forestall this enterprise Meredith's Iron Brigade,[1] and two of Cutler's regiments—the Fourteenth Brooklyn (Eighty-fourth New York) and the 147th New York—made a counter attack, aided by a volley from Buford's carbineers, who delivered a flanking fire from the woods on the Confederate right. Archer's men and their commander were in goodly numbers captured.

It was at the opening of this phase of the fight that Reynolds was killed. He had stationed his men, under Cutler's command, on the right of the pike, and had hastened to supervise the movement on the left. While pointing to the woods to be taken and inspiring his command by word and example he was hit by a sharp-shooter's bullet, and with a fatal wound in his neck he fell dead from his horse.

While the First Division had been thus engaged Robinson's division was hurrying along the Emmitsburg road to the field, where it arrived at about eleven, and was posted in reserve for a little while

---

[1] Meredith's Iron Brigade: Nineteenth Indiana, Twenty-fourth Michigan, Second, Sixth, and Seventh Wisconsin.

at the Seminary; then, danger threatening the right
of the line, it was hurried beyond the pike toward
the north, and there Baxter's brigade[1] extended the
line already formed by Cutler, and at once faced a
terrific assault from a newly aligned body of fresh
Confederate troops. This assault, twice repeated,
was repulsed, and the Confederates lost a thousand
men as prisoners who had ventured too far in their
charge.

Paul's brigade,[2] of this division, was at first occupied with preparing rifle-pits at the Seminary for
later use and extending the line of extemporized
fortifications up to the Chambersburg pike, or Cashtown road, and then, an opening intervening between
Baxter and Cutler, Paul's men were aligned in it,
soon to be involved in a fresh and dreadful artillery
and infantry conflict. General Hill had brought
into action nearly twenty batteries—all his reserve
artillery—and soon after two o'clock he brought his
sixty or eighty guns to bear on the Union line with
terrific effect.

Two brigades of the Third Division, which had
been led by Doubleday, but was now commanded by
Rowley, closely followed Robinson's, and were posted
on the left; Col. Roy Stone's Bucktail Brigade,[3]
from the mountains of their native Keystone State,
to the north of the Iron Brigade, near McPherson's

[1] Baxter's brigade: Twelfth Massachusetts, Eighty-third and Ninety-seventh New York, Eleventh, Eighty-eighth, and Ninetieth Pennsylvania.
[2] Paul's brigade: Sixteenth Maine, Thirteenth Massachusetts, Ninety-fourth and 100th New York, 107th Pennsylvania.
[3] Stone's Bucktails: 143d, 149th, and 150th Pennsylvania.

FIRST CORPS, SEMINARY RIDGE, 3·30 P.M., JULY 1

(From a print of the time)

Woods; and Biddle's First Brigade [1] to the left of
that organization, the former facing Davis's remnant,
and the latter in front of Pettigrew,[2] who, with Brockenbrough,[3] had not thus far been actively engaged,
but who were now brought forward from the reserve
line to join in a more determined attempt to drive
the Union forces back from their position in front of
Seminary Ridge.

By half after eleven o'clock both forces, after nearly
two hours of fighting, were ready for a halt, which
was had until about two in the afternoon, when, with
forces recruited and newly aligned, the battle was
undertaken again. By that hour things assumed a
threatening aspect on the Union right, where fresh
troops from Rodes's division had taken their post
in a location from which the right flank of the First
Corps was gravely endangered, three brigades [4] of
North Carolinians, just arrived from Carlisle after a
hurried march since daylight, suddenly appearing in
view. These brigades, in the order indicated in the
footnote, were marshaled from the railroad cut northeast in an arc of a circle inclosing the whole right
flank of the Union force, while O'Neal's Alabama
brigade [5] closed in from the north, ready to break to
pieces Cutler's right.

[1] Biddle's brigade: Eightieth New York, 121st, 142d, and 151st
Pennsylvania.
[2] Pettigrew's brigade: Eleventh, Twenty-sixth, Forty-seventh,
and Fifty-second North Carolina.
[3] Brockenbrough's brigade: Virginia troops; Fortieth, Forty-
seventh, and Fifty-fifth regiments, Twenty-second Battalion.
[4] Daniel's brigade: Thirty-second, Forty-third, Forty-fifth, and
Fifty-third regiments, Second Battalion. Iverson's: Fifth, Twelfth,
Twentieth, and Twenty-third. Ramseur: Second, Fourth, Fourteenth, and Thirtieth. Doles: Georgia; Fourth, Twelfth, Twenty-first,
Forty-fourth. [5] Third, Fifth, Sixth, Twelfth, and Twenty-sixth.

Supporting this array, in the rear of Hill's division, and brought forward to the front in the exigencies of the afternoon struggle was Pender's division of Hill's corps, one brigade of which, led by Thomas,[1] being held in reserve, while the other three brigades took part in the final advance movement of the day, Lane,[2] Perrin,[3] and Scales[4] forming along Willoughby Run and pressing forward toward Seminary Ridge.

The struggle was carried on under great disadvantages to the Union side, Doubleday being overnumbered from the start, and yet forbidden by the circumstances of the case from retreating until necessity urged him to take that step to keep himself and men from annihilation. To add to his perplexities and difficulties the Eleventh Corps, which had arrived at noon or a little later, found it impossible to close in with the right of the First Corps, the attack on their front and right flank by Ewell's corps making such a movement wholly out of the question. That part of the fight will be treated in some detail in the next section.

We may not attempt to rehearse the details of the terrific fight from two to four-thirty in the afternoon. The "forced reconnaissance," which Heth supposed the affair would be when it began, developed into one of the bloodiest fights of the whole war, in

---

[1] Thomas: Georgia; Fourteenth, Thirty-fifth, Forty-fifth, Forty-ninth.

[2] Lane: Seventh, Eighteenth, Twenty-eighth, Thirty-third, and Thirty-seventh North Carolina.

[3] Perrin: South Carolina; First, Twelfth, Thirteenth, Fourteenth, and First Rifles.

[4] Scales: North Carolina; Thirteenth, Sixteenth, Twenty-second, Thirty-fourth, and Thirty-eighth.

which some of his regiments suffered literally beyond parallel. The Twenty-sixth North Carolina, for example, had been freshly recruited up to the number of more than 800 present in line; its losses in killed and wounded were 588. General Heth notes that in one instance when that command "encountered the second line of the enemy" the dead of the North Carolinians "marked their line of battle with the accuracy of a line at dress-parade."

The regimental quartermaster, writing on July 4th to the governor of his State, testifies that on that day, after having been again engaged—this last time in the final charge under Pettigrew—only eighty men were present for duty. This stands as the largest record of losses sustained by any regiment, Union or Confederate, in any battle of the Rebellion. (*Official Records*, XXVII, 2:639–645.)

It is a singular circumstance that this Confederate regiment was in the force which immediately confronted the three Union regiments that lost more heavily in the battle than any other trio—the Twenty-fourth Michigan, 363; the 151st Pennsylvania, 337; and the 149th Pennsylvania, 336. It clearly appears, therefore, from these data that most deadly volleys were exchanged in that part of the field. In the Twenty-fourth Michigan all of the color-guard were killed or wounded, and the flag was carried by nine persons in succession, four of whom were killed and three wounded.

To sum up the outcome let us say that the whole Union line about four o'clock was pressed back and forced to escape to Cemetery Hill, some passing through the town and meeting the troops of the fleeing Eleventh Corps mixed with Confederates crowding after them, and some evading capture by going through the area around the town, having made an extraordinary record; amid great losses and often taken on the flank and finally in the rear for five or six hours, they did magnificent fighting, capturing many prisoners. Thus far, indeed, no historian has done justice to the devotion, steadfastness, and superior service rendered by the officers and men of this corps in this part of the battle. The veteran, General Wadsworth, later to give up his life in the Wilderness, with his two disciplined brigades under Meredith and Cutler; the Second Division, led by Gen. John C. Robinson—his First Brigade having five successive commanders, Paul, Leonard, Root, Coulter, and Lyle—stricken by wounds in the fierceness of the conflict; the Second, with Gen. Henry Baxter at its head, battered at and hammered to pieces in the encounter for hours; the Third Division, under General Rowley, with Col. Chapman Biddle leading the First Brigade, and Colonels Roy Stone, Langhorne Wister, and E. L. Dana in succession, commanding the Second Brigade; the Artillery Brigade, under Colonel Wainwright, its batteries holding their own until the Confederates in some cases were right at the guns—this was the combined force which, along Seminary Ridge and facing for hours the on-coming ranks of Hill's corps, maintained their ground at a heavy cost, until at last they were flanked and almost surrounded by the forces of Ewell coming in upon their right and rear from north and east. Then, and then only, did they give way.

XIV

HOWARD IN COMMAND

AT a little before eleven o'clock on that embattled morning Maj. Gen. Oliver O. Howard, with his own Eleventh Corps, after a forced march from Emmitsburg, arrived at Gettysburg, to find himself (as the senior general now present) by the death of Reynolds in command of the whole field. Apprehending at a glance, as Reynolds had done, the vital and evident strength and importance of Cemetery Hill as the center of the prospective Union line of battle, he directed Steinwehr's division [1] to occupy it directly it arrived, ordering that experienced engineer officer to dig rifle-pits, plant batteries, and otherwise dispose his forces so as to hold the heights until the other portions of the army could arrive.

Years afterward, in telling the story and reviewing the emergency, we heard Howard say: "As I saw the present peril and foresaw the impending danger I bethought myself of the resources of Him who has all power, and I said to myself, 'God helping me, I will hold this hill until Meade and the rest of the army shall come.'"

[1] STEINWEHR. Colonel Coster's brigade: 134th and 154th New York, Twenty-seventh and Seventy-third Pennsylvania. Col. Orland Smith's brigade: Thirty-third Massachusetts, 136th New York, Fifty-fifth Ohio, Seventy-third Ohio.

GETTYSBURG

Accordingly, a little after noon he sent out to cover the northern approaches to the town, on which thousands of Confederates were expected, his First Division, under Barlow, and his Third, under Schurz, the latter in charge of both. This small force had no protection for the right flank, and on the left could not quite connect with the First Corps, whose line was at right angles with that of the Eleventh. The situation of the latter was accordingly desperate from the start, and those who have censured these troops without mercy in earlier or later stories of the first day have done so without just cause. Its disadvantages were, as we shall see, insuperable from the start, and yet it was bound by all obligations at any cost to make its utmost effort to stay the Confederate forces in their onward march. Carl Schurz,[1] in his report, sums up the obvious features of the case as he saw them at noon that day, just before going out to the front of the town:

Of the enemy we saw but little, and had no means of forming a just estimate of his strength. Either the enemy was before us in

[1] Maj. Gen. Carl Schurz (1829–1906), commanding the two divisions of the Eleventh Corps in the fight of Wednesday afternoon, to the north of the town, was for half a century one of the notable contributions made by Germany to the patriotic life of the United States. Born in Prussia and educated in the University of Bonn, he came to this country in 1852, a friendless refugee, after having run many risks and suffered imprisonment as a young revolutionist in his native land. He became a leader of the Republican party, a helper of the Union cause, and a journalist. For some months in 1861 he was minister to Spain; then he accepted a commission as general in the Union Army, showing fine qualities in command of men. After the war he was an editor, United States Senator, Secretary of the Interior, and littérateur—in all his relationships showing deep convictions, knowledge of economics, and large patriotism. Among his notable productions are his political speeches, his *Life of Henry Clay*, and his three-volume *Autobiography*.

small force, and then we had to push him with all possible vigor, or he had the principal part of his army there, and then we had to establish ourselves in a position which would enable us to maintain ourselves until the arrival of reinforcements. Either of these cases being possible, provision was to be made for both. [*Official Records*, XXVII, 1:727.]

The first unit of the corps to arrive at Gettysburg, after four hours of rapid marching, without a halt, in dust and sweltering heat, was Schurz's own division,[1] which Schimmelfennig now led, as the first-named officer had been put in charge of the corps.

About one o'clock the troops of this division were in line, their left resting on the Mummasburg pike which leads to the northwest, but connection with the right of the First Corps (now engaged in a fierce fight), which also rested on that road, was found impossible at that juncture, the point to be occupied in order to make the connection being half a mile to the front and swept by an enfilading flank fire of the enemy.

Barlow's division,[2] on arrival from Emmitsburg, through the heat and dust, was also hastened through the town, and posted to cover the right of the field, the entire Eleventh Corps line now stretching from the Mummasburg pike on the left around the northern flank of the suburbs of the town to the York road, which comes in from the east, the center of its line being crossed by the Carlisle road.

[1] Van Amsberg's brigade: Eighty-second Illinois, Forty-fifth and 157th New York, Sixty-first Ohio, Seventy-fourth Pennsylvania. Krzyzanowski's brigade: Fifty-eighth and 119th New York, Eighty-second Ohio, Seventy-fifth Pennsylvania, Twenty-sixth Wisconsin.

[2] BARLOW. First Brigade: Colonel von Gilsa; Forty-first, Fifty-fourth, and Sixty-eighth New York, 153d Pennsylvania. Second Brigade: Ames; Seventeenth Connecticut, Twenty-fifth, Seventy-fifth, and 107th Ohio.

GETTYSBURG

On the Confederate side Rodes's division of Ewell's corps had arrived, as already intimated, a little after noon, and after studying the topography for a time to find a proper place whereon to locate his troops that leader had so posted his five brigades as to aid Hill on the one hand, then about to begin with fresh fury his attack on the troops of Doubleday, still

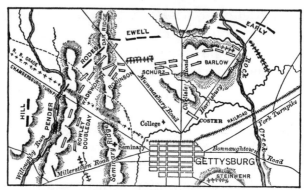

FIRST DAY AT GETTYSBURG, AT 3 P.M.
(Federal, ▭   Confederate, ■)

arrayed along the Seminary Ridge line, and at the same time assail both the front and the flank of the Eleventh Corps, now in place to cover the northern flank of Gettysburg.

This is probably the point in our narrative in which to afford room to a brief portraiture of this notable Confederate chieftain, as all the other division leaders in Lee's army find their proper place in the section on West Point, and Maj. Gen. Robert Emmet Rodes is the only officer in the Army of Northern Virginia holding such a command who was not a graduate of the Academy. He had, however, received military training in that famous institution

194

which contributed so many students to the Southern armies, the Viriginia Military Institute, from which he was graduated in the class of 1848. Born at Lynchburg, Virginia, March 29, 1829, when his schooling was completed he turned his attention to railroad service in the civil engineering department, locating finally at Tuscaloosa, Alabama, where he won rank in his vocation both as a technical expert and as an executive. Early in 1861 he organized the Fifth Alabama, from the command of which he was promoted in October, 1861, to be brigadier general, going one grade higher after Chancellorsville, for special skill in that fight, where he headed Jackson's assault on Hooker's right flank. It happened at Gettysburg that he was so placed as to be able to inflict another terrific flanking blow upon the men he smote at Chancellorsville—the Eleventh Corps. Rodes was one of Lee's reliable commanders in the Wilderness campaign; on September 19, 1864, he was mortally wounded while making a vigorous attack at Winchester.

An hour after Rodes's division had been posted Early's four brigades[1] had formed their line on the left of Rodes, encircling the two small brigades under Barlow so as to afford both a front and enfilading fire, and threatening even before the fight opened to cut them off completely from the town. Schurz, fore-seeing the peril, hurried a staff-officer to Howard, at

---

[1] EARLY. Hays's Louisiana brigade: Fifth, Sixth, Seventh, Eighth, Ninth. Wm. Smith: Thirty-first, Forty-ninth, and Fifty-second Virginia. Col. Avery: Sixth, Twenty-first, and Fifty-seventh North Carolina. Gordon's Georgia: Thirteenth, Twenty-sixth, Thirty-first, Thirty-eighth, Sixtieth, and Sixty-first.

GETTYSBURG

Cemetery Hill, pleading that reinforcements might be sent to safeguard the right flank of his struggling force, and at least preserve a way of escape back into the town if his forces had to retreat. In answer to this request Howard sent Coster's small brigade, the only reinforcement he could spare; but it reached the field only in time to stay for a few minutes the progress of the already victorious Confederates.

The artillery accumulated by the Confederates for that afternoon attack was of itself a guarantee of victory, as over against the small array of cannon which the Eleventh Corps was able to use, two of its batteries having been already stationed on Cemetery Hill; this left for use in the field in front of the town but sixteen guns, in the batteries[1] commanded by Dilger, Wilkeson, Wheeler—and, almost at the end of the fight, and during the retreat—Wiedrich. On the other side Jones's artillery battalion (24 guns) was strongly placed on a hill which commanded the right flank of Barlow; while to the northwest, on Oak Hill, Carter's artillery battalion (24 guns) was so stationed as to command Barlow's left flank, as well as the front of the other portions of Schurz's command, and also enfilade the whole line of the First Corps. What soldiers in the world could stand before such a concentrated fire of artillery, supplemented by an overpowering array of infantry?

Among the losses that day was one which had unusually tragic elements: Bayard Wilkeson, first lieutenant, in command of the regular battery indicated

[1] Battery I, First Ohio; G, Fourth United States Artillery; Thirteenth New York Battery, and Battery I, First New York.

above, was mortally wounded in the battle; entering the Regular Army in the fall of 1861, he had already won two brevets for gallantry in battle, a third for lieutenant colonel being added posthumously after Gettysburg. His father, a noted journalist, Samuel Wilkeson, was with the Union Army at Gettysburg caring for the interests of one of the great New York daily papers.

We have been thus explicit in making clear the foredoomed situation of the Eleventh Corps because it has been most unjustly abused for the work of that day. In a recent volume already noted in these pages, *The Gettysburg Campaign*, the author, page 150, speaks of—

the inglorious rout of the Eleventh Corps, the only body of troops which did not win laurels at Gettysburg. Since its disastrous defeat by Jackson at Chancellorsville about a month before the morale of the Eleventh Corps had left much to be desired. By a curious chance its opponents at Gettysburg were the same men who had driven the Germans in such terrible rout through the Wilderness. So great was the feeling of the rest of the army toward the Eleventh Corps, after its second stampede within a month, that it was considered best to break it up; this was done, and the brigades composing it were distributed among the other units of the Army of the Potomac.

As to this amazing series of allegations bearing against the character and conduct of a brave and faithful body of men let us say, in brief:

(*a*) No distribution of the Eleventh Corps among the other units of the Army of the Potomac was ever made. The Eleventh Corps and the Twelfth in September, 1863, intact, were sent under Hooker's command to Sherman's army near Chattanooga;

they remained intact until April 4, 1864, when the two were combined into the Twentieth Corps, still remaining with the same brigade organizations and under Hooker's orders. Similar redistributions were made of other army corps, and these reconstructions were never meant to be a discredit to them. For example, at the opening of the Wilderness campaign of the Army of the Potomac, in 1864, the First Corps and the Third were recombined with other corps, losing their beloved corps badges, number, and status; no one for a moment ever charged that this was done to disgrace them.

(b) The allusion to Chancellorsville shows that the author has either forgotten or ignored the fact that the fault there was not that of the regiments or their officers. Hooker and Howard were the chief ones at fault and responsible; they were warned again and again of the signs of danger, and they allowed the Eleventh Corps to remain faced south instead of west —the direction from which the attack came. There never was an army corps in the world which under such circumstances, left without warning, without instructions or opportunity to form line or fortify on the endangered flank, would have stood by their guns under the assault of Jackson's troops that day.

(c) In view of their conduct at Gettysburg thousands of the Eleventh Corps deserve—instead of denunciation — credit for making the stand they did with fidelity and courage until overwhelmed, flanked, and almost destroyed, before they finally, in order to avoid annihilation, made their way, in confusion and tumult inevitable, back to Cemetery

Hill—"all that was left of them." The First Corps avoided a part of this confusion and entanglement by using the way of retreat which was open to them through and around the western suburbs of the town. The Eleventh Corps had but one avenue of escape— through the narrow and enfiladed streets. Gen. Carl Schurz's *Autobiography* contains data and incidents which wholly relieve his corps from the charge of discreditable conduct, both at Chancellorsville and at Gettysburg.

(*d*) The testimony of the opposing generals whose forces faced the Eleventh Corps that day should be considered in order to appreciate the behavior of Schurz's troops. Rodes testifies that it required from Doles's troops, which faced one of Schurz's brigades, "a desperate contest in which his brigade acted with unsurpassed gallantry" at last to drive the enemy toward the town. John B. Gordon, who fought against Barlow's line, says:

> My brigade rushed upon the enemy with a resolution and spirit in my opinion rarely excelled. The enemy made a most obstinate resistance until the colors on portions of the two lines were separated by a distance of less than fifty paces, when his line was broken and driven back, leaving the flank which this line had protected exposed to the fire from my brigade. An effort was made here by the enemy to change his front and check our advance, but the effort failed.

Early says in his recent *Autobiography* that it was only after "an obstinate and bloody conflict" that the victory that afternoon was won. Ewell, the corps commander, writing of this phase of the fight against the Eleventh Corps, says that force made an "obstinate contest" before their line yielded. In view of these testimonies of the generals who won the fight that day, who will now intimate that the only phase of the work done by the unhappy Eleventh Corps to be recalled is that it ended in "an inglorious rout?"

About four o'clock the entire Confederate line, forming a semicircle inclosing the region round the town from the Hanover road on the east to the Hagerstown (or Fairfield) road on the southwest, made a united advance, bringing pressure to bear at once on the whole length of the Union forces; a gap intervened between the two Union corps near the Mummasburg pike, and the Confederates, crowding through that vacant place, enfiladed both flanks thus exposed; the Union lines gave way, the men of the Eleventh Corps were pressed back into the streets of Gettysburg, and hundreds of them were caught in the swirl and captured.

The town became a scene of slaughter, confusion, and terror; occasional cannon-shots, mingled with the rattle of musketry, the shouts of officers trying to stem the tide of retreat and rally their men, the yells of the victorious forces, crying: "Shoot the Yankees! Lay down your arms! Don't let one escape!" and the noise of cannon and caissons struggling to get through the mass of pursuers and pursued made up a spectacle never to be forgotten.

General Barlow was terribly wounded, and found by his opponent, Gordon, seemingly dying on the field; the sketch of the latter officer found later in this volume gives the touching interview that took place between them. Schimmelfennig, a brigade

commander under Schurz, was caught in the confusion and entangled in the town, but contrived to
hide from his pursuers till the fight was over, when the
two officers on the morning of the Fourth had break-
fast together in the town, now under Union auspices;
while the citizens of the place saw their town turned
into a hospital for thousands of wounded and dying
men, and in dismay and dread beheld a reign of terror
inaugurated, the outcome of which no man could
foretell.

It may be well to say just here that but little
property was destroyed in Gettysburg; although the
town was in the hands of the Confederates for over
two days, the people themselves and their homes were
not disturbed, and notwithstanding the fact that
much of the artillery fire involved the passage of hundreds of shot and shell over the town, but few of the
missiles lodged therein, and no conflagrations ensued.

One phase of that fight, seen in the hour of humiliation and retreat by the discomfited men of the two
withdrawing army corps, made its due impression on
those who pushed after them to the edge of the town
—the spectacle afforded by Buford's cavalry at the
foot of Cemetery Hill, aligned on the western flank
but facing the town. They had been helping on the
flanks all day, and now they were posted under
Buford himself, a magnificent body of expert carbineers, three thousand in number, in proud array,
with drawn sabers, ready to charge if the Confederates should press on after the retreating Union forces,
who had abandoned the town and the whole field
of battle held through the day, to the enemy.

GETTYSBURG

Some critics, including the Comte de Paris (*Civil War*, Vol. III, p. 565), have urged that General Howard was to blame for not withdrawing his own corps and the struggling men of the First Corps, under Doubleday, at possibly two o'clock, instead of later in the afternoon, when they were literally driven back. Gen. Carl Schurz, whose command suffered heavily in the attempt to resist the onset of the Confederates from the north and east that afternoon, urgently and sensibly contends in his *Autobiography* (Vol. III, p. 19) that this view of the case does not comport with the facts. He urges that an earlier retreat would have been to the distinctive advantage of the Confederates, who in that event would have been encouraged to press forward upon Cemetery Hill with an increased chance of capturing that commanding position. As the case turned out the resistance made by Doubleday and Schurz—the one in command on Seminary Ridge and facing the incoming tides from the west, and the other striving to hold in check to the very last extremity the troops that had arrived from the north and east—exhausted the attacking force for the time being, as the Confederate generals testify in their reports, quenched for a while their thirst for battle, and by the halt that was made imperative gave the Union forces a fresh opportunity to prepare Cemetery Hill to repel the later assaults.

XV

EWELL'S "LOST OPPORTUNITY"

HILL made no pursuit of the forces he had fought all day during the period from ten in the morning until half-past four in the afternoon after they had cleared the town, but allowed his exhausted troops to bivouac along Seminary Ridge, Anderson's division, which arrived in the evening from near Chambersburg, going into camp some two miles in the rear. He avows in his report that his men were exhausted and somewhat disordered by some six hours of hard fighting, that he was under the impression that the enemy was entirely routed, and that were he to press forward to the hill he would probably find it necessary to encounter fresh troops of the foe.

Ewell's corps in part occupied the town; they had followed the retiring infantry through Gettysburg to the edge of the town; here they were met by sharpshooters' musketry fire from the houses which they occupied in the suburbs and along the foot of Cemetery Hill, which bristled apparently with bayonets and was mantled with artillery. Not knowing what force was on the heights before them, the pursuing soldiers halted for orders; the conclusion was reached before night set in that it would be better not to press any further attack that evening, and the claim has been set up by writers on both sides of the line that this conclusion ignored and wasted a great opportunity to win a decisive victory by which the great central point of the Union line of battle might have been captured almost offhand. Some have gone so far as to say that "if Stonewall Jackson had been alive and in command of the corps, instead of Ewell, he would not have halted at the foot of Cemetery Hill, but would have followed up the retreating soldiers of the Union Army, and would have taken the embattled heights that evening." In the same spirit of hero-worship they have also said that had Stonewall been in command of the lines which made the final charge on Friday he would have won the fight in spite of all the opposition and all the difficulty that had to be faced—which is an absurd claim.

There are manifestly two sides to the case. Let us examine them.

Early was stationed at the close of the afternoon's fight immediately in front of the Hill, Avery's brigade in the fields facing the northern approaches, and Hays's men in the town, with Gordon's in reserve a little farther back. The latter records in his book of reminiscences his eagerness to press on and his conviction that the heights could have been carried by prompt and vigorous action that evening. Early, who was nearest to the enemy at the time, found that his brigades could not alone undertake the task, and sought to find Ewell, Rodes, or Hill in order to urge a combined movement of all forces present in order to carry the point. Rodes's troops, however, had not remained in the town after the victory, but had returned to Seminary Ridge to go into bivouac; Ewell, when found, gave a presentation of the case, to be related in a moment, and meanwhile time was flying, and it soon became too late to accomplish anything by an advance. Early's comment (*Autobiography*, page 271) is as follows:

> Perhaps that victory might have been made decisive, so far as Gettysburg was concerned, by a prompt advance of all the troops that had been engaged on our side against the hill upon and behind which the enemy had taken refuge, but a common superior did not happen to be present, and the opportunity was lost.

General Lee arrived at Seminary Ridge just in time to witness the retreat of the Union troops through the town, and when he found a standpoint from which he could see at a distance the hill south of the town, to which the pursued were fleeing, he sent a message to Ewell bearing on the imminent opportunity. Ewell records the fact in his report that Lee sent word by a staff-officer to press on "and attack Cemetery Hill if he could do so with advantage." Ewell surveyed the situation, saw the height before him occupied with infantry, defended by batteries, and fortified with rifle-pits, and concluded that he could not use artillery in the attack from his position in the edge of the town. Besides, Edward Johnson's fresh division was close at hand and rapidly approaching; the other two divisions of the corps were jaded with twelve hours' hard marching and fighting; at last, moreover, before Johnson could make any advance against Culp's Hill, commanding Cemetery Hill, night had come on. These are the reasons Ewell gives for not making an effort to press on after the retreating Union forces and endeavoring to capture the Hill on which they had found a refuge. (*Official Records*, XXVII, 2:445.)

Upon a resurvey of the facts in the case our judgment is that Ewell could not wisely or profitably have done any more than he did with regard to Cemetery Hill that evening. The height had been fortified by Steinwehr's division; about fifty cannon from the First, the Eleventh, and late in the evening from the Twelfth, and soon afterward twenty more from the Third, Corps were on or near the Hill, many of them protected by lunettes and posted so as to sweep all the approaches from the town. With this armament, thus protected, the destruction wrought out would have been terrific as against any force of infantry attempting to charge up the slopes. Moreover, reinforcements were at hand, and others were constantly arriving: Stannard's fresh brigade had come; the First Division of the Third Corps, with Sickles himself, were in sight; the Twelfth Corps was massing on the right on or near Culp's Hill; Buford's cavalry, ready to do work with both carbine and saber, were arrayed on the fields at the foot of the slope near where the Taneytown and the Emmitsburg roads unite; and in addition Generals Slocum, Hancock, Warren, and Howard were all at work forming and strengthening lines of battle, stationing the incoming troops, and making all possible preparations to thwart an attack of the enemy, should it be made.

In view of this situation on the Hill we cannot see that it can be claimed with reason that Ewell made any mistake in stopping at the foot instead of making an effort to get to the top of Cemetery Hill that Wednesday evening.

On the other hand, it does seem clear that Ewell had an opportunity to occupy Culp's Hill, and thus flank and command the adjacent height on that night. Edward Johnson's division of his corps arriving, after some delay, at dusk, was stationed at the foot of Culp's Hill. Ewell and Early[1] both discerned the advantage to be gained were the Hill seized before the Union troops took possession of it, and Johnson was ordered to venture through the darkness and occupy it. Johnson replied that he had found, through a reconnoitering party which had climbed almost to the summit, that the place was already "occupied by a superior force of the enemy." (*Official Records*, XXVII, 2:445, 446.)

The obverse phase of this incident is afforded by Major General Slocum, whose corps was just then making preparations to occupy Culp's Hill in force and fortify it. He testified, long afterward:

The fact is that the reconnoitering party to which Johnson refers came in contact with a small force sent here to protect our

[1] Closely associated with General Early in the work of this opening day was his assistant adjutant general, Maj. John Warwick Daniel, who, although then not quite twenty-one, gave token by his skill, courage, and all-round ability of the future that was before him. He had intermitted his college course to enter military service, and was wounded four times during the war. Later he studied law in the University of Virginia, and entered upon what proved to be a long and distinguished civic career, serving ten years in the Virginia House of Delegates and Senate, one term in Congress, and from 1887 until his death in 1910 as United States Senator. As an orator, a wise leader in his party, and a faithful patriot he achieved a notable record.

engineers, who were engaged in marking out the line to be occupied by the troops of the Twelfth Corps. The troops of Geary's division did not commence taking position here till about 3 A.M., and the last of Williams's division was not in position till after 8 A.M.

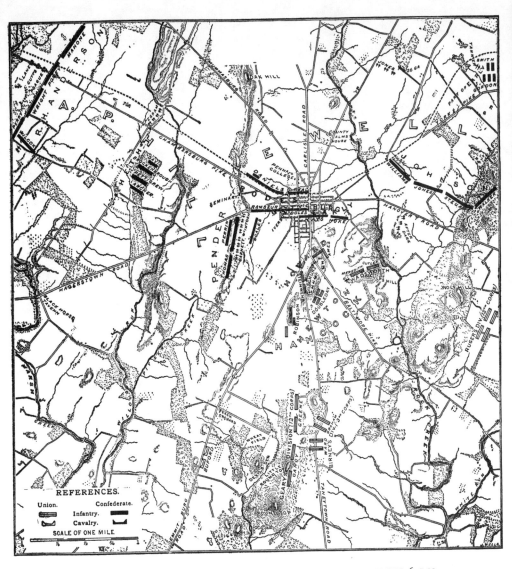

POSITIONS OF FEDERAL AND CONFEDERATE FORCES, JULY I, ABOUT 6 P.M.

XVI

HANCOCK STUDIES THE SITUATION

MEADE, at Taneytown, hearing of the encounter at Gettysburg, and later of the death of Reynolds, sent Hancock post haste in advance to take command of the forces then on the field, to survey the region, and to decide what in his judgment was best to do—stay and fight, or withdraw to a better position. Much more has been made, it seems to us, of the immediate effects of Hancock's arrival than the facts justify. He gave, it is true, by his magnificent presence and leadership, inspiration to the troops and he aided in doing that which Howard and his subordinates, as well as Slocum, were already doing—distributing the force at hand to advantage. But it should be recalled that on Cemetery Hill, to which Hancock came, was in good part a body of troops that had not yet been in the fight, and that the batteries already placed in position were ready for immediate service, and that Howard and Steinwehr had been busy for hours guarding against the very emergency that had occurred, the inevitable giving way of the troops in front of Gettysburg under the pressure of the advancing Confederate hosts, and that General Warren, chief engineer of the army, was there also hard at work. There is no reason for discounting the services of the others who were there that day in order to give additional honor to Hancock, who does not need it, for, without any exaggeration, he rendered most valuable help, and the two, Hancock and Howard, worked together without apparent friction in spite of the delicate and embarrassing circumstances.

Hancock sent Geary to Round Top to hold that commanding point, and he hurried Wadsworth's division—worn and broken from the struggles of the day at the front—to Culp's Hill, along with Hall's Fifth Maine Battery, and aided with soldierly insight in stationing other troops so as to insure the Cemetery position against attack. The work done in occupying Culp's Hill was of singular value. General Lee notes in his report that "in the mean time the enemy occupied the point [Culp's Hill] which General Ewell had designed to seize." It will be seen, therefore, at a glance how urgent was the task executed at the immediate and sagacious command of Hancock which resulted in securing offhand the wooded and precipitous height which at once became the impregnable right flank of the Army of the Potomac.

The relations between Howard and Hancock at this juncture have occasioned a vast amount of controversy. Howard felt the presence of his junior, Hancock, with enlarged powers, as a slight and an indignity, and to the very last, contrary to the obvious facts in the case, sought to interpret Hancock's authority as simply that of a staff-officer delegated to direct affairs in the crisis in behalf of Meade. Howard has written his version of the matter in an article in the *Atlantic Monthly*, July, 1876, and Hancock's story is found in the *Galaxy*, December, 1876. The latter is so fortified and illuminated by documentary evidence that no one can in reason doubt that it is correct, and that Hancock was present that afternoon to supersede Howard, to take entire charge of the field, and to act as commander of all the forces then present or arriving until Slocum, the next in rank, should come. Carl Schurz, who was a witness of the scene, thus portrays it:

> The appearance of General Hancock at the front was a most fortunate event. It gave the troops a new inspiration. They all knew him by fame, and his stalwart figure, his proud mien, and his soldierly bearing seemed to verify all that fame had told about him. His mere presence was a reinforcement, and everybody on the field felt stronger for his being there. This new inspiration of self-reliance might have become of immediate importance, had the enemy made another attack—an eventuality for which we had to prepare. And in this preparation Howard, in spite of his heart-sore, co-operated so loyally with Hancock that it would have been hard to tell which of the two was the commander and which the subordinate. [*Autobiography*, Vol. III, p. 14.]

Furthermore, it is not fair to give Hancock credit for selecting Gettysburg as the place of encounter. That officer reported to Meade by a staff-officer, late Wednesday afternoon, that Gettysburg afforded a suitable place for defense, but that it was somewhat exposed to be flanked on the left; but before any word had come from Hancock, Meade, at Taneytown, had made up his mind in the case. Data had been accumulating all day; and of his own accord, and in view of the light that now illuminated his judgment, he made his decision. At six o'clock in the evening,

July 1st, he sent a message to Hancock and Doubleday at Gettysburg: "A battle is now forced on us at
Gettysburg." An hour and a half later he dictated
the despatch to Sedgwick: "A general battle seems
to be impending to-morrow at Gettysburg . . . it is of
the utmost importance that your command should
be up." (*Official Records*, XXVII, 3 : 466, 467.)

The testimony of General Hunt, Meade's chief of
artillery, who had on the morning of July 1st been
engaged in reconnoitering the "country behind Pipe
Creek for a battle-ground," confirms our conclusion.
He says:

On my return I found General Hancock at General Meade's
tent. He informed me that Reynolds was killed, that a battle
was going on at Gettysburg, and that he was under orders to
proceed to that place. His instructions were to examine it and
the intermediate country for a suitable field, and if his report was
favorable the troops would be ordered forward. Before the re-
ceipt that evening of Hancock's written report from Cemetery
Hill, which was not very favorable, General Meade received from
others information as to the state of affairs at the front, set his
troops in motion toward Gettysburg, afterward urged them to
forced marches, and under his orders I gave the necessary instructions to the artillery reserve for a battle there. The move
was under the circumstances a bold one, and Meade, as we shall
see, took great risks. ["The Second Day at Gettysburg," *Battles
and Leaders of the Civil War*, Vol. III, p. 291.]

SECOND DAY

XVII

SOON after Hancock had returned to Taneytown and made his report, which simply confirmed the judgment and decision already made up on the part of the commander of the army, both generals rode to Gettysburg, arriving at midnight, and in the darkness, with Howard's aid, and in company with Hunt, the artillerist, they got some idea of the field and its chief strategic points of value. The line of battle, laid out by the topography of the region, and impressed on the landscape indelibly for all time, is in the form of a fishhook. The end of the handle is Little Round Top, the extreme Union left flank; the line runs north from the extremity for two miles or more to Cemetery Hill, occupying for the most of that distance an elevated backbone of rocky land, below and east of which, throughout its entire extent, runs the Taneytown road, which unites at an acute angle with the road from Emmitsburg near the point where the line of battle bends to climb Cemetery Hill.

Here, at the Cemetery the ground is high, overlooking the town and the territory beyond the village, as one glances to the north. The line then inclines to the right—the east—running along elevated ground, back of which runs the Baltimore pike, one of the chief lines of communication leading to the Union rear, and finally circles around to the point of the fishhook, where is located the rough, wooded, precipitous height known as Culp's Hill. The length of the line is nearly five miles; the distance across from point to end of handle, half that distance. This shape and location gave the Union commander the advantage of quick and easy communication between his wings and enabled him to keep promptly posted as to happenings all along the line.

The Confederate line was of similar shape, opposite the Union line at the distance of half a mile to a mile, along Seminary Ridge, on which it ran from south to north for three miles; at the Seminary it left the ridge, ran through the center of the town, and swung around to envelop Culp's Hill. It was an awkward, inconvenient, and disadvantageous line; critics have wondered why Lee held it so long. It was impossible for subordinates aptly to co-operate one with another on account of the distance—seven miles—between the ends; and there was no point from which the commander could get a glimpse of more than a fraction of the line—except from the cupola of the Seminary. Even here Culp's Hill was almost entirely hidden from sight.

Upon these lines, waiting for a fresh encounter, portions of the two armies rested on their arms, while thousands were arriving on both sides during the night and in the opening hours of the second day of the struggle.

The allegation has been ignorantly made, even within recent months, that Meade was to blame for unskilfully scattering his troops so widely that when they were needed they were not within reach. Even were it true that the various corps of the Union Army were not kept in hand so as to be of avail in case of sudden battle, it can easily be shown that Meade was not to blame, since he had to accept the army as he found it and do his best to concentrate it when he ascertained where his troops were located. But the accusation is not true. Both armies were scattered, and necessarily so; neither commander knew anything definite until the eve before the battle concerning the whereabouts or plans of his antagonist, and neither commander had the advantage of the other with regard to the policy of having his forces immediately in hand. As it happened, the forces were brought together as rapidly and skilfully as possible by both leaders, and neither one suffered injury by the fact that the scattered divisions had to be brought together at Gettysburg in good part after the battle opened. The truth is that on Thursday morning, long before noon, all of Meade's forces were on the field, except the Sixth Corps, and that body began to arrive shortly after noon. General Lee arrived late on Wednesday afternoon; and now, as we have already related, Meade was at his post, worn and haggard from anxiety, long riding, and loss of sleep, but spending his time and strength in forming and strengthening his lines, posting the arriving troops, and getting ready for the decisive struggle.[1]

[1] On the line thus held, starting at Culp's Hill, the commands thus followed in order: Twelfth Corps, Slocum; Eleventh Corps, Howard, at the Cemetery; the First Corps, Newton, near the junction of the

GETTYSBURG

General Schurz recalls his impressions of General Meade, on the morning of the second day (*Autobiography*, Vol. III, p. 20):

About eight o'clock General Meade quietly appeared at the Cemetery on horseback, accompanied by a staff-officer and an orderly. His long-bearded, haggard face, shaded by a black military felt hat, the rim of which was turned down, looked care-worn and tired, as if he had not slept that night. The spectacles on his nose gave him a somewhat magisterial look. His mind was evidently absorbed by a hard problem. But this simple, cold, serious soldier with his businesslike air did inspire confidence. The officers and men, as much as was permitted, crowded around and looked up to him with curious eyes, and then turned away, not enthusiastic, but clearly satisfied.

three chief roads, to Emmitsburg, to Taneytown, and Littlestown (the Baltimore pike); then came the Second Corps, Hancock; and finally the Third Corps, Sickles, the latter ordered to occupy with his left Little Round Top, the extremity of the Union line. The Fifth Corps was held in reserve, as also the Sixth, when it came on the field.

On the Confederate side the right, opposite Round Top, was held by Longstreet's corps; then came Hill's corps, in the center; while the left was in command of Ewell, whose corps stretched from the town to the region about Culp's Hill. Lee's headquarters were in a house on the Chambersburg pike, at the point where that road crosses Seminary Ridge; Meade established his in a little house on the Taney-town road, in rear of the left center of his line.

XVIII

THE morning and the early afternoon of Thursday, July 2, passed without any fighting, except now and then a little outbreak along the extended skirmish-line. Neither commander had gained sufficient knowledge of either the topographical or the military situation to warrant early action, and on both sides the arrival and stationing of troops in their tentative positions completely occupied the time and energies of them both. The silence, therefore, that prevailed nearly all day was not the stillness of inaction or repose; it was the hush that precedes the storm. The eyes of both Lee and Meade on that second morning were directed to Culp's Hill, the Union right flank. Meade for some hours considered the propriety of making an attack from that point upon the Confederate left flank, and his attention was absorbed with the risks that centered there—in view of the relation of that part of the line to the roads in the rear of his army and to the trains and parks of ammunition and artillery sheltered there—almost to the exclusion of other portions of the line which should have been kept in mind. It now appears that there was ground for his apprehensions of danger, although his first, and not sufficiently considered, idea of making an attack was speedily abandoned as unwise. He had gone so far in this direction as to give Slocum a tentative order to advance and assail the enemy in his front—a project which would have been full of peril. Slocum was at this time making his position impregnable by fortifying it; hence to leave this magnificent hill and venture down into the valley against an enemy whose position was not yet clearly known would have been to invite disaster. Slocum urged this fact so strongly that the plan was abandoned. But it is now demonstrable that the attention which Meade gave to this part of the line was warranted amply by the situation. General Lee's first thought was to mass his troops against Culp's Hill and carry the heights if possible. Colonel Taylor, Lee's adjutant general (*Four Years with General Lee*, pages 96 and 97), declares that late at night, after the battle of the first day, Lee's "mind was evidently occupied with the idea of renewing the assault upon the enemy's right with the dawn of day on the second." Meade therefore had good ground for his anxiety, and his prescience is shown in the fact that by military instinct he had rightly divined the intention of his antagonist.

This point was until the very end the point of extreme peril. From the extremity of the Union line on Culp's Hill to the Baltimore pike the distance was very short. Were the enemy to penetrate through this interval, almost irreparable disaster might ensue, as the hospitals, wagon-trains, lines of communication with the rear, and roads by which retreat must be made, should that desperate extremity be reached, would be at once endangered. As it happened, however, early in the morning the Fifth Corps was at hand, and it was used temporarily to strengthen the lines at Culp's Hill; and, on the other hand, Lee concluded not to make his attack on that point until later in the day, his attention having been attracted toward the Union left flank in front of the Round Tops as affording him better promise of success. With regard to this prospective part of the fight the question as between Longstreet and Lee properly comes up at this point for brief consideration.

The allegation was made by Gen. W. N. Pendleton, chief of artillery of Lee's army, in 1875—five years after the death of General Lee—that Longstreet was ordered to make his assault on the Union left, in the vicinity of the Round Tops, at sunrise of the second day, and that he, Pendleton, had reconnoitered in advance the region from which the attack was to be made. This charge is not supported by any testimony from General Lee, who gives no sign in anything he is reported to have said or in any of his written reports that he had ordered an early attack to be made. The fact is that Longstreet could not have attacked in the morning, for many of his troops were yet on the road; Law's brigade did not arrive until nearly noon, and one division, that of Pickett, did not get to the vicinity of Gettysburg until the fight for the day was about finished. Moreover, the reconnaissance which General Pendleton claims to have made on the evening of July 1st and on the early part of July 2d could not have been made then. The region which he claims to have traversed was until noon of the second in possession of Union forces, which did not withdraw from it until just after noon. Longstreet, it is true, was delayed in getting to his position—perhaps the charge that he was, "as usual," a little sluggish, has some truth in it; but we judge, after going over all the available data in the case, that he has been unjustly blamed for his so-called neglect to make his assault in the morning. In justification of our conclusion it may be said that Col. W. H. Taylor, the adjutant general, and Col. Charles S. Venable, and Col. Charles Marshall, aides-de-camp, and Gen. A. L. Long, military secretary, all on the staff of General Lee at Gettysburg, combine in the testimony that they never heard of any order or plan on the part of Lee looking toward an early attack to be made by Longstreet on the morning of July 2d. Perhaps it may not be worth while to say anything more with regard to this phase of the case; but in view of the fact that as competent a man as Gen. John B. Gordon, of the Confederate forces at Gettysburg, led astray by the charges in question, expressed himself in his volume with confidence as blaming Longstreet for gross dereliction in delaying his attack from morning to afternoon, what we have said has seemed to be due to justice and to truth.

XIX

WE may not enter into the controversy between Sickles and Meade at this point, nor try to decide as to its merits. The facts, however, may be briefly outlined. On Thursday morning the Third Corps was directed, through its commander, Maj. Gen. Daniel E. Sickles, to extend the line from Hancock's left to Little Round Top, occupying there the position which Geary had held on Wednesday night; but Geary's division had left Little Round Top before Sickles's troops were within reach, and the position was thus left undefined. The line roughly indicated to Sickles was altogether too long to be maintained by his two small divisions of the Third Corps; and no officer from army headquarters was designated, although it appears that Sickles made more than one request for one to be sent, to indicate more clearly the exact location which was to be occupied. The ridge running from Cemetery Hill to the Round Tops sinks away into a swale not far from Little Round Top, leaving the prospective line of battle at that point difficult to be held in view of an attack upon it from the direction of the more elevated ground in its front at the Peach Orchard. On studying the ground Sickles was apprehensive that the Confederates—who, as the morning wore away, gave signs of moving across his front and swinging around to his left flank—were about to occupy the higher ground along the Emmitsburg road. Moreover, skirmishing with the enemy, starting about nine in the morning, was kept up until eleven with increasing force. Indeed, two brigades of the Third Corps, arriving that morning from Emmitsburg by the direct road to Gettysburg, had been worried by the skirmishers of the enemy as they drew near to the position occupied by Sickles. In order to satisfy himself of the situation before him and to guard his troops against surprise, and fearing that the enemy might be concentrating under cover of the woods beyond the Emmitsburg road, Sickles sends out two regiments under Colonel Berdan, who find Wilcox's brigade moving toward its chosen place in the proposed line of battle. A sharp fight follows, and Berdan has to withdraw, but he has made an important discovery, worth all that it costs: Lee's army is moving against the Union left flank, and is plainly getting ready to attack that part of the line. Sickles, at this development, apprehends that an attack is to be made upon him on the low·ground where he has been stationed, and where he believed he could not aptly defend himself with artillery or withstand a heavy blow; he determines, therefore, to take possession of the Emmitsburg road in his front, including the Peach Orchard, first having made one more appeal to Meade for definite instructions. In answer to his request General Hunt, chief of artillery, was sent with him to survey the ground. Hunt refused to take final responsibility; indeed, he seems to have been in a state of mental equipoise as between the relative advantages and disadvantages of the proposed line which Sickles desired to occupy in view of the then evident movements of the enemy. The latter, therefore, without waiting any longer, advanced his force and occupied the front line. The sight was a glorious one, as we recall it: the two divisions advancing with banners waving, and with muskets gleaming in the sun, and in line of battle, the regiments in the rear marching massed by division front, across Plum Run, and up the grade toward the Peach Orchard and the region to the north of it along the Emmitsburg road.

The Peach Orchard, as may be easily seen by any close observer to-day, was the weak place in the new line; here the First Division bent back toward the Round Tops, leaving an angle in the Orchard, which in the course of the late afternoon was broken to pieces, thus giving the Confederates the chance to enfilade both lines—that occupied by Humphreys along the Emmitsburg road, and that held by Birney, extending from the Peach Orchard to the Devil's Den in front of Little Round Top. It was not until about three in the afternoon that Meade, at last, after a brief meeting of his corps commanders, became awake to the dangerous developments on his left flank. Soon after that hour he galloped with Sickles, who had come late to the meeting and in person urged once more the perils in his front, to the part of the field which was so soon to be the place of a desperate conflict. Arriving here, Meade realized now for the first time what had happened — his line was not in the place where he had ordered it located.

We cannot at this distance clearly apprehend why he should have been taken by surprise; for the movement in question, the advance to the Peach Orchard, had taken place two hours before his arrival, and it had been under consideration, as Warren and Hunt both knew, before noon. A glance at a map will help the reader to apprehend the situation. Meade's plan had been to maintain a straight line from the Cemetery to Little Round Top. Instead he finds a broken line, with an angle at the Peach Orchard, three-quarters of a mile in advance of his proposed position. In addition, he discovers, at the very moment when the Confederate cannon begin to open upon Sickles's advanced line, that Little Round Top has no troops stationed upon it and that his entire left flank is thereby in imminent danger.

The controversy as to this phase of the battle has furnished a voluminous amount of matter. Without assuming any dogmatic spirit in the case we may give a few luminous citations which may throw sidelights on the vexed questions involved. For example, we find in the *Memoirs of General Lee*, written by his military secretary, Gen. A. L. Long, this comment:

Cemetery Ridge at this portion of its extent is ill defined, and the movement of Sickles to occupy the advanced position was not without tactical warrant. Yet it was faulty from the fact that his line, to gain a defensive position for its left flank, had to be bent at a considerable angle at the advanced point known as the Peach Orchard. . . . The weak point in this line was the salient at the Peach Orchard, which formed the key of Sickles's position, and on this, when the columns of Longstreet moved to the attack at 4.30 P.M., the greatest vigor of the assault fell.

Later, in telling the story of the assault made by McLaws on this salient, breaking it and driving back the troops that held it, General Long says:

Whether the result would have been different had the original assault been made on this [first] line of battle is a question which it is impossible now to answer, and the advantage or disadvantage of Sickles's advanced movement cannot be determined except from the standpoint of military strategy. [Pages 283–286.]

A military expert of the British Army, Capt. Cecil Battine, in his recent admirable work *The Crisis of the Confederacy*, after a careful study of the whole case, comes to this conclusion:

The only merit of the new position was that it acted like a breakwater upon which the fury of the attack spent itself, and by the delay enabled all the Federal troops to come into line. [Page 216.]

The Comte de Paris, who sincerely admires Sickles and gives him credit for his courage and enterprise, devotes considerable space to this whole question. Conceding certain advantages gained by the advanced line, the Comte says:

Nevertheless, it presents such serious difficulties that one cannot approve of the initiative steps taken by General Sickles in planting himself there. [*The Civil War in America*, Vol. III, p. 604.]

General Doubleday, in his volume, *Chancellorsville and Gettysburg*, page 178, plainly evinces his final judgment that there are two sides to the case:

GETTYSBURG

The movement, disastrous in some respects, was propitious as regards its general results, for the enemy had wasted all their strength and valor in gaining the Emmitsburg road, which, after all, was of no particular benefit to them. They were still outside our main line.

Summing up the outcome of Sickles's movement, Lieut. Col. William F. Fox, of the 107th New York Infantry, says in his story of *New York at Gettysburg:*

The line of the Union Army was still intact. The Third Corps, by interposing itself in a strong position, had resisted an attack made by twice its number until the distant corps and divisions could march to that part of the field. But could it alone and unassisted have resisted a flank attack in its original position? Longstreet says it could not. Without a change of front no effective resistance could have been possible.

Concluding this survey, we may record our own conclusion, that Longstreet's blow, falling upon the Third Army Corps in its original position, as first stationed in a thin line from the left of the Second Corps to the northern slope of Little Round Top, could not have been warded off or withstood; it would have made a hole clean through the line to the Taneytown road.

XX

MEADE COMMANDS IN BATTLE

WHATEVER conclusion may be reached as to the policy of Sickles in this instance, there can be no question that the situation which the commanding general faced at half-past three o'clock that hot afternoon was one of peril, a situation, indeed, that was ominous with tokens of calamity. It is worth while to study the new commander in a crisis such as was now at hand. All military authorities agree that the supreme test of a general is his readiness to meet alarming developments which menace all his former calculations. The grade which a commander occupies, estimated by standards of the highest order, depends largely on his mastery of emergent circumstances, his poise and behavior when all his plans go awry, his quickness of insight and fertility of action when confronted by untoward happenings—in short, his ability to face the unexpected, to repair damages wrought in his lines and among his troops by disasters which burst like so many thunderbolts out of a clear sky upon him and his command. In this regard where shall we place General Meade in view of his conduct that afternoon?

This was his first opportunity in battle to command that army. Up to this moment he had only heard the thunder of cannon a dozen miles away on the previous day, which told him that his forces were engaged with the enemy. Now he is to command his army on the field! How will he behave? What stuff is he made of? What sort of leadership will he show now when his plans are disarranged and his troops are to be suddenly attacked on what he deems disadvantageous ground?

Three things he saw at once:

(1) Round Top must be instantly seized and held, for the artillery of the enemy, even while he conversed with Sickles, had opened, and that point, his extreme left and the most important part of his line, considered both tactically and strategically, was in deadly peril. He gave Warren, his chief engineer, charge of that business, and that officer at full speed hurried to fulfil his mission.

(2) He saw that Sickles could not be withdrawn. No retreat at that moment from that line, however disadvantageous the location was, could be carried out. The dangers to the corps were deadly. Its right flank was in air, a quarter of a mile in front of the left of Hancock's corps, with which it should have touched elbows. At the Peach Orchard the angle was already the portentous center of coming catastrophe, for when it was broken both lines could be swept by artillery and musketry fire. And, to finish the picture which the commander realized later, or possibly saw with intuitive military discernment that moment, the left flank of the Third Corps had no support. It lay in a hollow near the Devil's Den, and was, like the right flank, to use the customary phrase, wholly in the air.

VIEW FROM LITTLE ROUND TOP

(From a photograph taken in 1886. The view is from the position occupied by Vincent's brigade and Hazlett's battery.)

MEADE COMMANDS IN BATTLE

(3) Meade, not at his wit's end, not nonplussed or staggered or helpless, in view of this situation, saw what must be done: this little courageous Third Corps, with its brave commander, must be backed and reinforced with all the resources at command. The fight must be had—it was now on—even if it were to be attended at first with what might seem to be irretrievable damage.

It was in a crisis of this sort that Meade showed himself capable of commanding the great army which from that hour came to trust and love him. Under a weight of anxiety and mental concern almost intolerable, with his nervous system, chronically irritable and edgy, now worn to the quick and painful to the touch, yet he maintained his equipoise of judgment and his command of his faculties undisturbed. Three days ago a stranger to the whole army, except his own corps and the intimates who knew his abilities, now he had in mind and at immediate command, without a question or a moment of hesitation, all the resources of that great army. To Hunt he gave directions to bring up his reserve batteries and plant them along the original line, now half a mile in rear of where the fighting had begun; he brought Caldwell's division from the Second Corps and the three divisions of the Fifth Corps, until then held in reserve, and troops from the Sixth Corps, just arriving, and men from the First and the Twelfth corps, on the extreme right—from every part of the field, indeed, except that occupied by the Eleventh Corps— and hurled these brigades from time to time upon the enemy in the effort to withstand the assault which quickly assumed overwhelming proportions. Twice he led troops in person to their place in the line, urging them forward by his presence and example—something perhaps never before done by any other commander of that army. Once by his own hand he planted a battery that checked the advancing Confederates, almost sighting the guns himself, so immediate was his supervision of the fight.

From three-thirty that afternoon until the darkness of night shaded the field that dreadful encounter went on with terrific losses on both sides; but, although the Union forces were flanked and sometimes surrounded and driven, they kept steadfastly to their work — Humphreys's division, for example, making a change of front in the midst of the fighting as clean and true as though upon the parade-ground; and when the end came the original line was held intact. Not a Confederate passed through to the rear except as a prisoner! And Meade was on the spot, in the midst of the fighting, superintending the movement in person, and thus revealing himself as a man adequate to command the Army of the Potomac in one of the most critical emergencies that had ever befallen it in all its history! This part of the fight, so far as Meade's management is concerned, has evoked the most generous praise from accomplished critics. Gen. E. P. Alexander, for example, the Confederate expert artillerist, says, commenting on the work done by the Union commander that afternoon:

Meade saw the danger, and with military foresight prepared to meet it with every available man. There was not during the war a finer example of efficient command than that displayed by Meade on this occasion. He immediately began to bring to the scene reinforcements, both of infantry and artillery, from every corps and from every part of the line. . . . His work that afternoon presents perhaps the best example which the war produced of active supervision and efficient handling of a large force on the defensive. [*Military Memoirs of a Confederate*, pages 393, 403.]

To the same effect is an utterance of General Howard in regard to this phase of the case:

The reserves have never before during this war been thrown in at just the right moment. In many cases when points were just being carried by the enemy a regiment or brigade appeared to stop this progress and hurl him back. [*Official Records*, XXVII, 1:700.]

Major General Slocum, in his report of the Twelfth Corps, in commenting on the heroic conduct of the entire command during this campaign, both officers and men, has this to say:

Their confidence in the final result of this important battle was greatly increased by the fact, which soon became apparent to all, that in this battle, at least, all our forces were to be used; that a large portion of the army was not to remain idle while the enemy's masses were being hurled against another portion. [*Official Records*, XXVII, 1:762.]

XXI

THE SAFEGUARDING OF LITTLE ROUND TOP

WE have taken a general view of the situation as it stood just before the attack made by Longstreet at about three-thirty, Thursday afternoon, and have summarized the plans of Meade to meet that advance. Some of the details of the fight thus opening now command attention. And at the outset the services rendered by General Warren, the chief engineer of the army, demand recognition.

Just before the attack was made by Longstreet it was discovered by Meade, in conversation with Sickles on the ground where the Third Corps was located, that the left flank of the army was in grave peril. To Warren, who was present and heard the conversation and understood the danger, Meade turned and ordered him to look after Little Round Top; just before this Meade had given directions to Sykes to place his corps on the endangered flank, which Sickles alone up to that moment had been occupying. Warren, with three aides—to be noted a little later— rode as rapidly as the steepness of the hill, the rocks, and underbrush would permit, up to the summit, to find it defenseless. A little squad of signalmen and officers were there, but they were about to abandon as untenable the station, which they had been using for hours. Warren was told by them that they had discovered, as they thought, signs of a large body of troops massing in the woods, off to their left front, in the direction of the Emmitsburg road, for an attack on Sickles's line, then running from the Devil's Den to the Peach Orchard. Asking the signal-men to keep waving their flags for a little while, he sent an orderly down the hill to the captain of Smith's New York battery near the Den, and asked him to drop a shell over in the direction of the woods. When the shot was fired Warren, on the watch for what was about to happen, saw the light flash from bayo-nets and rifle-barrels in the woods, the soldiers who carried them having been slightly startled for the moment by the bursting shell and the sound of the cannon—the slight motion they had made caused the gleaming of their weapons to send a quiver of illumination through the forest. Warren by a glance discovered that the Confederate line thus revealed was overlapping the lines of Sickles, and that Little Round Top, as well as the whole left flank of Meade's force, was in imminent danger.

With Warren—quick, eager, intuitive—to see was to act; he despatched Lieut. R. S. Mackenzie, one of his aides, whose brilliant career is noted in our chapter on West Point, and who was brevetted major for his services in this battle, to ask Sickles for a brigade to hold this point; the aide, on being told by Sickles that he was overtaxed already to hold his ground, rode to Sykes, who at once directed that some of Barnes's division, then on their way to the front along Sickles's line, should be sent to the summit of

Little Round Top, and that Hazlett's battery also should be directed there.

Meanwhile Warren, tarrying to watch the situation on the hill and almost distracted with the urgent need, despatched Capt. Chauncey B. Reese, another aide, to Meade, telling him of the situation and intimating what had been done; this staff-officer also was a graduate of the Academy, and an engineer officer of gifts and promise of whom we have briefly written in another part of this volume; he was brevetted again and again for his various services.

A few minutes later Warren, catching sight of troops heading for Sickles's line to reinforce that part of the field, where the battle was now fiercely begun, accompanied by the remaining aide-de-camp, rode as rapidly as possible down the hill, with the hope of intercepting some of the troops in sight, in order that Round Top might have the needed succor.

This third staff-officer, on duty with Warren that notable day, deserves a paragraph. His name was Washington A. Roebling, a graduate of Rensselaer Polytechnic Institute, who, after having served as private and sergeant in the Eighty-third New York Infantry for six months, had been promoted to a lieutenancy in the Sixth New York Battery in January, 1862, and then had been assigned to duty as a military engineer on Warren's staff. In this campaign he was on duty at army headquarters, rendering skilful service to both Meade and Warren. In April, 1864, he was made major and aide with Warren, and he was brevetted two notches higher later in the war. In 1877 Warren wrote to a friend: "Roebling was on my staff, and, I think, performed more able and brave service than any one I knew."

His name now brings to mind two facts: his father, one of the great engineering architects of the world, died, from an accidental injury which befell him in the midst of his plans for construction of the great Brooklyn Bridge—a project then without a parallel in the world—in 1869. The son, Col. Washington A. Roebling, an assistant in the enterprise, and in complete touch with the colossal designs, undertook to finish the bridge. To this task he gave fourteen years of extraordinary labor, almost losing his life in the mission thus laid upon him, and in 1883 the completion of the achievement showed him to be a worthy son of an illustrious sire, and one of the most eminent of the constructive engineers of the time. The other fact to be noted is that Colonel Roebling was one of the victims of the *Titanic* disaster, in which he perished, April 14, 1912, at the age of seventy-five.

Let us leave Warren and Roebling for the moment, as they ride down from the summit of Little Round Top in search of troops, while we note what was at the same time going on in connection with the task of safeguarding that vital point in the battle.

It must be recalled that one of Warren's aides, Mackenzie, had been sent to get a brigade from Sickles, who could not respond to the appeal, and had then gone to Sykes and secured from him at once the promise of a brigade from Barnes's division, a staff-officer from Sykes being at once despatched to find Barnes and deliver the order. On the way that officer came upon Strong Vincent's brigade, of

GETTYSBURG

Barnes's division, on its way to the field in front of the hill, and stated the case to that discerning soldier. Vincent at once replied: "I will not wait to find Barnes; a brigade is ordered there, and the case is pressing, and I will take the responsibility and lead my men there." On the instant, therefore, this Third Brigade of Barnes's division was set upon its way, Vincent riding ahead to select the best position for his men. The post thus chosen by Vincent was a vital element in the fight for that part of the field. The brigade, ascending the height on its eastern flank, was quickly located in a circuitous shape about the southern and southwestern slopes of Little Round Top. At that very moment the Confederates were making their way through the woods to assail that portion of the hill; had there been any delay in the case, had Vincent not been alert and skilful in recognizing his opportunity, there would have been no salvation for that pivotal point; in a quarter of an hour it would have been occupied by the enemy as a location from which to enfilade and destroy the Union line. It became, however, an invincible stronghold of the Army of the Potomac.

We have been at pains to detail the order of events in this case, for the situation was a complicated one, and narrators have misapprehended it, and even the official reports do not fully co-ordinate.[1]

[1] A booklet by Oliver W. Norton, color-bearer for Colonel Vincent in this engagement, *Strong Vincent and His Brigade at Gettysburg*, issued in Chicago in 1910, and a book of 343 pages, with illustrations, *The Attack and Defense of Little Round Top*, New York, 1913, by the same author, furnish an unusually full and accurate array of data, official, historical, and of other sorts pertaining to this part of the battle.

SAFEGUARDING LITTLE ROUND TOP

Vincent's command,[1] in this enterprise, with Colonel Chamberlain's Maine soldiers in the lead, clambered up the eastern slopes of the hill and swung around toward the southern descent, and thence down into the intervale between the two Round Tops, reaching the defile just in time to form their line, send out skirmishers, and then come face to face with troops from Law's brigade[2] of Hood's division, forming the extreme Confederate right, and in their furious advance pressing up from below to capture the height which they had foreboded was strongly held by Union troops, but which they had within an hour or two discovered to be defenseless. They expected an easy victory, particularly as some of them had surmounted Big Round Top and had found it undefended; now they hoped to capture the smaller hill and from its summit sweep Meade's whole left flank with artillery.

As the lines clashed together a terrific struggle began between the men from Maine and the men from Alabama, Colonel Chamberlain[3] leading the one side and Col. W. C. Oates, with his Fifteenth Alabama, the other, each being at the extremity of his whole line of battle, now extending from that point

---

[1] Fifth Corps, First Division, Third Brigade: Twentieth Maine, Sixteenth Michigan, Forty-fourth New York, Eighty-third Pennsylvania.

[2] Law's Alabama men: Fourth, Fifteenth, Forty-fourth, Forty-seventh, Forty-eighth.

[3] General Chamberlain, now eighty-four years of age, has had a heroic and worthy civil and military career: he has been president and professor in his alma mater, Bowdoin College, Maine; governor of the State, and commander of its militia in a critical time of threatened anarchy. He was brevetted major general, commanded a division under Grant, was awarded the Congressional Medal of Honor for Gettysburg, and has written many books.

out into the valley, past the Devil's Den and the Wheat-field, to the Peach Orchard to their west. The engagement here, at various points on the hill, lasted nearly two hours, breaking out in fresh fury at intervals and extending around the base of Little Round Top and up its rocky sides. There were close encounters and hand-to-hand struggles, with the lines on the left at times not twenty paces apart. In the height of the contest Chamberlain led his men in a charge which pressed the Confederates back in confusion and secured the capture of a hundred or more who had pressed in their ardor too far inside of the Union lines. (See *Official Records*, XXVII, 1:599, 622.)

Colonel Oates, who is sketched elsewhere in this book in connection with his regiment, gives a vivid narrative of the work of the afternoon in his volume *The War Between the Union and the Confederacy*, and Gen. E. M. Law, commanding the division after Hood fell, is the author of an article in the *Century War Book* detailing his version of the engagement.

We need now to turn our attention to what was going on at the summit of Little Round Top and along its western face. The brigade of Vincent extended its line so as to circle the hill, facing really in three directions, so that while Chamberlain was fighting in the vale between the two Round Tops the adjacent regiments continued the line clean around the hill, faced by the Confederates from Alabama and Texas, who were crowding against the Union position. Vincent in person directed this part of the line, and while striving to mend a temporary breach made by

HAZLETT'S BATTERY ON LITTLE ROUND TOP
(From a print of the time)

a sudden and overwhelming advance of the foe from the valley in front of the hill he was fatally wounded, dying on July 7th. A message from the War Department giving him the commission of brigadier general arrived at his bedside just as he was about to pass away.

It is worth while to premise just here that Warren's position while studying the case from the western summit of the hill did not give him any opportunity to note the arrival of Vincent's troops, who had ascended on the eastern flank, and who in their location in line were hidden from his observation by the woods and rocky heights in his rear and to his left. Thus, although he had sent for them and urged their presence, he had not yet learned of their arrival when he left his post of observation at the signal station. Before he and Roebling hastened from the scene, however, one section of Hazlett's battery arrived, and the general and the staff-officer, with some stragglers near by, helped to pull the guns by hand into position, no room being found for the horses just at that point. Then Warren and Roebling hurried down the hill, as we have already told. As they struck the road leading across the foot of Little Round Top on its northern side they chanced upon a passing unit of Weed's brigade—the other three having passed that point in hastening to the front— the 140th New York, led by its colonel, Patrick H. O'Rorke, one of the most winsome and able of the young West - Pointers on the field and an intimate friend of Warren's. The general halted the regiment, explained the exigency, and asked O'Rorke to take his men to the summit and help save the hill. O'Rorke responded eagerly and turned his regiment up the slope, Roebling accompanying him, while Warren hastened off to tell Meade what had been done. The drivers, cannoneers, and horses of the section of artillery accompanying the regiment were all stalled in the effort to climb the hill on the rocky trail, and scores of the 140th gave help to the battery in order that it might, under the directions of its commander, Hazlett, and his assistant, Lieutenant Rittenhouse, quickly reach the place where it was needed. In a few minutes also the other regiments of Weed's brigade and Weed himself followed up the hill and formed their line, but it was the 140th New York and O'Rorke, under the guidance of Roebling, which reached the place of need in the very nick of time, and there found its great opportunity. Had they not come at the very minute when they did Little Round Top would have been in the hands of the foe.

The situation as they emerged on the summit was appalling. The valley below, extending from the base of the hill out toward the Wheat-field and Peach Orchard, was the scene of a dreadful struggle, the air filled with smoke and with exploding shells, while before them on the slope, scrambling up the hill, giving out their "rebel yells," were hundreds of Texas troops, intent on the capture of the summit. These troops had almost won their venture, when suddenly out of the woods above them and down over the steep places which they were covering appeared an embattled line of men in blue, shouting, charging bayonets, and led by a soldierly youth, the very incarnation of

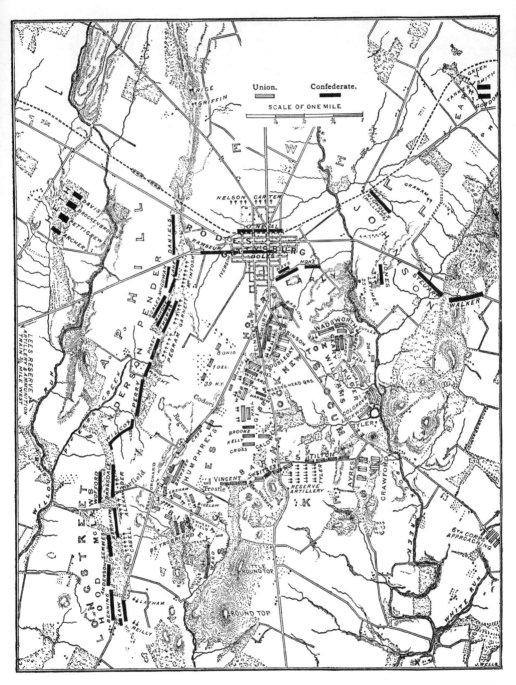

POSITIONS OF FEDERAL AND CONFEDERATE FORCES, JULY 2, ABOUT 3.30 P.M., WHEN LONGSTREET'S
ATTACK OPENED

martial prowess, his presence an inspiration, as, sword in hand, his ringing voice sounding above the storm of battle, he sent cheer into the hearts of those who saw and heard him. Thus did the 140th New York, under the kindling leadership of the splendid O'Rorke, burst like a sweeping torrent out of the rocky ledges and from the momentary covert of the underbrush down upon the lithe and sinewy Texas Rangers, who had all but captured the height before their course was arrested, and they were driven back to the foot of the hill.

Weed's brigade,[1] in adjusting itself to its position, touched elbows on its left with Vincent's men, now commanded by Col. J. C. Rice, of the Forty-fourth New York, who, after the death of Vincent, took the brigade.

Colonel O'Rorke, a man of singular gifts and attractiveness, a favorite in the army, and destined for large things in the estimate of his comrades and superiors, fell early in the struggle here. The commander of the battery, Lieut. Charles E. Hazlett, and O'Rorke had graduated together from the Academy in 1861, and both were now veterans, not in years— the former was twenty-seven and the latter twenty-five—but in service, for each had been in the war and in all its battles in the East since Bull Run; they had been intimate at the Point for four years; these two veterans and Weed, their commander, at the age of thirty, their close friend, and but a few years their

[1] Fifth Corps, Second Division, Third Brigade; Weed: 140th and 146th New York, Ninety-first and 155th Pennsylvania; Battery D, Fifth United States Artillery (Hazlett).

241

senior in years and service, and one of the leading soldiers on the field, were all to yield their lives that day on that rocky height, and thus consecrate it with their blood.

The fight was by no means at an end when O'Rorke and his men administered the terrible check to the Texans. Again and again the Confederates crowded forward and made the attempt to climb the hill. Their artillery played against the summit and the slope, and scores of sharp-shooters lodged in the rocks of the Devil's Den and in the trees near by used their rifles with fatal skill. Weed located his troops so as to shelter them as far as possible, but he and O'Rorke and Hazlett, who had used his cannon to advantage, were of necessity exposed to the keen-sighted riflemen in their front, and all of them fell. Weed was fatally wounded and lived but for a day; but Hazlett, leaning over his fallen comrade and leader to catch his words, fell dead on General Weed's body, pierced by a sharp-shooter's bullet.

Col. Kenner Garrard, of the 146th New York, another West-Pointer, who won a brigadier's commission that day, took Weed's brigade, and at its head in the hours that followed made a fine record for them as well as for himself.

The men on Round Top that afternoon, and also later at night, piled up rocks as barricades to shelter themselves from the terrific fire of the sharp-shooters; this gave them an advantage which was made still more effective at night when under engineering supervision the task was extended. Confederates who were located at the foot of the hill that night, or on the slopes of Big Round Top, across the ravine, and who escaped to tell the story, used to say in after years:

"When we heard the stones dropping into place, hour after hour, that night, and knew thereby that the Yankees were girdling the hill with a sheltering wall, we reckoned that our chances at that point were hopeless. We had done our best to carry the hill in the afternoon before it was terraced with rocky barricades, one after another—after that was done we knew better than to attempt to carry it by storm."

And now thousands every year stand on that height and say, as they look on these rough stone walls: "These are the shelters which protected the defenders of the Union in the storm of battle!"

That night Chamberlain, with a heavy skirmish-line, and supported by two regiments from the Pennsylvania Reserves—which by this time were holding the woods and fields in front of the Round Tops—advanced to the summit of the larger eminence and, finding no opposition, held the point, the Confederates in the morning giving up both of the heights as unattainable.

17

XXII

"ATTACK UP THE EMMITSBURG ROAD"

THE struggle for the Round Tops, although tragic and terrible, was but an episode in a complicated engagement, reaching in due time out to the Peach Orchard, a mile distant from the summit of the now historic height of which we have been writing, and then extending to the north, following the Emmitsburg road in a surging, swaying, serrate, and oft-broken line for another mile, until in the gathering darkness of the oncoming night the fires of battle were quenched at last. For three hours this almost incomparable death-grapple was marked by advances, rebuffs, hand-to-hand struggles, intervolutions of hostile lines, dreadful losses, and hundreds of captures on either side, forming altogether a chapter in the battle story which has thus far baffled every man who has attempted to weave the involved and constantly shifting incidents and movements into a complete and coherent narrative. Not even at Waterloo was there more appalling confusion to justify Victor Hugo's suggestion, "The artist who would paint a battle must have Chaos in his touch." Let us, therefore, if we may, bring out of the chaotic and havoc-breeding scenes of that afternoon in orderly array at least the outlines of what was done.

244

"UP THE EMMITSBURG ROAD"

Lee's orders to Longstreet with regard to the attack to be made on the Federal left flank were based on the erroneous impression that the line to be broken to pieces ended at the Peach Orchard, where it was, as he believed, without support—or, in other words, "in the air." He surmised, therefore, that it would be an easy task to assail this fancied exposed position and thus proceed to roll up the entire Federal line, from south to north, one division after another. Accordingly, his definite orders to Longstreet were thus literally phrased, "Attack up the Emmitsburg road."

It appears that Lee had not in person inspected this part of the Union line, and had not been correctly posted with regard to the location by his staff-officers who had undertaken the task of inspection, and, unfortunately, he was not present when the attack opened, having gone to the other end of the line, miles away, and hence when further advice was to be sought and reasons were to be presented for changing the plans the commander in chief was inaccessible, and the attempt was therefore made with doubt and hesitation in the mind of the leading officers, but with tremendous vigor, nevertheless, to carry out the orders that had been given.

Hood, in arraying his men to attack up the Emmitsburg road, found that his lines had to be changed. It was not feasible to align his brigades so as to cross that road almost at right angles, as at first was planned; that policy, he ascertained, would leave his right flank open to attack from the guns which in advance he opined were mounted on Little Round

245

Top. A little later, before the actual opening of the infantry fight, his scouts brought him important information; they had discovered that the Round Tops were unoccupied, and that a way was open (either through the intervale between them or by a roundabout course south of Big Round Top) to the rear of the Union Army. There, Hood believed—and always believed till the day of his death—*there* was the place to plant a mortal blow; there was the route by which he could endanger the trains and smite with panic the reserve artillery parked in that region just behind the two heights.

Hood, deeply moved with an unshakable conviction that Lee would see the facts as they were and change his plan if word could be got to him, held his orders in abeyance for the time, and before firing a gun made the facts clear to Longstreet, and three times urged, in person and by staff-officers, his conviction that his line of attack must be changed, that he could not "attack up the Emmitsburg road" without destroying his own lines and neglecting the opportunity which a movement to the rear of the Union position would afford. He protested further that the situation as it had been uncovered would make it imperative for him to swing his lines around eastward, so as to make a direct assault on the Round Tops, which he assumed were now occupied, an enterprise which would be evidently hopeless in view of their craggy and precipitous front. Three times in reply the corps commander reiterated Lee's orders as the only commands he was at liberty to follow—"Attack up the Emmitsburg road." Longstreet, in his book

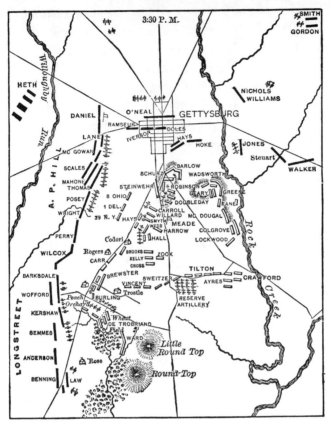

POSITION OF UNION AND CONFEDERATE TROOPS, 3.30 P.M., JULY 2

The situation shown here just precedes the assignment of Vincent to
Little Round Top and the advance of Hood against that point

From Manassas to Appomattox, page 368, explains
as follows: "If Lee had been with us General Hood's
messengers could have been referred to general headquarters, but to delay and send messengers five miles
in favor of a movement that he had rejected would
have been contumacious." On the other hand,
Hood in his *Advance and Retreat,* page 59, repeats his

conviction in a letter written to Longstreet, June 28, 1875: "I shall ever believe that had I been permitted to turn Round Top Mountain we would not only have gained that position, but would have been able finally to rout the enemy."

During this interchange of messages between the commander of the corps and his division leader the troops were being arrayed in order of battle; in fact, the batteries had been for almost an hour shelling the Peach Orchard and trying to make things uncomfortable for soldiers of the Union who might be in the neighborhood of the base of the Round Tops. Finally, when Hood gave signal to move forward he found, just as he had surmised, that he could not carry out his original directions, but that in order to come into contact with the Federal forces he must swing away from the Emmitsburg road altogether, changing direction, and extending his right flank so as to girdle Little Round Top's base. Early in the fight he was severely wounded and taken to the rear, and Gen. E. M. Law took command of the division.

XXIII

DEFENDING SICKLES'S LINE

THE two divisions of Longstreet's corps, under Hood and McLaws, which carried on his attack on Thursday afternoon—Pickett's division of three brigades being yet on its way from Chambersburg—were thus aligned at the opening of the infantry contest between three and four o'clock: Law's brigade, on the extreme right of Hood's attacking division, swung around, as we have already indicated, so as to face the Round Tops; next on its left was Robertson's brigade,[1] which soon after the opening of the fight changed direction so as to confront troops of Ward, at the Devil's Den, its right flank touching the base of Little Round Top; on Robertson's left was the brigade of G. T. Anderson;[2] while Benning,[3] at first in reserve, was brought up in the later stages of the fight to the front line.

These forces, at first ordered to advance up the Emmitsburg road toward the north, as already intimated, had to change direction and face almost due east and then toward the north as the phases of the fight developed.

[1] Robertson: Third Arkansas, First, Fourth, and Fifth Texas.
[2] Anderson: Seventh, Eighth, Ninth, Eleventh, and Fifty-ninth Georgia.
[3] Benning: Second, Fifteenth, Seventeenth, and Twentieth Georgia.

McLaws had four strong infantry brigades[1] adjoining Hood on the left of the latter; these forces were aligned at first on the ridge, almost parallel with the Emmitsburg road, but almost as soon as the engagement began some of his forces crossed that road, forming a semicircle roundabout the angle in which the Peach Orchard was located, so that his men in part assailed that point from the west and in part from the south; when the angle was broken the Union forces were enfiladed from two directions, the entire mass for a time, including both Union and Confederate troops, were merged together in a seething caldron of battle which raged and thundered in the woods and fields and among the rocks, and which did not subside until at last, in the darkening night, Longstreet concluded that it was not then possible to penetrate the original line of battle of the Union forces reaching from Little Round Top to Cemetery Hill.

R. H. Anderson's division of Hill's corps made connection with McLaws's left, and extended its ranks north along the ridge, with instructions to continue the fight in that direction as opportunity might present itself, as we shall hereafter show.

It is time to take a glance at the line which had been formed by Sickles to face the troops thus arrayed in his front. He had found it impossible to

---

[1] McLaws's division — Kershaw: South Carolina, Second, Third, Seventh, Eighth, Fifteenth regiments, and Third Battalion. Semmes: Tenth, Fiftieth, Fifty-first, and Fifty-third Georgia. Wofford: Georgia, Sixteenth, Eighteenth, Twenty-fourth; Cobb's Legion, Phillips's Legion. Barksdale: Mississippi, Thirteenth, Seventeenth, Eighteenth, and Twenty-first.

place any of his force on Little Round Top, and that portion of the line, as we have seen, was safeguarded by men from the Fifth Corps. Sickles's line began at the base of that eminence, at the Devil's Den where Ward's brigade[1] was stationed, with De Trobriand[2] to its right along the Wheat-field, touching toward the Peach Orchard with Graham's brigade,[3] which at that point made an angle, part of its line running back toward the Den and part of it facing west on the Emmitsburg road—the turn presenting to the enemy an opportunity to enfilade both lines when it was shattered and broken in, as happened later in the fight.

The Confederates had a strong array of artillery for their attack. Two batteries went with Hood's advancing division, while about forty guns were posted along the ridge crossed by the Emmitsburg road, the whole force under the direction of that fine artillerist, Col. E. P. Alexander. There were also during the fight of the afternoon perhaps the same number of guns stationed in defense of the Peach Orchard and at other places on Sickles's line, the chief of artillery of the Third Corps, Capt. George E. Randolph, in charge, while General Hunt, who had in mind the entire artillery force of the army, and General Tyler, commanding the artillery reserve, were in touch with the situation throughout the afternoon.

[1] Birney's division, Third Corps—Ward: Twentieth Indiana, Third Maine, Fourth Maine, Eighty-sixth and 124th New York, Ninety-ninth Pennsylvania, First and Second United States Sharp-shooters.

[2] Colonel de Trobriand: Seventeenth Maine, Third Michigan, Fifth Michigan, Fortieth New York, Eleventh Pennsylvania.

[3] Graham: Fifty-seventh, Sixty-third, Sixty-eighth, 105th, 114th, 141st Pennsylvania.

GETTYSBURG

There had been occasional exchange of shots between opposing batteries up to half-past three o'clock, when the Southern artillery opened in earnest, massing their guns from the west and the south against the Peach Orchard, while some of their batteries directed their fire against Little Round Top.

It was evident to both Sickles and Meade before the fight was opened that reinforcements were needed immediately. In addition to the help which succored Round Top from the Fifth Army Corps—the brigades of Vincent and Weed, already noted—there came from that corps all that remained of its troops, making four brigades, two from Barnes's division, led respectively by Col. Wm. S. Tilton,[1] Twenty - second Massachusetts Infantry, and Col. Jacob B. Sweitzer,[2] of the Sixty-second Pennsylvania. Altogether these two attenuated brigades did not number more than fifteen hundred officers and men. They were posted in the interval between the brigades of Ward and De Trobriand, in the neighborhood of the Wheatfield; and before they came out of the battle they had left half their number on the ground, for they were assailed very soon after they began their fight, not only in front, but on their flanks, and some of their regiments were entangled in close struggles with the assailing force, so that bayonets were used. Colonel Jeffords, of the Fourth Michigan, was thrust through with a bayonet in defense of his regimental colors.

[1] Tilton: Eighteenth and Twenty-second Massachusetts, First Michigan, and 118th Pennsylvania.
[2] Sweitzer: Ninth and Thirty-second Massachusetts, Fourth Michigan, and Sixty-second Pennsylvania.

DEFENDING SICKLES'S LINE

The pressure on Sickles's line becoming more and more terrific, additional reinforcements were hurried into the field—two more brigades, for instance, from Sykes's corps, the regulars from Ayres's division, commanded respectively by those veteran soldiers, Colonels Hannibal Day[1] and Sidney Burbank,[2] who were posted in the neighborhood of the Devil's Den, where a cross-fire cut them almost to pieces, and where they could not effectively fight back.

In addition, the two brigades of Crawford's division of Pennsylvania Reserves, led respectively by Colonels McCandless[3] and Fisher,[4] were brought from the rear and stationed on the northern flank of Little Round Top, where they did valiant service as the day was ending.

The emergency was so imperative that Hancock was also called on to lend aid to this struggling and almost baffled left flank of the army, and he immediately responded by despatching four brigades, constituting Caldwell's division,[5] and for these there were found places in the neighborhood of the Wheatfield, where death with his gory sickle was reaping a

[1] Day's brigade: Third, Fourth, Sixth, Twelfth, and Fourteenth United States Infantry.
[2] Burbank's brigade: Second, Seventh, Tenth, Eleventh, and Seventeenth United States Infantry.
[3] McCandless: First, Second, Sixth, Thirteenth Pennsylvania Reserves.
[4] Fisher: Fifth, Ninth, Tenth, Eleventh, Twelfth Pennsylvania Reserves.
[5] Caldwell's division — Cross's brigade: Fifth New Hampshire, Sixty-first New York, Eighty-first and 148th Pennsylvania. Kelly's brigade: Twenty-eighth Massachusetts, Sixty-third, Sixty-ninth, and Eighty-eighth New York, and 116th Pennsylvania. Zook's brigade: Fifty-second, Fifty-seventh, Sixty-sixth New York, 140th Pennsylvania. Brooke's brigade: Twenty-seventh Connecticut, Second Delaware, Sixty-fourth New York, Fifty-third and 145th Pennsylvania.

bloody harvest. Here fell Col. Edward E. Cross, of the Fifth New Hampshire, at the head of his brigade; here also was slain another brigade leader, General Zook (sketched in the chapter on "The Empire State"); and here prodigies of valor were performed in the midst of a contest which proved unavailing so far as holding the advanced ground was concerned, but which at last proved sufficient to maintain the original line of battle as at first laid out absolutely intact.

We may not tarry to tell the story of the movements back and forth made by the components of this line of battle, in which divisions from three army corps were crowded together. Sickles and Birney made a brave struggle to keep their men in place and hold their line unbroken; nevertheless, it was flanked and driven; Graham was wounded and captured in the Peach Orchard; and without exception all the organizations which had been stationed in front of Little Round Top were flanked, crowded back, and at last forced in more or less confusion toward the rear. The artillery was thus left without infantry support, and in due time had to withdraw to evade capture. The literal truth is that the batteries at the Peach Orchard stood their ground until their horses were all disabled or killed, and then the men that were left saved their guns by "firing with fixed prolonge" as they withdrew to the rear, loading and firing as they retreated, the Confederates pursuing with yells and sweeping the field with fresh batteries brought to the scene from their rear.

DEFENDING SICKLES'S LINE

Humphreys's Division[1] had been depleted during the early part of the fight, one regiment after another being sent at the request of Sickles to aid in the defense of the line at or east of the Peach Orchard, until Burling's brigade had but one regiment left, and from the Excelsior Brigade Brewster had sent the Seventy-third New York to the same region; Carr's brigade alone was intact. These thinned forces were aligned along the Emmitsburg road, running north from the point near the Peach Orchard, where they touched elbows on their left with the brigade of Graham in the First Division.

This division of Humphreys formed the extreme right of Sickles's line, and was without any support for its right flank, which rested "in air" opposite to the left flank of Hancock's line, which was on the ridge a quarter of a mile in the rear. Its position was therefore laid open to attack on that flank from the start, although the actual assault did not come until some time after the struggle of the other parts of Sickles's force and their co-adjutant brigades. Directly in front, across the Emmitsburg road, on the ridge, but concealed for the time from view, lay the troops in R. H. Anderson's division,[2] ready to join in the

[1] Humphreys; Second Division, Third Corps—Carr's brigade: First, Eleventh, Sixteenth Massachusetts, Twelfth New Hampshire, Eleventh New Jersey, Twenty-sixth and Eighty-fourth Pennsylvania (latter on train duty). Brewster: (Excelsior Brigade): Seventieth, Seventy-first, Seventy-second, Seventy-third, Seventy-fourth, 120th New York. Burling: Second New Hampshire, Fifth, Sixth, Seventh, and Eighth New Jersey, 115th Pennsylvania.
[2] R. H. Anderson's division—Wilcox: Eighth, Ninth, Tenth, Eleventh, Fourteenth Alabama. Perry (led by Lang): Second, Fifth, Eighth Florida. Wright: Third, Twenty-second, Forty-eighth Georgia regiments, and Second Battalion. Mahone: Sixth, Twelfth, Sixteenth, Forty-first, Sixty-first Virginia.

fight when the signal was given. That signal consisted in the advance of Barksdale's Mississippians across the Emmitsburg road against the Union forces. These eager fighters had been anxious to join in the fray ever since it started, and when the Peach Orchard angle was smashed they advanced in a charge which not only made their adversaries in front of them give way, but imperiled the left flank of Humphreys's force. He had to manœuver to meet this new attack, and in the heat of battle performed a task hardly ever undertaken on the field under fire: changing front by wheeling a part of his line to the left and rear, so as to face the new antagonist, Barksdale, who, the embodiment of an ancient warrior, sword waving in air, his hair, prematurely white, streaming in the wind, his words of cheer sounding through the smoke, was leading on his men.

At this very moment Humphreys was beset with a new peril: Wilcox and Lang took their cue from Barksdale's charge, and on the instant also pressed forward. Their movement brought them immediately against the unprotected right flank of Humphreys's division—what was left of it—Wilcox assailing his narrow front, and Lang flanking him on his right. It appeared even to Humphreys himself that the case was hopeless, although he changed front on his right to protect himself, if possible, against this new advance; but he speedily found himself forced toward the rear.

The writer of this narrative, in the midst of that scene under Humphreys, can never forget it. When our division began to fall back under the awful pressure which was incumbent from three directions it seemed to my distracted boyish vision that the Union was going to pieces, and that Lee was winning a decisive victory on the soil of my native State. I can recall Humphreys—without a superior on the field of battle—full of fire, and yet in absolute equipoise, carrying out his change of front so as to meet, if possible, the assault on his flanks, the troops obeying his directions, administered by his faithful staff— Major Hamlin, Captains McClellan and Chester, and Lieutenants Humphreys and Christiancy—as coolly as if they had been on dress-parade.

This change of front served only for a brief interval to stay the Confederate onset, which for the time swept the entire field, reaching out to the Emmitsburg road from the base of Little Round Top and the adjacent ridge running north, clean of Union troops. It looked for the moment as though the force of Longstreet would make its way through to the Taneytown road in the rear of the Union line.

Wofford's brigade, roused by the personal presence of Longstreet, who rode with Wofford, made one final, headlong effort to complete the work of the day by a desperate charge against the base of that hill, from which the Union troops had for the time being been crowded back. But on the northern crest of that point stood the Pennsylvania Reserves, eager to have the leash unloosed. They stood on the soil of their native State—one company, enlisted in Gettysburg, had passed by their own dooryards in the neighborhood on their way to the front. From the rocky height on which they stood a score of them could see now and then through the smoke of battle their own roofs. At once by officers and men it was clearly seen that the advancing troops of Wofford, pressing across the fields and heading for the foot of Little Round Top, would prove victorious unless they could at once be checked. Crawford, quickly determining that the hour had come for his gallant Reserves to move forward and meet the enemy half-way, seized a battle-flag and directed one flank of the line, while McCandless, also with a banner in hand, commanded the other flank, and with a tumultuous cheer, and the order flying from lip to lip along the line, "Charge down the hill, boys!" the division leaped down the slope. Over the crags, through the underbrush, and out to the Wheat-field, and into its blood-drenched borders where hundreds of dead and dying were scattered, bearing testimony of the fury of the preceding struggle, forward they swept with impulse irresistible.

By this advance of Crawford's division Wofford's men were checked; about the same time Humphreys's force, rallied and recruited by help from other portions of the line, formed line again and made a heroic advance; helped in the very opportune moment by the welcome appearance of the Sixth Army Corps pressing up from the rear, with heartening cheers, with waving flags, with eager mien, although they had been marching day and night for thirty-odd miles to get to the field in time to be of service — that was a sight never to be forgotten.

The vicissitude which developed when the Third Corps and the troops which had fought with it to sustain the assault on the left were pressed toward the rear was so alarming and commanding that Meade and Hancock and Doubleday at last were all drawn to the place of danger. Meade brought from the region near his headquarters two regiments of Lockwood's brigade, and in person assigned them to a post where they could render service; Doubleday brought his own division and a fragment of Robinson's, and stationed them along the original line of battle to help make it invincible; and Hancock aroused the troops by his presence and by regiments he brought along and led toward the enemy. This notable leader, after Sickles's disablement, was ordered by Meade to take under his care the battered Third Corps, as well as his own Second Corps. At one point of danger he put into action Willard's brigade,[1] and not far away the First Minnesota, these forces suffering great loss, but performing a timely work in aiding to stay the onset of the foe. Willard, an accomplished veteran officer of the Regular Army, was killed.

The final blow which arrested the crowding forces of Longstreet on the left was administered by Lieut. Col. Freeman McGilvery, of the First Maine Light Artillery, commander of a brigade in the artillery reserve. The juncture in which he accomplished his task he calls in his report "the crisis of the engagement," and he is not very far astray in his judgment. The entire force in front of Little Round Top, infantry as well as artillery, was being pressed irresistibly back toward the ridge behind which lay the Taneytown road, while the reinforcements from

---

[1] Willard; Third Brigade, Third Division, Second Corps: Thirty-ninth, 111th, 125th, and 126th New York.

other parts of the line had not yet fully arrived. McGilvery as a last resort planned a line of cannon just in front of this ridge to check the advancing foe and to afford a rallying place for the retreating men. But he needed time to do this, and the needed time was found by sacrificing one of his best forces, the Ninth Massachusetts Battery, Captain Bigelow. This battery had done notable service in the defense of the Peach Orchard, and at the last of that fight had to retire firing "by fixed prolonge," a manœuver used only *in extremis*, when no horses remain to pull the cannon, and when it is impossible to stop firing the guns without losing them while being withdrawn from the advancing foe. Under such circumstances the limber and the gun fastened together for the time by the rope called the prolonge are dragged toward the rear in retirement, the men loading and firing off the piece while moving. By this movement the sharp-shooters of the enemy were for the time kept at bay. In the Trostle yard, back toward the line which McGilvery was trying to form, Captain Bigelow was directed to mass his guns in battery and hold that point at all risks until other batteries could be planted in the rear. Only four guns could be used— the other two were sent to the rear—and for almost half an hour Bigelow and his men, under a terrible fire from the Confederates, served their four pieces in the effort to keep the Confederates back. When notified that the line in his rear was completed, Bigelow, severely wounded, and the men who were left alive fell back to the rear, leaving their guns for the time—these were brought in later that night. Bugler

Reed won a medal of honor by his gallantry in rescuing his wounded captain from the foe, mounted on a horse and holding the officer on another while they rode to the rear. When the oncoming Confederates, including Barksdale's Mississippians, had driven Bigelow's men back from the Trostle House they found themselves facing what that little band of men had for the time sheltered—a line of thirty cannon, now blazing in their faces.[1]

Longstreet withdrew most of his men from the region in front of Little Round Top to the region beyond the Peach Orchard for their bivouac when the night had closed in, after his terrific but unavailing assaults had proved abortive.[2]

[1] A booklet, *The Peach Orchard: Gettysburg*, by Maj. John Bigelow, of the Ninth Massachusetts Battery, makes clear the value of the work done by Colonel McGilvery on this occasion, the maps and citations from official reports helping to justify all the contentions in the case.

[2] Out of the tumult and confusion of that final hour there remains in my memory one indelible impression. In the very crisis of the fight, while we were struggling to press back the temporarily victorious Confederates, I happened to be facing south, toward the Devil's Den, when out against the sky, darkened by battle smoke and the on-coming night, there flashed the spectacle of an exploding caisson, the wheels, the arms and legs of dismembered human beings, and detonating shells, all mingling together in the instantaneous picture—and then the darkening heavens covered the awful scene with its merciful veil.

XXIV

THE ECHELON ASSAULTS BREAK DOWN

LEE'S plan for Longstreet's fight on Thursday afternoon was, technically speaking, an assault, or series of assaults, by brigades *en echelon*. A simple diagram will make clear what this expression means, and show what really happened when the fight which Longstreet waged came to a sudden stop at a certain point in the line—a phase of the case which we had not quite reached in our story in the preceding pages. We halted our narration, it may be premised just here, at the end of the movement on Humphreys, in which the brigades of Wilcox and Lang made a strenuous and temporarily successful advance, and then in turn were driven back to the ridge from which they had made their charge, having suffered heavy losses. The work done by one more Confederate brigade, that of Wright,[1] claims attention in connection with the task which was *not* done by the forces on his left in the Confederate line on the ridge, but which was intended to be done in the plan of Lee.

An echelon line or movement involves a formation in which the unit of manœuver — in this case a bri-

[1] Hill's corps, R. H. Anderson's division, Wright's brigade: Georgia, Third, Twenty-second, Forty-eighth regiments, and Second Battalion.

gade—takes its cue from a preceding one, occupying a parallel line, in advance of the one it holds. For example, in order to make clear the precise circumstances under which Lee's plans went to pieces on Thursday evening, we may indicate by a diagram the movements proposed, *en echelon*, by the brigades of Anderson's division of Hill's corps. The troops are supposed to be located on the ridge, facing toward the east—the Little Round Top region—the Peach Orchard being in the diagram located at the extreme right of the line.

```
                                      ————     Barks-
                                    Wilcox      dale.

                           ————
                          Lang

                  ————
                 Wright

————    ————     ————
Daniel¹  Mahone²   Posey³
```

The orders for the fight were explicit—namely, that each brigade commander should be governed in his advance by the movements of his brigade neighbor on his right; when that body had advanced and was engaged in the fight, then he was to follow, pressing forward against the troops in his front. Thus, as figured in the diagram, Wilcox was to watch the movements of Barksdale, and make a charge after that brigade had got well into the battle. In like manner Lang was to follow the movements of Wilcox, and when these had made their movement

[1] Daniel was in Pender's Division.
[2] Mahone: Sixth, Twelfth, Sixteenth, Forty-first, Sixty-first Virginia.
[3] Posey: Twelfth, Sixteenth, Nineteenth, Forty-eighth Mississippi.

then Wright was to go forward, and this echelon movement was to be continued five miles clean to the other end of the line of battle at Culp's Hill. It was expected by Lee that somewhere along the course his troops would find a weak spot in the Union line and break through, and thus inflict a fatal blow upon Meade.

Up to the point shown by Wright's location and forward movement in the diagram this plan succeeded fairly well; but it broke down at that juncture. Wright and his four regiments made a charge that is remembered to this day as one of phenomenal spirit and force. His apprehension of the plans for the hour are admirably given in his report:

> About noon I was informed that an attack upon the enemy's lines would soon be made by the whole division, commencing on our right by Wilcox's brigade, and that each brigade of the division would begin the attack as soon as the brigade on its right commenced the movement. I was instructed to move simultaneously with Perry's brigade [commanded by Lang], and informed that Posey's brigade, on my left, would move forward upon my advance.

Wright's command carried out its part of the program, and by its enthusiasm and valor and momentum made a deeper impression on the Union line than any other brigade that day. Gibbon in his report says:

> The enemy came on with such impetuosity that the head of his column came quite through a vacancy in our line to the left of my division, opened by detaching troops for other points. By the steadiness of our men, however, and the timely arrival of [help from] the Twelfth Corps the advance was checked and

driven back with considerable loss, the pursuit being continued for some distance beyond our lines, and all the guns overrun by the enemy retaken.

The brave Confederate brigadier, however, in spite of his seeming success (real success for the time, for his men laid their hands on twenty cannon belonging to the Union forces and broke through their line for one elated and promising moment), to his alarm and indignation, found that Lang's men on his right had been defeated and driven back, and that Posey's men, on his left when he started, had made no move, and that therefore his little brigade was absolutely without support, and that in his front and on either flank Union forces were crowding to capture or annihilate him and his heroic command. With a loss of six hundred and eighty-eight officers and men, including some of his ablest field-officers, Wright had to urge his way back again across the Emmitsburg road and to the ridge from which he had started. It turned out that Posey had misapprehended his orders, and had sent out only a line of skirmishers instead of advancing in force when Wright began to move; furthermore, Mahone, next to Posey in the line, seeing no movement made by Posey's brigade, did not feel called upon under his instructions to advance; still further, Pender, next to Mahone in line, when getting his forces ready to advance in turn was severely wounded, and no one at the instant appeared to take his command, and, as no supervising officer apprehended what under the circumstances should be done, no part of his division moved, the link was broken, and the policy of a "consecutive series of assaults *en echelon*" suddenly came to a stop before it had half finished its course around to Culp's Hill.

This same plan was used by Lee again and again in the battle, the instructions often being of a general character, and the onus of determining when to advance or attack being put upon division or corps commanders, as may be instanced in the instructions given to Rodes, who was ordered to "co-operate with the attacking force [on his right or left, as the case might be] as soon as any opportunity of doing so with good effect was offered." (*Official Records*, XXVII, 2:556, 557.) Wilcox's report is of the same sort: "My instructions were to advance when the troops on my right should advance, and to report this to the division commander, in order that the other brigades should advance in proper time."

It is difficult to study this plan without coming to the conclusion that it was blameworthy. The line was six miles long, and of such a character that the commander in chief could not supervise it in person. But was it necessary to let so many subordinates judge when the right opportunity in their front had come? Was it necessary to allow breaks in the line to go unheeded and unmended, as in the case of Posey and Pender? Why were there no staff-officers assigned to give signal when "the favorable opportunity" for an advance had arrived? The student of the battle can hardly fail to note that this phase of the engagement revealed a fatal defect in the plans of Lee. The best writers on the subject have noted an utter lack of co-ordination between the leading officers of Lee's army—not that there was disloyalty to him, or a disposition to evade responsibility, but that for one reason or another links were broken and the purposes of the commander in chief miscarried. This is the conviction of writers from both sides, as a few citations will show.

Maj. Gen. J. B. Kershaw, in an article in the *Century War Book*, Vol. III, p. 338, declares that the causes of the Confederate failure at Gettysburg may all be reduced to a single one—"the want of simultaneous movement and co-operation between the troops employed, between corps, divisions, and brigades, and, in some instances, regiments of the same brigade." The Comte de Paris in his great work similarly says that the radical fault was "the want of co-ordination." An ex-Confederate, Dr. Randolph H. McKim, in *A Soldier's Recollections* also testifies, page 179: "Splendid assaults were made at different points of the line; but in no instance were these supported. There seemed to be a paralysis of the co-ordinating faculty all along the line."

We have assiduously studied this general plan of Lee, and after long consideration we have failed to find in it the promise and elements of victory which that great general unmistakably did. To the very last venture of the last day of the fight his mind was set on the idea of "a general advance" all along the line from right to left. The dream that this policy would assure defeat for the opposing army clung to him, we venture to surmise, to the day of his death. We conclude this in view of a sentence in a letter which Lee wrote—cited in a biography of Lee—some years after the battle of Gettysburg, to a gentleman who desired information concerning that engagement, to the effect that he still believed that had circumstances been such as to give him the opportunity of one more assault "all along the whole line of battle," the victory would have been won for the Confederates.

Such an opinion is amazing, even at this far remove from the time of the battle. The Union line was shorter by two miles than Lee's; it was at certain points almost impregnable; along the slopes of Round Top and on Cemetery Hill and on Culp's Hill the advantages of the defensive positions there afforded multiplied the force of the defenders, in comparison with those who assailed, three times over; and in addition Meade had at least ten thousand more men in hand when the fight was over than Lee could possibly have mustered, with ammunition more than sufficient for another full day's battle; it is therefore astounding that a soldier of Lee's genius could, in view of the outcome of the battle, have cherished the belief that obsessed him in regard to this method of warfare.

Perhaps it is due to his fame to say that he did at one time, early in the engagement, suggest the plan of shortening his line by giving up the Culp's Hill region and swinging the troops who fought so bravely but so unavailingly in that part of the field over to Seminary Ridge, to join in the assaults made from that position, and that he was dissuaded from that half-formed purpose by the conviction that Ewell avowed with regard to his ability to carry the positions in his front on the Confederate left.

With regard to the policy of Lee, to which we have thus animadverted, it may be pertinent to quote a single sentence from Francis A. Walker's notable volume, *History of the Second Army Corps*, in which, after citing instances of the method which General Grant pursued during the battle-summer of 1864—from the opening of the Wilderness campaign to the time his army faced Petersburg, he says:

"To assault 'all along the line,' as was so often done in the summer of 1864, is the very abdication of leadership."

XXV

THE ATTACK ON CEMETERY HILL

THREE separate phases of the fight occurred under Ewell's direction, on the Confederate left, which had not, under its orders in pursuance of the "consecutive assaults" policy, found opportunity to co-operate with the work of the day; these now demand attention.

First, there was an attack, marked by great pluck and fortitude, made against the Union center, where the batteries were located on Cemetery Hill, immediately overlooking the eastern suburbs of the town. This attack was projected by Edward Johnson, in command of the division on Ewell's extreme left— the Culp's Hill region. That general determined to annihilate or demoralize the entire artillery force which was posted by the Federal commanders on the top of Cemetery Hill and upon the adjacent brow of Culp's Hill.

Accordingly, he instructed his chief of artillery, Maj. J. W. Latimer, "the Boy Major," a soldier of skill and courage, who, although but twenty years of age, had won his way up to the command of an artillery battalion, to mass his guns, twenty-four in number, on Benner's Hill, more than a mile in front of the Union cannon located near the Cemetery gateway and on the brow of Culp's Hill. Benner's Hill was not commanding in height, and it was unsheltered, so that most of the battery horses had to be taken to the rear for safety before the fight opened. Latimer's guns also were of short range, and directly he opened fire he became the concentric object of half a dozen or more batteries of rifled cannon, commandingly posted on the two hills in question, covering an arc of fifty degrees. It did not require much more than an hour of combined work on the part of these Union guns to demolish Latimer's entire outfit. Latimer himself, knowing as an expert in his arm of the service the inevitable result which would attend his enterprise, protested at last to Johnson, his division commander, that complete destruction was before him, his men, and his guns; and he was permitted to cease firing, but not until his opponents had made it impossible for him to continue much longer. The gallant young artilleryman was fatally wounded, lost an arm, and a few days later died of his injuries, lamented by the entire Confederate Army.

Maj. Robert Stiles, an officer in the Confederate Army at Gettysburg, in his recent volume, *Four Years with Marse Robert*, gives a thrilling picture of an incident which he encountered toward the close of this artillery duel. Serving temporarily on staff duty, he had offered to take a message from Gordon to Edward Johnson from the edge of the town, and his shortest path to his destination on the flank of Culp's Hill led him directly across the zone of fire. Recklessly he undertook to gallop straight through the storm of missiles which swept the region, not apprehending until he came into the midst of the tempest how dreadful a danger he was incurring. Benner's Hill was exactly in the path he had ventured upon, and in trying to get through the rolling fields he arrived at its base just when the climax of destruction had been wrought. He describes in his narrative most graphically the havoc, the slaughter, and the overthrow which the Union batteries had occasioned — dismantled guns, exploded caissons, wounded horses frantically kicking to get loose from the pieces to which they had been harnessed, dying men struggling under the cannon, shells exploding in the air and falling into the ruined mass, while the survivors were trying to extricate the wounded from the debris—a spectacle of confusion, slaughter, and suffering not to be forgotten, imagined, or reproduced. It need not be said, after this recital, that the bravery of the Confederate batterymen and their courageous leader was fruitless. They suffered disaster and loss without doing great damage.

The infantry assault on Cemetery Hill at about eight o'clock in the evening was another fruitless display of magnificent bravery, in which life and zeal were thrown away. Time and again in this battle the Confederate leaders sought out with seeming purpose the strongest positions along the Union line as the locations where their fiercest assaults were to be made. If the policy of the battle had been definitely announced—"Find out where the position of the enemy is naturally impregnable, where his batteries are most aptly located, and his infantrymen are most advantageously aligned, and there make

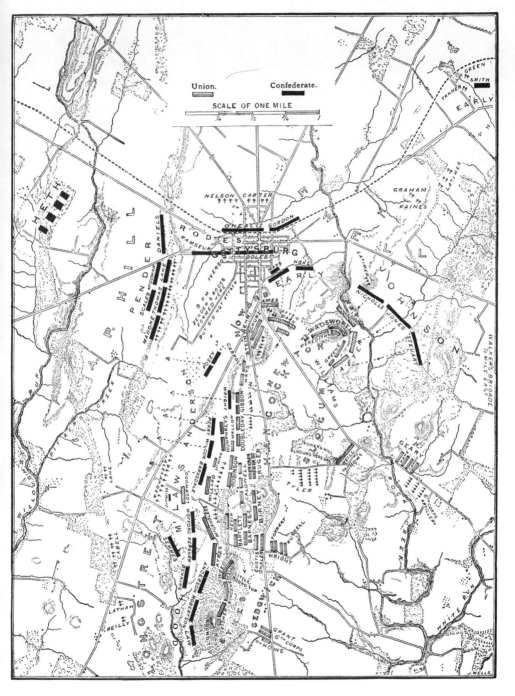

POSITIONS OF FEDERAL AND CONFEDERATE FORCES, JULY 2, AT DUSK

your attacks"—the story of the fight would not have been at all changed from the records as they stand. In this instance a chance visitor to the field may see for himself what an advantage the Union forces had, although just at that juncture—at dusk on Thursday evening—nearly all the infantry had been hurried to the Round Top region to help that struggling flank and had not yet returned. But the batteries occupied the brow of the hill against which the assault was levied, in strong force, magnificently located. It had been proposed that the troops on Early's right (Early facing Cemetery Hill, and his neighboring division, led by Rodes, facing the northwestern front of the hill) should move at the same time. At a little after dusk two brigades of Early's division, one led by Brig. Gen. Harry T. Hays,[1] and the other by Col. Isaac T. Avery,[2] marched out from the town in which they had been stationed for the day, and arrayed themselves in well-dressed line in the fields and behind the rolling hillocks at the base of Cemetery Hill. Had their advance been made under the circumstances by three times their number, instead of eight depleted regiments in all, it might have wrought tremendous damage. Their leaders had been told to expect co-operation by troops on their right and left, and it had been intimated also that their "victorious" comrades were to press across the eminence from the south and meet them on the hill. Alas for their hopes! There was no co-

---

[1] Hays: Fifth, Sixth, Seventh, Eighth, and Ninth Louisiana "Tigers."
[2] Avery: Sixth, Twenty-first, and Fifty-seventh North Carolina.

operation whatever. The Louisiana men and the North-Carolinians made their way across the fields—in spite of the fire from the batterymen on the hill, who could not depress their pieces, on account of the steepness of the ground, sufficiently to make their missiles effective, and who were hampered in their aim by the gathering darkness—made their way through the thin line of infantry at the base of the slope, surmounted the stone wall which was there, and with yells and steady efforts sought to climb to the top. The Louisianians were on the right and the North-Carolinians on the left in the movement; the latter found themselves enfiladed by a flank fire, as well as imperiled from the front by the batteries, and before they reached the top had to face terrific infantry volleys from troops which had been hurriedly summoned to defend the threatened line. Carroll's brigade from the Second Corps, furnished, under Carroll's own rousing leadership, three regiments, the Fourth Ohio, the Fourteenth Indiana, and the Seventh West Virginia, who came at a double quick, and in spite of the darkness found positions where they could lend instant aid. Perhaps not over a hundred out of the two Confederate brigades succeeded in surmounting the hill, and these were either captured or driven back again with other survivors still on the slope who had to retreat before achieving the ascent. Colonel Avery, at the head of his brigade, fell mortally wounded. The losses in the assailing force were heavy, but not so dreadful as they would have been had the attack been made in the open day.

Many incidents worthy of remembrance occurred

ATTACK ON CEMETERY HILL
(From a print of the time)

on Cemetery Hill during the fight of the afternoon and evening. In Cooper's Pennsylvania battery, for example, while the Latimer duel was being carried on, a shell exploded under one of Cooper's guns, killing or wounding all who were serving that piece; yet, as the artillery-brigade commander reports, "fire from that piece was reopened before all the wounded men were removed." In Rickett's battery, from the same State, the Texans in their advance, in the dusk, surmounted the lunette which inclosed the guns, and spiked one of the pieces in the midst of a hand-to-hand struggle, the cannoneers using handspikes, rammers, and side-arms in their effort to repel the assault. Lieut. Charles B. Brockway, in arresting the departure of a Confederate who was making off with a horse and the battery guidon, knocked his opponent down with a stone, and as he lifted the guidon, once more in Union hands, the staff was shot in two in the air.

An incident, full of pathetic tenderness, which took place in connection with this fight on Thursday night was this, which years after the battle came under my personal notice. The Texans, marching out through the streets of the town on their way to the fields from which they made their heroic advance, were chatting loudly of what they were expecting to do. A lady of devotion—who long afterward was known to the writer of this volume—heard them say as they passed her open window, "Boys, we are going to charge Cemetery Hill and take those batteries that have been troubling us all day." The woman, who had already passed through two days of

terror along with other residents of the town, was
smitten with dismay, as she foreboded a turn for the
worst for the defenders of the Union. For the moment she sat in speechless despair; then she bethought herself of the refuge of the faint and forlorn,
and dropped on her knees, crying out: "Almighty
God, save our flag! Help our boys on the hill! Oh,
may they save their guns, and maintain their ground,
and repulse this assault!" And, accordingly, for the
next hour, while the heroic charge was carried on
against the front of Cemetery Hill, that devout
woman was praying to God that the cause of the
Union might be succored and the cannoneers on the
heights might be helped to defend their guns and
guard the hill from capture.

XXVI

ASSAULTS ON CULP'S HILL

FOR many years after the battle the district included in the Union right flank at Culp's Hill contained frightful tokens of the havoc wrought by the bloody contests waged in the woods and among the rocks on Thursday evening and Friday morning. The Federal troops here in position occupied a strong and strongly fortified series of lines. The hill abounded in steep declivities, terraces of rock, and dense clumps of timber, which were made all the more formidable by breastworks and well-built rifle-pits and other forms of defensive works, under the skilled supervision of Slocum, the corps commander, Williams, a division leader who for some hours had charge of the corps, and Greene, a brigade commander, a veteran West-Pointer of the very largest engineering capacity and experience, as well as Geary, the remaining division commander. As soon as these distinguished officers were assigned to this point, on the evening of the first day and early in the morning of the second day, they recognized the natural advantages of the position, and began at once to fortify. Before the second day had ended they had transformed a natural fortress into one that could not be flanked or stormed. As we have already suggested in

the opening sentence of this paragraph, the woods
and rocks for many years bore tokens of the wreck
and ruin occasioned by the fight at that point. Trees
several inches in diameter were cut in two by cross-
firing of musketry, and the timber all over the hill
was hacked and gashed by bullets and shells and
grape-shot in an extraordinary way.

General Slocum in his report indicates a subsidiary
phase of the protected position which he had in
charge:

> As soon as the corps was established [on Culp's Hill] a strong
> force was detailed for the construction of breastworks and abatis,
> which subsequently proved of great value, as they enabled us at
> a critical moment to detach portions of the command to other
> points of the line.

In the arrangement of troops Wadsworth's division
of the First Corps occupied the Cemetery Hill front,
directly overlooking the fields east of the town, at
the point where the two hills adjoin; the Twelfth
Corps[1] with its left made connection with the right
of Wadsworth, Geary's division taking position here,
almost at right angles with the former; Williams's
division came next, commanded temporarily by
Ruger, while Williams had charge of the corps, this

---

[1] Twelfth Corps, Williams's division — Col. McDougall's brigade:
Fifth and Twentieth Connecticut, Third Maryland, 123d and 145th
New York, Forty-sixth Pennsylvania. Lockwood's brigade: First
Maryland (Potomac Home Brigade), First Maryland (Eastern
Shore), 150th New York. Ruger's brigade (led by Colgrove):
Twenty-seventh Indiana, Second Massachusetts, Thirteenth New
Jersey, 107th New York, Third Wisconsin.

Geary's division, Candy's brigade: Fifth, Seventh, Twenty-ninth,
and Sixty-sixth Ohio, Twenty-eighth and 147th Pennsylvania. Second Brigade (led by Kane and Cobham): Twenty-ninth, 109th, and
111th Pennsylvania. Greene's brigade: Sixtieth, Seventy-eighth,
102d, 137th, and 149th New York.

portion of the line extending around the brow of the hill through the woods and over the rocky acclivities almost directly south nearly to the Baltimore pike.[1]

Against this point of the Union line of battle occupied on Culp's Hill by the Twelfth Corps a series of vehement assaults was begun at nine o'clock on Thursday night by Edward Johnson's division.[2] Without knowing what an advantage he had unwittingly secured he chanced to advance against one portion of the fortified Federal line from which a large portion of the troops of this corps had been hurried away in the dusk of the night, in order to strengthen the struggling left flank near Round Top and to give backing and reinforcement to the command of Hancock, against which terrific charges were

[1] For a time Slocum was in command of the right wing, the Twelfth Corps then falling into the hands of Brig. Gen. Alpheus S. Williams, whose regular post was at the head of the First Division. General Williams was lieutenant colonel of the First Michigan Infantry in the Mexican War, and from that State was appointed brigadier general in April, 1861. He was brevetted major general, January 12, 1865, "for marked ability and energy." At Gettysburg his work was of value in fortifying and defending Culp's Hill. He died January 23, 1878.

[2] Edward Johnson's division—Steuart's brigade: First Maryland Battalion, First and Third North Carolina, Tenth, Twenty-third, and Thirty-seventh Virginia. Walker's "Stonewall" brigade: Second, Fourth, Fifth, Twenty-seventh, and Thirty-third Virginia. "Nicholls's brigade" (led by Williams): First, Second, Tenth, Fourteenth, and Fifteenth Louisiana. [Gen. Francis T. Nicholls, after whom the Louisiana command was called, lost a foot at Chancellorsville, and therefore did not get to Gettysburg. He had lost an arm in 1862. He was a graduate of West Point, 1855. He served after the war twice as governor of his State, and from 1893 till 1912—the date of his death—he was on the Supreme Bench, for thirteen years chief justice.] J. M. Jones's brigade: Twenty-first, Twenty-fifth, Forty-second, Forty-fourth, Forty-eighth, and Fiftieth Virginia. Daniel's brigade: Thirty-second, Forty-third, Forty-fifth, Fifty-third North Carolina regiments, and Second North Carolina Battalion. Colonel O'Neal's brigade: Third, Fifth, Sixth, Twelfth, and Twenty-sixth Alabama. (The Fifth was detached for the day in town.) Smith's brigade: Thirty-first, Forty-ninth, and Fifty-second Virginia.

being made. These troops did not return to Culp's Hill until nearly midnight, and when they did come back they found their breastworks occupied by Confederate soldiers.

The last three brigades detailed in the footnote, led by Daniel, O'Neal, and Smith, were added at night to Johnson's division in his effort to capture Culp's Hill.

One of the tragic phases of this part of the fight consisted in the fact that the Maryland organization in Steuart's brigade, given in the footnote, found itself confronted in the engagement by three regiments from the same State, in Lockwood's command. It thus happened, as at Winchester three weeks before, that members of the same family were arrayed against one another in deadly encounter. At Winchester, for instance, Major Goldsborough, of the Confederate "First Battalion," captured in battle his own brother, Major Goldsborough, surgeon of the Fifth Maryland, of the Union Army.

With regard to the assault which Johnson made on Thursday night he bears this testimony: "It was made with great vigor and spirit, and was as successful as could have been expected, considering the superiority of the enemy's force and position."

Before any advance was made that night Lieut. R. H. McKim, aide to General Steuart (at this writing, 1913, and for years rector of the Church of the Epiphany, in Washington City), who was accustomed to hold services in the army as occasion might offer, conducted a most impressive meeting in the bivouac of the Tenth Virginia, and then in the rendezvous of the Maryland battalion. Soon afterward he led the

First North Carolina in a furious stage of the battle forward to reinforce the line of assault. Dr. McKim has written two interesting volumes of Confederate reminiscences.

We cannot now divine why the assaults on Culp's Hill were delayed almost twenty-four hours, during which period the Union troops had full time and chance to dig their rifle-pits and build their breastworks—an opportunity which, as we have already pointed out, was skilfully utilized.

Some of the subordinate officers, as we have already noted, discerned the possibilities which were presented for the Confederate troops on the night of the first day. Colonel Brown, for instance, of the First North Carolina, sent word to Johnson soon after being posted on the eastern base of Culp's Hill, Wednesday night, that if he were reinforced he could make his way down the narrow Rock Creek Valley and cut the Union highway to the rear, the Baltimore pike. Smith's brigade was at once ordered thither, but that commander—whimsically known in his political career as "Extra Billy Smith"—had been seized with a notion that he was about to be attacked on the Hanover road, and his arrival at the new location was delayed, and hence no effort was made to carry out Brown's wise suggestion.

By the night assault Steuart, on the Confederate left, captured a line of breastworks and some prisoners, and Johnson's whole line pressed forward, close up to that of the Union troops. About midnight, to repeat what has already been summarized in advance, the portions of the Twelfth Corps which had been withdrawn from their position on this hill and swung to the other end of the Union line, returned to their former position, to find their breastworks occupied by Steuart's brigade and other forces from Johnson's division; they made an attempt to retake the works, but found it too difficult a task to be undertaken at night, and by midnight the lines were quiet for a time.

THIRD DAY

XXVII

SLOCUM RECAPTURES CULP'S HILL

LATE on Thursday night, when the fighting all along the line had ceased, General Meade called his corps commanders together to find out what the situation was in each command. Butterfield, chief of staff, had prepared certain questions to be answered by the assembled officers—the net result of the consultation being that the army should await an attack, and not venture out from its strong position to assail the army of Lee.

With regard to this council some misapprehension has been made of record, in view of the allegation that Meade was minded to retreat and that orders looking to that end had been prepared. Meade himself, before the Committee on the Conduct of the War, definitely declared that he had not at any time during the battle cherished or expressed any such intention, and there is no evidence worth considering to overcome his testimony and the almost unanimous testimony of his corps commanders.

It was clear to Meade that the first thing on Friday morning must be an attack upon Johnson's force, which had secured, by a conjuncture of circumstances already related, possession of a portion of Culp's Hill. Accordingly, at four o'clock on Friday morning, July 3d, Slocum opened fire upon the opposing lines at that point. By that time the reinforcements assigned to Johnson, as indicated in our last section, were all in place, and the assaults were renewed on the Union position. The fight here lasted for seven hours, charge alternating with countercharge, the Union troops now and then venturing out from their breastworks to attack the foe, and all the phases of the engagement proving most vehement in their intensity, and dreadfully slaughterous, if we may coin an expression adequate to the havoc which was wrought. Two general assaults were made by Johnson, reaching throughout the extent of his line of battle against the base of the hill, and against troops screened by solid walls of rock, skilfully built breastworks, barricades of timber and abatis, which formed an impregnable position. The Union situation at Fredericksburg was reversed, and the madness exhibited under Burnside by his hopeless assaults up the steep and wall-crowned hills in that battle was reproduced by the assailing Confederates. One cannot think or speak of such military policy now either with patience or admiration. The only question to be settled was: How long will men endure such treatment? How long will they submit to be urged and driven against fortified positions, when five times their numbers could do nothing more than perish in the assault?

By eleven o'clock that morning the troops of Johnson, finding their task impossible, under orders ceased making any further effort to attack, retraced their steps from the immediate front of the hill, and occupied the Rock Creek intervale.[1]

It may be recalled at this juncture that the temporary indentation in the Union lines made on Thursday evening and occupied by Johnson till nearly noon on Friday, and then regained by the Twelfth Army Corps after desperate efforts had been made by the Confederates to retain them and capture the entire Culp's Hill—an achievement which would have put the parks of reserve artillery, the wagon-trains, and the entire rear of Meade's army at the command of his opponent—was the only break made in the entire line of battle as laid out by Meade, reaching from Culp's Hill to the Round Tops. In spite of utmost pressure and repeated assaults, that original line remained unbroken. What more could Lee do? He had lost more than twenty thousand men, and expended a vast amount of ammunition, a precious article just then; he had assailed the left flank of his foe, the left center, the center, and the right flank in vain. Was there yet a weak point where a break could be made? Could he bring himself to withdraw in the face of this situation as it then stood? Was it possible to lure Meade out to attack? Or was there rational ground for hope that the Confederates might

[1] Among the leading Maryland officers at Gettysburg, where he was wounded and captured, was Maj. Henry Kyd Douglas, assistant adjutant general on the staff of Maj. Gen. Edward Johnson. Later he was made a brigadier general. After the war he became the major general commanding the militia of Maryland, and also the adjutant general of the State. He served for years with widely recognized ability as judge of the Fifth Judicial Circuit of Maryland, and died, at the age of sixty-three, in 1903.

make one last, irresistible onset and thus win a victory?

There remained, of course, the plan thus far untried, suggested by Longstreet—march south toward Emmitsburg, threaten the left flank and the com-

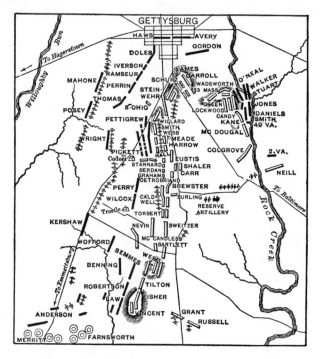

POSITIONS OF FEDERAL AND CONFEDERATE FORCES, JULY 3
(Federal, ⊏⊐   Confederate, ▬)

munications of the Union Army, and thus induce Meade to attack. But at this juncture that venture would have opened Lee's own flank and rear to assailments; it was not to be thought of. To Lee's mind there remained but one thing yet to do—make a final assault.

XXVIII

UNION CAVALRY ON THE FLANKS

IT is necessary to divert attention for the moment from the preliminaries of the final movement to note the work of the cavalry on the flanks of the armies on Friday afternoon, almost exactly at the time of the artillery and infantry engagements, to be detailed in succeeding pages.

On the left flank of the Union Army Kilpatrick was at work tackling the skirmishers which Longstreet had arrayed, along with a stronger line under Law, to protect his right flank while arrangements were in progress for the charge under Pickett. This protecting line ran for some distance along the base of Big Round Top, and then extended westward from Plum Run to the Emmitsburg road. It was occupied by artillery and otherwise made strong by stone-fence barricades and other safeguards against an advance of the enemy. Besides, this part of the field was irregular in formation, and abounded in boulders and other impediments, making it an unusually formidable ground for anything like a cavalry movement. After having carried on a prolonged skirmish with Law's troops during two hours in the afternoon (part of the time during the struggle then going on between

Pickett and the Union left center) the two brigades [1] which Kilpatrick had with him on that part of the line were ordered to press forward late in the day.

It is not easy to discern now what was to be accomplished by this move, the fight having closed farther along the line. An hour earlier, and at another point farther west, there was really an opportunity for the cavalry to do some aggressive and damaging work. It should have been clear to those on the spot that it was an untimely juncture and an unfortunate place for a charge to be made. Confederate writers acquainted with the situation at the time have declared, substantially, that had Kilpatrick skirted around the right flank of the Confederate force to the rear of that part of their line (a mile or two, or perhaps farther, west) the way was open at that moment—just following the defeat of Pickett—for a panic-smiting blow to be delivered among the trains and artillery parks of the army of Lee.

Nevertheless, Kilpatrick recklessly ordered Farnsworth to charge against the lines of Law. That junior officer, it is said, intimated that it was not the place to make a charge, and it appears well established that Kilpatrick taunted the gallant young fellow with being too timid. It had been well for him had he maintained his ground and refused to act the part of a madman; but he was brave and proud and highstrung and loyal to present duty, and with two small

[1] Merritt's cavalry brigade: Sixth Pennsylvania, First, Second, Fifth, Sixth Regulars. Farnsworth's cavalry brigade: Fifth New York, Eighteenth Pennsylvania, First Vermont, First West Virginia.

regiments, the First Vermont and the First West Virginia, he led an impetuous advance. There were three lines of infantry behind stone fences and granite boulders, and then there were batteries to face and a flanking fire of other forces to meet. Farnsworth, pressing through these lines, followed by gallant squads of officers and men, made a half circuit among the opposing forces, and at last in the midst of the foe fell covered with wounds. His men were in part captured, in part slain; with great difficulty and after a hand-to-hand fight the survivors made their escape, having discerned in advance of the climax of the struggle that unless they turned to the right or left, as the case might be, and got back to their own line in haste the entire body of them would be killed or captured.

Gen. Elon J. Farnsworth, thus killed at the opening of his career as a general officer, had been promoted from a captaincy just four days before. He was the first adjutant of the Eighth Illinois Cavalry; after his captaincy was reached he served on the staff of Major General Pleasanton, the head of the cavalry corps, and here, under the immediate eye of the commander, he revealed such gallantry, such military intuitions, such aptitudes for command in mounted service that he was at the suggestion of both Meade and Pleasanton made a brigadier general at one leap from the post of captain. Pleasanton, in his report of the case, thus wrote:

Gifted in a high degree with a quick perception and a correct judgment, and remarkable for his daring coolness, his comprehensive grasp of the situation on the field of battle and the rapidity of his actions had already distinguished General Farnsworth among his comrades in arms. In his death was closed a career that must have won the highest honors of his profession.

A cavalry fight of a vitally important character took place that same afternoon—during the struggle of the infantry forces near the center—between Stuart (and his cavalry forces, four brigades, led by Hampton,[1] Fitzhugh Lee,[2] Colonels Chambliss[3] and Jenkins[4]), and Gregg,[5] with three brigades of Union cavalry under Colonels McIntosh, J. Irvin Gregg, and Custer. The field of encounter was a mile or two east of Culp's Hill, which marked the limit of the Confederate left, where Ewell was in command; and the fight on the part of the Confederates was intended to guard that flank, and if possible break through the Union line and start a panic among the trains and artillery parks near the Baltimore pike.

Gregg and Stuart were comrades at West Point, and they had met before the battle at Gettysburg more than once in bloody conflict, and they were destined to meet again and again in the months that followed. In this particular engagement on the Union right flank they were fairly well matched—each com-

[1] Hampton: Cavalry, First North Carolina, First and Second South Carolina; Cobb's, Jeff Davis's, and Phillips's "legions."

[2] Fitzhugh Lee: First Maryland Battalion, First, Second, Third, Fourth, and Fifth Virginia.

[3] Colonel Chambliss: Second North Carolina, Ninth, Tenth, and Thirteenth Virginia.

[4] Jenkins: Fourteenth, Sixteenth, Seventeenth Virginia regiments, Thirty-fourth and Thirty-sixth Virginia battalions.

[5] Gregg's Union Cavalry—McIntosh: First Maryland; Purnell Legion, Maryland; First Massachusetts, First New Jersey, First and Third Pennsylvania, Third Pa. Heavy Artillery, section of Battery H. Col. J. I. Gregg: First Maine, Tenth New York, Fourth and Sixteenth Pennsylvania. Custer: First, Fifth, Sixth, and Seventh Michigan.

mander had with him about five thousand sabers—
and for about two hours there was a most spirited and
vehement conflict in which close encounters with
pistol and saber, advances and retrogressions, mag-

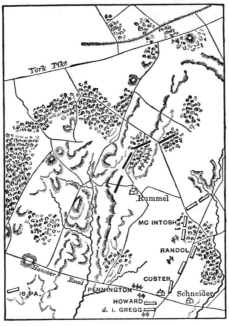

GREGG'S FIGHT WITH STUART

nificent charges and retreats, and many displays of
personal gallantry and soldierly skill took place.
Had Stuart succeeded in his venture the conse-
quences would have been serious for the Union Army;
his cavalry would have created confusion and damage in the very midst of the artillery reserves, the
hospitals, and the trains which were located near the
Baltimore pike, not far from which the struggle
occurred. The net results of the contest were that

the effort of Stuart was arrested; each force with-drew to the edges of the disputed territory, and that night Stuart drew back within the lines of Lee's main army.   In this fight Wade Hampton, in a hand-to-hand encounter, was wounded by a saber cut on the head—a very narrow escape from instant death.

XXIX

THE brief success won by Wright's brigade on Thursday evening in its charge against Hancock's position seems to have suggested to Lee that at the point where the line yielded for a moment in that movement an opportunity possibly offered for new pressure to be brought upon the left center of the Union Army, where it might be broken to pieces. Accordingly, while the fight of Johnson was going on at Culp's Hill the Southern commander made his plans, arrayed his troops, and outlined his movement. Under the direction of Col. E. P. Alexander, Longstreet's chief of artillery, co-operating with Pendleton, chief of that branch in Lee's army, about forty batteries were put in position—a hundred and fifty cannon, smooth bores, rifled pieces, light and heavy guns— very few of the latter, however—along Seminary Ridge for full three miles, starting south of the Peach Orchard and running northward to Oak Hill, northwest of the town. To a considerable extent the guns were aimed at the Cemetery and at the line of battle adjacent to that point extending southward, the locality where Hancock was in command.

Meanwhile, the Union commander and his chief of artillery, Hunt—a master in his profession—were busy making arrangements to meet the plans of Lee. Meade had foreseen the threatened movements of his antagonist; indeed, he had indicated the night before to Gibbon and Hays, in an offhand way, that Lee would probably aim an attack on their front next day. Hunt and his staff with their glasses had kept track of the operations on the other side, and had noted that batteries were being planted along its front, and that the preliminaries were being arranged for a forward movement. Accordingly, fresh batteries were stationed on the entire Union line, guns of long range were planted on Little Round Top, the whole interval between that point and the Cemetery was filled in with cannon, and Cemetery Hill was mantled with them, fixed at such points that they might with some success aim over their own infantry and into the field in their front. Arrangements were made to have fresh batteries near at hand, and vast supplies of ammunition within reach. Moreover, Meade had so shrewdly anticipated the movements of the foe that he had massed his infantry in great strength in the rear of Hancock, along the Taneytown road, to be ready for whatever crisis might develop during the afternoon. These plans were so magnificently carried out that when the closing phases of the fight began to open up nothing was needed except to fill in with fresh guns the vacancies occasioned by batteries which had to be withdrawn on account of damage, or to be restocked with grape and canister. Hardly a brigade of infantry needed to change its place in view of the cannonade and the last charge. This prescient generalship shown by Meade has never been fully appreciated. It was one of the signal marks of his ability in the battle.

From eleven in the morning till one in the afternoon occurred an interval of silence, mysterious, oppressive, ominous—strangely contrasting with the terrific musketry and artillery resonance which had for seven hours been echoing from Culp's Hill—a stillness which awoke in every mind a sense of apprehension, and seemed to people the breathless air with portents of doom, a hush like that which in the tropics precedes the outbreak of a tornado.

Two cannon-shots in quick succession from a Napoleon gun, in Smith's battery of the Washington artillery (of New Orleans), broke the silence at exactly one o'clock—it was the signal for a hundred and twenty men who held the lanyards of that many cannon to "let go!" For over an hour the noise was infernal. Two hundred field-pieces can make a furious concourse of appalling explosions when they go off in concert, as was the case when Meade's guns joined with the Confederate cannon in unison that afternoon. No such a spectacle had ever before taken place on American soil. Each different missile had its own peculiar dissonance—shell and round shot, of various caliber, from smooth bores or rifled pieces, from twelve-pounder bronze guns called Napoleons, and from Parrott cannon, whizzing, shrieking, swishing, and exploding in numbers faster than could be counted—all this made confusion worse confounded indeed. This writer recalls especially the fiendish wailings of certain oblong, convoluted, heavy projectiles which came from a few Whitworth pieces on the Confederate side, which broke now and then into the horrible discord, sounding like the predatory howls of demons in search of their prey.

The aim of the Confederates was to focus their fire on the left center of the Union forces, demoralize the infantry, dismantle the batteries, and thus open a way through which an infantry charge might penetrate. Concerning this purpose General Alexander, already cited, complains that Pendleton did not aptly carry it out, that he made but little use of commanding points near the town and to the north and east of the village, and that the guns did not focus on the predestined portion of the Union lines.

On the Federal side General Hunt found it possible at first to use with profit only about seventy-five guns; others, to advantage, were added later. The damage done was severe among the batteries, but the infantry lay on the ground, used slight barricades of rails and earth, found shelter here and there behind stone walls, and thus escaped great harm, while quantities of shot and shell went clean over the lines of battle into the valley along the Taneytown road. At the opening of the artillery firing the headquarters of Meade, just in the rear of the point where the final blow was levied, formed the concentric point where for the time being a storm of shot and shell swept down, making it impossible for horse or man to tarry. The instant flight of all whose duty it was to be stationed at headquarters just at that moment made up a scene of panic and commotion which an Irish orderly—whose horse had been disemboweled by a shell, and who had run for shelter and crouched behind a rock by the roadside—thus commented upon: "Begorra, wherever there is a gatherin', there must be a scatherin'!"

Some of the Union batteries were greatly damaged before the cannonade ended; but, by Hunt's prescient plans, and by quick co-operation with the reserve artillery commander and his helpers, other guns were brought forward on the gallop to fill into the vacant places. Many men who still recall that terrible hour will possibly think of the work done by those batteries—by officers, horses, and men as they hurried at forced speed across the fields and up the Taneytown road, the buglers giving signal by their instruments, resounding in the air above the sounds of shells and grape, the captains and lieutenants urging their steeds forward, aides coming toward them to hurry them up and lead them to posts they were to fill, while now and then on the way a caisson would explode, and the smoky air would be filled with the spectral fragments of dismembered horses, drivers, and cannoneers. It was a token, a supreme token, of steadfastness and discipline that that great force— particularly the infantry who had to lie down and keep still and face the music till they were needed to take part—could preserve its nerve and equipoise without any sign of demoralization in the midst of such appalling circumstances. At one critical moment, in order to assure the temper of his men, General Hancock, with two or three of his staff, rode deliberately along the front of his corps from end to end. That officer knew how to give his men in a crisis superhuman bravery.

GETTYSBURG

The artillery duel, after it had occupied an hour and a half, was abated by the sound judgment of Meade and Hunt, whose military foresight suggested to each of them, at about the same moment in different parts of the line, the conclusion that in order to cool the guns, save ammunition, clear the atmosphere, and thus give a better chance to aim at an advancing foe when he might come, the batteries would better slow down. The impression made on the Confederates by this policy was a delusion; they fancied that the Union forces were demoralized, the batteries dismantled, and the lines broken so that an advance of the Southern infantry—for which preparations had been going forward all day—might now penetrate to the rear of Meade's army. That, at least, was the first blush thought of some of the leaders. An hour later they realized how dreadfully they were mistaken. Nevertheless, the order was now transmitted for the chosen troops, the flower of the Confederate Army, to emerge from their shelter behind Seminary Ridge, advance across the rolling plain to the Emmitsburg road, stop for a moment and dress their lines, and then charge the position in their front.

XXX

CUI BONO?

BEFORE we rehearse afresh the story of the final movement of the Confederate commander in chief let us ask once more, what wisdom was manifested in this last heroic effort of the Army of Northern Virginia? Can this movement be justified as viewed from any standpoint? What reasonable expectation, what rational hope, could have been cherished that such a stroke could possibly succeed? What conclusion must candidly be written concerning the sanity and the inevitable outcome of such an enterprise?

The recorded judgment of the officers who took part in the battle under Lee, while it is true that they have spoken usually with great reticence because of their affection and reverence for their commander, does not show that they believed victory possible. Longstreet, as is well known, protested against the charge, believed that not even forty thousand soldiers could win against such a position as the Union Army occupied in his front, and against such a force as that which manned the Union lines that day. Wade Hampton, wounded in the cavalry battle that afternoon on the Confederate left under Stuart, wrote a few days later from Charlottesville, Virginia, where he was undergoing treatment, to Senator Wigfall at

Richmond: "Our army is in good condition after its terrible and useless battle. . . . We could better have stormed the heights of Stafford than those of Gettysburg."

Gen. E. P. Alexander, who occupied a leading part in the conduct of the cannonade, and whose function particularly that afternoon it chanced to be to study the effect of his artillery on the Union lines, and to indicate the time when the advance was to be made, records his judgment, again and again, concerning the hopelessness of the venture. He says:

> It seemed madness to order a column in the middle of a hot July day to undertake an advance of three-fourths of a mile over open ground against the center of that line. . . . No formation could have been successful to win at that point. . . . Of the third day it must be said, as was said of the charge of the Six Hundred at Balaklava—"Magnificent, but not war!" [*Military Memoirs*, p. 412.]

Just before the advance was ordered General Alexander chatted with a brigade commander, Gen. A. R. Wright, who had at this very point on the preceding day led an assault on Hancock's corps, asking the question, "What do you think of it? Is it as hard to get there as it looks?" Wright replied: "The trouble is not in getting there. I went there with my brigade yesterday. There is a place where you can get breath and re-form. The trouble is to stay there after you get there, for the whole Yankee army is there in a bunch!"

This same writer recalls an amusing myth which had currency in the Confederate ranks after the close of the engagement, to the effect that the attacking force had "run up against all creation" in its advance, and had heard the command given on the Federal side as it neared Hancock's line: "Attention, Universe! Nations into line! By kingdoms right wheel! March!"

The truth is that this final effort at Gettysburg was a monumental act of heroic desperation. It belongs with the reckless assaults made by Lee on the Union position at Malvern Hill, in 1862, the charges forced by Burnside against the heights of Fredericksburg, and the attack against Lee's impregnable position made by Grant at Cold Harbor—these were all dreadful blunders costing thousands of lives without any countervailing return. Can anything else be fairly said of this fatal and desperate venture at Gettysburg? When that choice body of men under Pickett and Pettigrew was ordered forward against the line which Hancock occupied that Friday afternoon— against a position magnificently occupied by men and guns—were they not sent to their death? They had no possible chance to do anything except make an immortal record of their gallantry and their willingness to die at Lee's bidding.

Furthermore, this charge, when compared with the other assaults in the same battle, cannot fairly be declared to be an exceptional display of courage, discipline, and devotion.

The Confederates who made their unflinching advance on the first day; the soldiers of Hood, McLaws, and Anderson, in their attacks on the Peach Orchard and on the Devil's Den; the troops of Hays, Avery, and George H. Steuart in their repeated charges at Cemetery Hill and Culp's Hill—these all exhibited a forgetfulness of self, a loyal spirit of discipline, and a reckless courage fully equal to the similar qualities which were revealed by the soldiers who were marshaled by Pickett and Pettigrew. The last charge at Gettysburg was a culmination of tremendous attacks, adding the climactic touch to three days of terrific fighting; and it was, in addition, surcharged with romantic, spectacular, and dramatic elements; but, although it has been glorified by historians of the engagement and celebrated in poetry and portrayed by gifted painters on canvas, it by no means stands alone as an example of self-sacrificing heroism. Humphreys's three charges at Fredericksburg deserve in all respects—in skill, determination, and daring—to stand alongside of it. But fairness to the truth of history and to the dead who were sacrificed that bloody day requires it to be said that the effort was a forlorn hope, an absolutely hopeless enterprise. Had Lee withdrawn all his forces from Culp's Hill and from the town, and massed the bulk of them for that last advance, then possibly the blow by its momentum might have opened up a gaping avenue of ruin through Meade's line of battle; but for a single division aided by half a dozen shattered brigades to make the attempt meant simply the erection of a lasting memorial to utterly unavailing valor.

XXXI

FIFTEEN Virginia regiments, as choice an array of soldiers as the Southern Army could muster, and aggregating a little over five thousand officers and men, constituted Maj. Gen. George E. Pickett's division[1] at Gettysburg. Up to the hour of three o'clock on Friday afternoon, July 3d, when that force was ordered forward on its final advance, it had had no active part in the battle, duties in the Cumberland Valley having detained it in its work and movements so that it did not reach the field until late in the afternoon of the second day. As formed for the advance the brigade led by Brig. Gen. J. L. Kemper held the right of the line; that which Brig. Gen. Lewis A. Armistead commanded was in the center, ranging slightly behind the front formation, prepared to crowd forward and fill up the space when the troops in front should spread out and make more room. Brig. Gen. R. B. Garnett's brigade occupied the left of the division.

Making connection on Pickett's left and extending

---

[1] Garnett's brigade: Eighth, Eighteenth, Nineteenth, Twenty-eighth, and Fifty-sixth Virginia. Kemper's brigade: First, Third, Seventh, Eleventh, and Twenty-fourth Virginia. Armistead's brigade: Ninth, Fourteenth Thirty-eighth, Fifty-third, and Fifty-seventh Virginia.

the line northward were the following organizations, constituting the battered and broken remnants of two divisions which had been torn to pieces in the first day's fight under Hill, a brigade in most cases hardly containing enough men to make a full-sized regiment. One of these small divisions was led by Pettigrew,[1] Heth, their former division commander, having been wounded; the four brigades were formed in the following order, from right to left: next to Pickett's men came Col. B. D. Fry's force; then Col. J. K. Marshall's North Carolinians, their leader a magnificent-looking soldier, well mounted, and destined to perish at the head of his men; then came Gen. J. R. Davis's quota, and on the extreme left Col. J. M. Brockenbrough's Virginia regiments.

Behind, and in support of Pettigrew's right, were two small forces: Scales's brigade, led by Col. W. L. J. Lowrance, their former leader having been wounded on the first day; and Gen. J. H. Lane's brigade, for the time in the hands of Col. C. M. Avery, of the Thirty-third North Carolina, Lane having been assigned to take charge of the division, as Pender had been fatally wounded the day before.

In this order the lines were formed, and Lane, up to the very moment when the word "Forward" was sounded, expected to lead the last-noted division.

[1] Heth's division (led by Pettigrew)—Brockenbrough's brigade: Fortieth, Forty-seventh, and Fifty-fifth Virginia regiments, and Twenty-second Virginia Battalion. Marshall's brigade: Eleventh, Twenty-sixth, Forty-seventh, and Fifty-second North Carolina. Col. B. D. Fry's brigade: Thirteenth Alabama, Fifth Alabama Battalion, First Tennessee, Seventh Tennessee, and Fourteenth Tennessee. Davis's brigade: Second, Eleventh, and Forty-second Mississippi, Fifty-fifth North Carolina.

THE CHARGING FORCE MAKES READY

Just as the movement was about to begin, however, Maj. Gen. I. R. Trimble[1] rode up with an order in his hands from Lee putting him in command of the division, and thus sending Lane back to his brigade and Avery back to his regiment.

Trimble, a man of years and ability, a West Point graduate who had been for many years in railroad management in Baltimore, and who in the opening part of the current campaign had been ill, arrived at Gettysburg after the battle had begun and served on staff duty with Lee for a day or two. He was intensely anxious, however, to be in command of troops once more, and made his desires known to Lee, who granted his request, as we have noted, at the very last moment. Half an hour later Trimble, desperately wounded, was a prisoner.

The line as finally formed on the slopes of Seminary Ridge, running through the woods and orchards, facing eastward toward Hancock's front, with which at the start it was not quite parallel, may be roughly depicted by the following diagram—Wilcox's brigade, not shown here, being on the right toward the south:

Brocken-brough Davis Marshall Fry		Garnett Kemper
PETTIGREW'S DIVISION		Armistead
Lane Lowrance		PICKETT'S DIVISION
TRIMBLE'S DIVISION		

Early in the day Lee, Longstreet and Pickett had quietly inspected Pickett's force, and had heartily

[1] Trimble's division—Lowrance's brigade: Thirteenth, Sixteenth, Twenty-second, Thirty-fourth, and Thirty-eighth North Carolina. Lane's brigade: Seventh, Eighteenth, Twenty-eighth, Thirty-third, and Thirty-seventh North Carolina.

approved its equipment and appearance as it was arrayed along the ridge, screened for the time from the observation of the vigilant foe a mile away to the eastward front.

Wilcox's Alabama brigade, to the right of the point where the charging force was arrayed on the Ridge, had been posted since early morning somewhat in front of the regular line of battle to support the artillery attack; but there is no intimation given in any of the reports that it was to form at the outset a part of the advancing line. Wilcox tells us in his report that no orders came to him to advance in support of Pickett until half an hour after the start of the latter had been made, at a time when the Virginians had been broken and scattered in their fatal enterprise. Wilcox, however, to anticipate the outcome, even in that extremity made the attempt to charge; but the field was so tempest-swept with the Union cannon in his front and against his flanks that it was impossible to proceed very far, and his brigade was ordered back by Longstreet in order to escape absolute destruction.

Without counting Wilcox, therefore, the entire force arrayed for the charge was as follows: Virginia, nineteen regiments; North Carolina, fifteen; Alabama, two; Tennessee, three; Mississippi, three—forty-two in all, possibly twelve thousand men. There is no evidence on record in the reports of the battle that General Lee had in mind any larger force than this for the movement, or that orders were issued for any troops at other portions of the line to co-operate simultaneously with this charge, except in the instance of Stuart's cavalry attack, which we have already outlined.

We make this averment with confidence, having gone over the data in the case, and, in full view of the hints and vague accusations as to the lack of support, which had been ordered and arranged for in advance—accusations found in the writings of some of Lee's staff-officers, for example, in *Four Years with General Lee*, by Col. Walter H. Taylor, who intimates, pages 107–108, that other forces were under definite orders to co-operate and move forward with Pickett and Pettigrew; but there are no orders or reports on record to justify this charge. It was fully understood that Hood's and McLaws's divisions of Longstreet's corps must be held in hand to protect the extreme right flank of Lee's army; and hence they could not be a part of the charging force. Anderson's division, therefore, is the only component of Lee's army that could have been drawn upon for that purpose, being close by in the line on Seminary Ridge. What were Anderson's orders? He tells us in his report (*Official Records*, XXVII, 2:614, 615). Speaking of the cannonade, he says:

After about an hour's continuance of this conflict the enemy's force seemed to subside, and troops of General Longstreet's corps were advanced to the assault of the enemy's center. I received orders to hold my division in readiness to move up in support, if it should become necessary. . . . Wilcox's and Perry's brigades had been moved forward so as to be in position to render assistance or to take advantage of any success gained by the assaulting column, and at what I supposed to be the proper time I was about to move forward Wright's and Posey's brigades, when Lieutenant General Longstreet directed me to stop the movement, adding that it was useless and would only involve unnecessary loss, the assault having failed.

Certainly the instructions which Anderson received did not make it incumbent on him to move forward when Pickett did.

According to the narrative given by Mrs. Pickett in her interesting volume *Pickett and His Men,* her husband, not long after the battle, wrote out a report in which it appears he made some severe reflections against some of the other generals of the Confederate Army. When Lee received and read it he returned the document to Pickett, suggesting to him that it should not be allowed to appear. The request to Pickett from Lee is as follows, without date:

> You and your men have crowned yourselves with glory; but we have the enemy to fight, and must carefully at this critical moment guard against dissensions which the reflections in your report would create. I will, therefore, suggest that you destroy both copy and original, substituting one confined to casualties merely. I hope all will yet be well. [*Official Records,* XXVII, 3: 1075.]

There is, we believe, no correct record of casualties in Pickett's division; from the Government records no adequate idea of the losses can be secured. We have elsewhere added to these the names furnished by Mrs. Pickett in her volume, which include only a score or so of field-officers.

In view of the extent of the disaster which resulted from this attempt on the part of Lee—against the protests of Longstreet and possibly others—to break through the Union center at a point where the line was impregnable, and in the face of an overwhelming force arrayed at that spot against him, it is no wonder that some of his staff after the war were anxious to put the blame on other shoulders than those of their beloved chieftain; but after thorough search we have been unable to find any evidence to justify their allegations.

XXXII

HANCOCK'S LINE IN VIEW

IT is time now to glance at the preparations which have been made on the Union side to meet this advance of the Confederates. Happily for the Army of the Potomac and for the cause which was to be decided in the impending struggle, Hancock had command over the front which was to be directly assailed. His line and its adjacent positions were closely crowded with batteries from the western foot of Cemetery Hill clean to the Round Tops. On Cemetery Hill, overlooking much of the field, were thirteen batteries so posted that many of the guns could fire over the heads of the troops which defended that point, and thus damage the forces of the enemy when they might advance. Some of these batteries belonged to the reserve artillery, and others to the Eleventh Corps, whose infantry forces girdled a part of the hill itself.

Immediately facing the open ground over which the advance was made, and near the point where the blow with all its force fell, were five batteries—twenty-six guns — commanded by men who made a record of valor that day never surpassed in the history of the Republic—Woodruff's Battery I, First United States; Arnold's A, First Rhode Island; Cushing's

310

A, Fourth United States; Brown's B, First Rhode Island; and Rorty's B, First New York.

Of the five just noted Woodruff was on the extreme right at Ziegler's Grove, on the eastern foot of the Cemetery. Along his front, from north to south, ran a stone wall extending past Arnold's position, where it turned westward for a short distance, and again south, forming at the latter turn what is now known as the "bloody angle." Here Cushing was located, the "clump of trees," still preserved as one of the notable landmarks, being immediately to his left. Beyond him came Brown and Rorty, the stone wall giving place in their front to a rail fence which had been thrown down to offer some slight protection to the infantry. The front of these five batteries covered some two thousand feet.

It may also advantage the reader to recall that the Emmitsburg road was diagonal to the two lines of battle, being well within the Union lines near Ziegler's Grove, and running thence in a southwesterly direction until it entered the Confederate territory in the neighborhood of the Peach Orchard a mile and a half away.

Continuing the line southward were forty guns under McGilvery, who had on the preceding afternoon massed with such appalling effect his guns against the charging troops of Barksdale and Wofford; while on Little Round Top were two batteries, one of them of long range and fitted to do deadly work against the right flank of the enemy that was to advance. Thus in all seventy-five guns of the best sort were here so skilfully arrayed that they could either by a direct or a flanking fire sweep every square rod of the landscape before them.

Those who have traversed that field, or who have studied the maps which exhibit this tremendous line of guns, and who have in addition dwelt on the fact that scores of cannon in reserve were close by, ready to be hurried in time of need at once into position, cannot cease to wonder how any man survived after being exposed to the scathing effects of that dreadful artillery ordeal.

The infantry line was made up of an extraordinary body of soldiers, as choice as any that were ever mustered under any flag, marshaled either in the front or the supporting lines by such division leaders as Hays, Gibbon, Caldwell, Doubleday, Birney, Humphreys, and Robinson, with such brigade commanders as Webb, Hall, Harrow—types of skill and patriotic devotion worthy of any land or age. On their left were the troops of the Fifth Corps, and near them massed in reserve stood the Sixth Corps, held ready for any critical advance which might later develop near and on Little Round Top.

Against this solidly massed and magnificently posted body of batteries and this great force of infantry, occupying lines in part defended by stone fences and in part by hastily constructed barricades on a slightly elevated ridge which almost completely overlooked the rolling fields across which an assailing force must approach, the charge of the forlorn hope was now to be made.

XXXIII

THE LEADERS IN THE MOVEMENT

BEFORE we reproduce the final advance of the Confederate forces arrayed for the last charge it may help to make the picture a vivid one if we take a glance at the notable personalities identified with the memorable spectacle. Some of them, such as Pettigrew, Lane, Davis, Fry, and Marshall, heading the men who had already on the first or second day been "stormed at with shot and shell" in previous phases of the fight, have been already sketched, but the Virginians in the division of Pickett now come before us in the battle for the first time, and their foremost men claim attention.

The circumstances which led to the appointment of George E. Pickett to West Point are of striking interest. Pickett's uncle, Andrew Johnston, of Richmond, in 1841 had legal business with Abraham Lincoln at Springfield, Illinois, and it chanced that by this relationship Mr. Lincoln learned that the lad, whom he had met and liked, desired to be a soldier, and that there was no likelihood of any early vacancy in the cadetships due to Virginia, and at once the friendly interest of the Western lawyer was awakened. It further chanced that at that time Mr. Lincoln's law partner John T. Stuart, had been elected to Congress, and that he had no application for a cadetship from his district. Accordingly, at Mr. Lincoln's request, Young Pickett was nominated as a cadet, and the friendship thus begun lasted until the death of President Lincoln sundered it on earth.

Mrs. Pickett, in her vivid volume *Pickett and His Men*, tells how Mr. Lincoln, visiting Richmond in April, 1865, after its evacuation by the Confederate Government, took pains to call at the residence of his old friend, Andrew Johnston, to inquire after him, and also in a homely way to ask for "George Pickett's wife." The story is made graphic when we recall that "George Pickett" at that very moment was struggling with the ragged remnants of his division against desperate odds in the retreat to Five Forks. And under these circumstances Abraham Lincoln took the baby, which Mrs. Pickett brought with her into the room, in his arms, spoke gracious words to the young mother, and left a kindly message for "George" when he should get back from the front.

A lasting touch of pathos is added to the picture when we pause for a moment to reflect on the fact that this baby, grown long ago to manhood, after years of service in the United States Army, returning on sick leave from the Philippine Islands, in 1911, died at sea—Maj. George Edward Pickett, Jr.

In the class of Pickett at West Point (1846) among other notable soldiers were McClellan and Stonewall Jackson; while among his classmates also were some of the officers who confronted his force in the final charge, such as Lieut. Col. Nelson H. Davis, assistant inspector general on Meade's staff, one of the officers who helped to rally the Union forces at the very point where Pickett's heaviest blows lodged in that culminating struggle; while Generals Gibbon, Griffin, Ayres, and Neill, comrades at the Point, although not in his class, were close at hand.

Pickett, in the critical assault made by Scott's army in the Mexican War, was the first man to raise the Stars and Stripes on the tower of the Castle of Chapultepec, September 13, 1847, winning thereby his brevet captaincy. Longstreet, some years older than Pickett, but then a lieutenant in the same regiment, fell by Pickett's side in the assault, severely wounded, and also winning brevet rank by his gallantry that day. The comradeship between these two ever after was very close and tender.

Pickett was a man of notable figure, erect and commanding, with long hair which curled over his shoulders in auburn ringlets. Socially he was the embodiment of courtesy, cheer, and gallantry.

The brigade commanders of this division of Pickett's were men of mark. Gen. Richard Brooke Garnett had been for twenty-two years, since his graduation at West Point, an officer of distinction in the old army, serving chiefly on the frontier and in the Far West. He was a captain when he resigned to enter the Southern force, in which he established his fame first as a major of artillery and then as a leader of a brigade. On the way to Gettysburg he had been very ill, and had had to ride in an ambulance part of the time. He was so worn and weak on the afternoon of the charge that he could not mount his horse without assistance; but in the crisis he called into his service all his natural self-poise and strength of will, and was the picture of a heroic spirit, as, close up to his advancing line, aided by his staff, and exerting himself to conserve his physical strength and keep his lines well dressed, he rode forth, escaping harm until within a few paces of the stone wall behind which "the enemy" was installed; and here he was shot to death in the very climax of the struggle. The whole brigade was impressed during the tempest of fire that swept upon them by the "cool and handsome bearing" of their commander, as Major Peyton, the surviving field-officer of the brigade, who makes the record in the case, suggestively puts it. One of General Garnett's kinsmen, an officer of ordnance in the battle, has recently written for the *Dial*, of Chicago, an article on the battle, in which he declares that Garnett's body was never recovered.

The Second Brigade in this division was under the orders of Brig. Gen. James Lawson Kemper (1823–1895), a Virginian of rank, educated at the Virginia Military Institute and at Washington College, as it was then called; a trained lawyer; a captain in the Mexican War; for a decade a member of the House of Delegates, and for two years its speaker. He was a soldier of fine repute, and in nearly all the battles in which the Army of Northern Virginia shared he was a noble figure. In the fight at Gettysburg he was desperately wounded, and captured. When he recovered his strength and returned to the field he was made a major general. From January 1, 1874, till January 1, 1878, he was governor of Virginia.

A veteran soldier with twenty-five years of military training and experience to his credit led the Third Brigade, Brig. Gen. Lewis Addison Armistead, born in North Carolina in 1817, the son of one of the distinguished soldiers of the United States Army, Gen. Walker Keith Armistead, who was one of the earliest graduates of the Military Academy, and who rose to the post of chief engineer of the army. The son was anxious also to be a soldier, and served as a cadet at West Point from September, 1834, until February, 1836, when, on account of a tussle in the messroom with a fellow-cadet (later known as Gen. Jubal A. Early, over whose head a plate was broken in the scuffle), young Armistead was sent home. He pleaded month after month for another chance to be a soldier, and at last was appointed a lieutenant, July 10, 1839, reaching in 1855 the captaincy which he resigned to enter the army of Lee in 1861.

In the assault on Chapultepec at the gateway to the city of Mexico Armistead led one of the storming parties, and was the first man to leap into the moat surrounding the fortress and advance against the gate to be broken at that point. Hancock was a lieutenant in the same regiment, and not far away from him was Pickett at the same juncture carrying the United States flag to plant it on the top of the castle.

The deliberate courage of Armistead was proverbial among his former comrades. An incident which illustrates this characteristic is told by a retired officer

of the United States Army, Lieut. Col. A. B. Kauff-
man, at the time a first sergeant under Armistead and
a sharer in the peril involved. The Mojave Indians
had been, in the summer of 1858, making forays in
southern California, butchering or capturing women
and children. An officer who led an expedition
against them with six companies of infantry and two
mountain-guns reported on his return that it would
not be wise to attack the savages with less than a
thousand men. Later, August 4, 1859, Captain
Armistead collected a force of fifty men, half of them
veteran soldiers, and started out on a counter-foray.
At daybreak he attacked the Mojave encampment,
defeated three hundred Indians, scattered the rest to
the four winds, left twenty-three dead on the ground,
and returned to his camp, leaving the Indian problem
for the time settled in that quarter.

At Gettysburg he commanded the admiration of
all who, on both sides of the line, witnessed his leadership. In advance of the charging force at the last
(although he started out in command of the supporting lines), with his hat on his sword, he waved his
men forward, pressing on until he set his feet on the
stone barricade of the Union lines, and there fell
fatally wounded into the hands of men commanded
by his former comrade, Hancock, who in the Mexican
battles fought by his side again and again in the
Sixth Infantry, where, as we have said, they were
both lieutenants.

Among the regimental commanders were noted
men, one of whom, Col. Eppa Hunton, who was
wounded, and whose horse was killed under him,

was a lawyer of rank, later a member of Congress for eight years and for three years a United States Senator from his State of Virginia.

The horror of it all may be stressed by summarizing the loss of leading officers. Two of the three brigade commanders were killed, and one was terribly wounded; every field-officer but one in the division went down, killed or wounded, and among them eight of the most efficient and admirable leaders of regiments furnished by Virginia in the entire war: Colonels R. C. Allen, W. D. Stuart, Lewis B. Williams, W. T. Patton, John C. Owens, James C. Hodges, E. C. Edmonds, and John Bowie Magruder—all killed!

XXXIV

THEN COMETH THE END

IT had been left to the chief of artillery of the First
Confederate Corps, Gen. E. P. Alexander, to indicate the time when the apparent havoc wrought on
the forces in Hancock's command should denote the
opportune moment for Pickett's advance to open.

Longstreet had in vain protested against the project, and was under such pressure of foreboding under
his conviction that a useless slaughter of the best men
in the Confederacy had been ordained by Lee that
he had no voice to give the final command to the
general who had been selected to direct the forlorn
hope, and Pickett, having received word from Alexander to come at once, that the Confederate ammunition was about exhausted, and that if the charge was
to be made it must now be undertaken, saluted Longstreet and said, "I shall move forward, sir." The
corps commander, unable to speak, nodded his head,
and Pickett gallantly rode away to start his forces
forward.

Before starting his men he took a single moment
to draw from his pocket a pencil and a letter, ready
to be sealed, and added a postscript to his sweetheart,
to whom he had told the story of the plan up to that
moment: "If Old Pete's nod [this was the pet-name

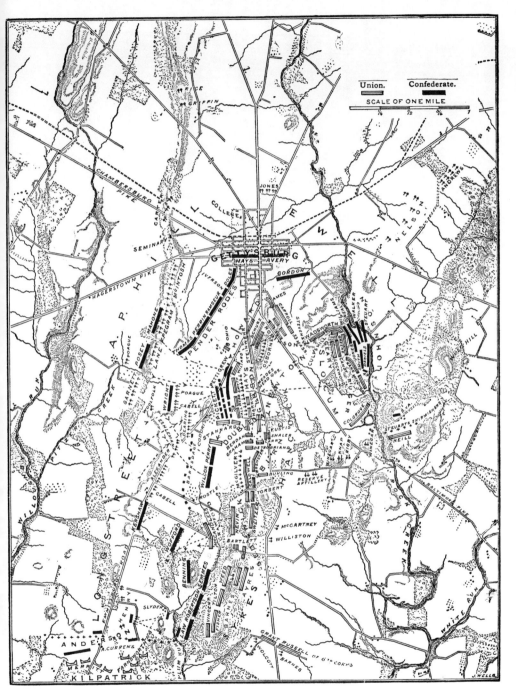

POSITIONS OF FEDERAL AND CONFEDERATE FORCES, JULY 3, ABOUT 4.30 P.M.
(At the climax of the final charge)

THEN COMETH THE END

by which Longstreet had been known familiarly in the old army] means death, then good-by, little one, and God bless you." Then the words, "Forward, guide center!" were heard and repeated down the line, and "March!" followed; and the men, their muskets at a right-shoulder shift, started to execute their desperate adventure.

The scene, as viewed on that sultry, sulphurous July afternoon from Hancock's line, was one of the incomparable tragedies of history, when all the elements of the occasion were considered. The cessation of the Union artillery fire and the partial subsidence of the cannonade on the part of the Confederates, as well as the partial clearing of the atmosphere, had united to give token that the climax of the day was in sight. As we look out over that landscape we see emerging from the distant woods and orchards on Seminary Ridge a line of men in gray and butternut with battle-flags waving and muskets gleaming in the sun. When the first line comes forth from its shelter and aligns its ranks and moves forward, another follows behind, and then another, with steady, determined tread and well-aligned front. There was displayed no sign of impetuous, reckless valor, but a cool, disciplined steadiness which won the admiration of those who beheld the heroic spectacle and will long command the attention of history.

In length from north to south along the ridge as they emerged from their shelter, they occupied three-quarters of a mile, and had to march almost a mile from the wooded ridge behind which for hours they had lain concealed. None of them could see the

321

extent and character of the undertaking with which they had been intrusted until they had covered one-third of the distance across the rolling plain, although some indication of its desperate nature had been conveyed to them before they started. For a time they were screened by the depressions which intervened between the Seminary Ridge and the one in front, crossed diagonally by the road to Emmitsburg. When they reached that elevation the panorama of terror burst on their vision. Up to that hour there had opened for a few brief minutes before their eyes farewell vistas into the Southland, into Virginia, the Carolinas, Alabama, through which the faces of sweetheart, sister, mother, bright with love, for a moment shone; now that vista closed, and the soldiers were smitten breathless with the first awful realization of what was before them, for as these desperate men looked they saw the Union line full two miles in extent, bristling with bayonets and massed with batteries, the latter planted so close together that no space was left for another gun.

Now the men in gray are across the road, where they halt for a few moments in a semi-depression to align their ranks—broken by the effort to tear down fences and to pass other obstacles—and to make a swing so as to bring the whole line parallel, if possible, to the Union position; then they press forward again. Long-range guns occasionally play upon them, and we can see a slight disturbance wrought underneath the shells exploding above them here and there; but it is clear that the artillery is not checking the advance. As one man falls others crowd up to take his place; clouds of smoke obscure the view, but as a puff of air clears away the scene we still see that unwavering, embattled line pressing across the plain.

Round Top, nearly a mile to the south, has begun to enfilade their right flank; the guns on Cemetery Hill have got the range of their center and left flank; the cannon in front have been reinforced by fresh batteries, and shells from these are exploding all about them.

And now upon these gleaming, dusty, steady lines of men holding themselves in serene self-poise, and only showing by their blanched cheeks and an occasional tremor of the lips that they were appalled by the work before them, came a tempest of solid shot, shell, canister, and grape-shot; and a little later, as the Union infantry rose from their extemporized shelter of stone fences, rails, and slight ditches here and there, volleys of musketry mowed down the advancing ranks of Pickett and Pettigrew as the scythe sweeps down the grass, swath by swath, in its resistless motion.

The momentum was broken under the havoc-making Union fire long minutes before the lines came together. A courageous resistance was made by the strong skirmish-line thrown out in front, and by two or three batteries which occupied a post near the Emmitsburg road; and when these were savagely driven back the oncoming forces mistakenly apprehended that an impression had been made on the Union front. But they had not yet touched the main line.

Two or three mounted officers are seen in the assailing ranks, but quickly horse and rider disappear. On the Union side two staff-officers of Hancock and one of Gibbon ride up and down the line regardless of the missiles that fly; wounded, frenzied horses gallop riderless to and fro; caissons are exploding; a fresh battery is hurried to position, and its horses are shot down before the guns can be put in place; Hancock, Gibbon, Hays, and staff-officers by the dozen are giving messages and encouraging the men.

In the very crisis of the battle, as the Confederate forces, crowded together by the exigencies of their advance and by virtue of the flanking fire upon both their wings, came upon Gibbon, General Stannard's Vermont brigade had its great opportunity.

This brigade had spent its time since enlistment in the defenses of Washington; the men marched for seven days over bad roads to arrive at Gettysburg on the evening of July 1st, hearing during the afternoon the noise of battle afar off, but fearing that they might be too late to get a taste of it. Had the ears of these eager men been opened to hear the voice of Fate, perhaps they might have discerned a message on this wise: "Cheer up, Green Mountain Boys! You shall not miss your chance! In the storm of battle a great opportunity shall flash before your vision, and you shall be privileged to strike one of the culminating blows in behalf of the Union. Possess your souls in patience." That opportunity was now at hand.

The Thirteenth, Fourteenth, and Sixteenth regiments on the last day were massed in Doubleday's division, close to Gibbon's lines. As Pickett's men came near that point both Hancock and Stannard, the two happening to be near each other, saw a fine chance for a flank attack on the charging Confederates. Hancock suggested the move, and Stannard was eager to use it.

Above the storm of battle were heard the commands: "*Second Vermont Brigade—change front—forward. . . . Double quick—march!*" And with the coolness and steadiness of battalion drill the regiments wheeled to the right and poured at short range into the Confederate ranks a destructive fire.

At about the same time an equally devastating fire was poured into the left flank of the charging force by the Eighth Ohio, under Lieut. Col. Franklin Sawyer, and a skirmish-line from the One Hundred and Twenty-fifth New York, led by Captain Samuel C. Armstrong (later brigadier general, and still later founder of Hampton Institute), this double pressure crowding both flanks in upon the center.

An advance line was reached in Webb's brigade, where a stone-fence angle gave shelter for a time to the defenders of the Union batteries. Here the pressure created by the seemingly irresistible ranks of Pickett and Pettigrew, which, assailed on both sides by flank and enfilading fire, were crowded together into the apex of a triangle, forced some Union regiments back for a bit, and it appeared that an opening had been made in the main line of the Army of the Potomac. Into and near that apparent opening pressed a gallant remnant, led by Trimble, Armistead, and Garnett, and at the very mouth of the Union cannon, on which some of the Confederates had already laid their hands in the vain confidence that these were now their captured guns, a hand-to-hand encounter took place.

Armistead—facing the old army comrades with whom he had stood shoulder to shoulder at El Molino del Rey sixteen years before—his hat on the top of his sword, and shouting, "Give them cold steel, boys!" falls at the barricade which he tries to surmount, almost at the mouth of the field-piece which stood there, at the very moment when Lieut. Alonzo H. Cushing, Battery A, Fourth Regular Artillery—whose organization had been almost destroyed in the fight —cried to Hancock, chancing to be at his side, "I'll give them a final blast." Then the gallant youth drew the lanyard with one hand, while with the other he sought to hold his own body together for the moment to keep it from collapsing, as, disemboweled, he falls dead at the post he had held so well, and near him Meade, Gibbon, and other leaders direct the whirlwind and regulate the storm—while the cannoneers, their ammunition exhausted, their guns dismantled, and their caissons exploding behind them, spring to the mouth of their pieces and beat the enemy back with rammer and sponge-staff.

And then over the hill from behind Hancock's line rushed other batteries into the faces of the assailants, along with fresh troops which had been massed by the thousand along the Taneytown road ready for this very emergency.

Then, at last, the Confederates are stayed in their onset. They have done all that martial valor can accomplish. As General Sorrel, Longstreet's assist-

ATTACK OF PICKETT'S AND PETTIGREW'S DIVISIONS

(From a print of the time)

ant adjutant general, describes it: "We broke, tearing back pell-mell, torn by shot and shell, across the width of that bloody plain, a sight never before witnessed— part of the Army of Northern Virginia in full, breath- less flight."

Flanked on the right and on the left, lines of skir- mishers going out to gather them in, their cause lost, their hopes blighted, their generals dead or dying, their flags captured, hundreds fling themselves to the ground to escape the tempest of fire that sweeps the field, or turn to the rear in the despairing hope of making escape across the plain over which they had come so proudly an hour before.

And thus, half surrounded, flags taken, officers fallen, leaders nearly all dead or dying or captured, hundreds biting the dust in the effort to escape the tornado from hell that lays waste the field, the Union troops gathering prisoners by the thousands, and only the forlorn remnant that had not reached the front able to escape—thus, in unspeakable disaster, the charge of Pickett and Pettigrew, the last forlorn effort of Lee to smite into defeat and despair the army of Meade, thus the effort came to an end, and the great charge took its place in the pages of history, an enduring picture of courage, of unavailing hero- ism, of surpassing martial splendor, excelled only by the spectacle afforded years afterward, when on this same spot hundreds of survivors of the awful struggle met and greeted one another in glorious friendship, shook hands across the stone fence which had been stained in Sixty-three by the blood of two armies, looked with tearful vision on the Stars and Stripes waving above them, symbol of a reunited nation, and blended their voices in song, as they sent out over the battle-field the hymn:

Our father's God, to thee,
Author of Liberty,
To thee we sing!
Long may our land be bright,
With Freedom's holy light,
Protect us by Thy might,
Great God, our King!

XXXV

WE do not care to reopen the discussion concerning Lee's retreat, Meade's over-cautious pursuit, and the final escape of the Army of Northern Virginia across the Potomac, although the facts in the case may be briefly summarized. Hancock and Butterfield urged upon the Union commander an immediate advance against Lee's army on Friday afternoon, at the end of the assault made by Pickett and Pettigrew. Meade was afraid—that is the term—to risk an advance in view of the circumstances—the strong line still held by his opponent, occupied by a hundred guns, and by thousands of men who had not taken part in the charge; the field in front covered with dead and wounded by the thousand; the possibilities of a reverse; the exhausted condition of the Army of the Potomac; and the traditional specter of Lee's transcendent generalship, from the spell of which thus far no one in the Union forces had as yet been able to escape. It may be taken for granted that a counterstroke in front, an attempt at once to follow up the remnant of the assaulting divisions, might not have been wise; but surely an advance from the Round Top region made by a strong body of cavalry and urged by the Fifth and Sixth corps could have turned the right flank of Lee, occupied the Fairfield road, and created confusion and panic in his rear, had it been undertaken promptly. However, the work already done was so great that Meade dreaded to endanger it by an assault which might become a reverse, and a heavy rain that night and on the next day made an engagement just then out of the question.

Meanwhile Lee, waiting behind his fortified Seminary Ridge, where he had concentrated his remaining troops to receive an attack should one be ventured upon, prepared to retreat, and late in the afternoon of the Fourth of July sent forth his trains toward the two nearest passes through the South Mountain Range—by Fairfield and Cashtown—and although threatened by the advancing Sixth Corps, and by the Union cavalry which did serious damage to the trains laden with supplies, ammunition, and wounded, contrived to reach Hagerstown, Maryland, in the evening of July 6th and the morning of July 7th, to find the Potomac River swollen with floods, and the pontoon bridge on which he had planned to cross partially destroyed by an expedition sent by General French, from Frederick, during the battle at Gettysburg. When Meade's army, on the 10th, reached its place confronting its adversary, it was found that Lee was occupying a range of hills near Hagerstown affording a position of extraordinary strength, which he had made still more formidable by skilful fortifications. This front, which covered the pontoon bridges at Falling Waters and the ford at Williamsport—neither place being available as yet, however, the river being too high to be forded, and the bridges not yet being repaired—was surveyed as closely as possible by Meade, Warren, and Humphreys, and their united judgment was that its flanks could not be turned, and that it presented no vulnerable points. President Lincoln, Halleck, and Secretary Stanton, however, urged upon Meade the necessity of destroying Lee's army, which at the distance of Washington looked like an easy task, that army being almost surrounded, its ammunition depleted, the river in its rear at a flood, the pontoons wrecked—"Why not close in on it now and annihilate it?" That was the inevitable question. Meade desired to carry out the injunctions of his superiors; he ordered his corps commanders to make a reconnaissance in force all along the line, and endeavor to find a weak point in Lee's front where an attack might break through. The position, however, was of such tremendous and portentous strength that the corps commanders were almost unanimously opposed to an advance movement, and the plan was called off for twenty-four hours, and then was held in abeyance for another day on account of storm and fog; and when finally, on the morning of July 14th, the Union forces advanced it was discovered that Lee's army had escaped during the previous night, in part by the extemporized pontoon bridges, and in part by the ford.

Major General Humphreys, chief of staff to Meade at that time, and one of the most skilful and heroic soldiers of the army, declared after careful inspection of the position repeatedly made not only at the time, but afterward, that the intrenchments at Fredericksburg in the battle of December, 1862—where he had led three desperate charges on Marye Heights all in vain—"were not more formidable than those of Williamsport," and declared that an assault by Meade at that point "would have resulted disastrously." Accordingly remembering the fruitless assaults made under Grant in 1864, we may be grateful that the victory at Gettysburg was not frustrated by an attempt at Williamsport to storm a position which was too strong to be victoriously assailed.

It is a singular coincidence that each leader, soon after the escape of the Confederate army, sought to be relieved from command: Meade, stung and mortified by Halleck's censure, spoken in behalf of Lincoln; and Lee, burdened by the sense of failure, and imploring that some stronger and younger man might be found to lead the Army of Northern Virginia. Fortunately for the final fame of both commanders, their requests were not heeded, and they were permitted to hold their posts until their work was done.

THE LOSSES

Army of the Potomac: The official statement is as given here: killed, 3,155; wounded, 14,529; captured or missing, 5,365; total, 23,049. The list of killed was increased during the weeks after the battle by the number of fatally wounded who died from their injuries, making an aggregate of killed, 5,091. This would make a total Union loss of 24,985.

Army of Northern Virginia: killed, 2,592; wounded, 12,709; missing, 5,150; total, 20,451.

In comparing these data it must be recalled that by Lee's orders none of those who were but slightly wounded were reported in the lists. Further, many were actually killed or wounded who were simply counted as "missing" in the lists officially reported. There were 12,227 captured by the Union Army; of these 6,802 were wounded, and out of this number 2,810 died. No return of the fatally wounded who died during Lee's retreat was ever made. When Lee's figures are modified by a consideration of all the facts in the case it will be evident that the losses were nearly equal.

PART THREE

THE OPPOSING ARMIES — EN MASSE AND IN DETAIL

WITH BRIEF PERSONAL MEMORANDA, STATISTICS, ILLUSTRATIVE DATA, AND COMMENTS

I

WEST POINT AT GETTYSBURG

(*A*) GRADUATES OF THE MILITARY ACADEMY IN THE ARMY OF THE POTOMAC

WITH regard to the share which West Point had in the entire struggle of 1861–65, Gen. George W. Cullum, editor of the *Biographical Register* of the Military Academy, furnishes the authoritative data. In 1861, according to the official estimates, there were 1,245 graduates alive; added to this list the classes which received diplomas during the war made up an aggregate of 1,448. Out of this number 197 officers in the army and 99 from civil life—counting in the few who in 1861 and 1862 upon graduation cast their fortunes in with those of the Confederacy—made up the muster-roll of 296 graduates in all who served in the Southern armies.

On the other hand, there were graduates as follows who served the Union:

From the old army	636
From civil life	110
From classes '61 to '64	190
Total	936

In addition there were scores of officers who had been living in retirement, advanced in years, not fit for active service, but who rendered in various ways efficient labors to the cause of the nation. Thus the list of graduates in the service of the Union during those years of struggle probably reached nearly a round thousand. Of the entire number of those in the Union armies General Cullum says one-fifth laid down their lives and one-third were wounded in defense of their country's flag.

These graduates were distributed far and wide in the armies of the United States during the war. Heretofore no effort has

GETTYSBURG

been made, so far as we are aware, to make up a published list of all West Point graduates who were present in any one great battle. In view of that fact the list we have compiled in this volume, for both armies, in regard to Gettysburg, has, we judge, peculiar value. Diligent search through Cullum's *Biographical Register*, and Heitman's *Historical Register and Dictionary of the United States Army*, and the published lists of students of the Academy from the beginning, has been made, and it is believed that the list we have undertaken to make is accurate and complete. Summarized, the category stands thus for the Army of the Potomac:

> *The Commanders in Chief and Corps Leaders:* Hooker, Meade, Reynolds, Doubleday, Newton, Hancock, Wm. Hays, Sykes, Sedgwick, Howard, Slocum, Pleasanton 12
>
> *Division Commanders:* Gibbon, Alex. Hays, Humphreys, Barnes, Griffin, Ayres, Wright, Howe, Ames, Ruger, Buford, D. M. Gregg, Kilpatrick 13
>
> *Brigade Commanders:* Paul, Webb, Hall, Carroll, Day, Burbank, Weed, Garrard, Torbert, Russell, Neill, Eustis, Lockwood, Greene, Merritt, Custer 16
>
> *Engineer Department:* Warren (chief engineer), Mackenzie, Benham, Haupt, Pettes, Mendell, Turnbull, Reese, Barlow, Gillespie, Howell, Cross 12
>
> *Signal Corps:* Nicodemus. *Ordnance:* Flagler, Edie, Schaff 4
>
> *Headquarters Staff:* Williams, Schriver, Davis, Ingalls, Sawtelle, Clarke, Patrick 7
>
> *Other Staff - officers:* Bankhead, Morgan, Poland, Ryan, Kent, Platt, Beaumont, Andrews, Best, Norris, McQuesten 11
>
> *Artillery:* Chief, Hunt; commander of reserve, Tyler; brigade commander, Tidball, and battery officers 20
>
> *Cavalry* officers, 10; *Infantry* officers, 14; total . 24
>
> Aggregate 119

The order in which the names occur follows the army-corps designation usually, except that the lists of officers in batteries

and in the infantry and cavalry regiments are arranged alpha-
betically.

It does not require much insight to discern that the posts
occupied by this array of educated officers in the campaign and
battle were pivotal and fundamental in their relation to the
organization, activity, and efficiency of the Army of the Potomac.
Moreover, a little study in the case will suggest how large a part
of the work done at Gettysburg and the victory wrought there
is due to the efficiency of the West Point graduates, who occupied
so many places of vast responsibility in the army in which they
served.

THE ARMY COMMANDER AND THE CORPS
LEADERS

The Commanding General:—GEORGE GORDON MEADE

General Meade,[1] who led the Army of the Potomac from June
28, 1863, until the work of that embattled host was finally done,
and its fame had become historic in the early summer of 1865,
was born December 31, 1815, in Cadiz, Spain, where his parents
were then residing, his father being naval agent for the United
States, and at the same time engaged in business there. In 1820
the family came back to this country, and after some years spent
in Washington returned to their long-time home in Philadelphia.

Young Meade was graduated from the West Point Military
Academy, and appointed a brevet second lieutenant of artillery
July 1, 1835. After spending two years in the war with the
Seminoles he resigned to enter Government service as a civil
engineer in a survey of the Mississippi Delta, the Texas boundary, and the northeastern boundary of the United States. In
1842 he re-entered the army as a lieutenant of topographical engineers; he rendered service in the military occupation of Texas
and in the Mexican War, winning his first brevet—that of first
lieutenant—"for gallant conduct in the several conflicts at
Monterey," to date from September 23, 1846, and receiving
praise from Generals Taylor, Worth, and Scott for his courage
and skill, as shown in the field and engineering operations through
which he had served.

Meade was occupied during the period between the close of the

[1] A sketch of Maj. Gen. Joseph Hooker has been already given
in the opening section of Part Two.

GETTYSBURG

Mexican War and the outbreak of the Rebellion in the construction of light-houses, and the geodetic survey of the northern lake region, which for four years was under his personal direction, attaining his captaincy in 1856. Captain Meade was made brigadier general August 31, 1861, and placed in command of one of the brigades of the then organizing division of Pennsylvania Reserves, Brig. Gen. John F. Reynolds being in command of one of the other brigades; thus these two men, who won their first brevets at Monterey, but had not served together since that time, now had a chance to get acquainted; they quickly found themselves closely intimate, although Reynolds was, so far as graduation at the Point was concerned, six years junior to Meade. They grew up together in the Army of the Potomac, counseling and supporting each other, and acquiring military experience and prestige in similar increments.

General Meade developed his capacities for service in the field without a break or a misfortune, being promoted from brigade to division command, and then to the head of the Fifth Army Corps; he was severely wounded at Glendale, on the Peninsula; after Chancellorsville, and the singular collapse of Hooker, at the very time when victory should have been within reach, Meade was one of the four men under consideration as possible commanders of the Army of the Potomac, should a change become necessary, Couch, Reynolds, and Hancock being the other three, particularly Reynolds, whom Meade would have been glad to see thus recognized.

Meade became major general of volunteers November 29, 1862; brigadier general, U.S.A., to date from his victory at Gettysburg, July 3, 1863; and major general U.S.A., August 18, 1864, the latter recognition being in view of his strenuous and skilful work of that dreadful battle summer. From the opening of the Wilderness campaign, May 14, 1864, down to the collapse of Lee's army, April, 1865, the presence of Grant with the Army of the Potomac, although Meade was continued at its head and Grant's orders usually went through him to the forces employed, was a complication and an embarrassment to all concerned. The judgment of many who had an inside view of the situation at that time is that it would have been much better for Meade to have been untrammeled by the presence of the commander in chief; that certain things could not have happened, and certain policies would not have been followed, had Meade been absolute master of the situation. Still, after long delay, dreadful front assaults, and consequent appalling losses, in due time Grant's sledge-hammer blows were modified, and through his attrition plans victory came at last; and history records the fact that in association with Grant George G. Meade was the man who led the Army of the Potomac to its crowning triumph.

A cruel blow was allowed to fall on Meade a little later, an instance of inequity which can never be extenuated or wiped out, when he was overslaughed by the advancement of Sheridan, his junior in many ways, and his inferior in the largest sense (except as a terrific fighter on the field, where Sheridan stood almost alone as an incarnation of martial fury and insight), to the vacated post of lieutenant general of the army, a crowning honor which was due to Meade as the senior major general, as the long-time commander of the Army of the Potomac, as the victor of Gettysburg, and as the one man whose complete record and culminating services denoted him as beyond comparison, among the generals then surviving, worthy to rank next to Grant and Sherman. It was Grant's inordinate partisanship for Sheridan which prompted him as soon as he became President to make this promotion, which was an unspeakable humiliation—indeed, almost a death-blow—to Meade's high-strung and sensitive soul.

General Meade in his personal appearance was the embodiment of knightly and scholarly leadership; he was tall and rather spare, and, in spite of a slight stoop of the shoulders, endowed with a commanding mien; his piercing eye, Roman nose, dignified presence, pallid complexion, full and rather straggly beard, and quick, alert habit, giving token of the salient phases of his character. He had, however, a nervous nature which was easily disturbed, and a temper which when aroused was imperious; but when the storm of battle raged, and in critical moments when something had to be done with lightning-like celerity, this quick, passionate, furious habit of his became an added element of power in bringing things to pass. Meade lacked the personal magnetism which sends thrills of fervor and enthusiasm through great masses of men; he never stooped to play to the galleries, and yet his army trusted him even in advance of the triumphant hour when he demonstrated his ability to lead it to victory. Perhaps we may not yet be able to indicate in the corridors of generalship and fame his exact niche; but it can never be forgotten that he was able to sustain himself at the head of the Army of the Potomac for nearly two years, and was the one leader who proved himself able finally to cope with Lee.

GETTYSBURG

The Commander of the Left Wing: — JOHN FULTON
REYNOLDS

This officer, born in Lancaster, Pennsylvania, in 1820, upon graduation in 1842 entered the artillery, where he won brevets as captain and major in the war with Mexico; in 1860 he was stationed at West Point as commandant of cadets and instructor in tactics. As brigadier general in 1861 he was assigned to a brigade in the Pennsylvania reserves, which notable body of troops he commanded a little later, with the added rank of major general. He steadily won distinction in military circles from the opening of the contest, although he had no opportunity on the field in any great battle to show adequately what was in him, being in the reserve at Chancellorsville, and called to Pennsylvania by Governor Curtin during the Antietam campaign to organize and command the Pennyslvania militia in that period of alarm and peril. Still his fellow-officers had insight to discover in him what they reckoned to be the genius of a great commander, and had they been allowed to vote, and had he been willing, when Hooker was removed, by an almost unanimous choice he would have been selected as the one notable soldier fit to command the Army of the Potomac. He was modest, generous, highly equipped with professional knowledge and experience, beloved by his men, and trusted by the Government. It was, however, by his own distinct approval that in the hour of need the lot fell upon Meade, and not upon himself, although he might have had the chief command could he have secured the assurance that the army would really be under his direction, untrammeled by its close connection with the War Department at Washington. Like Meade, he went from the head of a brigade to the Pennsylvania reserves to command the division, and then, November 29, 1862, he took the First Army Corps, which he commanded until June 29, 1863, when he was put in command of the advanced wing of the army, made up of his own corps along with the Third and the Eleventh; in exercising that command and posting his men in the opening hour of the infantry fight at Gettysburg he was instantly killed.

Thus, defending his native State, occupying the foremost place in a critical hour of danger, all his abilities and devotion, with his superb qualities as a man and a general, became at once pinnacled for all time in full view of the world. By his early and heroic death he was lifted into enduring fame.

WEST POINT AT GETTYSBURG

THE CORPS COMMANDERS

First Army Corps:—(1) ABNER DOUBLEDAY

Maj. Gen. Abner Doubleday (1819–1893), a native of New York, was graduated from the Academy in 1842; he served until 1861 in the artillery, taking part in several battles in Mexico, and showing his gallantry and patriotism in Forts Moultrie and Sumter during the stirring time which immediately preceded the outbreak of the Civil War. Approaching Gettysburg he commanded the Third Division, First Corps, and succeeded Reynolds at the head of the corps when the latter directed the advancing wing of the army.

Doubleday, by the death of Reynolds, was unexpectedly left in command of the field of conflict to the northwest of the town, where all day long with skill and energy he carried on the fight against steadily increasing opposition. Howard, misapprehending the situation, and not having the chance to see what was actually going on under Doubleday, remarked to Hancock, when the latter arrived, that the "First Corps had given way." Hancock wrote the news to Meade, who offhand adjudged Doubleday unequal to the responsibilities of the command of a corps, and that night sent Newton to relieve Doubleday from his post. In so far as this change involved the thought that Doubleday had in conducting the fight on the first day showed himself in any way inadequate to the work assigned, it was a piece of injustice which left Doubleday for months sore-hearted and outraged. He was relieved from command, with his own consent, and given work in Washington.

It may be worth while to record here that the misunderstanding was relieved later. In April, 1864, just before the opening of the Wilderness campaign, as related to us by one who was present, Maj. E. P. Halstead, a long-time staff-officer of Doubleday, the latter was visited by Meade in Washington. In this interview Meade expressed his sense of the injustice which had been unintentionally perpetrated, and spoke his sincere wish that in the approaching campaign of the Army of the Potomac Doubleday might be willing to accept an appropriate command in that army once more. It was not deemed well at that time for Doubleday to be relieved from duty in Washington, but the wound, at any rate, was healed.

Doubleday's *Chancellorsville and Gettysburg*, in the " Campaigns

GETTYSBURG

of the Civil War" series, is a valuable work, barring its occasional sneers at Howard, which, in view of the facts as we have indicated them, are not to be wondered at. Doubleday was brevetted brigadier general and major general, U.S.A., in 1865, for "gallant and meritorious conduct during the rebellion."

First Army Corps:—(2) JOHN NEWTON

The prophecy afforded in the case of this officer, when, in July, 1842, he was graduated from the Academy number two in a class of fifty-six and assigned to the corps of engineers, was amply fulfilled in his whole career. Born in Norfolk, Virginia, in 1823, he grew to be recognized as one of the great engineers of the age, constructing fortifications, improving harbors, and demolishing obstructions to navigation—the removal of the "Hell Gate" ledges, which had been for a century a menace to ships entering or departing from the harbor of New York, being one of his greatest achievements, in connection with his labors in building the forts which defend that harbor, and his professional labors as Chief of Engineers, U.S.A., which crowned his career. He was brevetted lieutenant colonel of engineers for his gallantry at Antietam, and colonel for services at Gettysburg, and brigadier general for the Atlanta campaign, and major general for meritorious services in the field during the Rebellion. He had been in command of a division in the Sixth Corps for months previous to the battle of Gettysburg, when he was promoted to the leadership of the First Corps, on July 2d. General Newton died in 1895.

Second Army Corps:—(1) WINFIELD SCOTT HANCOCK

This unsurpassed corps commander was born in Pennsylvania in 1824, and on graduation from the Military Academy, 1844, entered the infantry; he won his first brevet in the battles in front of the City of Mexico in August, 1847, and became captain in the quartermaster department in 1855, serving on the frontier and in California; brigadier general, September 23, 1861; major general, November 29, 1862; brigadier in the Regular Army, August 12, 1864; brevet major general, U.S.A., for gallantry at Spottsylvania, and full major general in the Regular Army in 1866. The story of his services would form an essential part of the record of the Army of the Potomac. He was sent, as has been already indicated, in advance by Meade to report the situation at Gettysburg on the afternoon of the first day; he helped to reorganize the forces after the reverse of that day; he aided in checking the tide of disaster on the second day, and in annihilating Pickett's charge on the last day, in the midst of which action he was severely wounded. He was one of the most remarkable men on the field of battle America ever produced; endowed with a majestic physique, extraordinary martial insight, and personal magnetism of an unusual sort—indeed, there was no quality which a corps commander needs in order to be perfect in his function which was denied to this distinguished fighter. Whether he would have ranked high in command of an army, whether he possessed the lofty scientific attainments, the broad technical accomplishments which an army commander requires for his highest success, may be doubted; but we judge that he was never surpassed in the history of American warfare in respect of the skill, courage, military intuitions, and varied qualities needed by the commander of an army corps. He was the unsuccessful candidate of the Democratic Party for the presidency in the fall of 1880. His death occurred in 1886.

Second Army Corps:—(2) WILLIAM HAYS

When Hancock was wounded, late in the engagement of the last day, he asked Brig. Gen. J. C. Caldwell, of the First Division of the Second Corps, to assume command. It seemed good to General Meade to assign Brig. Gen. William Hays to this post instead of General Caldwell, who returned that evening to his division. Hays was a member of the class of 1840; in the Mexican War he won brevets of captain and major, and was wounded in the engagement at Molino del Rey; from a captaincy in the Second Artillery he was appointed to a staff position involving the rank of lieutenant colonel in 1861, reaching the rank of brigadier general in the following year, in which capacity he commanded a brigade in the Second Corps at Fredericksburg and Chancellorsville, where he was captured. He had just returned from his imprisonment in the South and rejoined the Army of the Potomac when this opportunity occurred, and he assumed command of the Second Army Corps, holding the post until September 13th following, when Warren assumed the place. General Hays was a man of singular personal courage, fine leadership, and high character. After the war, in which he won five promotions by brevet or otherwise, he served as major, Fifth Artillery, until his death in 1875.

GETTYSBURG

Fifth Army Corps:—GEORGE SYKES

Major General Sykes, born in Delaware in 1822, and appointed to West Point from Maryland, was graduated in 1842, and won a brevet captaincy at Cerro Gordo; he spent years in dangerous service among the Indians on the plains, making two long expeditions into Texas and New Mexico. In 1861 he had reached the post of major, Third Infantry, when he was made a brigadier general to command a brigade of Regular Infantry, winning a brevet colonelcy in the battle of Gaines's Mill, and reaching the rank of major general of volunteers, November 29, 1862. When Meade became commander of the army, Sykes, who had been at the head of the Division of Regulars for some months, was assigned to direct the corps. He won the brevet rank of brigadier general in the Regular Army for gallant and meritorious services at Gettysburg, and the higher brevet rank at the end of the war. His work in leading and directing the movements of his corps on the left in aid of the troops fighting for the safety of Round Top, Thursday afternoon, was of great value. General Sykes died in 1880.

Sixth Army Corps:—JOHN SEDGWICK

Major General Sedgwick's nickname, in common use by the army, suggests some of the kindly qualities of this noble officer —"Uncle John" Sedgwick. He was a tremendous fighter as well as a manly, heroic, gentle-hearted, straightforward soldier, not particularly gifted for independent command, but intelligent, obedient, enterprising, and loyal as a corps commander. He was born in Connecticut, September 13, 1813, and graduated from West Point in 1837 into the artillery. He learned some of the duties of an officer while fighting the Seminoles in Florida, and others scouting along the Canadian frontier, and later in the Mexican War, where he served his battery so handsomely that he rose to be both captain and major by brevet for his gallantry in that conflict. When Robert E. Lee resigned the colonelcy of the First Cavalry, in 1861, Sedgwick became his successor in that post, and later in the year he was made a brigadier general, and next year a major general. He was one of McClellan's division commanders on the Peninsula, was wounded at Glendale and again at Antietam; when he recovered he was advanced to lead the Ninth Corps, and then finally the Sixth. His magnificent conduct when left to fight for his life

344

at Salem Church, while Hooker at Chancellorsville, six miles away, stood still and kept his army in the leash lest it might fall on Lee and get entangled in a fight, was a test and a revelation of Sedgwick's courage and skill. His forces at Gettysburg were held in reserve; the best students of the battle now think they might have been hurled to advantage upon the discomfited forces of Lee when Pickett's charge failed. However, Sedgwick was sent after the retreating foe, and it was not Sedgwick's fault that no serious attack was made during the withdrawal. He was killed at Spottsylvania while posting his artillery, May 9, 1864. When at West Point, October 28, 1868, George William Curtis spoke one of his noblest orations in commemoration of Sedgwick, the orator wisely and truly said: "This almost ideal American soldier had all the cardinal soldierly qualities, the positive masculine, manly traits, but with them that depth of tenderness and sweet humor which complete the finest natures."

Eleventh Army Corps:—OLIVER OTIS HOWARD

Major General Howard was Maine's chief contribution to the military service of the Union during the Civil War. He was born in that State November 8, 1830, finished his college course in Bowdoin College, and in 1854 was graduated from West Point. He served in the ordnance department, and as professor of mathematics at West Point till the outbreak of the War, when he accepted the colonelcy of the Third Maine, and on September 3, 1861, the post of brigadier general. He did brave service on the Peninsula; lost an arm at Fair Oaks; became major general November 29, 1862, and took part in the battles and movements of the Army of the Potomac until September, 1863, when he went with the Eleventh Corps, which he had commanded since April 1st, to join the army of Grant and Sherman at Chattanooga. From that time he was one of Sherman's best men, commanding the Army of the Tennessee, May 3d to December 21, 1864, and having part in the movements under Sherman till Johnston surrendered and the war was over.

He won the brevet of major general, U.S.A., for gallantry during the campaign against Atlanta. At Gettysburg, by the death of Reynolds, he was left in command of the field and of the operations of the first day; and, although he has been criticized, yet the final judgment will be, we doubt not, that he served the best interests of the army and the nation by his policy and deeds that day.

345

For some years after peace returned he had charge of the Freed-men's Bureau. He died in 1909.

His volume of *Reminiscences* and other occasional volumes are creditable productions. From early manhood he was a devoted Christian and an active worker in religious services, and on the platform outspoken as a witness for Christ. Efforts have been made to depreciate his military ability on that account, but without success.

Twelfth Army Corps:—HENRY WARNER SLOCUM

Major General Slocum, born in New York, 1827, was graduated from West Point July 1, 1852, entering the First Artillery, in which he served for two years in the hostilities against the Seminoles, and then in Fort Moultrie until October 31, 1856, when he resigned to enter the profession of law. He was for one year a member of the New York House of Representatives, and meanwhile gave two years of service to the militia as instructor in artillery, with the rank of colonel. On May 21, 1861, he accepted the command of the Twenty-seventh New York Volunteers, in leading which organization he was badly wounded at Bull Run; was promoted to be brigadier general August, 1861, and major general July 4, 1862; served on the Peninsula and in the second Bull Run campaign; he led the Twelfth Corps from October 15, 1862, until April 13, 1864, and was in command of the Army of Georgia under Sherman, in the Atlanta campaign and in the March to the Sea, till the end.

After the war he stood high as a counselor-at-law in Brooklyn, served three terms in Congress, and rendered services of a very valuable type to the city of which he was by rights the first citizen, as president of the Brooklyn Board of Public Works. He died in 1894.

His combined prudence and courage, his reserve stock of knowledge and fidelity, and his capacity to meet an unexpected situation with readiness and skill gave him high standing in the army. At Gettysburg he commanded the right wing for a little while, held the region at Culp's Hill with an invincible grip, and so directed his men that, in spite of the several bloody assaults made upon his position and their temporary success, that part of the field finally remained in Union hands.

The Cavalry Corps:—ALFRED PLEASANTON

Maj. Gen. Alfred Pleasanton (born in Washington, D. C., in 1824, graduated in 1844; entered the dragoons; brevetted for gallantry in two battles in the Mexican War), after long service on the frontier and the Pacific coast, had become a captain in the Second Cavalry in 1861; was made brigadier general in 1862, and major general June 22, 1863, two weeks after he had been promoted to the command of the entire cavalry force of the Army of the Potomac. He was brevetted lieutenant colonel, U.S.A., for services at Antietam; his work at Gettysburg gave him the brevet of colonel, and two higher brevets followed later. In 1868 he resigned from the army; for a while he was collector of internal revenue, and then president of a railroad company. He died in 1897.

HEADQUARTERS STAFF

It is difficult for those who have not had the opportunity to study the operations of an army in war-time to apprehend the worth of the service rendered to the commander in chief by a corps of well-trained staff-officers such as was stationed at the headquarters of the Army of the Potomac, where some of the most competent, alert, and industrious men ever graduated from the Point were on duty. Their work was for the most part incorporated in the mass; in no case is it possible to indicate the individual component which each man may have contributed toward the results achieved in any single campaign or in the final victory; a reference is made now and then by the commander, and a general acknowledgment is noted, or a brevet or two may be awarded —that is all the recognition they get in the very nature of things. But it is worth while to say here that the work of the staff-officers at Gettysburg was of the very highest order, measured by the best standards of military efficiency, and that the men in question, whose record we are now to glance at, were made capable of rendering this magnificent service chiefly because, in view of their natural aptitudes, they were thoroughly equipped for their special tasks by the training which they received at West Point. To the alma mater of these men, therefore, there is due the amplest recognition.

The Adjutant General:—SETH WILLIAMS

Gen. Seth Williams, born in Maine, graduated 1842, brevetted captain First Artillery for gallantry at Cerro Gordo, enjoyed peculiar opportunities of equipment for his special duties in his earlier training as adjutant at the Military Academy for three years, and as assistant for six years in the adjutant general's office at Washington. This training, imparted to a temperament and character peculiarly fitted to deal with the peculiarly delicate and responsible tasks and problems which arise at the headquarters of an army in an active campaign, helped to make him an ideal officer for the position which he occupied. General Meade, with whom he served so long, and who had such intimate relations with him, in the order announcing his death (General Williams died March 23, 1866, in his prime, at the age of forty-four) used the following language, and doubtless the men who had preceded Meade in commanding the Army of the Potomac—McClellan, Burnside, and Hooker—would have gladly underwritten the testimony: "There was hardly an engagement in which he did not take part; there is not a portion of the records or written history of the Army of the Potomac which does not bear witness to his ability and fidelity; and to its officers and soldiers he was specially endeared by a never-failing patience and kindliness of heart that made no labor irksome, that could promote their interests and welfare."

The War Department indicated its appreciation of the services rendered by General Williams at Gettysburg by the brevet rank of colonel; in addition he received the brevet rank of major general of volunteers to date from August 1, 1864, for services "from Gettysburg to Petersburg," and then at the end he was brevetted brigadier general, United States Army, for "gallant and meritorious conduct in the field during the rebellion." We have therefore good cause to keep in mind, to use the words of General Meade once more, "the public career and the private virtues of this distinguished soldier."

The Inspector General:—EDMUND SCHRIVER

This veteran officer, born in Pennsylvania, appointed from New York, graduated 1833, after serving six years in the artillery and seven in the adjutant general's office in Washington went into civil life and railroad employment, returning to the army as lieutenant colonel Eleventh Infantry in 1861. After a year or two of special services at the headquarters of the First Army Corps he became a colonel and inspector general of the Army of the Potomac, March 13, 1863. After the battle of Gettysburg he was especially honored by being made the representative of the victorious army to convey to the War Department details of the engagement and thirty-one captured battle-flags and other trophies. In 1865 he was brevetted brigadier general and major general for distinguished services in the field during the Rebellion. Died February 10, 1899.

MAJ. NELSON H. DAVIS, class of 1846, assistant inspector general, served as one of Meade's most confidential and efficient staff-officers throughout the campaign and battle, his "gallant and meritorious services" in the engagement bringing him the brevet rank of lieutenant colonel. Other brevets for service in the Mexican War and bravery in Indian warfare and for his work throughout the civil conflict were also conferred; he became inspector general in the Regular Army in 1885, with the rank of brigadier general, with which he was retired that year. He died May 15, 1890.

The Chief Quartermaster:—RUFUS INGALLS

General Ingalls, born in Maine, graduated 1843, and brevetted for gallantry in the war with Mexico, served in the dragoons till 1848, when he entered the quartermaster's department. He was in the defense of Fort Pickens, April–July, 1861; was appointed lieutenant colonel and aide-de-camp late that year, and was chief quartermaster for the Army of the Potomac from the very beginning, remaining in that post till the war was over. He was made a brigadier general May 23, 1863, and was brevetted four times, ending with the rank of major general for "meritorious and distinguished services" during the war. On February 23, 1882, he was appointed by President Grant to be quartermaster general of the army. He died in 1893. Charles A. Dana, who knew him well, wrote at the time of his decease: "There was no more valuable and competent service rendered to the cause of the Union than that of Rufus Ingalls. He refused to recognize difficulties and surmounted them often in a marvelous fashion. Grant once said of him: 'Ingalls in command of men would, in my opinion, have become a great and famous general. If the command of the Army of the Potomac had ever become vacant, I would have given it to Ingalls.'"

In the Gettysburg campaign General Ingalls had four thousand wagons and more than twelve thousand horses, which had to be cared for in the rear, guarded against raids, and yet kept at such a convenient distance from the army as to be serviceable with supplies when these were needed. The trains were not seen by the troops; not a wagon or horse was lost (the captures made by Stuart in his raid were taken from trains on the way from Washington to Ingalls, and many miles from the point where his jurisdiction over them began). Not an hour's delay occurred through scarcity of supplies, and throughout the campaign ample portions of forage, clothing, and other impedimenta were always within reach. Ingalls was a man of extraordinary administrative capacity and military attainments, a great patriot, and a most lovable man.

Assistant Chief Quartermaster:—CHARLES G. SAWTELLE

Lieut. Col. Charles G. Sawtelle, born in Maine, 1834, graduated 1854, served in the Sixth Infantry till the outbreak of the war, when he became captain and assistant quartermaster. As assistant chief quartermaster of the Army of the Potomac he superintended the stupendous task of removing the supplies and stores of various sorts from Acquia Creek Landing, which had been in use for six months as the storehouse of the army, when the forces started northward in June from Falmouth; and then he undertook successfully the mission of forwarding supplies from Washington to the army en route. He was afterward brevetted major, lieutenant colonel, colonel, and brigadier general. For thirty years after the war ended he rendered service in the department which he had done much to develop, attaining the post of quartermaster general of the army some months before his retirement, February 16, 1897.

The Chief of Commissariat:—HENRY F. CLARKE

General Clarke, born in Pennsylvania, graduated 1843, assigned to the artillery, wounded at Molino del Rey, and brevetted captain for gallantry in the storming of Chapultepec, did expert service as chief of commissariat to the Utah Expedition, 1857 to 1860, and served as chief of commissariat to the Army of the Potomac from July 2, 1861, till January 8, 1864. He was made a brevet brigadier general "for gallant and meritorious services at Gettysburg," and a final brevet of major general, U.S.A., was awarded at the close of hostilities.

To feed an army of a hundred thousand men scattered over a vast region on the march, in bivouac, and in battle; to keep supplies within reach and yet out of danger from the foe; to distribute the wagons so that they can reach the troops on demand, and yet not impede them in their movements; and to contrive so skilfully that no man shall go hungry after a day's march or a day in battle—that was General Clarke's task, and he accomplished it with a phenomenal skill and success. He retired from the army, colonel and assistant commissary general, November 9, 1884. He died May 10, 1887.

The Provost Marshal General:—MARSENA R. PATRICK

General Patrick (1811–1888; graduated 1835, and brevetted major in the war with Mexico) resigned from the army June 30, 1850, to enter civil life, in which as farmer, railroad president, and head of the New York State Agricultural College he rose to prominence. In 1862, when inspector general New York State militia, he was appointed brigadier general; he was brevetted major general March 13, 1865. From October 15, 1862, till the Army of the Potomac had completed its work, he served as its provost marshal general. His task at Gettysburg was one that required knowledge, discipline, tact, integrity, and utmost fidelity—guard duty, care of prisoners, the prevention of straggling, secret-service details, and matters of that nature. There was not much glory in a work of this sort; but it required abilities of a high order and of a peculiar kind, all of which this veteran officer possessed.

ARMY HEADQUARTERS: Maj. Gen. Gouverneur K. Warren, Chief Topographical Engineer (New York, class of 1850), was brevetted colonel, U.S.A., for his services in this battle, which are fully treated in connection with the story of Little Round Top. The blight cast upon him by Sheridan, with the sanction of Grant, at Five Forks, in the full tide of victory, when he was sent to the rear in disgrace, was lifted by the high court which fourteen years later fully cleared him from censure. Warren's faults were those of a sensitive, high-strung, proud, and nervous temperament; but he was one of the bravest and most accomplished men in the service; his death in 1882, when but fifty-two years of age, was hurried if not occasioned by the long years of heartbreak and brooding which preceded it when he was pleading in vain for a hearing.

The aides and assistants in this department of engineers were all graduates:

GETTYSBURG

First Lieut. Ranald S. Mackenzie, born in New York; class of 1862, at the top; who won brevet of major at Gettysburg. He was a brevet major general when the war ended, and had become colonel of the First Infantry in 1889, when by a premature death his career was cut short. He was recognized as one of the most gifted men in the army.

The commander of the Engineer Brigade, an expert in his profession, in civil as well as military life, Gen. Henry W. Benham, was a member of the class of 1837. His bridge-building exploits are noted in military history. Died 1884.

Col. William H. Pettes, 50th New York (Engineers), born in Vermont; class of 1832; resigned as a lieutenant in 1836 to serve the Government as a civil engineer. He and his regiment gave service of a high order in the line to which they were devoted. He died February 29, 1880.

Capt. George H. Mendell, a Pennsylvanian, class of 1852 (brevetted colonel at the end of the war; retired colonel of engineers 1895; died 1902); Capt. Charles N. Turnbull, born in District of Columbia, graduated in 1854, brevetted colonel at the last; Capt. Chauncey B. Reese, an engineer officer on Warren's staff and a conspicuous figure in saving Round Top, brevetted up to brigadier general in 1865; First Lieut. John W. Barlow (Wisconsin, class of 1861; in 1901 chief of engineers and brigadier general); Lieut. George L. Gillespie, brevetted lieutenant colonel and awarded a medal of honor for gallantry at Bethesda Church in 1864; Lieut. Charles W. Howell, a graduate just from the Point, class of 1863, who had a chance to join in the after-battle campaign; and Capt. Charles E. Cross, class of 1861, born in Massachusetts (killed in the earliest move of the campaign while he was directing the erection of a bridge below Fredericksburg); and Col. Herman Haupt, class of 1835, a notable railroad engineer and projector, who had in charge the railroads and transportation service of the army in the field—all these officers in their proper sphere gave service— in the battle or on the march, in crossing streams, and in other departments of engineering operations—worthy of record and of admiration.

THE ORDNANCE AND SIGNAL OFFICERS: In this sphere of service were the following graduates:

The Chief, Capt. Daniel W. Flagler, class of 1861, from New York, who rose to be Chief of Ordnance, U.S.A., from January 23, 1891, to his death, March 29, 1899. Lieut. John R. Edie, class of 1857, a Pennsylvanian, who a little after the battle found place on Meade's staff as an aide; brevetted captain and major for later services; and died in 1874. First Lieut. Morris Schaff, Ohio; class of 1862; brevetted captain for gallantry in the Wilderness in May, 1864, of which battle he has lately written an engaging volume, in addition to articles on West Point life. Maj. W. J. L. Nicodemus, the Chief Signal Officer (in later years commander of the Signal Corps at Washington), graduated in 1858.

DIVISION COMMANDERS

SECOND CORPS: *Second Division*, John Gibbon (1827–1896), born in Pennsylvania; class of 1847; captain, Fourth Artillery, when the war began; brigadier general in 1862; brevetted up to major general in the war; colonel in the Regular Army for Gettysburg; was severely wounded; rose to be corps commander; died 1896. *Third Division*, Brig. Gen. Alexander Hays, a Pennsylvanian; class of 1844; brevetted first lieutenant 8th Infantry at Palo Alto; resigned in 1848, and became a famous iron-master at Pittsburg; early in the war was re-appointed in the army, captain, 6th Infantry, and also made colonel, 63d Pennsylvania; brevetted colonel for Gettysburg; had been made brigadier general in September, 1862; a man of extraordinary courage, coolness, and insight on the field; killed, at the age of forty-four, in the Wilderness, May 5, 1864.

THIRD CORPS: *Second Division*, Brig. Gen. Andrew A. Humphreys, a Pennsylvanian; class of 1831; major of engineers in 1861; as chief topographical engineer of the Army of the Potomac under McClellan he rendered notable services, one of them being the planning of the defensive works on Malvern Hill and the order of battle; he was made brigadier general, April 28, 1862; won the brevet of colonel at Fredericksburg, where he led three historic charges; he was brevetted brigadier general for his extraordinary services at Gettysburg, and his commission as major general, dated July 8th following the battle, when he became chief of staff of that army, was a further recognition. He commanded the Second Corps from November 25, 1864, till the end of the war, and was foremost in the plans and movements which brought the end about. On the 8th of August, 1866, he was made Chief of Engineers, U.S.A. He died December 27, 1883, with a renown in both hemispheres as one of the most accomplished and richly equipped military minds in the world.

GETTYSBURG

FIFTH CORPS: *First Division*, (1) James Barnes (Mass.; class of 1829); went into railroad service from his first lieutenancy, Fourth Artillery, 1836; in the Civil War from the colonelcy of the 18th Mass. he was made a brigadier; was brevetted major general at the end of the conflict; died February 12, 1869. (2) Brig. Gen. Charles Griffin (Ohio; class of 1847) relieved Barnes on the evening of the last day of the battle, the latter having been slightly wounded the preceding day. Griffin was advanced eight times by brevet or regularly from his captaincy in the Second Artillery in 1861 from Bull Run to Five Forks, and was major general when the war ended. At the age of forty-seven, he died September 15, 1867. *Second Division*, Brig. Gen. Romeyn Beck Ayres (1825–1888); New York; class of 1847; served in the Mexican War; captain, Fifth Artillery, 1861; brigadier general, November 29, 1862; brevetted major in the Regular Army for Gettysburg. His six brevets were at last crowned with that to major general, U.S.A.

SIXTH CORPS: *First Division*, Brig. Gen. Horatio G. Wright (Conn.; class of 1841) became major of engineers August 6, 1861, and brigadier general in the following September. His division was in line of battle, but not seriously engaged. General Wright became a great corps commander, and won seven promotions by brevet or in regular sequence during the war, reaching the rank of major general, U.S.A. From 1879 to his retirement in 1884 he was Chief of Engineers of the army. Died July 2, 1899. *Second Division*, Brig. Gen. Albion P. Howe (Maine; class of 1841) gained a brevet captaincy in artillery service in Mexico; promoted from a full captaincy in that branch to be brigadier general, June 11, 1862. His division was held in reserve at Gettysburg. He won six advancements in rank, by brevet or otherwise, during the war; died in 1897.

ELEVENTH CORPS: *First Division*, Brig. Gen Adelbert Ames, born in Maine, 1835; class of May 6, 1861; served with his battery, Fifth Artillery, in the first Bull Run battle; then was made colonel 20th Maine, and then a year later a brigadier general, winning brevet to colonel for Gettysburg, and up to major general for later battles, and also a medal of honor. In reconstruction times he was governor of Miss., and also Senator from that State. In the Spanish-American War he was a brigadier general. At Gettysburg for a time he was in command of his brigade; but when Barlow was wounded he took the division.

TWELFTH CORPS: *First Division*, Brig. Gen. Thomas H. Ruger

(1833–1907); New York; appointed from Wis.; class of 1854; resigned soon after graduation to become a lawyer; early in 1861 he was made colonel of the 3d Wis., and then, November 29, 1862, a brigadier general. For his services at Gettysburg he was brevetted brigadier general, U.S.A. His usual command in the corps was a brigade, but when Williams, the division leader, temporarily took the corps, Ruger led the division. After the war he served as military governor of Georgia, and from 1871 to 1876 he was superintendent of the Military Academy. In 1897 he was retired with rank of major general.

CAVALRY CORPS: *First Division*, John Buford (born in Ky., appointed from Ill., class of 1848) was major and assistant inspector general, November, 1861; and brigadier general, July 27, 1862. This notable man, in command of a division of cavalry, was on urgent duty from the opening of the campaign to its close. His services during the week preceding the battle, scouting, exploring the mountain passes, uncovering the whereabouts of the Confederate forces, and keeping them at bay on the first morning, till the infantry could come up, were invaluable. He had extraordinary discernment, energy, courage, and skill. He died December 16, 1863, at the age of thirty-seven, his commission as major general reaching him on his death-bed. The nation never had a more generous-hearted, loyal, gifted cavalry commander than Buford. *Second Division*, Brig. Gen. David McM. Gregg (Penn.; class of 1855) at the outbreak of the war was captain, Sixth Cavalry; was made colonel 8th Penn. Cavalry, January 24, 1862; and brigadier general, November 29, 1862; throughout 1863 he commanded a division of cavalry in many skirmishes and engagements with Stuart, with whom he had been closely associated at West Point for three years. He was brevetted major general August 1, 1864, "for highly meritorious and distinguished conduct" throughout the Wilderness and Petersburg campaigns. He commanded the Union cavalry in the terrific action on the Federal right flank on the afternoon of the closing day at Gettysburg, when he prevented Stuart's forces from gaining the rear of Meade's army. General Gregg was U. S. Consul at Prague, 1874, and auditor general of Pennsylvania in 1891. He has served for years as commander in chief of the Military Order of the Loyal Legion. He passed his eightieth birthday anniversary, April 10, 1913. *Third Division*, Brig. Gen. Judson Kilpatrick, born in New Jersey, graduated from the Academy May 6, 1861; was made colonel 3d N. Y. Cavalry, December 6, 1862; brigadier general, June 13, 1863;

was brevetted major for Aldie, June, 1863, and lieutenant colonel for gallantry at Gettysburg; major general, U.S.A., for campaign in the Carolinas. He was one of the notable "dashing" cavalry commanders of the war. At Gettysburg he was in command of the Third Division, Cavalry Corps. After the war he served as U. S. Minister to Chile, 1865–70, and again in 1881, when he died in Valparaiso.

———

The following BRIGADE COMMANDERS were graduates of the Academy:

Brig. Gen. Gabriel R. Paul (1834), wounded and lost sight of both eyes on the first day; brevetted brigadier general for Gettysburg.

Brig. Gen. Alexander S. Webb, class of 1855, won six brevets, two of which were for this battle; his brigade received a heavy part of the brunt of the final charge; he was at the end of the war a brevet major general, U.S.A., and a full officer of that rank in the volunteers; from January to June, 1865, he was chief of staff to Meade; from 1869 to 1903 president of the College of the City of New York; he wrote *The Peninsula: McClellan's Campaign*, in the "Campaigns of the Civil War" series. Died in 1910.

Col. Norman J. Hall, class of 1859, was brevetted lieutenant colonel for this fight, in which his brigade helped to repel Pickett's charge. Died at the age of thirty, 1867.

Col. Samuel Sprigg Carroll, 8th Ohio, class of 1856, won seven brevets before the end of the war, and was several times desperately wounded. He was retired as major general in 1869, and died in 1902.

Col. Hannibal Day, class of 1823, entered on the day he led his brigade at Gettysburg on his forty-first consecutive year of service in the army; he died in 1891.

Col. Sidney Burbank, of the 2d Infantry, of the class of 1829, won in the battle the brevet of brigadier general. Died 1882.

Brig. Gen. Stephen H. Weed, class of 1854, died at the age of thirty at the head of his men on Little Round Top—an unusually expert artillerist. He was made brigadier general three or four weeks before Gettysburg for gallantry at Chancellorsville.

Col. Kenner Garrard (1851), 146th N. Y., brevetted lieutenant colonel for Gettysburg, was promoted to the next grade at Meade's request just after the battle.

Brig. Gen. A. T. A. Torbert, class of 1855, was finally a brevet major general who served after the war as a foreign minister for some years.

Brig. Gen. David A. Russell, brevetted colonel for Gettysburg, and killed at the age of forty-two, in 1864, at Opequan.

Brig. Gen. Thomas H. Neill, class of 1847, who won five brevets during the war.

Col. Henry L. Eustis, class of 1842, who became brigadier general in September, 1863.

In the Twelfth Corps were Brig. Gen. Henry H. Lockwood, class of 1836, for years a professor in the Naval Academy, and Brig. Gen. George S. Greene, of the class of 1823, the great engineer officer to whom due tribute is paid in the record of the fight on Culp's Hill.

CAVALRY CORPS

FIRST DIVISION: *Reserve Brigade*, Brig. Gen. Wesley Merritt (1836–1910; born in N. Y.; graduated 1860; 1st Lieut., 2d Cavalry, in 1861, and captain, April 5, 1862) served on the staff of Pleasanton, and proved so capable that Meade's first request on taking command of the army, prompted by Pleasanton, was that three staff-officers—Capt. George A. Custer, Capt. Wesley Merritt, and Capt. Elon J. Farnsworth—should be appointed brigadier generals and assigned to command brigades of cavalry. This was done without delay. In this battle Merritt was brevetted major, five other brevets followed, and at the end of the war he was major general of volunteers. He proved himself a famous Indian-fighter after the war; served five years as superintendent of the Military Academy; commanded the first expedition to the Philippines, and added to his fame by the work he did there; and reached the retired list in 1900 with the rank of major general, U.S.A. He died in November, 1910.

THIRD DIVISION: *Second Brigade*, George A. Custer (Ohio; class of June 24, 1861; captain and aide to McClellan on the Peninsula; later, aide to Pleasanton, brigadier general, June 29, 1863; commanded cavalry brigade from that date in the campaign) was brevetted major for gallantry in the battle; served in many cavalry battles and commanded a cavalry division at the end, when he had won eleven promotions, including brevets, from graduation day till, at the end of the war, at the age of twenty-six, he was a major general of volunteers and a brevet major general, U.S.A. General Custer was killed in a tragic engagement with an overwhelming

357

GETTYSBURG

force of Sitting Bull's Sioux Indians on the Little Big Horn River, in the Northwest, June 25, 1876.

GRADUATES IN THE ARTILLERY

The Chief of Artillery, Gen. Henry J. Hunt, won two brevets in the Mexican War in view of his skill and courage in handling his battery. His work in his department, under McClellan and his successors, before Gettysburg, had revealed his mastery of that arm of the service, and his work in the battle of Gettysburg, where he had under his eye and command about 320 cannon, brought him two brevets; two others afterward crowned him brevet major general, U.S.A. He was from Ohio and a member of the class of 1839. He died in 1889.

The commander of the reserve artillery, Brig. Gen. Robert O. Tyler, class of 1853, won the brevet of lieutenant colonel in the Regular Army at Gettysburg; five later recognitions made him at last major general, U.S.A.; he died in 1874.

Capt. John C. Tidball, class of 1848, led a brigade of horse artillery, and won in the war six brevets, ending with major general. He was retired as colonel, First Artillery, 1889.

Lieut. Col. Edward R. Warner, class of 1857, was brevetted twice for services at Gettysburg. He was inspector of artillery for the entire army. His specialty in the fight was the reorganization of batteries withdrawn and the furnishing of new ones.

BATTERY OFFICERS IN ALPHABETICAL ORDER

NAME AND RANK	CLASS AT WEST POINT	BREVET
Calef, Lieut. John H.		
Battery A, 2d Artillery	1862	Captain
Cushing, Lieut. Alonzo H.		
Battery A, 4th Artillery	June 24, 1861	Killed
Egan, Lieut. John		
Battery I, 1st artillery	1862	Captain
Fuller, Lieut. William D.		
Battery C, 3d Artillery	June 24, 1861	Major
Hamilton, Lieut. Frank B.		
3d Artillery, Horse Battery	1862	Captain
Hazlett, Lieut. Charles E.		
Battery D, 5th Artillery	May 6, 1861	Killed
Lancaster, Lieut. James M.		
Horse Battery C, 3d Artillery	1862	

WEST POINT AT GETTYSBURG

NAME AND RANK	CLASS AT WEST POINT	BREVET
McCrea, Lieut. Tully		Captain; brigadier gen-
Battery I, 1st Artillery	1862	eral, 1903
McIntire, Lieut. Samuel B.		
2d Artillery	1862	
Martin, Lieut. Leonard		
Battery F, 5th Artillery	May 6, 1861	
Pennington, Lieut. Alex. C. M.		Major; retired, 1899;
Battery M, Horse Artillery	1860	brigadier general, U.S.A.
Randol, Alanson M.	1860	Major
Sanderson, Lieut. James A.		Mortally wounded,
Battery H, 1st Artillery	1862	Pleasant Hill, La., April 9, 1864
Warner, Lieut. Charles N.	1862	1st Lieutenant
Watson, Lieut. Malbone F.	May 6, 1861	Major
Woodruff, Lieut. George A.	June 24, 1861	Killed; 22 years old

CAVALRY OFFICERS

Baker, Eugene M.		
Captain, 1st Cavalry; brevetted major and lieutenant colonel for former services	1859	
Bryan, Timothy M.		
Colonel 18th Penn. Cavalry	1855	
Claflin, Ira W.		
Captain, 6th Cavalry	1857	Major
Davis, Benjamin F.		
Captain, 1st Cavalry, and Colonel 8th N. Y. Cavalry	1854	Killed at Beverly Ford, Va., June 9th
Kellogg, Josiah H.		
Col. 17th Penn. Cav., and Capt. 1st U. S. Cav.	1860	Major
Loeser, Charles McK.		Disabled at Beverly
Captain, 2d Cavalry	May 6, 1861	Ford; captain from that fight
Lord, Richard S. C.		Wounded in the pursuit
Captain, 1st Cavalry	1856	of Lee
McKee, Samuel		Died of wounds at Cold
Captain, 1st Cavalry	1858	Harbor, June 3, 1864
Noyes, Henry E.		Retired as brigadier gen-
Bvt. Capt., 2d Cavalry	June 24, 1861	eral, 1901
Whiting, Charles J.		Served in command of
Major, 2d Cavalry	1835	regiment and brigade in early stages of the campaign

INFANTRY OFFICERS

Adams, Julius W.		Died from exposure and
Capt., 4th Infantry, commanding regiment	June 24, 1861	wounds, November 15, 1865, at age of 25

NAME AND RANK	CLASS AT WEST POINT	BREVET
Bush, Edward G.		Wounded; brevetted
Captain, 10th Infantry	1859	major; died Colonel 12th Infantry, 1892
Carter, Eugene		
Bvt. Major, 8th Infantry	June 24, 1861	Died February 10, 1877
Floyd-Jones, De Lancey		
Major, 11th Infantry, commanded regiment	1846	Colonel
Freedley, Henry W.		
Captain, 3d Infantry; commanded regiment; wounded	1855	Lieutenant colonel
Hancock, David P.		Major and lieutenant
Captain, 7th Infantry; commanded regiment	1854	colonel
Lynn, Daniel D.		
1st Lieut., 6th Infantry	1860	Captain and major
McCleary, John		
Captain, 6th Infantry	1854	Major
Martin, James P.		
Captain, 7th Infantry	1860	Major
O'Rorke, Patrick H.		Killed; posthumous
1st Lieut., Engineers, and Colonel 140th N. Y. Vols.	June 24, 1861	brevet to colonel
Remington, Philip H.		
1st Lieut., 8th Infantry	June 24, 1861	
Upham, John J.		
Captain, 6th Infantry	1859	Major
Upton, Emory		Brevetted up to major
1st Lieut., 4th Artillery, and Col. 121st N. Y. Vols.	1861	general, U.S.A., at end of war; died March 15, 1881

OTHER STAFF-OFFICERS

Andrews, John N.		
Bvt. Capt., 8th Infantry; Com. Musters, 6th Corps	1860	Died, 1903; on retired list; brig. gen., U.S.A.
Bankhead, Henry C.		
Capt., 5th Infantry, Lieut. Col. and Assist. Insp. Gen.	1850	Major
Beaumont, Eugene B.		
1st Lieut., 4th Cavalry; Capt. and A. D. C.	May 6, 1861	
Best, Clermont L.		Lieut. col.; died, 1897;
Capt., 4th Artillery; Lieut. Col. and A. I. G.	1847	colonel 2d Artillery
Kent, Jacob Ford		Major general com-
1st Lieut., 3d Infantry; Col. and A. I. G. 6th Corps	May 6, 1861	manding division in 1898
Morgan, Charles H.		
Capt., 4th Artillery; Lieut. Col. and A. I. G.	1857	Major

WEST POINT AT GETTYSBURG

NAME AND RANK	CLASS AT WEST POINT	BREVET
Platt, Edward R.		
Capt., 2d Artillery; Lieut.	1849	
Col. Staff, 6th Corps		
Poland, John S.		
Capt., 2d Infantry; Lieut.	1862	Brig. general in 1898; died same year
Col. and C. M. 3d Corps		
Ryan, George		Killed; col. 140th N. Y.
Capt., 7th Infantry	1857	Vols., May 8, 1864, aged 29

CAVALRY CORPS

McQuesten, James F.		
Lieut., 2d Cavalry, on Merritt's staff	May 6, 1861	Killed, September 19, 1864, at Opequan
Norris, Charles E.		
Capt., 2d Cavalry; on staff of Buford	1851	Major

(*B*) WEST POINT GRADUATES IN THE ARMY OF NORTHERN VIRGINIA

The extent to which the Army of Northern Virginia was officered by men whose native capacity had been developed by military schooling, as well as by experience in camp, on the march, and in battle, has thus far never been adequately portrayed. This feature is so fundamental, it has such bearing on the character and history of the organization, which was informed and attempered throughout by the spirit and ministrations, the instruction and example, of a large number of carefully equipped, widely experienced professional soldiers—that one marvels to find out how little has been made of it.

When the records have been explored it becomes apparent that the corps and division commanders, the leaders of brigades, and also in many cases the colonels of regiments, were examples of the military proficiency which can be secured only under the auspices of a great institution like the United States Military Academy at West Point, or, in smaller measure, in the Virginia Military Institute, or in one of the half-dozen similar schools of lower rank which were in existence in the South in the fifties or earlier, and which, taken en masse, made an extraordinary contribution to the efficiency of Lee's army.

In view of these facts it has seemed to the writer to be imperative that a complete study of the campaign and battle, and an adequate portrayal of the personnel and capacity of the two armies which faced each other at Gettysburg, must include answers, at least in brief, to such questions as these: "What sort of officers, on either side, led the rank and file? In what way were they trained? What was the military equipment of an intellectual and technical sort with which they were furnished in advance of the outbreak of the war? To what extent were the leading officers in the two armies graduates of the Military Academy at West Point? And, further, what proportion of the leading officers were advantaged by previous experience in militia service, or in State military schools, or in the Mexican War?"

362

WEST POINT AT GETTYSBURG

These comments are in some measure anticipated by the personal sketches which elsewhere set forth the training and history of commanders other than the ones who were educated at West Point, including in these pen-portraits an account also of those officers who spent some time at that institution, but who for one cause or another did not finish the course. It remains, therefore, for us to indicate the West Point graduates in the Army of Northern Virginia, and to tell something of their personal characteristics and gifts.

We may further anticipate our inquiries by saying that when the facts are before the reader he will have secured the data for an extraordinary claim in behalf of technical and professional training, education in general, and military education in particular. It will be seen at a glance that none of the Southern political orators who were so prominent on the stump and in the secession conventions, and in Congress during the decade before 1861, but who were lacking in military training, amounted to anything worth while as commanders of armies. Only one civilian soldier in the whole of Lee's army revealed the qualities of a great commander— John B. Gordon. Every other man who showed the capacity to command a division or an army corps was a trained soldier.

With this preliminary word let us set before our vision the array of notable soldiers furnished by West Point to the Army of Northern Virginia, suggesting meanwhile that the Confederate Government had an advantage to begin with, in the knowledge and experience of Jefferson Davis, who was a graduate of West Point; had seen service and received wounds in the Mexican War, where he did courageous work; and had been Secretary of War, and also a member of the United States Senate Committee on Military Affairs. There was also at hand that venerable and erudite soldier, Gen. Samuel Cooper, an army officer ever since his graduation from the Point in 1815, and for twenty-five years of that time in the adjutant general's office at Washington, and for a decade the adjutant general of the United States Army, who held the same office at the opening of the Confederate administration in the Southern military organization. Moreover, Beauregard, Joseph E. Johnston, and Lee were all within reach, each one of them acquainted with the personnel of the old army, and in particular with its Southern representatives.

Moreover, Mr. Davis and the others whom we have mentioned understood, as the North did not, and we might say, does not to-day, understand the fundamental importance of military

GETTYSBURG

training. For a long while in the administration of the war from the Union side the name West Point conveyed with it a fling and a sneer, implied a lack of energy, and suggested deficiency in loyalty to the Government and an intimation of mere military pedantry, instead of a capacity to organize and lead men in actual and aggressive warfare. The Confederate Government had therefore, at the start, no necessity of overcoming a prejudice against West Point training; it was endowed, rather, as one of its chief advantages, with a spirit of appreciation, of insight, of foresight in that it recognized the value of that equipment, and was ready to give ample opportunity at the outset for largest service to those who had been favored with a military education. These suggestions will throw light, we judge, on the data now presented in this regard.

The data in question may be made more luminous when summarized as we have done in the case of the graduates in the Army of the Potomac, so that we may see at a glance how the West Point men were distributed, and to what extent, in the Army of Northern Virginia. Thus marshaled they appear in the following order:

(1) *Commander in Chief and Corps Commanders:*
Lee, Longstreet, Ewell, and Hill 4
(2) *Division Commanders:* McLaws, Pickett, Hood, Early, Johnson, R. H. Anderson, Heth, Pender, Trimble, Stuart 10
(3) *Brigade Commanders:* Bryan, Garnett, Steuart, J. M. Jones, Daniel, Ramseur, Wilcox, Baker, Robertson, Fitzhugh Lee, W. E. Jones, J. R. Chambliss 12
(4) *Artillery:* Chief Pendleton. *Battalion Commanders:* Alexander, Henry, Huger, Beckham 4
(5) *Miscellaneous:* Cols. Lomax, Davis, Mercer, Williams; and Lee's staff: Long, Corley, Cole, Smith 8
Total 38

In addition Gen. Thomas L. Rosser and Col. Edward Willis, Maj. James Dearing, Col. B. D. Fry, and Col. Pierce M. B. Young were at the Point for a part of the course. The two first-named had practically finished the course, but resigned just at the outbreak of the war.

A full array of the graduates of the Virginia Military Institute

364

and of various colleges among the officers in Lee's army would add to this showing of educated leadership. Among the general officers thus equipped were the following: Rodes, Jenkins, Kemper, Walker, Benning, Mahone, Law, Gordon, Iverson, Pettigrew, Thomas, and Lane. Col. Walter H. Taylor, Lee's aide or assistant adjutant general for the whole war, and author of *Four Years with Lee*, and Col. R. L. Walker, chief of artillery in Hill's corps, and Colonel Herbert, later Secretary of the Navy, may be added to the list, which is, even as thus outlined, far from complete, although the category of West Point graduates is, we believe, full and correct as above given.

THE GENERAL IN CHIEF AND THE CORPS COMMANDERS

The Commanding General:—ROBERT EDWARD LEE

Robert Edward Lee (born January 19, 1807; graduated 1829, number two in a class of forty-six) revealed in his youth a winsome personality. His well-poised spirit, cheery and brave temperament, and blameless life gave early token of his fundamental qualities; when to these were added his singular fitness for the career of a soldier and his easy mastery of its technical details it is no wonder that he won almost at the start the admiring friendship of General Scott as well as the confidence of his fellow-officers.

In the siege of Vera Cruz, March 9–29, 1847, Lee, a captain of engineers, and Meade (who emerged from the Academy six years later than Lee) a brevet first lieutenant in the same arm of the service, were closely associated in the technical operations of that strenuous month of peril and victory, little dreaming that in a little less than sixteen years thence they two would stand pinnacled in history for all time as the leaders of opposing armies in one of the most critical battles of the centuries.

In the early fifties Lee was for three years superintendent of the Academy at West Point; in 1855 he was transferred to the cavalry, and then saw service in Texas; and on March 16, 1861, he received his final promotion in the old army, the commission as Colonel of the First Cavalry being signed by Abraham Lincoln, the newly inaugurated President. On the 25th of April in that year he resigned his place in the United States Army, and also declined the proffer, as it appears, of the command of the Union

GETTYSBURG

Army for the war as yet inchoate, and heeded the call of Virginia, and then of the Confederacy, in whose service he became finally recognized as one of the world's great generals.

This is not the place in which his development can be even outlined—the skill with which he baffled McClellan, with little more than half the forces directed by the Union commander; the ability with which he contrived to make Antietam a drawn battle; the ingenuity and audacity combined whereby he and Jackson outwitted Hooker and brought the at first glance splendid plans of the latter to utter confusion at Chancellorsville; nor need we reiterate the reasons which prompted him to undertake an invasion of the North in June, 1863.

Lee was fifty-six at Gettysburg; whatever conclusions may be reached as to his plans in that battle, no one can question the superb character of his manhood, the irresistible personal attractions which drew countless thousands to trust and adore him, his composure in calamity, his equitable temper under burdens and trials which would have crushed a housand ordinary men, and the mixture of prudence and audacity which marked his larger military exploits. Then, who can indeed fail to note his temper at the end, when his hungry and ragged veterans laid down their arms at his bidding, and when he, the commander of a defeated and surrendered army and the representative of a "lost cause," quietly, prayerfully, and benignantly set himself to achieve peace, to build up the stricken Commonwealth of Virginia, and to help as a college president the new generation of young men to honor God, the flag, and the nation?

LEE'S CORPS COMMANDERS

First Army Corps:—JAMES LONGSTREET

Lieut. Gen. James Longstreet (1831–1904), born in South Carolina, was graduated 1838, Newton, Doubleday, and Sykes, whom he confronted at Gettysburg, being among his classmates.

In 1843 Ulysses S. Grant, just graduated from the Academy, was assigned to Jefferson Barracks, where Longstreet was then serving. The latter introduced his cousin, Miss Julia Dent, to the young lieutenant, and she a little later became Mrs. Grant. Thus began a long friendship, interrupted for a quadrennium, and renewed after the war, between the two notable soldiers.

Longstreet won two brevets in the Mexican War and was severely wounded. He led his company in the battle of Monterey, September 22, 1846, and it serves to vivify the record to know that the storming party that morning was led through the mists and darkness to its post of duty by Lieut. George G. Meade, of the Topographical Engineers. Longstreet resigned his office of major and paymaster in the United States Army, June 1, 1861, to enter the Confederate service, in which he became in succession brigadier general, major general, and lieutenant general. His history is imperishably bound up with that of the Army of Northern Virginia. He possessed a phlegmatic temperament, and in the estimate of other generals was hard to move; but when he was ready and once in battle he was a sturdy, terrific, and tremendous fighter. He was wounded desperately in the Wilderness, in 1864, in the midst of a movement which he had headed, and which threatened serious inroads on the Union line. Personally he was a conspicuous figure, vigorously developed, and a fine horseman; he had keen blue eyes, a full, dark beard, and a winsome face. After the war Longstreet served the United States Government in several important posts, among them that of Minister to Turkey and of Commissioner of Pacific Railroads. His volume of reminiscences, *From Manassas to Appomattox*, is a valuable contribution to war-time literature.

Second Army Corps:—RICHARD STODDERT EWELL

Lieutenant General Ewell, born in the District of Columbia in 1817, was graduated in 1840, Sherman and Thomas being among the notable men in the class. He served in the war with Mexico, in Texas and other frontier districts for the twenty years that intervened between his graduation and the Civil War, a life which left its ineffaceable mark upon his habits and methods of speech and action. He won a brevet captaincy for meritorious conduct at Churubusco, and had been a full captain of dragoons for a dozen years when he resigned, May 7, 1861, to enter the Confederate service, where a little later he became brigadier general, and in the fall of that year a major general. In the engagement at Groveton, in the second Manassas campaign, he lost a leg; but, full of pluck, he refused to allow that disablement to keep him from active service, and after convalescence he returned to the field undaunted, although in order to ride a horse he had to be helped into the saddle and strapped there. He led the advance into Pennsylvania, and commanded the Confederate left at Gettysburg. At Spottsylvania his horse was killed under

GETTYSBURG

him, May, 1864, and he was hurt by the fall so severely as to incapacitate him for further field service, although he was in command of the defenses of Richmond toward the close of the conflict. He died in Tennessse, January 25, 1872.

General Ewell was bald, and had an aquiline nose and a piercing eye; he spoke with a lisp, abounded in eccentricities of speech and conduct, possessed an outrageous temper, and carried into his later life the habit of intolerant and profane speech. Before the conflict ended, however, he changed his manners in a wonderful way, and after his conversion he revealed a spirit of hearty religious devotion. On the field of battle he was a leader full of electrifying energy.

Third Army Corps:—Ambrose Powell Hill

Lieutenant General Hill, born in Virginia, November 9, 1825, was assigned to the artillery service when, in the class of 1847, he emerged from the Academy, having among his classmates Gibbon, Ayres, Griffin, and Neill—generals whose commands were opposite his in the lines at Gettysburg—as well as Heth, one of his own division commanders in that battle. Young Hill spent a year or two in Mexico toward the close of the struggle there, several years in the war with the Seminoles, and in Texas, and five years in the office of the Coast Survey in Washington. He was a lieutenant in the First Artillery in 1861, when he resigned to accept the colonelcy of the 13th Virginia; as brigadier general and major general he commended himself to the affection and confidence of Lee, and after Chancellorsville he was promoted to the rank of a lieutenant general and the command of a corps. General Sorrel says of him: "Hill was of medium height, had a light, good figure, and a most pleasing soldierly appearance." General Hill began his service at Bull Run, and finished his course, April 2, 1865, at the very close of the war in front of Petersburg, where he was fatally shot. The burial occurred without notice or display while Petersburg and Richmond were in flames and the army of Lee was crowding toward its doom at Appomattox.

DIVISION COMMANDERS

First Army Corps

First Division:—McLaws

Maj. Gen. Lafayette McLaws (1821–1898), born in Georgia, entered the 6th Infantry from the Military Academy in 1842.

His whole term of service was occupied with duties on the frontier, with the exception of the time spent in Mexico during the war with that country, the decade of the fifties being largely taken up with work done in the behalf of emigrants then crossing the plains to the Pacific coast. Resigning his captaincy in 1861 to become colonel of the 10th Georgia Infantry, within two years he was a major general, and had proved himself a fighter of resource and courage. At Gettysburg he commanded Longstreet's center at the Peach Orchard, with Barksdale, Kershaw, Semmes, and Wofford as his brigade commanders, whose assaults made under his direction were furious and desperate. After the war McLaws became in succession collector of internal revenue, postmaster, and port warden at Savannah, where his death occurred.

Second Division:—PICKETT

Maj. Gen. George Edward Pickett (1825–1875) was born in Richmond; he was, as we have related elsewhere, appointed to West Point at the suggestion of Abraham Lincoln, of Springfield, Illinois, and was graduated with the class of 1846—just in time to see service in the Mexican War, where as a lieutenant in the 8th Infantry he won two brevets. He became a full captain March 3, 1855, and after strenuous frontier service in Texas and in the Northwest he resigned, June 25, 1861, to enter the Confederate Army, in which he rose from the rank of major to that of major general. He was one of the foremost figures at the very last in Lee's despairing effort to escape with the remnants of his Army of Northern Virginia from surrender to Grant. His services at Gettysburg are, of course, historic, and require no comment here.

Third Division:—HOOD

John Bell Hood, born in Kentucky in 1831, was graduated from the Academy in 1853, McPherson, Schofield, and Sheridan being among his classmates. He was engaged chiefly in warfare with Indian tribes—in one battle with Indians being dangerously wounded in a hand-to-hand encounter—and on the frontier until 1861, when he resigned to enter the Confederate service, in which he rose to be a lieutenant general, showing himself to be a relentless, desperate, and sometimes reckless fighter. He lost a leg at Chickamauga; was pressed back by Sherman to Atlanta, which he was forced to abandon, and was finally overwhelmed at

GETTYSBURG

Nashville with his army near the end of the strife. At Gettysburg he opened the assault in the afternoon of the second day with his four brigades, led by Law, Robertson, G. T. Anderson, and Benning, attacking the Round Tops and the Devil's Den; but early in the fight fell with a severe wound in the Peach Orchard, and had to be taken to the rear, leaving the division in charge of Gen. E. M. Law.

General Hood was unfortunate in his career in that he was forced by his superiors to undertake desperate enterprises with inadequate forces at command, as when he was crowded into the task of relieving Joseph E. Johnston in the Atlanta campaign, and later when forced to attempt the capture of Nashville and the defeat of Schofield and Thomas. He makes a skilful effort to demonstrate his side of the case in his volume *Advance and Retreat*. His death occurred in 1879. General Sorrel pictures Hood as "tall and somewhat loose-jointed, with a long, oval face shaded by a yellowish beard, with hair of the same color, and a voice of great compass and power."

SECOND ARMY CORPS

First Division:—JUBAL ANDERSON EARLY

General Early (born in Virginia, November 3, 1816) after graduation in 1837 spent but one year in the army, resigning to enter the profession of law in his native State. He was a member of the legislature in 1841–1842, served as Commonwealth's attorney for eight years, and was a major of Virginia volunteers in the Mexican War. He became colonel of the 24th Virginia Infantry, commanded a brigade at Bull Run, and rapidly rose to the head of a division, and then of an army corps, with the rank of lieutenant general. He headed the forces which captured Winchester in the opening of the Gettysburg campaign, and in the battle was in charge of the lines in front of the Cemetery after the opening day, in which his division took a leading part. One of his most daring ventures was his advance into Maryland in July, 1864, at the head of Ewell's corps, and his partial investment of the city of Washington.

Early had a striking face, piercing eyes, clear-cut features, a full beard, rather straggly, a high, bald forehead, and a good presence; in command of troops, notwithstanding a slight stoop, occasioned by chronic rheumatism, he presented an impressive

370

figure, and was always a capable and brave leader. His long-time comrade and friend, Gen. D. H. Hill, said long after the war that Early was considered the wittiest man in the Confederate Army. Early's bachelor habits, however, and his sufferings from the disease just mentioned, which he contracted by exposure in the Mexican War, combined with his native temperament to confirm an acrid manner of speech and a fitful temper which often exasperated those who had to deal with him.

When the collapse of the Confederacy finally came Early was one of the men who stubbornly refused to accept the situation; after a long and perilous ride through the South from Virginia to Texas he managed to find temporary refuge in Mexico, and then in Havana, thence going to Canada. After a few years he returned to this country, residing for a time in New Orleans, and then in Virginia, dying at Lynchburg, March 2, 1894. His effervescent caprices of speech and action were sometimes ludicrous and sometimes tragic; they certainly helped to cloud his life with bitterness and trouble.[1]

Second Division:—EDWARD JOHNSON

Maj. Gen. Edward Johnson (1816–1873; born in Kentucky; graduated in 1838) won a brevet captaincy at Molino del Rey in the Mexican War, and was brevetted major for gallantry at Chapultepec. He gave large service on the frontier in the Utah expedition, and on the march to California, and to work on the coast, resigning June 10, 1861, to accept the command of the 12th Georgia, from which he was promoted to be brigadier general, December 13, 1861, and major general, May 5, 1863. With a large part of his division he was captured in the Bloody Angle, in May, 1864, by the forces of Hancock, who had served side by side with him in the 6th Infantry in the battles in front of the City of Mexico in the fall of 1847. He and a good part of his division were captured at Franklin and Nashville, November-

---

[1] A posthumous volume, illustrated, *General Jubal A. Early: An Autobiographical Sketch, and Narrative of the War Between the States,* issued in the fall of 1912, forms a worthy contribution to the extraordinary body of literature pertaining to the struggle in the sixties. By its candid spirit, its luminous comments, and its keen descriptions it helps to throw light on the battles and course of events in which from Bull Run till the end Early was a heroic figure, and at the same time it furnishes a fresh standard by which his character and convictions may be adjudged.

December, 1864. He engaged in the life of a planter after the war in Virginia.

At Gettysburg he directed with terrific vigor half a dozen assaults on the Union positions on Culp's Hill, where he would have won a great victory had it been possible for military skill and desperate valor to overcome the advantages possessed by the Union forces in their fortified stronghold and in the courage and steadiness whereby it was defended.

THIRD ARMY CORPS

First Division:—RICHARD H. ANDERSON

Major General Anderson, born in South Carolina, was graduated 1842, and entered the First Dragoons as a brevet second lieutenant. Standing next in number to him on graduation day was George Sykes, who served with him later in Mexico, and who at Gettysburg commanded the Fifth Army Corps, immediately opposite his position as the lines were there arrayed. After the Mexican War Anderson had much experience on the plains and in Texas. He was a captain of dragoons when, March 3, 1861, he resigned to enter the Confederate service. From one rank to another he rose until he reached that of lieutenant general and corps commander, succeeding Longstreet when that leader was wounded in the Wilderness in May, 1864. At Gettysburg two of his brigades were foremost in the impressions they made in assaults upon the Union line commanded by Hancock—the brigades of Wilcox and Wright. General Anderson died June 26, 1879.

Second Division:—HENRY HETH

Major General Heth, born in Virginia in 1825, entered the First Infantry on graduation in 1847. When he resigned his commission as captain of the 10th Infantry in 1861 he had spent the years of his army service chiefly on the frontier. He became major in the army of the Confederate States, colonel of the 45th Virginia, brigadier and major general in successive promotions; was several times wounded, receiving one severe wound at Gettysburg in the opening part of the battle on the first day. His brigades made the opening attack, on Wednesday, July 1st, led by Pettigrew, Archer, Davis, and Brockenbrough, on the Chambersburg pike, aided by the troops of Pender's division. After the war General

Heth engaged for some years in insurance business in Richmond. He died September 7, 1899.

Third Division:—WILLIAM DORSEY PENDER

General Pender, born in North Carolina, February 6, 1834, and graduating in 1854, gave two years of service to the artillery branch, and was then transferred to the First Dragoons, in which he was a lieutenant when he resigned to enter the Confederate Army, March 21, 1861, as colonel of the 13th North Carolina Infantry. He reached a brigadiership in 1862, and on May 27, 1863, was made a major general. His promotion from a colonelcy was made by President Davis in person, at Seven Pines, in the Peninsula campaign, as a reward for the skill and gallantry the young officer had shown.

An officer who served under him wrote long afterward: "Colonel Pender was one of the coolest and most self-possessed and absolutely fearless men under fire I ever knew." General Pender's division took a leading part in the operations of the first day; on the afternoon of July 2d, when the attack was being made on Hancock's line by the troops of Wright and others adjacent, Pender was in the act of arraying his men to join in the advance when he was fatally wounded by a fragment of a shell.

In the retreat he was taken to Staunton, Virginia, where he died, July 18, 1863. General Pender's military endowments, his youthful and manly graces, his religious devotion, his coolness in battle, and his combined modesty and dignity gave him an unusual status in the army. General Lee said of him: "His promise and usefulness as an officer were equaled only by the purity and excellence of his private life."

Pender's Division:—ISAAC RIDGEWAY TRIMBLE

Maj. Gen. Isaac Ridgeway Trimble, born in Virginia, 1802, was graduated 1822. After spending ten years in ordnance, topographical, and garrison details, he resigned, May 31, 1832, to enter railroad service, in which he attained high repute as chief engineer and general superintendent until May 31, 1861, when he entered the army of the Confederacy as colonel of engineers, winning rapid promotion to the grade of brigadier and major general.

At the opening of the Gettysburg campaign General Lee put Trimble in command of the Valley of Virginia, with special organizing duties assigned to perform, but giving him somewhat reluctant permission, because of his age, depleted physique, and recent wound, to join the army in Maryland should he find himself able to do so. Trimble, however, was not disposed to make years, debility, or wounds an excuse, and accordingly he presented himself at Gettysburg as soon as the army reached there, and for two days served on Lee's staff as engineer. On the third day Pender's division was at Lee's disposal, that officer having been fatally hurt the evening before, and Trimble asked that he might be assigned to lead it in the charge about to be made. Although it had been provided that Gen. James H. Lane, who had already aligned it for battle, should lead it forward, General Lee made the change and allowed Trimble to take command. Accordingly, Lane went back to his brigade, and Trimble led the charge; but fell at the very climax of the movement with a dreadful wound which resulted in his capture and the amputation of his leg.

Some of the Union authorities at Washington, cautioned by Simon Cameron, deemed Trimble, because of his knowledge of railroad connections in Maryland and Pennsylvania, which he had administered for years, a "dangerous man," and he was retained as a prisoner of war in Fort Warren till February, 1865. At the end of the war he returned to his former home in Baltimore, where he resided until his death, January 2, 1888.

The Cavalry Division:—JAMES EWELL BROWN STUART

Maj. Gen. "J. E. B." Stuart, one of the world's great cavalrymen, born in Virginia, February 6, 1833, was graduated in 1856, entering the mounted riflemen, and later reaching the rank of Captain, First Cavalry. His services were largely among the Indians on the Western plains, and he was a member of the famous Utah Expedition in 1858.

At the time of the John Brown episode he was a volunteer aide on the staff of Col. R. E. Lee. He resigned his captaincy May 7, 1861, and accepted the colonelcy of a regiment of Virginia infantry, from which he was speedily promoted to the rank of brigadier general, and later to that of major general. He developed qualities of dash and venturesomeness, and the strategic and tactical ability to handle large bodies of horsemen in skirmishes, in raids, and in battle, which quickly gave him commanding fame.

His part in the Gettysburg campaign consisted in a venturesome skylarking expedition which led him around the Army of the Potomac—between that body and Washington—separating him from the rest of Lee's army for a full week, depriving Lee of the services of the cavalry, and bringing the mounted division to Gettysburg on the afternoon of the second day to little purpose, after days and nights of exhausting forays and several fierce encounters with Pleasanton's forces.

The judgment of the Army of Northern Virginia was nearly unanimous to the effect that this raid was a damage and hindrance, and not a help to Lee's plans.

The cavalry fight on the left flank of the Confederate position, Friday afternoon, led by Stuart on the one hand and Gregg on the other, was a remarkable engagement in which saber-cuts were frequent and many hand-to-hand conflicts occurred. In connection with this battle it may be recalled that Gregg and Stuart were together at West Point for three years of their course, and that during the war they faced each other in hostile combats more than a score of times, almost literally crossing sabers in deadly strife. In character Stuart was the embodiment of knightly chivalry, with manifold attractions; he was finely formed, had a ruddy, cheery face, a bushy red beard, the frolicsome spirits of a boy, the soul of a hero, and yet on occasion the dignity of a commander; he was fond of fanciful plumes and dashing accoutrements, and withal was an ensample of the nobler virtues—clean of speech, with a devotional habit, and exquisitely courteous to women—while at the same time in the hours of leisure in the camp, although never touching liquor or tobacco, he was able to give himself with zest and cheer to jovial songs, amateur minstrel performances, and the music of the banjo.

Stuart's irrepressible jocosity was illustrated early in 1863 when, after a successful raid in which he temporarily captured a station of the military telegraph-line and took considerable spoil in addition, he sent this message to Quartermaster General Meigs at Washington: "In future you will please furnish better mules to the Yankee Army. Those you have furnished recently are very inferior." These complex characteristics, almost irreconcilable with one another, attracted to him with affection, admiration, and devotion men, women, and children in society, in the home circle, and in camp; while his superiors trusted him, his fellow-officers loved him, and his men adored him; altogether he won a unique place in the annals of the war.

After his fatal hurt in the Wilderness campaign at Yellow

GETTYSBURG

Tavern, Virginia, May 11, 1864, he died with the words upon his lips: "I am resigned; God's will be done."

BRIGADE COMMANDERS

A goodly sprinkling of West Point graduates was to be found among the commanders of brigades in Lee's army, as this list will show.

Col. Goode Bryan, of the 16th Georgia, took command of the Second Brigade, McLaws's division, when the brigade commander, General Semmes, fell mortally wounded. Bryan was promoted to be a brigadier general immediately after the battle of Gettysburg. Born in Georgia, and graduated in 1834, he remained but a year in the army, resigning to enter railroad engineering. He served as colonel in the Alabama militia, and in the House of Representatives of that State, and became a planter, 1835–1846; then he was in the Mexican War as major of the First Alabama Volunteers, and later as staff-officer under General Worth. Returning from Mexico, he resumed plantation life in Georgia, but kept up his interest in military affairs through his captaincy in the militia, 1853–1861. He died in Augusta, Georgia, August 15, 1885.

Brig. Gen. Richard Brooke Garnett, who led the First Brigade in Pickett's division, born in Virginia, was graduated in 1841. After long service on the frontier in the Utah Expedition, in California, and New Mexico he resigned his captaincy in the Sixth Infantry, May 17, 1861, to enter the Confederate service. He was advanced rapidly from the position of major of artillery to that of brigade commander, and had distinguished himself in half a score of battles before he perished not far from the Union breastworks, in Pickett's charge. He led his brigade into the fight with 140 officers and 1,287 men. About 300 altogether escaped to the rear when the division was broken to pieces that afternoon. Maj. Chas. S. Peyton, the only field-officer left that day to command the brigade, notes in his report (*Official Records*, XXVII, 2:387) the example of General Garnett, who, totally devoid of excitement or rashness, rode immediately in the rear of his advancing line, endeavoring by his personal efforts and by the aid of his staff to keep his line well closed. He was shot from his horse while near the center of the brigade, within about twenty-five paces of the stone wall.

Brig. Gen. Stephen Dodson Ramseur, who led the Fourth Brigade in Rodes's division, born in North Carolina, May 31, 1837, was graduated in 1860, and resigned his lieutenancy in the Fourth Artillery, April 6, 1861, to accept the captaincy of the Ellis Light Artillery (North Carolina), in which he served for a year. Later he became colonel of the 49th North Carolina Infantry, and in October, 1862, rose to the rank of a brigadier. The work of his men at Gettysburg is told elsewhere. After showing gallantry and skill in several battles he was made major general in 1864. He was severely wounded several times. In October, 1863, he was married to Ellen S. Richmond, of Milton, North Carolina. A year later, October 19, 1864, at Cedar Creek, he fell mortally wounded, after leading his division with admirable skill, and was taken prisoner, dying the next day at the age of twenty-seven. Word came to him on the day before the battle that a daughter had been born in his home.

Brig. Gen. George H. Steuart, commanding a brigade in Edward Johnson's division, was one of the leading Maryland soldiers in Lee's army. Born in Baltimore, August 24, 1828, he was graduated in 1848 and assigned to the Second Dragoons, transferring later to the cavalry. Indian warfare, scouting on the plains, the Utah Expedition, and varied forms of frontier labors occupied him till he resigned in April, 1861, to accept the lieutenant colonelcy of the First Maryland, from which post he was promoted to be colonel, and then in March, 1862, to be brigadier general. He directed several assaults fruitlessly, but with valor, against Culp's Hill under Johnson's command, Thursday night, July 2d, and Friday morning. With a large body of Johnson's division he was captured in the Bloody Angle at Spottsylvania, May, 1864.

Brig. Gen. John M. Jones, who led a brigade in Johnson's division, was born in Virginia, July 26, 1820, and graduated in 1841. He spent much time on the frontier in Michigan; was on duty at the Academy for seven years as an assistant instructor in infantry tactics; and on May 27, 1861, resigned his captaincy to become an officer in the Southern Army. He was a lieutenant colonel of artillery, then assistant adjutant general under Ewell, and in May, 1863, a brigadier general. He was wounded in one of the assaults made by his brigade on Culp's Hill, and was fatally shot in the Wilderness, May 5, 1864.

Brig. Gen. Junius Daniel led a brigade in Rodes's division. He was born in North Carolina, June 27, 1828; graduated in 1851. In 1858, when a first lieutenant of infantry, he resigned to take charge of his father's plantation in Louisiana. In the spring of 1861 he was colonel of the 24th North Carolina Infantry, and in September, 1862, he rose to be a brigadier general. He was mortally wounded in the Bloody Angle at Spottsylvania, May 12, 1864.

The First Brigade in R. H. Anderson's division was commanded by Brig. Gen. Cadmus M. Wilcox, a North-Carolinian, who was graduated in 1846. In Mexico as a lieutenant in the Seventh Infantry he won a brevet at Chapultepec. He served five years as instructor in infantry tactics at the Point, had two years of study in Europe, and then did work on the frontier, resigning June 8, 1861. He was the compiler of a volume on rifle practice and the translator of another on infantry evolution. At Gettysburg he led his brigade with great gallantry in two heroic advances across the Emmitsburg road against the Union line. General Wilcox became a major general a month after the battle of Gettysburg. He died in 1890, the last four years of his life being occupied with duties in the Land Office in Washington. A posthumous work on the *Mexican War* from his pen, published in 1892, is a volume of distinctive value, the personal reminiscences and the list of officers and organizations associated with the Mexican campaigns being of particular interest.

BRIGADE COMMANDERS IN STUART'S CAVALRY

Brig. Gen. Fitzhugh Lee, born in Virginia, November 19, 1835, was graduated from West Point in 1856, entering the Second Cavalry, in which he had three or four years of service against the Indians in Texas before he resigned, May 21, 1861. He was promoted rapidly in the Confederate service from lieutenant colonel of Virginia cavalry to be colonel, brigadier general, and then major general—the latter commission coming just after the brilliant service he did at Gettysburg. He raided with Stuart in that campaign, and took part in the cavalry engagement on the last day. Later he was terribly wounded in a fight with Sheridan's cavalry at Winchester. He served as chief of cavalry onward to the end of the war.

After the conflict he won high civic distinction as governor of Virginia, consul general in Havana, major general United States volunteers, and military governor of Cuba, being a conspicuous figure in the Spanish-American War. He was promoted to be brigadier general in the Regular Army, and retired with that rank in 1901. He died in 1905. He was a nephew of Robert E. Lee.

Brig. Gen. William E. Jones, born in Virginia in 1824, was graduated in 1848, and served in the mounted riflemen on the plains and in the Far West till January 26, 1857, when he resigned and became a farmer. He led a company of mounted riflemen to Manassas in July, 1861, was made colonel of the First Virginia Cavalry, then was transferred to the Seventh, and later was promoted to a brigadiership. He was particularly skilled in out-post duty, scouting, and on the skirmish-line. His brigade of cavalry, united with Robertson's, and under the chief command of the latter, served in the rear of the advancing Confederate Army during the Gettysburg campaign, as related in the sketch of Robertson in the next paragraph. Jones was killed in the battle at Piedmont, West Virginia, June 5, 1864.

Brig. Gen. Beverly Holcombe Robertson, Virginia born (1827–1910), entered the Second Dragoons upon graduation from West Point in 1849, and spent years in frontier service in the South and Far West. He was a captain when he left the army in 1861 to accept the colonelcy of the Fourth Virginia Cavalry, later becoming a brigadier general. In the Gettysburg campaign Stuart left Robertson in Virginia with his own and Jones's brigades of cavalry to guard the rear, observe the movements of the Army of the Potomac, and follow up the forces of Lee. In that work these brigades were chiefly occupied in the Cumberland Valley, and did not cross the South Mountain toward Gettysburg until the battle was nearly over, July 3d, when they reported for duty at Cashtown and Fairfield. From that time during the next twelve days they were incessantly engaged in skirmishing with the Union cavalry day and night until the Confederate forces were "safe on the other shore" of the Potomac. In recent years General Robertson was engaged in real-estate operations in Washington City.

Col. Lawrence S. Baker, who took charge of Hampton's brigade[1] when that leader was wounded, was a graduate of the Academy (1851), serving in the mounted riflemen much of the time in the Far West. As first lieutenant he resigned, May 10, 1861, accepting the lieutenant colonelcy of the First North Carolina Cavalry. In 1862 he became colonel, and soon after Gettysburg

[1] Col. P. M. B. Young, of Cobb's Legion, in Hampton's brigade, was for two years, 1857–1859, a cadet at West Point.

GETTYSBURG

he was promoted to a brigadiership. He proved himself worthy to rank among the distinguished cavalry commanders on whom J. E. B. Stuart and Fitzhugh Lee relied in their forays and battles. For years he served at Suffolk, Virginia, after the war as agent of the Seaboard Air Line. His death occurred in 1907.

Col. Solomon Williams, Second North Carolina Cavalry, killed June 9, 1863, in the cavalry fight at Fleetwood, Virginia, at the opening of the campaign, was a member of the class of 1858, and resigned his lieutenancy in the Second Dragoons, May 3, 1861, to enter the Confederate service.

Col. John R. Chambliss, Jr. (afterward brigadier general), born in Virginia, January 23, 1833, graduated with the class of 1853—to which McPherson, Sheridan, Schofield, and Hood belonged—and served at Carlisle Barracks, Pennsylvania, until March 4, 1854, when he resigned to become a farmer in Virginia. Nevertheless, he maintained constant interest in military affairs as a member of the governor's staff, the colonel of a regiment, and acting brigade inspector in the State militia. He became colonel of the 13th Virginia Cavalry, and in the Gettysburg campaign commanded the brigade ordinarily led by Brig. Gen. W. H. F. Lee, who had been severely wounded at Brandy Station, June 9th. General Chambliss was slain at the head of his men at Deep Bottom, Virginia, August 16, 1864.

Col. J. Lucius Davis, commanding the 10th Virginia Cavalry in this campaign in Chambliss's brigade, was graduated from the Academy in 1833; he resigned to enter civil life three years later, and served throughout the Civil War in the regiment just noted. He died May 11, 1871.

In Gen. William E. Jones's brigade was another West-Pointer, Lunsford Lindsay Lomax, colonel of the 11th Virginia Cavalry, and afterward brigadier general. He finally commanded a division of cavalry in Lee's army, with the rank of major general. He was born in Newport, Rhode Island, November 4, 1835, of an old Virginia family, graduated from the Academy in 1856, and spent some years fighting Indians, escorting emigrants, and guarding the frontier before resigning his lieutenancy in the First Cavalry, April 22, 1861, to enter the Confederate service, where he reached distinction as a cavalry leader. In recent years he has rendered valuable service in the War Department in compiling and editing the *Official Records*. He is now (1912) a member of the Gettysburg Battle-field Park Commission.

Col. John T. Mercer, of Georgia, a member of the class of 1854, was first lieutenant in the Second Dragoons in 1861, when he resigned, April 26th, to become colonel of the 21st Georgia Infantry, which served in Doles's brigade, Rodes's division, at Gettysburg. Colonel Mercer was killed April 19, 1864, in the fight at Plymouth, North Carolina.

THE ARTILLERY

The Chief of Artillery, Army of Northern Virginia:—Brig. Gen.
WILLIAM NELSON PENDLETON

Brig. Gen. William Nelson Pendleton, born in Virginia, December 23, 1809, was graduated 1830, and served as a lieutenant of artillery for about three years, when he resigned to become a college professor, a clergyman of the Protestant Episcopal Church, and rector of the diocesan school of his denomination at Alexandria, Virginia. His long-time friendship for Jefferson Davis and Robert E. Lee began when they were cadets together at the Point.

Pendleton organized a battery of artillery at Lexington, Virginia, and went with it to Manassas, where he served as chief of that arm under Joseph E. Johnston; later he occupied the same post under Lee till the end. Under his directions Lee's artillery was reorganized just before the Gettysburg campaign. Longstreet, Gordon, and Pendleton were the three commissioners appointed at Appomattox to arrange the details of the surrender. During the war General Pendleton did not intermit his clerical duties; but when opportunity served he administered the ordinances and preached the Gospel. After the war he resumed ministerial duties at Lexington, Virginia, where Lee was president of the University, and thereby kept up his affectionate and confidential relations with his great chief. He died January 15, 1883.

Chief of Artillery, First Army Corps:—ALEXANDER

Edward Porter Alexander (1835–1910), born in Georgia, was graduated into the corps of engineers from the Point in 1857, and served as instructor in military engineering in the Academy. In the Confederate service he rose from a captaincy of artillery to be brigadier general, serving finally as chief of ordnance in the Army of Northern Virginia. At Gettysburg Longstreet intrusted Colonel Alexander with the duty of massing the artillery for the final cannonade to prepare the way for Pickett's charge; in this capacity Alexander arrayed sixty-five guns on Seminary Ridge, July 3d, and gave the signal for the cannonade to cease and the infantry to advance. After the war he served as a college professor for some years, and then gave his attention to railroad management and direction, in the large sense, and to great engineering enterprises. His *Military Memoirs of a Confederate* is the ablest volume on the critical aspects of the war that has been furnished by any Southern writer. It deals in an unbiased way with the large campaigns, and brings into view the merits and defects of leaders on both sides.

OTHER WEST POINT ARTILLERISTS

Among the commanders of battalions of artillery in Lee's army there were three others besides General Alexander who were trained in the Academy. In the corps of Longstreet the artillery battalion of Hood's division was under

Maj. MATHIS W. HENRY,

a Kentuckian, who belonged to the class of May 6, 1861, but who resigned his commission of second lieutenant in the Third Cavalry August 19, 1861, and who was advanced in Lee's army to be major and commander of four batteries constituting a battalion of that branch. Died November 28, 1877.

Serving in the First Corps, also, under Colonel Alexander, chief of artillery, was

Maj. FRANK HUGER,

a Virginian, who graduated from the Academy in 1860, and who resigned his lieutenancy in the 10th Infantry to enter the Confederate service, May 21, 1861, rising in due time to be lieutenant colonel and head of an artillery battalion in this corps—a position which he held at Gettysburg. He died June 10, 1897.

Another young Virginian in this branch of the army at Gettysburg was

Maj. ROBERT F. BECKHAM,

of the class of 1859, who gave up his lieutenancy of engineers, May 3, 1861, and later became commander of a battalion of horse artillery in Stuart's cavalry, in which capacity he served at Gettysburg. He was killed in the battle of Franklin, Tennessee, November 30, 1864.

WEST POINT AT GETTYSBURG

LEE'S STAFF-OFFICERS

The military secretary, colonel, and afterward brigadier general, Armistead Lindsay Long, of the class of 1850, an officer of the old army in artillery service until his resignation, June 10, 1861, served also with his commander as engineer and confidential staff-officer in many battles. After the war he was chief engineer of the James River and Kanawha Canal Company in Virginia; but for twenty years before his death, April 29, 1891, he walked in darkness without the use of his eyes. During this period happily he utilized his enforced leisure, with the help of an amanuensis, by composing his observations and experiences in wartime, which were embodied in his interesting volume, *Memoirs of Lee*.

The Chief Quartermaster, Col. James M. Corley, born in South Carolina, and graduated from the Academy in 1850, after years of service on the Plains and in the Northwest, resigned his lieutenancy in the 6th Infantry, May 4, 1861. He was honored with Lee's affection and confidence in his long and faithful service as chief at the head of his department in Lee's army.

The Chief Commissary of Subsistence, Robert G. Cole, born in Virginia, and a member of the class of 1850, was on duty as a lieutenant of the 8th Infantry in Texas and the Indian Territory chiefly, until his resignation from the service, January 28, 1861.

Lee's Chief of Engineers, Col. William Proctor Smith, a Virginian, served as a lieutenant of engineers after his graduation from the Point in the class of 1857 until he resigned, April 27, 1861.

OTHER STAFF-OFFICERS

Abner Smead, of Georgia, on graduation from the Academy July 1, 1854, entered the artillery branch and served at various eastern seaboard points, reaching a first lieutenancy, First Artillery, in 1860. In the spring of 1861, after proffering his resignation, he became a Confederate officer, rising to the rank of colonel and assistant inspector general, in which capacity he served in Ewell's corps at Gettysburg.

William T. Magruder, of Maryland, of the class of 1850, served in the cavalry and continued in the service of the United States until October 1, 1862, when he resigned his captaincy in the First Cavalry. He was made captain and assistant adjutant general in the Confederate Army, and, at Gettysburg, on duty with Gen. J. R. Davis's brigade, was killed in the final charge.

II

ROSTER OF THE ARMY OF THE POTOMAC

ORGANIZATION

The Maj. Gen. commanding, George Gordon Meade (W. P.).[1]

GENERAL HEADQUARTERS

Command of the provost marshal general, Brig. Gen. Marsena R. Patrick (W. P.).

93d New York, Col. John S. Crocker (brvt. brig. gen. March 13, 1865). The regiment served as headquarters guard under McClellan, Burnside, Hooker, and Meade for nearly two years. From March, 1864, it served in the Second Corps.

8th U. S. Infantry (8 companies), Capt. Edwin W. H. Read (brvt. maj. for gallantry in this battle).

2d Pennsylvania Cavalry, Col. R. Butler Price (brvt. brig. gen. March 13, 1865).

6th Pennsylvania Cavalry, companies E and I, Capt. James Starr (later maj. of the regiment), and detachments from 1st, 2d, 5th, and 6th U. S. Cavalry (regulars).

Signal Corps, Capt. Lemuel B. Norton (brvt. maj. for gallantry in this fight, also later brevets).

Guards and Orderlies, Oneida (N. Y.) Cavalry, Capt. Daniel P. Mann.

Chief of Artillery, Brig. Gen. Henry J. Hunt (W. P.).

ENGINEER DEPARTMENT

Chief Engineer of the Army, Brig. Gen. G. K. Warren (W. P.).
Engineer Brigade, Brig. Gen. Henry W. Benham (W. P.).
15th New York (3 companies), Maj. Walter L. Cassin.
50th New York, Col. William H. Pettes (W. P.).
U. S. Battalion, Capt. George H. Mendell (W. P.).
The engineers were not engaged in the fight; part of them were ordered to Washington when on their way to the field; some of the regular battalion were sent to guard trains after arrival at Gettys-

---

[1] The letters (W. P.) thus bracketed refer to the sketch of the officer in question in the section devoted to West Point Military Academy, where the record of every graduate in both armies will be found.

burg; and Capt. Mendell with other officers did notable service in building pontoon bridges for the army en route.

Adjutant General, Brig. Gen. Seth Williams (W. P.), brevetted for gallantry in this battle.

Chief Quartermaster, Brig. Gen. Rufus Ingalls (W. P.).

Chief of Commissariat, Col. Henry F. Clarke (W. P.).

Chief of Staff, Maj. Gen. Daniel Butterfield (sketched in "The Empire State in the Battle").

FIRST ARMY CORPS

(1) Maj. Gen. John F. Reynolds (W. P.).

(2) Maj. Gen. Abner Doubleday (W. P.).

(3) Maj. Gen. John Newton (W. P.).

(Doubleday commanded, June 30 and July 1; Newton took charge on the morning of July 2d).

HEADQUARTERS ESCORT AND GUARD

1st Maine Cavalry, Co. L, Capt. C. Taylor.

FIRST DIVISION

Brig. Gen. James S. Wadsworth. For sketch see "The Empire State in the Battle."

First Brigade: Brig. Gen. Solomon Meredith (an Indiana soldier, made brig. gen. October 6, 1862; brevetted maj. gen. in 1865; died 1875). He was severely injured by the falling of his horse, shot in the battle; then Col. William W. Robinson, 7th Wisconsin, led the command, which was known as the "Iron Brigade."

19th Indiana, Col. Samuel J. Williams. Losses, 210 (including Lieuts. Crockett T. East and Richard Jones among the killed) out of 288 taken into the fight. Lieut. Col. William W. Dudley lost a leg; was brevetted colonel and brigadier general for gallantry here; later achieved celebrity in law and politics, and served for a while as Commissioner of Pensions; then in law practice in Washington, D. C.

24th Michigan, Col. Henry A. Morrow, wounded; followed by Capt. Albert M. Edwards. Losses, 363, the largest regimental Union loss in the battle. The dead included eight officers: Capts. M. J. O'Donnell and Wm. J. Speed, and Lieuts. Gilbert A. Dickey, Newell Grace, Reuben H. Humphreville, Winfield S. Safford, Lucius L. Shattuck, and Walter H. Wallace. In addition Lieut. Col. Mark Flanigan lost a leg, and Maj. Edwin B. Wight an eye. Col. Morrow was brevetted up to major general later in the war, entering the regular service afterward; he died in 1891, colonel of the 21st Infantry.

2d Wisconsin. Losses, 233. Lieut. Col. George H. Stevens was mortally wounded; Lieut. William S. Winegar killed. The regiment was led in succession by Col. Lucius Fairchild, wounded; Maj. John

Mansfield, wounded (brevetted brig. gen. 1865; died 1896); and Capt. George H. Otis. Corpls. Davidson and Brisbois took the colors when they were shot down and bore them at last from the field. Col. Fairchild (1831–1896), who gallantly led his men till his elbow was smashed by a bullet—causing the loss of his arm—was made brigadier general in October, 1863, in recognition of his service here; but his strength gave way later, and he resigned from the army. He filled some notable places afterward: governor of Wisconsin, consul at Liverpool, consul general at Paris, minister to Spain, commander in chief Grand Army of the Republic.

6th Wisconsin, Lieut. Col. Rufus R. Dawes (col. July 5, 1864; brevetted brig. gen. March 13, 1865; died 1899). Losses, 164, including Capt. John Ticknor and Lieut. O. D. Chapman, killed. Corpl. Francis Asbury Waller won a medal of honor by the capture of the colors of the 2d Mississippi.

7th Wisconsin. Col. William W. Robinson, taking the brigade, was followed in command by Maj. Mark Finnicum, Lieut. Col. J. B. Callis having been wounded. Sergt. Jefferson Coates won a medal by his gallantry, and Color-bearer McDermott showed unusual heroism in keeping the shattered colors when the staff was shot in two, and he himself was badly wounded. Losses, 178.

Second Brigade: Brig. Gen. Lysander Cutler, a native of Massachusetts, colonel of the 6th Wisconsin, July, 1861; brigadier general, November 29, 1862; brevet major general, 1864; died 1866.

7th Indiana, Col. Ira G. Grover (brvt. brig. gen. March 13, 1865; died 1876). Losses, 10. This regiment escaped the first day's fight, being on special duty guarding Emmitsburg. That night Sergt. Hussy, scouting in the woods on Culp's Hill, captured an officer of the 25th Virginia, and scattered his squad of twenty men, reconnoitering from Edward Johnson's division. (See *Official Records,* XXVII, 2:531).

76th New York. Losses, 234. Maj. Andrew J. Grover, leading the regiment, was killed; Capt. John E. Cook took the command. Capt. Robert B. Everett killed; Capt. Robert Story and Lieuts. Philip Keeler and Robert G. Nixon mortally wounded.

84th New York—the "Fourteenth Militia"—Col. Edward B. Fowler (later brevetted brig. gen.). Losses, 217.

95th New York. Col. George H. Biddle, when wounded, gave place to Maj. Edward Pye. Losses, 115.

147th New York. Losses, 296, including Lieuts. Guilford D. Mace, Sylvester J. Taylor, David G. VanDusen, Wm. P. Schenck, and David McAssy, killed or fatally injured. Lieut. Col. Francis C. Miller, severely wounded, gave place to Maj. George Harney. In the retreat Sergt. W. A. Wybourn, although severely wounded, caught the regimental colors from the fallen standard-bearer and brought them safely inside the Union lines.

ROSTER OF ARMY OF THE POTOMAC

56th Pennsylvania, Col. J. William Hoffman (brevetted brig. gen. August 1, 1864; died 1902). Losses, 136, including Lieut. John D. Gordon, killed. This was the first infantry regiment to deliver a volley against the advancing foe at the opening of the fight. It was then flanked and severely damaged, the chief losses coming in its early experience.

SECOND DIVISION

Brig. Gen. John C. Robinson. (For personal sketch see "The Empire State in the Battle.")

First Brigade: Led in succession by Brig. Gen. Gabriel R. Paul (W. P.), who was dreadfully wounded and lost his eyesight from the bullet's hurt; Col. Samuel K. Leonard, 13th Massachusetts, wounded; Col. Adrian H. Root, 94th New York, wounded and captured; Col. Richard Coulter, 11th Pennsylvania, wounded (brevetted brig. gen. and maj. gen. 1864–1865); and Col. Peter Lyle, 90th Pennsylvania (brvt. brig. gen. 1865).

16th Maine. Losses, 232; Capts. Oliver H. Lowell and Stephen G. Whitehouse killed. At different times it was led by Col. Charles W. Tilden, Maj. Archibald W. Leavitt, and Lieut. Col. A. B. Farnham.

13th Massachusetts. Col. Samuel H. Leonard, wounded, was succeeded by Lieut. Col. N. W. Batchelder. Losses, 185. In one of its charges it captured 132 prisoners; in the final retreat it lost a hundred by capture.

94th New York. After Col. Adrian R. Root (brevetted brig. gen. and maj. gen. in 1865) was wounded and captured the command fell to Maj. Samuel A. Moffett. Losses, 245—167 of them missing, probably captured.

104th New York, Col. Gilbert G. Prey. Losses, 199, including Lieut. James Johnston, killed. In one crisis the colors, after three bearers had fallen, were stripped from the staff, and hidden under his coat by Sergt. Joseph Wallace, who thus brought them from the field.

107th Pennsylvania. Lieut. Col. James MacThomson (brevetted col. and brig. gen. for this battle) was wounded; Capt. Emanuel H. Roath following him in command. The losses were 165 out of 255.

Second Brigade: Brig. Gen. Henry Baxter. Gen. Baxter (1821–1873), born in New York, in his youth a "Forty-niner," adventuring himself on the Pacific coast, rose from a captaincy in the 7th Michigan to be its colonel, then a brigadier general, and at last a brevet major general. After the war he served as the United States minister to Honduras.

12th Massachusetts. Col. James L. Bates, twice wounded, left his command in the hands of Lieut. Col. David Allen, Jr. Losses, 119, including among the slain Lieuts. Charles G. Russell and Francis Thomas.

26   387

83d New York (9th Militia), Lieut. Col. Joseph A. Moesch, who, finely mounted and a commanding figure, led several charges. Losses, 88, including Capt. Thomas W. Quirk and Lieut. Charles A. Clark, killed.

97th New York. Col. Charles Wheelock (brvt. brig. gen. in 1864), when disabled, was followed by Maj. Charles Northrup. Losses, 125, including among the killed or mortally wounded Lieuts. Wm. J. Morrin, James H. Stiles, and Rush R. Cady. This is one item in the colonel's report: "We captured 213 of the 20th North Carolina, with their colors." Wheelock was captured, but escaped on his way from Gettysburg. Lieut. Col. Spofford was taken to Richmond, and suffered months of imprisonment.

11th Pennsylvania. When Col. Richard Coulter commanded a brigade the command fell to Capts. B. F. Haines and John H. Overmeyer in succession. Losses, 132. Coulter was wounded, and in 1864 and 1865 brevetted both brigadier and major general.

88th Pennsylvania. Maj. Benezet F. Foust was stricken down while cheering on his men (brevetted col. for his gallantry); the command then fell to Capt. Edmund A. Moss, later lieutenant colonel, who was captured; then Capt. Henry Whiteside took charge. Losses, 110.

90th Pennsylvania. Col. Peter Lyle (brvt. brig. gen. 1865) was for a time in charge of the brigade; then Maj. Alfred J. Sellers took charge. He won a medal of honor for his gallantry. Losses, 94, including Chaplain Howell, killed in the town in an unfortunate altercation with a Confederate.

THIRD DIVISION

Brig. Gen. Thomas A. Rowley. (For sketch see "Pennsylvania Officers in the Foreground.")

First Brigade: This body was usually directed by Rowley; when Doubleday took the corps Rowley had charge of the division; in that case Col. Chapman Biddle commanded the brigade. Sketches of Biddle, and also of Cols. Stone, Wister, and Dana, commanders in succession of the second brigade, will be found in the chapter on "Pennsylvania Officers" just referred to.

80th New York (20th Militia), Col. Theodore B. Gates (afterward brevetted brig. gen.). Losses, 170, including among the slain Capts. Ambrose N. Baldwin and Joseph S. Corbin, and Lieut. George W. Brankstonc. Doubleday declared afterward that this regiment held the post of honor, guarding the rear in the final retreat on the first day.

121st Pennsylvania. In the intervals when Col. Chapman Biddle was at the head of the brigade Maj. Alexander Biddle led the regiment. Both are mentioned by Rowley for their bravery. Losses, 179. Sergt. Robert F. Bates, of Company D, distinguished in the battle, was promoted to a first lieutenancy in 1864, and after the war went into the Regular Army; when retired in 1899 he was major, 2d Infantry. He was brevetted first lieutenancy for Gettysburg.

142d Pennsylvania. The commander, Col. Robert P. Cummins, killed early in the engagement, was followed by Lieut. Col. Alfred B. McCalmont, later brevet brigadier general. Losses, 211, including among the deaths Capt. Charles H. Flagg and Lieuts. Edward B. Hurst and Andrew G. Tucker.

151st Pennsylvania. Lieut. Col. George F. McFarland, gallantly leading his men, was desperately wounded, losing his right leg, and crippled incurably in the other; Capt. Walter L. Owens then took charge. Losses, 337—more than any other regiment in that army except the 24th Michigan, mentioned above. Officers slain: Lieuts. Aaron S. Seaman and George A. Trexler. When this regiment started out, nine hundred strong, in October, 1862, its ranks contained one hundred and thirteen school-teachers.

Second Brigade: Col. Roy Stone, 149th Pennsylvania (brevetted brig. gen. for bravery at Gettysburg), served in the Spanish-American War in 1898 as brigadier general; when Stone was wounded at Gettysburg Col. Langhorne Wister succeeded him; when that officer fell Col. Edmund L. Dana followed in command. Both of these were brevetted for Gettysburg.

143d Pennsylvania. Lieut. Col. John D. Musser directed the regiment when Dana took the brigade. (Musser was killed in the Wilderness, May 6, 1864). Losses, 253 out of 465. Officers killed: Lieuts. Charles W. Betzenberger and Lyman R. Nicholson.

149th Pennsylvania, "First Bucktails." Lieut. Col. Walton Dwight, wounded, was followed by Capt. James Glenn, afterward lieutenant colonel of the regiment. Losses, 336, including among the slain Capt. Alfred J. Sofield.

150th Pennsylvania, "Second Bucktails." When Col. Langhorne Wister headed the brigade Lieut. Col. Henry S. Huidekoper commanded the regiment; when he was wounded Capt. Cornelius C. Widdis was his successor. Losses, 264. Lieuts. Charles P. Keyser, Elias D. Weidensaul, and Henry Chancellor, Jr., were killed. Col. Huidekoper lost an arm, and won for his extraordinary gallantry the Congressional Medal of Honor. Col. Stone, in the tribute which he pays to this brigade, nobly says in his report, "They all fought as if each man felt that upon his own arm hung the fate of the day and the nation."

Third Brigade: Brig. Gen. George J. Stannard. This officer (1820–1886), after serving as colonel of the 9th Vermont, became brigadier general March 11, 1863, and brevet major general October 28, 1864. He led in the defense of Fort Harrison against a terrific assault made by the Confederates before Petersburg, September 30, 1864, and lost an arm. He held several important government positions in Burlington, Vt., and in Washington, D. C., after the war. The brigade

GETTYSBURG

marched from Washington to join the Army of the Potomac, arriving at Gettysburg late in the evening of the first day. It did extraordinary service on the next two days, as is related elsewhere in this volume.

12th Vermont, Col. Asa P. Blunt (brvt. brig. gen. 1865).

13th Vermont, Col. Francis V. Randall; when Stannard was wounded Randall took the brigade; and the regiment was directed in part by Lieut. Col. Wm. D. Munson, and for a time by Maj. Joseph J. Boynton. Losses, 113, Lieut. John T. Sennott being mortally wounded.

14th Vermont, Col. William T. Nichols. Losses, 107, including Lieut. Wm. H. Hamilton, killed.

15th Vermont, Col. Redfield Proctor (1831–1908), who, a graduate of Dartmouth, after a creditable career throughout the war, achieved high civic distinction as member of both houses of the State legislature, lieutenant governor, governor, Secretary of War, and United States Senator. He died in the midst of his fourth term in the Senate.

16th Vermont, Col. Wheelock G. Veazey. Losses, 119, including among the slain Lieut. Cyrus G. Lawton. Col. Veazey (1835–1898) was a graduate of Dartmouth, and of the Albany Law School. For years he was reporter for the Supreme Court of his State; then Senator, commissioner to revise the code, judge of the Supreme Court of Vermont, and member of the Interstate Commerce Commission. In 1890 he was commander in chief of the Grand Army of the Republic.

Artillery Brigade: Brigade commander, Col. Charles S. Wainwright, of the 1st New York Light Artillery. This officer, beginning his military service in the fall of 1861 as major in his regiment, was promoted to be lieutenant colonel and then colonel, serving a long while with credit as chief of artillery of the First Army Corps; brevetted brigadier general August 1, 1864, for special service in the campaigns of that year.

Maine Light, 2d Battery B, Capt. James A. Hall. Losses, 22.

Maine Light, 5th Battery E. Capt. Greenleaf T. Stevens and his assistant, Lieut. G. C. Hunt, were wounded, and the guns were left in charge of Lieut. Edward N. Whittier. Losses, 23.

1st New York Light, Batteries L and E. Capt. Gilbert H. Reynolds, severely wounded in the first day's fight, was followed in command by Lieut. George Breck, aided by Lieuts. B. W. Wilbur and W. H. Bower. Losses, 19. Bugler Mastin Smith, when a connoneer was wounded, dismounted and took his place for the time.

1st Pennsylvania Light, Battery B, Capt. James H. Cooper. Losses, 12.

4th U. S., Battery B, Lieut. James Stewart. Losses, 36.

SECOND ARMY CORPS

Maj. Gen. Winfield S. Hancock (W. P.).[1] (On the first day, while for a few hours Hancock was in temporary command of the whole

[1] See Addendum, page 454.

ROSTER OF ARMY OF THE POTOMAC

field, Brig. Gen. John Gibbon (W. P.) had charge of the corps. At the end of the third day, when Hancock because of his wound had to relinquish the corps, Brig. Gen. William Hays (W. P.) was put over it.)

General Headquarters

6th New York Cavalry, Companies D and K, Capt. Riley Johnson. Losses, 4.

First Division

Brig. Gen. John Curtis Caldwell. Gen. Caldwell, a Vermonter, born in 1833, a graduate of Amherst, was for five years principal of an academy in Maine before he became, in 1861, colonel of the 11th Maine Regiment. In April, 1862, he was made a brigadier general, and later was brevetted one notch higher. After the war he became a lawyer, a member of the Maine Senate, consul at Valparaiso, Chile, United States minister to Uruguay and Paraguay, and consul in Costa Rica. He made a most creditable record in military service.

First Brigade: Col. Edward E. Cross, 5th New Hampshire (killed at the head of the command); followed by Col. H. B. McKeen.

5th New Hampshire, Lieut. Col. Charles E. Hapgood. Losses, 80. Lieut. Ruel G. Austin mortally wounded.

61st New York, Lieut. Col. K. Oscar Broady. Losses, 62. Lieut. Franklin K. Garland mortally wounded.

81st Pennsylvania, Col. H. Boyd McKeen (killed at Cold Harbor, 1864). When this officer took the brigade Lieut. Col. Amos Stroh commanded the regiment. Losses, 62.

148th Pennsylvania, Lieut. Col. Robert McFarlane. Losses, 125. Capt. Robert M. Forster killed, and Lieut. John A. Bayard mortally wounded. The colonel of this regiment, James A. Beaver, recovering from Chancellorsville wounds, was at this time in command of Camp Curtin, Harrisburg, Penn., helping Couch and Curtin to organize the militia for defense of the State. Beaver, a college graduate and an able lawyer, after the war, in which he received serious injuries, losing a leg in one battle, served as governor of his State, and since 1896 (at this writing, 1913) has been on the bench of the Superior Court of Pennsylvania.

Second Brigade: Col. Patrick Kelly, killed, June 16, 1864, in front of Petersburg.

28th Massachusetts, Col. R. Byrnes (commissioned lieut., 17th Infantry, May, 1861, after five years of "regular" service before the war; mortally wounded at Cold Harbor, 1864). Losses, 100.

63d New York (2 companies). Lieut. Col. Richard C. Bentley, wounded, was followed in command by Capt. Thomas Touhy. Losses, 23.

69th New York (2 companies), Capt. Richard Maroney, wounded; followed by Lieut. James J. Smith. Losses, 25.

391

GETTYSBURG

88th New York, Capt. Denis F. Burke. Losses, 28. Lieut. Wm. McClelland killed.

116th Pennsylvania (4 companies), Maj. St. Clair A. Mulholland. Losses, 22. (Maj. Mulholland was brevetted maj. gen. before the war closed. He died in Philadelphia in 1910, after a career in his home city crowded with civic service and distinction.)

Third Brigade: Brig. Gen. Samuel K. Zook, mortally wounded in the Wheat-field, Thursday afternoon, followed in command by Lieut. Col. John Fraser, 140th Pennsylvania. Zook is sketched in the New York chapter.

52d New York. Lieut. Col. Charles G. Freudenberg, wounded, was followed by Maj. Edward Venuti, mortally wounded, and then by Capt. Wm. Scherrer. Losses, 38.

57th New York, Lieut. Col. Alfred B. Chapman (killed in the Wilderness, May 5, 1864). Losses, 34.

66th New York. Col. Orlando H. Morris, and Lieut. Col. John S. Hammell, both wounded, were followed by Maj. Peter Nelson. Losses, 44, including among the slain Capts. George H. Ince and Elijah F. Munn.

140th Pennsylvania. Col. Richard P. Roberts, shot at the head of his command, was succeeded by Lieut. Col. John Fraser, who later took the brigade. Losses, 241, including Capt. David Acheson and Lieut. Alex. M. Wilson among the killed.

Fourth Brigade: Col. John R. Brooke, in later years major general, U.S.A., sketched in chapter on Pennsylvania officers.

27th Connecticut (2 companies). Lieut. Col. Henry C. Merwin "fell in the thickest of the fight," said Brooke, in his report; Maj. James H. Coburn took charge. Losses, 37, including the colonel and Lieut. Jedediah Chapman, killed.

2d Delaware, Col. William P. Bailey; later Capt. Chas. H. Christman commanded. Losses, 84. Lieut. Hamill W. Ottey and Lieut. George G. Plank killed.

64th New York. Col. Daniel G. Bingham was wounded, dying a year later from the effects of the injury; Maj. Leman W. Bradley took command. Losses, 98. Capt. Henry V. Fuller, and Lieuts. Willis G. Babcock, Alfred H. Lewis, and Ira S. Thurber killed.

53d Pennsylvania, Lieut. Col. R. McMichael. Losses, 80.

145th Pennsylvania. Col. Hiram L. Brown and Capt. John W. Reynolds wounded; Capt. Moses W. Oliver then commanded. Losses, 90. Capt. George G. Griswold and Lieuts. Horatio F. Lewis and George H. Finch killed or mortally hurt.

SECOND DIVISION

Brig. Gen. John Gibbon (W. P.). When Gibbon took charge of the corps Brig. Gen. William Harrow, of the First Brigade, was ad-

392

vanced to the post of division commander. Gibbon was wounded at the close of the third day.

First Brigade: Brig. Gen. William Harrow. This officer was advanced from the colonelcy of the 14th Indiana to be brigadier general, November 29, 1862. When he was put over the division temporarily in the battle Col. Francis E. Heath took the brigade.

19th Maine, Col. Francis E. Heath (brvt. brig. gen. 1865); when Heath had the brigade Lieut. Col. Henry W. Cunningham took the regiment. Losses, 203, including among the killed Capt. George D. Smith and Lieut. Leroy S. Scott.

15th Massachusetts, Col. George H. Ward, mortally wounded in trying to check the advance of the Confederates Thursday afternoon; Lieut. Col. George C. Joslin took the vacated place. Capts. Hans P. Jorgenson and John Murkland were also killed; Lieut. Elisha B. Buss was mortally wounded. Losses, 148.

1st Minnesota. This regiment was made a stop-gap in a critical hour late Thursday afternoon by Hancock in person, in the attempt to arrest the charge of the Confederates against the Union line. The command was literally cut to pieces. The field-officers, Col. William Colville, Jr. (brvt. brig. gen. 1865), Lieut. Col. Charles P. Adams (also brevetted to the same rank), and Maj. Mark W. Downey, were wounded, and the next in command, Capt. Nathan W. Messick, was killed, along with Capt. Louis Muller and Lieut. Waldo Farrar, while Capts. Wilson B. Farrell and Joseph Periam, and Lieuts. David B. Demarest and Charles H. Mason were mortally wounded. Capt. Henry C. Coates was the final commander. Losses, 224.

82d New York, Lieut. Col. James Huston, killed on Thursday afternoon on the Emmitsburg road when Humphreys's men were pressed back; Capt. John Darrow then took command. Losses, 192. Capt. Jonah C. Hoyt, and Lieuts. John H. McDonald and John Cranston killed or fatally hurt.

Second Brigade: Brig. Gen. Alex. S. Webb (W. P.).

69th Pennsylvania. Col. Dennis O'Kane was mortally wounded during Pickett's assault, and also Lieut. Col. Martin Tschudy; then Capt. Wm. Davis commanded. Other officers killed: Capts. M. Duffy and George C. Thompson, and Lieut. Charles F. Kelly. Losses, 137.

71st Pennsylvania, Col. Richard Penn Smith. Losses, 98. Capts. John M. Steffan and W. H. Dull killed.

72d Pennsylvania, Col. De Witt C. Baxter (wounded; brvt. brig. gen. 1865), Lieut. Col. Theodore Hesser (killed at Mine Run, November 27, 1863). Losses, 192. Capt. Andrew McBride and Lieuts. James I. Griffith and Sutton Jones killed.

106th Pennsylvania, Lieut. Col. Wm. L. Curry (mortally wounded at Spottsylvania, May, 1864). Losses, 64. Lieut. F. M. Pleis mortally hurt, and Lieut. W. H. Smith killed. It may be recalled

GETTYSBURG

that the position held by this small Philadelphia brigade was the point where the brunt of the charge of Pickett and Pettigrew fell on Friday.

Third Brigade: Col. Norman J. Hall (W. P.) (7th Michigan).

19th Massachusetts, Col. Arthur F. Devereux (brvt. brig. gen. 1865). Losses, 77. Lieuts. Herman Donath and Sherman S. Robinson killed. Medals of honor were awarded to Corpls. J. H. De Castro and B. F. Falls, and Privates B. H. Jellison and John Robinson, for capturing battle-flags in the closing struggle.

20th Massachusetts, Col. Paul J. Revere (a grandson of the Revolutionary Paul Revere), wounded mortally, brevetted brigadier general for his gallantry; Lieut. Col. George N. Macy was wounded, and Capt. Henry L. Abbott followed next in command. Losses, 127. Lieuts. Sumner Paine and Henry Ropes killed. Capt. Oliver Wendell Holmes, now (1913) a justice of the Supreme Court, was an officer in this regiment, but at the time of this battle was still laid up with a wound incurred at Chancellorsville.

7th Michigan. Lieut. Col. Amos E. Steele, Jr., killed, was followed by Maj. Sylvanus W. Curtis. Losses, 65, including Lieut. Albert Slafter, killed.

42d New York, Col. James E. Mallon. Losses, 74.

59th New York, Lieut. Col. Max A. Thoman (mortally wounded), followed by Capt. Wm. McFadden. Losses, 34. Lieut. William H. Pohlman killed. A medal of honor was granted to Sergt. James Wiley for capturing one of the flags of the 48th Georgia.

1st Company, Massachusetts Sharp-shooters, led by Capt. Wm. Plumer and Lieut. Emerson L. Bicknell, lost 8.

THIRD DIVISION

Brig. Gen. Alexander Hays (W. P.).

First Brigade: Col. Samuel Sprigg Carroll (W. P.).

14th Indiana, Col. John Coons. Losses, 31.

4th Ohio, Col. Leonard W. Carpenter. Losses, 31. Lieuts. Addison H. Edgar and Samuel W. Shoub killed. Capt. John S. Jones, later brevet brigadier general, was after the war a member of Congress, and so was Archibald Lybrand, later a captain in the 73d Ohio.

8th Ohio. Col. Carroll, in command of the brigade, was of this regiment; Lieut. Col. Franklin Sawyer (brvt. brig. gen.) had the regiment. Losses, 102. Lieut. Elijah Hayden killed. This command did much to cripple Pickett's charge by a flank attack as the Confederates drew near to Hays's division. Sergt. Daniel Miller and Private James Richmond received medals of honor for capturing Confederate colors on the last day.

7th West Virginia, Lieut. Col. Jonathan H. Lockwood. Losses, 47.

Second Brigade: Col. Thomas A. Smyth, 1st Delaware (brig. gen.

October 1, 1864; brvt. maj. gen. April 7, 1865, for gallantry at Farm-ville on that date, when he was mortally wounded). Wounded in command of the brigade this day, and followed by Lieut. Col. Francis E. Pierce.

14th Connecticut, Maj. Theodore G. Ellis. Losses, 66.

1st Delaware was led successively by four officers—Lieut. Col. Edward P. Harris, Capt. Thomas B. Hizar, wounded; Lieut. William Smith, killed; and Lieut. John T. Dent. Losses, 77. Capt. Martin W. B. Ellegood was also killed.

12th New Jersey, Maj. John T. Hill. Losses, 115. Capt. Charles K. Horsfall and Lieut. Richard Townsend killed.

10th New York (a battalion), Maj. George F. Hopper. Losses, 6. (On special duty as rear guard, and at division headquarters.)

108th New York, Lieut. Col. Francis E. Pierce (brvt. brig. gen. 1865; died, November 4, 1896, capt. 1st Infantry, U.S.A.). Losses, 102, including among the killed Lieuts. Carl. V. Amiet, Dayton T. Card, and Robert Evans. Pierce took the brigade when Smyth was hurt.

Third Brigade: Col. George L. Willard, a veteran officer of the old army, lost his life in command of this body Thursday afternoon. When twenty years of age he had led as first sergeant his company in the 15th U. S. Infantry in scaling the walls of Chapultepec. Cadmus M. Wilcox, whose Confederate brigade Willard's men were engaged with at Gettysburg when Willard fell, won a brevet that day at Chapultepec, at the very hour when Willard won a lieutenancy by his gallantry. The latter was a major in the 19th Infantry, as well as colonel 125th New York, when he fell. He was a commander of gifts and princely presence, greatly beloved. Col. Eliakim Sherrill, 126th New York, took the brigade and fell at its head next day, when Lieut. Col. James M. Bull, of the same regiment, succeeded to the command.

39th New York (4 companies), Maj. H. Hildebrand. Losses, 95. Lieuts. Theodore Paush killed, and Adolph Wagner mortally wounded.

111th New York, Col. Clinton Dougall McDougall (wounded); Lieut. Col. Isaac M. Lusk (injured) and Capt. Aaron P. Seeley fol-lowed in command. Losses, 249, including Lieuts. John H. Drake, Erastus M. Granger, and Augustus W. Proseus, killed.

125th New York, Lieut. Col. Levin Crandall. Losses, 139, includ-ing Col. Willard, noted above, and Capt. Ephraim Wood. At the time when the troops were about to clinch in the final fight on Friday, Capt. Samuel C. Armstrong rallied the skirmish-line of 75 men to the right of the line, quickly formed them at right angles to the charging force, thus facing its left flank, and then poured a destructive enfilading fire into it; as Sawyer was at the same time doing with a portion of his 8th Ohio. Capt. Armstrong (maj. of his regiment in November, 1863, and later col. 8th U.S.C.T., following the heroic Fribley, killed at Olustee, and still later brevetted brig. gen.) became a great

GETTYSBURG

educational leader after the war. He was a graduate of Williams College, and for thirty years, until his death in 1892, he was at the head of the Hampton Institute, which he founded. During that period he had no rival as pioneer in the task of educating the Indian and the negro.

126th New York. Losses, 231, including the commander, Col. E. Sherrill, at the head of the brigade, killed during the charge; followed in regiment and brigade command by Lieut. Col. James M. Bull. Other officers killed or mortally hurt: Capts. Orin J. Herendeen, Isaac Shimer, Charles M. Wheeler; Lieuts. Rufus P. Holmes and Jacob Sherman. Medals of honor for capturing Confederate colors were awarded to Capt. Morris Brown, Jr., Sergt. George H. Dore, and Private Jerry Wall.

Artillery Brigade: Capt. John G. Hazard, 1st Rhode Island Light Artillery (later brevetted lieut. col., col., and brig. gen. for services during the war).

1st New York Light, Battery B, with 14th New York Battery attached, Capt. James McKay Rorty, killed; Lieut. Albert S. Sheldon wounded; Lieut. Robert E. Rogers followed in command. Losses, 26, including the captain just named.

1st Rhode Island, Battery A, Capt. William A. Arnold. Losses, 32.

1st Rhode Island, Battery B. Lieut. Fred T. Brown, wounded, was followed by Lieut. Walter S. Perrin; Lieut. Joseph S. Milne, serving for the time with Cushing, Battery A, 4th U. S. Artillery, was mortally wounded. Losses, 28.

1st U. S., Battery I, Lieut. George A. Woodruff (W. P.), mortally wounded, followed by Lieut. Tully McCrea (W. P.), brevetted captain for this battle; retired brigadier general, U.S.A., February 22, 1903.

4th U. S., Battery A, Lieut. Alonzo H. Cushing (W. P.), killed; brevetted lieutenant colonel for gallantry in this fight. Sergt. Frederick Fuger, a private and non-commissioned officer in this battery for seven years, won a medal of honor, and a little later a commission, by his extraordinary gallantry, taking the command when the officers were killed or wounded, and five guns disabled, and in the very climax of Pickett's charge, working the remaining gun till the end.

THIRD ARMY CORPS

Maj. Gen. Daniel E. Sickles (sketched in "The Empire State in the Battle") commanded this corps until he fell in the early evening of July 2d, with a wound which necessitated the amputation of his leg. Maj. Gen. David B. Birney (sketched in "Pennsylvania Officers in the Foreground") then took the command.

FIRST DIVISION

Birney had this division till he was assigned to lead the corps; then the body was led by Brig. Gen. J. H. Hobart Ward.

396

ROSTER OF ARMY OF THE POTOMAC

The First Brigade was led by Brig. Gen. Charles K. Graham (sketched in chapter on "Empire State") until he was wounded and captured; then Col. Andrew H. Tippin took command.

57th Pennsylvania (8 companies). Col. Peter Sides, when wounded, was followed in command by Capt. Alanson H. Nelson. Losses, 115 out of 209; scores were snared in the Sherfey buildings near the Peach Orchard, which they occupied as skirmishers; of these 44 died as prisoners of war. Lieuts. John F. Cox and Henry Mitchell were killed.

63d Pennsylvania, Maj. John A. Danks. Losses, 34. The regiment, from dawn till the battle began, Thursday afternoon, was in an incessant skirmish.

68th Pennsylvania. Losses, 152. Officers killed or fatally wounded: Capt. George W. McLearn; Lieuts. Lewis W. Ealer, Andrew Black, and John Reynolds.

105th Pennsylvania, Col. Galvin A. Craig. Losses, 132 out of 274, including Lieut. George W. Crossley, killed, and Lieut. Isaac A. Dunsten, mortally wounded.

114th Pennsylvania (the "Collis Zouaves"). Lieut. Col. Frederick F. Cavada, when captured, was followed by Maj. E. R. Bowen. Losses, 155.

141st Pennsylvania. Col. Henry J. Madill, the commander, was later brevetted both brigadier and major general; 149 were lost out of 209 in the battle. Maj. Israel P. Spaulding was mortally wounded. Color Corpl. Berry, wounded three times, would not give the flag to another until helpless from a fourth wound.

Second Brigade: This brigade was usually led by Brig. Gen. J. H. Hobart Ward, who took the division when Birney had to assume charge of the corps. (For sketch of Ward see "The Empire State in the Battle.")

20th Indiana. Col. John Wheeler, a noble soldier, was shot through the head in the battle; Lieut. Col. Wm. C. L. Taylor then led the regiment, which lost 156. Lieut. Ezra B. Robbins, in addition to the colonel, was killed.

3d Maine, Col. Moses B. Lakeman. Losses, 122 out of 210. This loss was in part incurred in a fight with two Alabama regiments at noon Thursday, the conflict assuring the fact to Sickles that the Confederates were moving to attack him. Killed: Capt. John C. Keene.

4th Maine. Col. Elijah Walker at the head was wounded, and Capt. Edwin Walker took his place. Losses, 144, including the following officers dead or mortally wounded: Maj. Ebenezer Whitcomb, Lieuts. George M. Bragg, Charles S. McCobb, and Orpheus Roberts.

86th New York. Lieut. Col. Benjamin L. Higgins, severely wounded, was followed by Maj. Jacob H. Lansing. Sergt. Maj. W. B. Van Houten is singled out for special praise. Losses, 66, including Capt. John N. Warner, killed.

GETTYSBURG

124th New York. Col. A. Van Horne Ellis was killed; Lieut. Col. F. M. Cummins was severely wounded; Maj. James Cromwell, Capt. Isaac Nichols, and Lieut. Milnor Brown were slain. Total losses, 92.

99th Pennsylvania, Maj. John W. Moore. Out of 339 the loss was 120, including Lieut. John R. Nice, killed. Color Sergt. H. M. Munsell was specially mentioned.

1st U. S. Sharp-shooters. Col. Hiram Berdan, who organized this corps, was brevetted brigadier general for Chancellorsville and major general for Gettysburg. For a time he had command of the brigade; then Lieut. Col. Casper Trepp led the regiment. Losses, 49, including Capt. Chas. D. McLean and Lieut. George W. Sheldon among the killed.

2d U. S. Sharp-shooters (8 companies), Maj. Homer R. Stoughton. Losses, 43.

Third Brigade: Col. P. Regis de Trobriand (sketched in "The Empire State in the Battle").

17th Maine, Lieut. Col. Charles B. Merrill. Losses, 133, including among the killed or mortally wounded Capts. Almon W. Fogg and Milton M. Young, and Lieut. Hiram R. Dyer.

3d Michigan. Losses, 45. Col. Byron Root Pierce was one of the officers who remained mounted in the fiercest fire of the battle; he lost a leg; and Lieut. Col. Edwin S. Pierce then took charge. Col. Pierce was brevetted to major general; was honored by high offices after the war in the Loyal Legion, and when these lines were written in 1913 was still in government employ in Grand Rapids, Mich.

5th Michigan, Lieut. Col. John Pulford. Losses, 109, including Capt. Peter Generous and Lieut. John P. Thelen, killed.

40th New York, Col. Thomas W. Egan. A composite organization made up of veterans from the 37th, 38th, 55th, and 101st, along with those of the 40th who re-enlisted. Col. Egan was brevetted both to brigadier general and major general. Losses, 150, including Lieut. William H. H. Johnson, slain.

110th Pennsylvania (6 companies). Lieut. Col. David M. Jones, when wounded, was followed by Maj. Isaac Rogers. Losses, 53 out of 152. Rogers, promoted to lieutenant colonel, was killed at Spottsylvania, May, 1864.

SECOND DIVISION

Brig. Gen. Andrew A. Humphreys (W. P.).

First Brigade: Brig. Gen. Joseph B. Carr (sketched in "The Empire State in the Battle").

1st Massachusetts, Lieut. Col. Clark B. Baldwin. Losses, 120. Lieut. Henry Hartley killed.

11th Massachusetts, Lieut. Col. Porter D. Tripp. Losses, 129. Capt. Edwin Humphreys killed, and Lieut. William B. Mitchell mortally wounded.

16th Massachusetts was first led by Lieut. Col. Waldo Merriam (killed in the Wilderness, May, 1864); when he was wounded Capt. Matthew Donavan commanded. Losses, 81. Officers killed or mortally wounded: Capts. Leander G. King, David W. Roche, Charles R. Johnson; Lieut. George F. Brown.

12th New Hampshire, Capt. John F. Langley (the three field-officers, Col. J. H. Potter (W. P.), Lieut. Col. John F. Marsh, and Maj. George D. Savage, being detained by wounds received at Chancellorsville). Losses, 92, including Lieut. Henry A. L. French, killed.

11th New Jersey. Losses, 153; Capts. Andrew H. Ackerman, Doraster B. Logan, and Luther Martin, killed; Maj. Philip J. Kearny mortally wounded. No less than six officers commanded in the exigencies of the fight. Col. Robert McAllister (later brevetted brig. and maj. gen.), when severely wounded, was followed by Capt. Martin, killed; Capts. W. H. Lloyd and S. T. Sleeper, wounded, and Lieut. John Schoonover, who, although twice wounded, stuck to his work to the end. Corpl. Thomas Johnson, after two color-bearers had been shot, took the flag, advanced to the front, and thus marked a new line to which the regiment rallied.

26th Pennsylvania, Maj. Robert L. Bodine (afterward brevetted col. and brig. gen.). Losses, 213 out of 365 engaged, including Lieuts. Benjamin R. Wright and Frank B. Bird.

84th Pennsylvania, Lieut. Col. Milton Opp. (This regiment was on special duty at Westminster, Maryland, guarding trains from June 30th to July 8th. The author of this volume, detached from the regiment and on special duty in the battle, may be permitted to express his judgment that this body of Pennsylvanians was not surpassed in intelligence, skill, and unflinching courage by any regiment in the Army of the Potomac.)

Second Brigade: Col. (afterward brvt. brig. gen.) Wm. R. Brewster, 73d New York, led this famous "Excelsior Brigade," portions of which, under his lead, recaptured three of the Union guns in the turmoil of the late afternoon of July 2d. Sergt. Thomas Hogan on this occasion took the colors of the 8th Florida.

70th New York, Col. J. Egbert Farnum (later brvt. brig. gen.). Losses, 117.

71st New York, Col. Henry L. Potter. Losses, 91. Lieut. Andrew W. Estes killed.

72d New York. Col. John S. Austin, wounded, was followed by Lieut. Col. John Leonard (brevetted maj. in the Regular Army for Gettysburg). Losses, 114. Lieut. Charles A. Foss mortally wounded.

73d New York, Maj. Michael W. Burns. Losses, 162. Capt. Eugene C. Shine, and Lieuts. William L. Herbert, James Marksman, George P. Dennen, and Martin E. Higgins killed or mortally wounded.

74th New York, Lieut. Col. Thomas Holt (brvt. col. and brig.

gen. in 1865). Losses, 89. Capt. William H. Chester mortally wounded.

120th New York. Lieut. Col. Cornelius Westbrook, when wounded, was followed by Maj. John R. Tappan. Losses, 203. This command suffered a greater loss in officers than any other New York command; eight were killed—Capts. Ayres G. Barker and Lansing Hollister; Lieuts. John R. Burnham, Jason Carle, Michael E. Creighton, Fred Freelewick, or Freileweh, Ed. H. Ketchum, and William J. Cockburn. Col. George H. Sharpe, of this regiment, was on duty at the headquarters of the Army of the Potomac as deputy provost marshal general; the work he did, particularly in gathering intelligence for Meade, was valuable.

Third Brigade: Col. George C. Burling, 6th New Jersey (brevetted brig. gen. for this battle).

2d New Hampshire. Col. Edward L. Bailey, wounded, and the following were killed or mortally wounded: Capts. Joseph A. Hubbard and Henry N. Metcalf; Lieuts. George W. Roberts, William W. Ballard, Edmund Dascomb, Charles W. Patch, and Charles Vickery. Losses, 193. From Col. Bailey's report: "They did their duty as become sons of the old Granite State."

5th New Jersey, Col. William J. Sewell (1835–1901), wounded; he was brevetted brigadier general and major general, and received a medal of honor. Born in Ireland, he gave, after coming to this country in 1851, a half-century of service to New Jersey and to the nation as a railroad executive, soldier, financier, president of the State Senate, United States Senator, and World's Columbian Exposition commissioner. Capts. Healy (wounded), Woolsey (wounded), and finally Godfrey took charge when Sewell was hurt. Losses, 94. Capt. Thomas Kelly and Lieut. Henry R. Clark were killed, and Capt. Edward P. Berry mortally hurt.

6th New Jersey, Lieut. Col. S. R. Gilkyson. Losses, 41.

7th New Jersey. Col. Louis R. Francine, distinguished for rank as a citizen and standing as a soldier, was mortally wounded at the head of his men. A posthumous brevet as brigadier general was given him. Lieut. Col. Francis Price, Jr., was also wounded (and likewise brevetted), and Maj. Frederick Cooper was left in command. Sergt. Charles A. Monks is specially mentioned for gallantry. Lieut. Charles F. Walker was killed. Losses, 114.

8th New Jersey, Col. John Ramsey (later brevetted brig. gen. and maj. gen.). Losses, 47, including Capt. Andrew S. Davis, mortally wounded. Col. Ramsey was wounded, and was followed in command by Capt. John G. Langston.

115th Pennsylvania, Maj. John P. Dunne (promoted soon after the battle to be lieut. col.). Losses, 24.

Artillery Brigade: Capt. George E. Randolph, chief of artillery of the Third Army Corps, had under him the following batteries (Capt.

Randolph was wounded in the battle, but did not leave the field, being aided in the command of the artillery by Capt. Clark, mentioned below):

New Jersey Light Artillery, 2d Battery. Capt. A. Judson Clark, when aiding Randolph, was followed in his own battery by Lieut. Robert Sims. Losses, 20. Their six 10-pounders were posted near the Peach Orchard on Thursday afternoon, and did not give way until the infantry had been driven back and no support was left for the gunners.

1st New York Light, Battery D. Capt. George B. Winslow, with Lieuts. Crego, Richardson, and Ames, used their six 12-pounders in the Wheat-field, near the base of Little Round Top. Losses, 18.

New York Light, 4th Battery, Capt. James E. Smith. Four of the six 10-pounder Parrotts were with great difficulty dragged onto the rocks of the Devil's Den, where, when the infantry were pressed back on the Union side, three of the guns had to be left behind in order that the gunners might escape captivity. No one blamed the officers or men; they had done their utmost. Losses, 13.

1st Rhode Island Light Artillery, Battery E. The brigade commander, Randolph, was the captain of this battery. Lieut. John K. Bucklyn, who was wounded, and then Lieut. Benj. Freeborn had command. Losses, 30. The fire of the enemy in its destructiveness may also be inferred from the havoc among the horses—17 killed and 23 disabled and abandoned.

4th U. S. Artillery, Battery K. Lieut. Francis W. Seeley, until wounded, commanded this battery on the Emmitsburg road, north of the Peach Orchard. When Seeley was wounded Lieut. Robert James took the guns. Both officers were expert artillerists from the old army. Gen. Humphreys says the "gallantry, skill, and good judgment" of Seeley awoke his admiration. Losses, 25.

FIFTH ARMY CORPS

Maj. Gen. George Sykes (W. P.).

GENERAL HEADQUARTERS

12th New York Infantry, Companies D and E, Capt. Henry W. Rider.

17th Pennsylvania Cavalry, Companies D and H, Capt. William Thompson.

FIRST DIVISION

Brig. Gen. James Barnes (W. P.). Gen. Barnes was slightly wounded in the battle, and was relieved from duty with the division at the end of the third day, when Brig. Gen. Charles Griffin (W. P.), who had been on sick leave, arrived and was assigned to the command.

GETTYSBURG

First Brigade: Col. William S. Tilton, 22d Massachusetts.
18th Massachusetts, Col. Joseph Hayes. Losses, 27.
22d Massachusetts, Lieut. Col. Thomas Sherwin, Jr. Losses, 31.
Lieut. Charles K. Knowles mortally wounded.
1st Michigan, Col. Ira C. Abbott, and Lieut. Col. William A.
Throop. Losses, 42. Lieut. Amos M. Ladd killed.
118th Pennsylvania, Lieut. Col. James Gwyn (col. of the regiment
December 5, 1863; later brevetted brig. gen. and maj. gen.). Losses,
25. Capt. Richard W. Davis killed.
Second Brigade: Col. Jacob Bowman Sweitzer (sketched in Pennsylvania chapter).
9th Massachusetts, Col. Patrick R. Guiney (brvt. brig. gen. March
13, 1865). Losses, 7.
32d Massachusetts, Col. George L. Prescott (brevetted brig. gen.
June 18, 1864, for special gallantry in leading an assault on the enemy's
works at Petersburg, where he was mortally wounded). Losses, 80.
Lieut. Wm. H. Barrows killed.
4th Michigan. Col. Harrison H. Jeffords was pierced fatally with
a bayonet in striving to save the colors; Lieut. Col. George W. Lum-
bard then commanded. Losses, 165.
62d Pennsylvania. The colonel, Sweitzer, led the brigade; Lieut.
Col. James C. Hull the regiment. The latter was fatally wounded in
the Wilderness, dying May 22, 1864. Losses, 175. Maj. William
G. Lowry, Capts. Edwin H. Little and James Brown, and Lieuts.
Scott C. McDowell, Josiah C. Mouck, and Patrick Morris were
killed or mortally wounded.
Third Brigade: Col. Strong Vincent, 83d Pennsylvania, mortally
wounded; Col. James C. Rice, 44th New York, then took the brigade
(brig. gen. August 17, 1863; killed in the Wilderness May, 1864).
20th Maine, Col. Joshua L. Chamberlain (sketched in "Safeguarding the Round Tops"). Losses, 125. Capt. Charles W. Billings and
Lieuts. Warren L. Kendall and Arad H. Linscott mortally wounded.
16th Michigan, Lieut. Col. Norval E. Welch. Losses (including 9
at Upperville, in June, where Capt. Judd M. Mott was mortally
wounded), 60. Lieuts. William H. Borden, Butler Browne, and
Wallace Jewett were killed.
44th New York, Col. James C. Rice, who, on taking the brigade,
was followed in regimental command by Lieut. Col. Freeman Conner.
Losses, 111. Capt. Lucius S. Larrabee and Lieut. Eugene L. Dun-
ham killed, and Lieut. Benjamin N. Thomas mortally wounded.
83d Pennsylvania, Capt. Orpheus S. Woodward. Losses, 55. Capt.
John M. Sell killed.

SECOND DIVISION

Brig. Gen. Romeyn B. Ayres (W. P.). (Two brigades of regular
infantry.)

ROSTER OF ARMY OF THE POTOMAC

First Brigade: Col. Hannibal Day (W. P.).

3d Infantry (6 companies), Capt. Henry W. Freedley (W. P.), wounded; brevetted lieutenant colonel for this fight; Capt. R. G. Lay followed; brevetted major and lieutenant colonel. Losses, 73.

4th Infantry (4 companies), Capt. Julius W. Adams, Jr. (W. P.). Losses, 40.

6th Infantry (5 companies), Capt. Levi C. Bootes. Losses, 44.

12th Infantry (8 companies), Capt. Thomas S. Dunn. Losses, 92. Lieut. Silas A. Miller killed.

14th Infantry (8 companies), Maj. Grotius R. Giddings, brevetted lieutenant colonel in part for this fight; and colonel for Gettysburg alone. Losses, 132.

Second Brigade: Col. Sidney Burbank (W. P.).

2d Infantry, Maj. Arthur T. Lee (wounded); army record dated back to 1838; brevetted lieutenant colonel for Gettysburg; followed in command by Capt. Samuel A. McKee (killed by guerrillas April 11, 1864). Losses, 67. Lieut. Frank C. Goodrich killed.

7th Infantry (4 companies), Capt. David P. Hancock (W. P.); brevetted to major and lieutenant colonel. Losses, 59. Lieut. Wesley F. Miller killed, brevetted captain; and Lieut. Richard R. Crawford mortally wounded, brevetted captain.

10th Infantry, Capt. William Clinton (brevetted maj.). Losses, 51. Lieut. William J. Fisher killed, and Lieut. Michael C. Boyce fatally wounded. Fisher was brevetted to captain.

11th Infantry (6 companies), Maj. De Lancey Floyd-Jones (W. P.); brevetted colonel. Losses, 120. Killed or mortally wounded: Capt. Thomas O. Barri, brevetted to major; Lieut. Matthew Elder, brevetted captain; Lieut. Henry Rochford, Lieut. Herbert Kenaston, brevetted captain; Lieut. Amaziah J. Barber, brevetted first lieutenant. Capt. John C. Bates, of this regiment, was aide to Gen. Meade; after a long record of distinction he was retired in April, 1906, from the post of lieutenant general, U.S.A.

17th Infantry (7 companies), Lieut. Col. J. Durell Greene, afterward brevet brigadier general. Losses, 150. Lieut. Edward S. Abbott (brvt. capt.) mortally wounded, and Lieut. William H. Chamberlain (brvt. capt.) killed.

Third Brigade: Brig. Gen. Stephen H. Weed (W. P.), mortally wounded on Little Round Top, followed by Col. Kenner Garrard (W. P.), brigadier general for this battle.

140th New York, Col. Patrick H. O'Rorke (W. P.), killed; followed by Lieut. Col. Louis Ernst. Losses, 133.

146th New York, Col. Kenner Garrard (W. P.). When he took the brigade Lieut. Col. David T. Jenkins led the regiment. Losses, 28.

91st Pennsylvania, Lieut. Col. Joseph H. Sinex. Losses, 19.

156th Pennsylvania, Col. John H. Cain. Losses, 19.

GETTYSBURG

THIRD DIVISION

(Pennsylvania Reserves), Brig. Gen. Samuel W. Crawford (maj. 13th U. S. Infantry, sketched in Pennsylvania chapter).
First Brigade: Col. William McCandless.
1st Pennsylvania Reserves (9 companies), Col. William C. Talley (brevetted brig. gen. 1865). Losses, 46.
2d Pennsylvania Reserves, Lieut. Col. George A. Woodward (brevetted col., U.S.A., for this battle); served in the regulars from 1866; retired as colonel 15th U. S. Infantry in 1879. Losses, 37.
6th Pennsylvania Reserves, Lieut. Col. Wellington H. Ent (col. of this regiment from date of this battle; brevetted brig. gen. for battles in the Wilderness). Losses, 24.
13th Pennsylvania Reserves, Col. Charles F. Taylor (brother of Bayard Taylor), killed July 2d; Maj. William R. Hartshorne then taking command. This regiment was also known as the "First Rifles." Losses, 48. Lieut. Robert Hall killed.

NOTE.—The Second Brigade was in the Department of Washington.

Third Brigade: Col. Joseph W. Fisher (brvt. brig. gen. November 4, 1865).
5th Pennsylvania Reserves, Lieut. Col. George Dare. Losses, 2.
9th Pennsylvania Reserves, Lieut. James McK. Snodgrass. Losses, 5.
10th Pennsylvania Reserves, Col. Adoniram J. Warner (brvt. brig. gen. March 13, 1865). Losses, 5.
11th Pennsylvania Reserves, Col. Samuel M. Jackson (brvt. brig. gen. for gallantry in the Wilderness fights). Losses, 41.
12th Pennsylvania Reserves, Col. Martin D. Hardin (W. P.). Losses, 2.
Artillery Brigade: Capt. Augustus P. Martin, 3d Massachusetts Battery.
Massachusetts Light Artillery, 3d Battery, C, Lieut. Aaron F. Walcott. Losses, 6.
1st New York Light Artillery, Battery C, Capt. Almont Barnes. Losses: in position for hours under fire, but ordered not to fire until so instructed, without losing a man.
1st Ohio Light Artillery, Battery L, Capt. Frank C. Gibbs. Losses, 2.
5th U. S., Battery D, Lieut. Charles E. Hazlett (W. P.), killed; followed by Lieut. Benjamin F. Rittenhouse. Losses, 13.
5th U. S., Battery I, Lieut. Malbone F. Watson (W. P.), brevet major for this battle, in which he was severely wounded, losing his right leg; Lieut. Chas. C. McConnell then commanded. Losses, 22.

ROSTER OF ARMY OF THE POTOMAC

SIXTH ARMY CORPS[1]

Maj. Gen. John Sedgwick (W. P.).

HEADQUARTERS GUARD AND ESCORT

Capt. William S. Craft; 1st New Jersey, Company L; 1st Pennsylvania Cavalry, Company H.

FIRST DIVISION[2]

Brig. Gen. Horatio G. Wright (W. P.).
First Brigade: Brig. Gen. A. T. A. Torbert (W. P.).
1st New Jersey, Lieut. Col. William Henry, Jr.   No losses.
2d New Jersey, Lieut. Col. Charles Wiebecke.   Losses, 6.
3d New Jersey, Lieut. Col. Edward L. Campbell.   Losses, 2.
15th New Jersey, Col. William H. Penrose (brevetted maj. for Gettysburg in Regular Army; commissioned brig. gen. of volunteers June 27, 1865).   Losses, 3.
Second Brigade: Brig. Gen. Joseph J. Bartlett (sketched in "Empire State in the Battle").
5th Maine, Col. Clark S. Edwards (brvt. brig. gen. March 13, 1865). No losses.
121st New York, Col. Emory Upton (W. P.).   Losses, 2.
95th Pennsylvania, Lieut. Col. Edward Carroll.   Losses, 2.
96th Pennsylvania, Maj. William H. Lessig.   Losses, 1.
Third Brigade: Brig. Gen. David A. Russell (W. P.), brevet colonel, U.S.A., for this battle.
6th Maine, Col. Hiram Burnham (brig. gen. 1864; killed in battle, Chapin's Bluff, Va., September 30, 1864).   No losses.
49th Pennsylvania (4 companies), Lieut. Col. Thomas M. Hulings (promoted col. April 22, 1864; killed at Spottsylvania May 10, 1864; in Regular Army, capt., 12th Infantry).   No losses.

---

[1] This corps, leaving Manchester, Maryland, immediately on receiving word that the fight was on at Gettysburg, late Wednesday evening, July 1st, made a forced march of from thirty to thirty-five miles that night and the next day, arriving on the field Thursday afternoon, the time varying for the different brigades at from 3.30 to 5 P.M.   The command was arrayed in line on the left, near Little Round Top, where some of the brigades were at once ushered into battle to aid in repulsing the advance of Longstreet's men; the remaining troops of the corps by their very presence, without firing a gun, did much to encourage the struggling Union force, and to impress the Confederates, catching a glimpse of the newly arriving lines, with a sense of the increasing strength of the Federal Army.   It chanced that the larger part of the Sixth Corps, although day and night in line and under arms, ready to advance at command, was held in reserve during the afternoon of Thursday and most of Friday, but was used after the fight to follow up the retreating Southern Army and utilize what opportunity might appear to assail it.

[2] Seven companies of the 4th New Jersey Infantry, under Maj. Charles Ewing, served as train-guard for the Artillery Reserve.   On Friday, during the cannonade and later fight, they were aligned in the rear of the army to prevent straggling, and to organize those who had been separated from their commands into companies for service in the fight.   The other three companies formed the provost guard of the division under Capt. Wm. S. Maxwell.

GETTYSBURG

119th Pennsylvania, Col. Peter C. Ellmaker. Losses, 2.

5th Wisconsin, Col. Thomas S. Allen (brvt. brig. gen. March 13, 1865). No losses.

SECOND DIVISION

N. B.—There was no First Brigade in this division in this fight.

Brig. Gen. Albion P. Howe (W. P.).

Second Brigade: Col. Lewis A. Grant; afterward brevetted major general, and awarded medal of honor; served under Harrison as Assistant Secretary of War. He and his men as already noted, at Franklin's Crossing, at the opening of the campaign, did fine service, with a loss of fifty. In following the retreat at Gettysburg, in a fight near Funkstown, Md., Gen. Sedgwick said of their service: "The remarkable conduct of this brigade deserves high praise." The loss at Gettysburg consisted of one man shot in the 4th Vermont.

2d Vermont, Col. James H. Walbridge.

3d Vermont, Col. Thomas C. Deaver (after the war a probate judge at Woodstock, Vt.).

4th Vermont, Col. Charles B. Stoughton (brvt. brig. gen. March 13, 1865).

5th Vermont, Lieut. Col. John R. Lewis (later col. and brvt. brig. gen.).

6th Vermont, Col. Elisha L. Barney (mortally wounded, May 5, 1864, in the Wilderness).

Third Brigade: Brig. Gen. Thomas H. Neill (W. P.).

7th Maine (6 companies), Lieut. Col. Selden Connor. (This officer, born 1839, a graduate of Tufts College, entered service as a private in 1861, and rose to be a brigadier general; he was wounded in the Wilderness; and after the war he served three terms as governor of Maine, and for years was Pension Agent at Augusta. He has often held high office in the Loyal Legion and in the G. A. R.) Losses, 6.

33d New York (a detachment), Capt. Henry J. Gifford. No losses.

43d New York, Lieut. Col. John Wilson. Losses, 5. Capt. William H. Gilfillan killed.

49th New York, Col. Daniel D. Bidwell (brig. gen. August 11, 1864; killed at Cedar Creek October 19, 1864). Losses, 2.

77th New York, Col. Winsor B. French (brvt. brig. gen. 1865). No losses.

61st Pennsylvania, Lieut. Col. George F. Smith. Losses, 2.

THIRD DIVISION

Maj. Gen. John Newton, on the morning of July 2d, became commander of the Second Army Corps; Brig. Gen. Frank Wheaton took the division. Wheaton was a Rhode-Islander who was appointed to a lieutenancy in the 1st Cavalry in the Regular Army in 1855, and colonel of the 2d Rhode Island Infantry in 1861, and brigadier general in November, 1862. He won several brevets, and, continuing in service after the war, rose to be major general, U.S.A., April 2, 1897; was retired that year, and died in 1903. In the Wilderness, and at Cedar Creek, and in the capture of Petersburg he showed courage and skill, for which special brevets were given.

First Brigade:[1] Brig. Gen. Alexander Shaler (for sketch see "Empire State in the Battle").

65th New York,[2] Col. Joseph E. Hamblin (brevetted brig. gen. 1864, and maj. gen. 1865, for gallantry in battle; commissioned brig. gen. May 19, 1865; died July 3, 1870). Losses, 9.

67th New York, Col. Nelson Cross (brevetted brig. gen. and maj. gen. 1865). Losses, 1.

122d New York, Col. Silas Titus. Losses, 44.

23d Pennsylvania, Lieut. Col. John F. Glenn. Losses, 14. Lieut. Joshua S. Garsed killed.

82d Pennsylvania, Col. Isaac C. Bassett (brevetted brig. gen. December 12, 1864). Losses, 6.

Second Brigade: Col. Henry L. Eustis (W. P.).

7th Massachusetts, Lieut. Col. Franklin P. Harlow. Losses, 6.

10th Massachusetts, Lieut. Col. Joseph B. Parsons. Losses, 9.

37th Massachusetts, Col. Oliver Edwards (brevetted brig. gen. and maj. gen. 1864 and 1865; full brig. gen. May 19, 1865). Losses, 47.

2d Rhode Island, Col. Horatio Rogers, Jr. (brvt. brig. gen. 1865). Losses, 7.

Third Brigade: Brig. Gen. Frank Wheaton for a time led the division; then Col. Nevin had the brigade.

62d New York, Col. David J. Nevin. When he was in command of the brigade Lieut. Col. Theo. B. Hamilton took the regiment. Losses, 12.

93d Pennsylvania, Maj. John I. Nevin. Losses, 10.

98th Pennsylvania, Maj. John B. Kohler. Losses, 11.

102d Pennsylvania, Col. John W. Patterson. (Guarding trains at Westminster.)

139th Pennsylvania, Col. Frederick H. Collier (brvt. brig. gen. 1865; when Collier was accidentally wounded on the third day Lieut. Col. William H. Moody led the regiment). Losses, 20. This brigade on Thursday afternoon joined lines with the Pennsylvania Reserves and advanced in a charge against the Confederates at the close of the evening fight, holding their ground till the end.

---

[1] This brigade, held in reserve near Round Top Thursday afternoon and evening, was sent to Culp's Hill early Friday morning, where it gave needed help to Geary's division, Twelfth Corps, in the fight to expel troops from Edward Johnson's division from the Union breastworks which they had occupied in the night battle.

[2] Charles Libbens Hodges was a private in this regiment at Gettysburg, and sergeant major at the end of the war. Enlisting in the Regular Army at the end of the war (when he was but eighteen and a half years of age), he was retired March 13, 1911, with the rank of major general. Died 1911.

GETTYSBURG

Artillery Brigade: Col. Charles H. Tompkins, 1st Rhode Island Light Artillery (brvt. brig. gen. August 1, 1864, for meritorious service in current campaigns).

1st Massachusetts Battery, Capt. W. H. McCartney. Posted for a time on Cemetery Hill, but not engaged. No losses.

New York Light Artillery, 1st Battery, Capt. Andrew Cowan (chief of corps artillery, closing part of the war). Losses, 11. The battery helped in Webb's front to break Pickett's charge.

New York Light, 3d Battery, Capt. Wm. A. Harn (posted in rear of Hays's division, Second Corps, to repel last charge of the foe). No losses.

1st Rhode Island Light Artillery, Battery C, Capt. Richard Waterman, and Battery G of the same regiment, Capt. George W. Adams, were held in reserve, and had no losses.

2d U. S., Battery D, Lieut. Edward B. Williston, and Battery G, same regiment, Lieut. John H. Butler, and 5th U. S., Battery F, Lieut. Leonard Martin.

ELEVENTH ARMY CORPS

Maj. Gen. Oliver O. Howard (W. P.).[1]

At corps headquarters the following troops were on guard and escort duty: 1st Indiana Cavalry, Companies I and K, Capt. Abram Sharra; 8th New York Infantry (1 company), Lieut. Hermann Foerster.

FIRST DIVISION

Brig. Gen. Francis C. Barlow (sketched in "The Empire State in the Battle") was severely wounded; Brig. Gen. Adelbert Ames (W. P.) then took direction of the division.

First Brigade: Col. Leopold von Gilsa, 41st New York.

41st New York (9 companies), Lieut. Col. Detleo von Einseidel. A score of the officers were veterans of German wars, and seven hundred of the men had seen service in their own country. The regiment, detained by duty at Emmitsburg, arrived at Gettysburg after the first day's fight was over. Losses, 75. Lieut. Reinhold Winzer was killed.

54th New York, "The Schwartzer Yaeger," Maj. Stephen Kovacs. Losses, 102.

68th New York, Col. Gotthilf Bourry. Losses, 138, including Capt. Otto Freidrich, killed.

---

[1] During the interval between the death of Gen. Reynolds and the arrival of Gen. Hancock, on the afternoon of July 1st, all the troops on the field of battle were commanded by Gen. Howard, Gen. Schurz taking command of the Eleventh Corps, and Gen. Schimmelfennig of the Third Division.

153d Pennsylvania, Maj. John F. Frueauff. Losses, 211 out of a total of 569. Lieut. William H. Beaver killed.

P. S.—This brigade was exposed almost from its entrance on the field, Wednesday afternoon, to a deadly flanking and enfilading fire, to which but little effective counterfire could be opposed.

Second Brigade: This body was ordinarily commanded by Brig. Gen. Adelbert Ames (W. P.); when he commanded the division, toward the close of the first day, Col. Andrew L. Harris, 75th Ohio, led the brigade. This officer was brevetted brigadier general in 1865; in the years since the war he has been a probate judge, member of the Ohio Senate and of Congress, lieutenant governor of Ohio, and later (1906–1909) governor. As these lines are written (1913) he is still living in an honored old age at Eaton, Ohio.

17th Connecticut, Lieut. Col. Douglas Fowler, killed; Maj. Allen G. Brady followed in command. He was wounded, but stayed at the front with his men. In addition to the colonel, Capt. James E. Moore was killed. Losses, 197.

25th Ohio. Losses, 184 out of 220. Lieut. Lewis E. Wilson killed. No other Ohio organization had such a large proportionate loss. Lieut. Col. Jeremiah Williams, Capt. Nathaniel J. Manning, Lieut. Wm. Mahoney, and Lieut. Israel White, in turn, were stricken down while leading this force.

75th Ohio. When Col. Andrew L. Harris took the brigade, Capt. George B. Fox led the regiment. Losses, 186 out of 269. Capts. James C. Mulharen and Mahlon B. Briggs killed, and Lieut. Thomas Wheeler mortally wounded.

107th Ohio. Col. Seraphim Meyer led for a time, and then was followed by Capt. John M. Lutz. Losses, 211 out of 480.

SECOND DIVISION

Brig. Gen. Adolph von Steinwehr. This officer is sketched in "The Empire State in the Battle."

First Brigade: Col. Charles R. Coster, 134th New York (capt., 12th Infantry, Regular Army).

134th New York, Lieut. Col. Allan H. Jackson (in regular service from 1866 to retirement as maj. and paymaster, 1898; brevetted capt. for Gettysburg). Losses, 252. Lieuts. Henry I. Palmer and Lucius Mead killed.

154th New York, Lieut. Col. Daniel B. Allen. Losses, 200.

27th Pennsylvania, Lieut. Col. Lorenz Cantador. Losses, 111. Lieuts. Walter S. Briggs and John Kuempel killed.

73d Pennsylvania, Capt. Daniel F. Kelly. Losses, 34 out of 332. (This brigade reached the field when the corps was being pressed back, and in the effort to keep a path of retreat open for the survivors suffered greatly in the struggle Wednesday afternoon.)

GETTYSBURG

Second Brigade: Col. Orland Smith, 73d Ohio (brvt. brig. gen. 1865).

33d Massachusetts, Col. Adin B. Underwood (brig. gen. November 6, 1863; brvt. maj. gen. August, 1865). Losses (including 3 at Beverly Ford), 48.

136th New York, Col. James Wood, Jr. (brevetted brig. gen. and maj. gen. 1865). Losses, 109.

55th Ohio, Col. Charles B. Gambee (killed at the head of his regiment, Resaca, Ga., May 15, 1864). Losses, 49 out of 375.

73d Ohio, Lieut. Col. Richard Long. Losses, 145 out of 338. Capt. Geo. M. Doherty mortally wounded.

THIRD DIVISION

Maj. Gen. Carl Schurz. (It will be recalled that on the first afternoon this officer was in charge of the corps, and Schimmelfennig of the division in front of the town.)

First Brigade: Brig. Gen. Alex. Schimmelfennig (sketched in "Pennsylvania Officers in the Forefront").

82d Illinois, Lieut. Col. Edward S. Salomon (brevetted col. and brig. gen. at the end of the war). Losses, 112.

45th New York, Col. George von Amsberg. (On Wednesday evening in the retreat Schimmelfennig was caught in the tumult, but contrived to secrete himself during the next two days, and thus escape capture. Meanwhile Von Amsberg led the brigade, and Lieut. Col. A. Dobke the regiment.) Losses, 224.

157th New York, Col. Philip P. Brown, Jr. (brvt. brig. gen. 1865). Stationed at the extreme left of the corps, it was enfiladed and torn to pieces, losing 27 killed, 166 wounded, and 114 captured, a total of 307. Officers killed or mortally wounded: Lieut. Col. George Arrowsmith, Capts. Jason F. Backus, Harrison Frank, and George A. Adams; Lieuts. Joseph F. Heeney and Randall D. Lower.

61st Ohio, Col. Stephen J. McGroarty (brvt. brig. gen. 1865). Losses, 54. Capt. James M. Reynolds and Assist. Surg. William S. Moore killed, and Lieut. Daniel W. Williams mortally wounded.

74th Pennsylvania. Col. Adolph von Hartung, Lieut. Col. Alexander von Mitzel, Capt. Gustav Schleiter, and Capt. Henry Krauseneck, in succession, commanded the regiment, one after another being stricken with wounds. Losses, 110 out of 381. Capt. Anton Heilig and Lieut. Wm. Roth killed.

Second Brigade: Col. Wladimir Krzyzanowski, 58th New York (for sketch see "Empire State in the Battle").

58th New York (2 companies only in the first day's fight). The commander, Lieut. Col. August Otto, detailed for staff duty on the second day, was followed by Capt. Emil Koenig. Losses, 20. Lieut. Louis Deitrick killed; Capts. Edward Antonieski and Gustave Stoldt mortally wounded.

ROSTER OF ARMY OF THE POTOMAC

119th New York, Col. John T. Lockman, wounded; followed in command by Lieut. Col. Edward F. Lloyd. (Lockman was brevetted brigadier general in 1865. He was a well-known citizen of New York. Before the war he was an active member of the New York (Volunteer) Fire Department. Subsequently he was a lawyer identified with the care of estates. He was a vestryman of Trinity Church. He died in 1912.) Losses, 140, including Capt. Otto Trumpelman and Lieuts. Emil Trost and Matthias Rasemann, killed or mortally wounded. The Adj. Lieut. Theodore Ayrault Dodge suffered the loss of his right leg; he was brevetted major for his gallantry, and other brevets followed. He died in 1909, at the age of seventy-seven, having achieved fame as an author of works of travel, military biography and criticism. Col. Dodge's ablest works are *History of the Art of War* (12 volumes) and *The Campaign of Chancellorsville.*

82d Ohio. Col. James S. Robinson (brig. gen. January 12, 1865, and brvt. maj. gen. March 13, 1865; later member of Congress from Ohio, and for two years secretary of the Commonwealth; died January 14, 1892) was wounded, and followed by Lieut. Col. David Thompson in command. Losses, 181 out of 258, including among the killed or mortally wounded Capts. John Costen and William D. W. Mitchell, and Lieuts. Stowell L. Burnham, Henry Jacoby, George W. McGary, and Philander C. Meredith.

75th Pennsylvania. Col. Francis Mahler, a compatriot and prison comrade with Carl Schurz in the German struggle for liberty before they came to this country, was mortally wounded. The two bade each other farewell while the gallant colonel was lying helpless on the field. Maj. August Ledig followed in command. Losses, 111 out of 258 present. Other officers slain: Lieuts. Henry Hauschild, Louis Mahler, and William J. Sill.

26th Wisconsin. Losses, 217, including among the killed Capt. Wm. Smith and Lieut. Martin Young. Lieut. Col. Hans Boebel and Maj. Henry Baetz were both wounded and captured; then Capt. John W. Fuchs and, later, Col. W. H. Jacobs led.

Artillery Brigade: Maj. Thomas W. Osborn, 1st New York Light Artillery, commanding.

1st New York Light, Battery I, Capt. Michael Wiedrich. Losses, 13.

New York Light, 13th Battery, Lieut. William Wheeler. Losses, 11.

1st Ohio Light, Battery I, Capt. Hubert Dilger. Losses, 13.

1st Ohio Light, Battery K, Capt. Lewis Heckman. Losses, 15.

4th U. S., Battery G, Lieut. Bayard Wilkeson (killed), Lieut. Eugene A. Bancroft. Losses, 17.

The list of losses of this corps, when duly scanned, should forever silence the voice of calumny and ignorance concerning the behavior of these heroic regiments. Most of those who retreated did not take

GETTYSBURG

a step backward until they had been overpowered in front and flanked on either side. Schurz, the soul of candor and honor, and a man of unyielding courage, says in his report as to the retreat: "In this part of the action, which was almost a hand-to-hand struggle, officers and men showed the highest courage and determination." The nation should by this time realize the truth that no more valuable services were given on the field of Gettysburg than those rendered by the First and Eleventh corps on the first day. The epitaph might aptly be written for the victims of that part of the struggle: "These brave men died—driven, flanked, defeated—and yet they died victorious, for they helped to make sure the final victory."

TWELFTH ARMY CORPS
Maj. Gen. Henry W. Slocum (W. P.).[1]

PROVOST GUARD
10th Maine (4 companies), Capt. John D. Beardsley.

FIRST DIVISION
Brig. Gen. Alpheus S. Williams. While Williams was in command of the corps Brig. Gen. T. H. Ruger (W. P.) took the division.
First Brigade: Col. Archibald L. McDougall, 123d New York.
5th Connecticut, Col. Warren W. Packer. Losses, 7.
20th Connecticut, Lieut. Col. Wm. B. Wooster. Losses, 28.
3d Maryland, Col. Jos. M. Sudsburg. Losses, 8. Capt. Henry Fenton killed.
123d New York, Lieut. Col. James C. Rogers and, at intervals, Capt. Adolphus H. Tanner. Losses, 14. Capt. Norman F. Weer killed.
145th New York, Col. E. Livingston Price. Losses, 10.
46th Pennsylvania, Col. James L. Selfridge (brvt. brig. gen. 1865). Losses, 13.
Second Brigade: Brig. Gen. Henry H. Lockwood (W. P.).
1st Maryland, Potomac Home Brigade, Col. Wm. P. Maulsby. Losses, 104. Lieuts. Charles E. Eader, James T. Smith, and John L. Willman killed.
1st Maryland, Eastern Shore, Col. James Wallace. Losses, 25.[2]

---

[1] For a few hours on the evening and through the first half of the night of the first day—between the departure of Hancock and the arrival of Meade—Slocum was by his seniority in command of all the troops that had then arrived on the field. For a part of the second day he commanded the right wing. During these intervals Williams commanded the corps. The latter is sketched in connection with the section in the Battle Narrative which describes the "Assaults on Culp's Hill."

[2] These two Maryland regiments found themselves on the second and third days of the fight on Culp's Hill confronting the First Maryland Battalion in Johnson's division of Ewell's corps, made up in part of old friends, former neighbors, and, in some cases, blood kinsmen.

150th New York, Col. John H. Ketcham (later brig. gen. and brvt. maj. gen. He was elected to Congress in the fall of 1864, and had from that time a notable political career). Losses, 45.

Third Brigade: Brig. Gen. Thomas H. Ruger (W. P.). When Ruger took the division Col. Silas Colgrove, 27th Indiana (brvt. brig. gen. August 7, 1864), headed the brigade.

27th Indiana, Lieut. Col. John R. Fesler (following Colgrove). Losses, 110.

2d Massachusetts. Losses, 136. Lieut. Col. Charles R. Mudge was slain—"a most brave and gallant officer who fell in leading his men." Maj. Chas. F. Morse then held the command. Capts. Thomas B. Fox, Jr., and Thomas R. Robeson, and Lieut. Henry V. D. Stone killed or mortally wounded.

13th New Jersey, Col. Ezra A. Carman (brvt. brig. gen. March 13, 1865). Losses, 21.

107th New York, Col. Nirom M. Crane (brvt. brig. gen. March 13, 1865). Losses, 2.

3d Wisconsin, Col. William Hawley (served a year in the Mexican War; brevetted brig. gen. in 1865; was lieut. in regular infantry 1866 to 1873, the date of his death). Losses, 10.

SECOND DIVISION

Brig. Gen. John W. Geary. Gen. Geary's career is sketched in the chapter on "Pennsylvania Officers in the Foreground."

First Brigade: Col. Charles Candy, 66th Ohio (served ten years up to 1861 in the Regular Army; brvt. brig. gen. March 13, 1865).

5th Ohio, Col. John H. Patrick. Losses, 18, including Lieut. Henry C. Brinkman, killed.

7th Ohio, Col. William R. Creighton (killed at Ringgold, Ga., November 27, 1863). Losses, 18.

29th Ohio, led by Capts. Wilbur F. Stevens and Edward Hayes. Losses, 38, including Lieuts. George Hayward and John H. Marsh, killed.

66th Ohio, Lieut. Col. Eugene Powell (later col. 193d Ohio, and brvt. brig. gen.). Losses, 17. Maj. Joshua G. Palmer mortally wounded.

28th Pennsylvania, Capt. John Flynn. Losses, 28.

147th Pennsylvania (8 companies), Lieut. Col. Ario Pardee, Jr. (col. March 19, 1864; brvt. brig. gen. 1865). Losses, 20, including Lieut. Wm. H. Tourison, killed.

Second Brigade: Gen. Thomas L. Kane, who had been very ill, took turns with Col. George A. Cobham, Jr., 11th Pennsylvania, in leading this brigade. Cobham was brevetted brigadier general in part for this battle, and was killed in the fight at Peach Tree Creek, Ga., July 20, 1864. Kane is noticed in the chapter on "Pennsylvania Officers."

GETTYSBURG

29th Pennsylvania, Col. William Rickards, Jr.   Losses, 66, including Lieuts. Edward J. Harvey and John J. McKeever, killed.

109th Pennsylvania, Capt Frederick L. Gimber.   Losses, 10.

111th Pennsylvania.   While Cobham led the brigade Lieut. Col. Thomas M. Walker commanded the regiment.   Losses, 23.

Third Brigade: Brig. Gen. George S. Greene (W. P.).

60th New York, Col. Abel Godard.   Losses, 52.   Lieut. Myron D. Stanley mortally wounded.

78th New York, Lieut. Col. Herbert von Hammerstein.   Losses, 30.

102d New York, Col. James C. Lane, wounded; was followed by Capt. Lewis R. Stegman.   Losses, 29.   Capt. John Mead and Lieut. Josiah V. Upham killed.

137th New York, Col. David Ireland.   Losses, 137, including among the killed Capts. Oscar C. Williams and Joseph H. Gregg, and Lieuts. Henry G. Hallett and John H. Van Emburg.

149th New York, Col. Henry A. Barnum, later brigadier general and brevet major general.   For some hours, while Col. Barnum was disabled by an old wound, Lieut. Col. Chas. B. Randall was in command. He was severely wounded on the third day.   Losses, 55.

Artillery Brigade: Lieut. Edward D. Muhlenberg, 1st lieut., 4th Artillery, in command.

1st New York Light, Battery M, Lieut. Charles E. Winegar.   Was protected by breastworks and did damage without suffering any casualties.

Pennsylvania Light, Battery E, Lieut. Charles A. Atwell.   Losses, 3.

4th U. S., Battery F, Lieut. Sylvanus T. Rugg.   Loss, 1.

5th U. S., Battery K, Lieut. David H. Kinzie (retired in 1903 brig. gen., U.S.A.).   Losses, 5.

CAVALRY CORPS[1]

Maj. Gen. Alfred Pleasanton (W. P.).

FIRST DIVISION

Brig. Gen. John Buford (W. P.).

First Brigade: Col. William Gamble, 8th Illinois Cavalry (later brig. gen.).

8th Illinois,[2] Maj. John L. Beveridge.   (This officer—1824–1910— born in the State of New York, spent nearly all his life in Illinois, where he practised law.   After four years' service in the army in the

---

[1] The losses as noted in this section are, in most cases, for the entire campaign, the cavalry fighting commencing with Brandy Station, June 9th, and coming to an end with the skirmishes attending the pursuit of the Confederate Army, which closed only when the two forces once more reached the Rappahannock River, about the end of July.

[2] Louis Henry Rucker, 1st sergeant, Company G, of this regiment, serving in the Gettysburg campaign, rose in the years following the battle in the Regular Army to the rank of brigadier general, with which he was retired in 1903.   He died in 1906.

cavalry he was brevetted brigadier general; in civil life he served as sheriff of Cook County, State senator, Congressman-at-large, lieutenant governor and governor of his State, and Assistant Treasurer of the United States at Chicago. In 1864 he was colonel 17th Illinois Cavalry.) Total losses for the campaign, 76. Maj. Alpheus Clark and Capt. John G. Smith were mortally wounded at Beverly Ford, and Maj. W. H. Medill at Williamsport at the close of the campaign. Surgn. Abner Hard, of this command, was division surgeon, and commended by Buford.

12th Illinois (4 companies), and 3d Indiana (6 companies), under Col. George H. Chapman, of the Indiana contingent (brig. gen. July 21, 1864, and brvt. maj. gen. 1865). Lost as follows: Illinois, 52, including Lieut. Isaac Conroe, killed; Indiana, 61.

8th New York, Lieut. Col. Wm. L. Markell. Losses: Brandy Station, 50 (officers killed or mortally wounded: Col. Benj. F. Davis, Capt. Benj. F. Foote, Lieut. Henry C. Cutler, Lieut. Benj. C. Efner, and Lieut. James E. Reeves); Gettysburg, 34 (Capt. Charles D. Follett killed).

Second Brigade: Col. Thomas C. Devin (sketched in story of opening of the cavalry fight first day).

6th New York, Maj. Wm. E. Beardsley. Lieut. W. W. Phillips killed at Brandy Station. Losses, 26.

9th New York, Col. Wm. Sackett (brevetted brig. gen. for gallantry at Trevillian Station, where he was mortally wounded, June 11, 1864). Losses, 27.

17th Pennsylvania, Col. J. H. Kellogg (W. P.). Losses, 15.

3d West Virginia (2 companies), Capt. Seymour B. Conger. Losses, 7.

Reserve Brigade: Brig. Gen. Wesley Merritt (W. P.).

6th Pennsylvania, Maj. James H. Haseltine. Losses: Beverly Ford, June 9, 147, including Capt. Charles B. Davis, killed, and Maj. Robert Morris, wounded and captured, and dying in Libby prison a few weeks later; at Gettysburg, 12.

1st U. S., Capt. Richard S. C. Lord (W. P.). Losses, 70. (Col. Benj. F. Davis, 8th New York Cavalry, killed at Beverly Ford, was a capt. in this regiment).

2d U. S., Capt. T. F. Rodenbough (brevetted later up to brig. gen.). Losses, 83, including Capt. Charles W. Canfield, killed at Beverly Ford, and Lieut. Geo. De Vere Selden, mortally wounded at Gettysburg, and dying September 17th following. Merritt was captain in this regiment when made brigadier general three days before the battle.

5th U. S., Capt. Julius W. Mason (brevetted maj. and lieut. col. for Beverly Ford and Brandy Station). Losses, 44.

6th U. S. Losses, 424, as follows: Beverly Ford and Upperville, 75; Fairfield, 200; Funkstown, 59. Officers killed or mortally wounded: Lieuts. Isaac M. Ward and Christian Balder. Five officers

GETTYSBURG

led the regiment: Maj. Samuel H. Starr, a veteran of twenty years' experience in the army before the war, brevetted lieutenant colonel for Upperville and colonel for Gettysburg, where he was severely wounded; Lieut. Louis H. Carpenter, now (1913) on the retired list of brigadier generals in the Regular Army, one of the most distinguished of our living officers; Lieut. Nicholas Nolan, a brave Irishman, a private in the army in 1852, dying in 1885 as major, 3d Cavalry; Capt. Ira W. Claflin (W. P.), brevetted major for this campaign; and Capt. George C. Cram, brevetted major for Beverly Ford. Second Lieut. Adna R. Chaffee won his first brevet in this campaign, an honor which pioneered his way until in 1906 he became lieutenant general of the army.

SECOND DIVISION

Brig. Gen. David McM. Gregg (W. P.).

HEADQUARTERS GUARD

1st Ohio, Company A, Capt. Noah Jones.

First Brigade: Col. John B. McIntosh (1st lieut., 5th U. S. Cavalry; brvt. lieut. col., U.S.A., for this battle; brig. gen. July 21, 1864).

1st Maryland, Lieut. Col. James M. Deems. Losses, 66—most of them at Stevensburg, Va., June 9th. Lieut. Jacob A. Metz was killed near Williamsport.

Purnell Legion (Md.), Company A, Capt. Robert E. Duvall.

1st Massachusetts, Lieut. Col. Greely S. Curtis. Losses for the campaign, 167.

1st New Jersey, Maj. M. H. Beaumont. Losses: at Brandy Station, 52 (Lieut. Col. Virgil Brodrick and Maj. John H. Shelmire killed); at Gettysburg, 9.

1st Pennsylvania, Col. John P. Taylor. Losses: Brandy Station, 35; Gettysburg, 2. Col. Taylor was brevetted brigadier general 1865.

3d Pennsylvania, Lieut. Col. E. S. Jones. Losses, 21.

3d Pennsylvania, Heavy Artillery, Section Battery H, Capt. W. D. Rank. No losses.

Second Brigade: Col. Pennock Huey (sketched in Pennsylvania chapter). On duty guarding the flanks and rear, and not at Gettysburg.

2d New York, Lieut. Col. Otto Harhaus. Losses: at Brandy Station, 39; at Aldie, June 17th, 50 (Lieuts. A. F. Martensen and Daniel Whittaker killed; at Upperville, 6.

4th New York, Lieut. Col. Augustus Pruyn. Col. L. P. Di Cesnola was wounded and captured at Aldie, where the loss was 42; at Upperville, 27.

6th Ohio (10 companies), Maj. William Stedman. Losses for the campaign, 44. Maj. Benj. C. Stanhope mortally wounded at Aldie.

8th Pennsylvania, Capt. William A. Corrie. (The regimental commander, Pennock Huey, led the brigade.) Losses for the campaign, 23.

Third Brigade: Col. John Irvin Gregg, 16th Pennsylvania Cavalry (sketched in Pennsylvania chapter).

1st Maine (10 companies), Col. Charles H. Smith (brvt. brig. gen. August 1, 1864). Losses: Brandy Station, 35; Aldie, 29, including Col. Calvin S. Douty and Capt. George J. Summat, killed; Middleburg, including Lieuts. George S. Kimball, Ephraim H. Taylor, and Mark Neville, killed; Upperville, 9; Gettysburg, 5—a total of 147.

10th New York, Maj. M. Henry Avery. Losses: at Brandy Station, 82, including Lieut. William J. Robb, killed, and Lieut. John B. King, mortally wounded; at Middleburg, 26 (Lieut. Horatio H. Boyd killed and Lieuts. Bronson, Beardsley, and Edward S. Hawes mortally wounded); at Gettysburg, 9—an aggregate of 117.

4th Pennsylvania,[1] Lieut. Col. William E. Doster (brvt. brig. gen. March 13, 1865). Losses, 28.

16th Pennsylvania, Lieut. Col. John K. Robinson (brvt. brig. March 13, 1865). Losses, 17. Lieut. Wm. H. Billmeyer mortally wounded.

THIRD DIVISION

Brig. Gen. Judson Kilpatrick (W. P.).

First Brigade: Brig. Gen. Elon J. Farnsworth (killed on the third day leading a charge against the Confederate right flank). Col. Nathan P. Richmond followed in command.

5th New York, Maj. John Hammond, later colonel and then brevet brigadier general. Losses from June 9th to July 8th, 141. Private Thomas Burke, later a sergeant, received a medal of honor for capturing a flag in the fight at Hanover. Lieuts. Alexander Gall, adjutant, and Elam S. Dye were killed.

18th Pennsylvania, Lieut. Col. William P. Brinton. Losses, 127 from June 30th to July 9th. Capt. William C. Lindsey was killed at Hagerstown.

1st Vermont, Lieut. Col. Addison W. Preston. Losses from June 29th to July 13th, 117. Col. Preston was killed at Salem Church, Va., June 3, 1864. On July 10th Col. Edward B. Sawyer, for some time necessarily separated from his command, took the regiment, and two weeks later the brigade. Capt. John W. Woodward was killed July 6th at Hagerstown.

1st West Virginia (10 companies), Col. Nathaniel P. Richmond

---

[1] Maj. Samuel B. M. Young, of this regiment, mentioned in one phase of the campaign for "distinguished conduct," entered the service in 1861 as a private; was finally colonel of his regiment and brevet brigadier general; then, entering the regular service, he rose by regular stages to the head of the U. S. Army, August 8, 1903. At twenty-one a private soldier, at sixty-three the lieutenant general commanding—what a record is that!

GETTYSBURG

(followed at the head of the regiment, when summoned to take the brigade, by Maj. Charles E. Capehart). Losses for the campaign, 61. Capt. William N. Harris, Lieut. Irvin C. Swentzel, and Lieut. Sidnier W. Knowles killed; Lieut. Henry W. Clark mortally wounded.

Second Brigade: Brig. Gen. George A. Custer (W. P.).

1st Michigan, Col. Charles H. Town. Losses, 124. Capts. William R. Elliott and Charles J. Snyder and Lieut. James S. McElhenny killed or mortally hurt.

5th Michigan, Col. Russell A. Alger. Losses, 56, including Maj. Noah H. Ferry, killed. (Col. Alger was brevetted maj. gen. before the war ended; he died in 1907, after a notable career in finance, politics, and war, serving as governor of Michigan, commander in chief of the Grand Army of the Republic, Secretary of War during the Spanish-American conflict, and United States Senator, dying at the end of his term in the latter office. He had at one time a considerable following in view of the Republican nomination for the presidency.)

6th Michigan, Col. George Gray. Losses, 28, including the following officers, killed on the Potomac in pursuit of Lee's forces: Capts. Peter A. Weber and David G. Royce, and Lieuts. Aaron C. Jewett and Charles E. Bolza.

7th Michigan (10 companies), Col. William D. Mann. Losses, 100. (Col. Mann during the war was the inventor of certain improved accoutrements for troops in active service; he pioneered the manufacture of cotton-seed oil after the war was ended; became the inventor of the Mann boudoir car, and a noted journalist in charge for a while of the *Mobile Register*, and later the owner of the *Smart Set* and of *Town Topics* in New York City.)

HORSE ARTILLERY

First Brigade: Capt. James M. Robertson. (This expert artillerist, after having served in the 2d Artillery for ten years in the ranks, won a commission in 1848, and reached his captaincy in that regiment in 1861, and was retired as maj. in that arm of the service in 1879; he was brevetted lieut. col. for Gettysburg, and brig. gen. at the end of the war for distinguished services as chief of the horse artillery of the Army of the Potomac. He died in 1891.)

9th Michigan Battery, Capt. Jabez J. Daniels. Losses, 5.

6th New York Battery, Capt. Joseph W. Martin. Loss, 1.

2d U. S., Batteries B and L, Lieut. Edward Heaton. Losses, 3— in early part of campaign.

2d U. S., Battery M, Lieut. A. C. M. Pennington (W. P.); brevetted major for this campaign, and brigadier general at the end of the war; retired brigadier general, U.S.A., in 1899. Loss, 1.

4th U. S., Battery E, Lieut. Samuel S. Elder (a soldier of the old army, with five years of service to his credit before he won his commission; brevetted thrice in after years). Loss, 1.

Second Brigade: Capt. John C. Tidball (W. P.), brevetted up to major general for varied services.

1st U. S., Batteries E and G, Capt. Alanson M. Randol (W. P.), brevetted major for Gettysburg; brigadier general for the war.

1st U. S., Battery K, Capt. William M. Graham (served in the old army, beginning with 1855; captain of artillery in 1861; brevetted colonel for Gettysburg; retired in 1898 as major general). Losses, 3.

2d U. S., Battery A, Lieut. John H. Calef (W. P.), brevetted captain for gallantry in this battle. Losses, 12.

3d U. S., Battery C, Lieut. William D. Fuller (W. P.), brevetted major for Gettysburg; on duty guarding rear and flank.

ARTILLERY RESERVE

Brig. Gen. Robert O. Tyler (W. P.), brevetted major and lieutenant colonel for this battle; when his horse was killed and he was temporarily injured by the fall Capt. J. M. Robertson had charge of the command.

HEADQUARTERS GUARD

32d Massachusetts Infantry, Company C, Capt. Josiah C. Fuller.

First Regular Brigade: Capt. Dunbar R. Ransom, 3d U. S. Artillery, brevetted lieutenant colonel for Gettysburg. This officer had over three years'—1847-1850—training in West Point, and was commissioned in the army in 1855; severely wounded.

1st U. S., Battery H, Chandler P. Eakin, severely wounded in the cannonade Thursday afternoon; brevetted major for this battle. Losses, 10. Lieut. Philip D. Mason, killed at Trevillian Station, June, 1864, took the battery when Eakin was hurt.

3d U. S., Batteries F and K, Lieut. John G. Turnbull, brevetted major for this battle, in which he was wounded. Lieut. Manning Livingston, of the battery, was killed. He was brevetted posthumously to a captaincy.

4th U. S., Battery C, Lieut. Evan Thomas (brevetted maj. for this battle; killed April 25, 1873, in fight with the Modoc Indians, Lava Beds, Cal.). Losses, 18.

5th U. S., Battery C, Lieut. Gulian V. Weir. Losses, 16.

First Volunteer Brigade: Lieut. Col. Freeman McGilvery, 1st Maine Light Artillery (died September 2, 1864, of wounds received at Deep Bottom, Va.).

Massachusetts Light Artillery, 5th Battery E, with 10th New York Battery attached, Capt. Charles A. Phillips. Losses in the New York contingent, 5; other losses, 16.

GETTYSBURG

Massachusetts Light Artillery, 9th Battery, Capt. John Bigelow, severely wounded; followed by Lieut. Richard S. Milton. Lieut. Christopher Erickson was killed, and Lieut. Alexander H. Whitaker was mortally hurt, dying of his injuries July 20th. Losses, 28.

New York Light Artillery, 15th Battery, Capt. Patrick Hart. Losses, 16.

Pennsylvania Light Artillery, Batteries C and F, Capt. James Thompson. Losses, 28. Lieut. Joseph L. Miller died August 9th of wounds received in this battle.

Second Volunteer Brigade: Capt. Elijah D. Taft, of the 5th Battery, New York Light Artillery.

1st Connecticut Heavy Artillery, Battery B, Capt. Albert F. Brooker. (Not engaged.)

1st Connecticut Heavy Artillery, Battery M, Capt. Franklin A. Pratt. (Not engaged.)

Connecticut Light Artillery, 2d Battery, Capt. John W. Sterling. Losses, 5.

New York Light Artillery, 5th Battery, Capt. Elijah D. Taft. Losses, 3.

Third Volunteer Brigade: Capt. James F. Huntington, 1st Ohio Light Artillery.

New Hampshire Light Artillery, 1st Battery, Capt. Frederick M. Edgell. Losses, 3.

1st Ohio Light Artillery, Battery H, Lieut. George W. Norton. Losses, 7.

1st Pennsylvania Light Artillery, Batteries F and G, Capt. R. Bruce Ricketts. Losses, 23.

West Virginia Light Artillery, Battery C, Capt. Wallace Hill. Losses, 4.

Fourth Volunteer Brigade: Capt. Robert H. Fitzhugh, Battery K, 1st New York Light Artillery (maj. of the regiment September, 1863; brevetted lieut. col. for this battle; maj. and chief com. sub. in Spanish-American War).

Maine Light Artillery, 6th Battery, F, Lieut. Edwin B. Dow (later promoted capt.). Losses, 13.

Maryland Light Artillery, Battery A, Capt. James H. Rigby. Losses, 9.

New Jersey Light Artillery, 1st Battery, Lieut. Augustin N. Parsons. Losses, 9.

1st New York Light Artillery, Battery G, Capt. Nelson Ames. Losses, 7.

1st New York Light Artillery, Battery K, with 11th New York Battery attached. Losses, 7.

Train Guard: 4th New Jersey Infantry (7 companies), Maj. Charles Ewing.

ADDENDUM: AN EXTRAORDINARY RECORD

The following list of thirty subalterns in the regular forces at Gettysburg who in later years rose to the ranks of general officers—chiefly during the emergent period of 1898—1900, when large work had to be done in Cuba and in the Philippine Islands, and when men were needed fit to command brigades, divisions, and army corps—is worthy of record and study.

We omit from the list the young West-Pointers who in their early or late twenties became in the Civil War generals in command—such as Kilpatrick, Custer, Merritt, Upton, Mackenzie, who made their record at Gettysburg and in later battles; their names are to be honored and remembered for the years to come. But just here we emphasize the fact that out of the little group of a few score of young officers of the Regular Army serving at Gettysburg, chiefly with the broken infantry or cavalry regiments, or with batteries, there were a score and a half of lieutenants of the very finest military gifts and acquirements who were in due time found worthy of handling large affairs at home or abroad, and who made thereby a notable record. We have made out the list in order to suggest what sort of material in subordinate posts of service the Regular Army contained in that battle.

We omit in the following list the intermediate stages of promotion and the brevets received from time to time—these data have their proper place of record; but this collection which we are now making has never before been done. The rank attained finally by these young officers, as they were then at Gettysburg, is that of brigadier general, unless otherwise indicated.

Engineers: Capt. John W. Barlow (W. P.), brigadier general and chief of engineers, U.S.A., April 30, 1901. Lieut. George L. Gillespie (W. P.), chief of engineers, U.S.A., May 3, 1901, and major general and assistant chief of staff, January 23, 1904; retired 1905.

Second Infantry: Capt. John S. Poland (W. P.) (on staff duty in the battle with the rank of lieut. col. of volunteers). Lieut. Daniel W. Burke.

Third Infantry: Brvt. Capt. John Henry Page. First Lieut. Daingerfield Parker. First Lieut. Jacob Ford Kent (W. P.) (on staff duty at Gettysburg with volunteer rank of lieut. col.).

Sixth Infantry: Second Lieut. John Walter Clous, commissioned after five years in the ranks in November, 1862; retired as judge advocate, U.S.A., with the rank of brigadier general, May 24, 1901. First Lieut. Hamilton S. Hawkins. In 1898 led a brigade, and was wounded at Santiago, and won a major general's commission. First Lieut. Harry Clay Egbert. In 1898 wounded at Santiago at the head of his brigade; killed in battle at Malinto, Philippine Islands, March 26, 1899; a brigadier general. First Lieut. Emerson H. Liscum. Wounded at Santiago in 1898, at the head of his brigade; killed leading his command, July 13, 1900, at Tientsin, China, in the advance of the allied forces toward Pekin.

Seventh Infantry: Second Lieut. Richard Comba, a brave Irishman, was commissioned after eight years of service, February 19, 1863; won three brevets at Gettysburg; was made brigadier general in 1898, and served as such in Cuba and in the Philippine Islands.

Eighth Infantry: First Lieut. William S. Worth, aide to Gen. Hunt, chief of artillery. At San Juan, when Col. Chas. A. Wikoff, leading the brigade, was killed, Worth, then lieutenant colonel 13th Infantry, took command, and was himself severely wounded. He was made colonel and then brigadier general for his gallantry.

Eleventh Infantry: Capt. John C. Bates (on Meade's staff), in 1898, after years of service, for gallantry at Santiago, became major general, and on February 1, 1906, lieutenant general, and chief of staff, U.S.A. Lieut. Abram A. Harbach was retired in 1902 as brigadier general after service in Cuba and the Philippines.

Twelfth Infantry: First Lieut. Evan Miles; promoted after service in Cuba, in 1898, to be brigadier general.

Fourteenth Infantry: Capt. John J. Coppinger, later colonel, 15th New York Cavalry; in 1898 major general of volunteers in the war with Spain.

Seventeenth Infantry: Capt. Edward P. Pearson, who at Gettysburg was aide on Howard's staff, led a brigade at Santiago in 1898 as colonel of the 10th Infantry, and won the stars of a brigadier.

This record, to be adequate, must also contain from other arms of the service the names of young officers at Gettysburg who later became brigadier or major generals.

First Artillery: Capt. William M. Graham (W. P.), in 1898 major general commanding Second Army Corps in Spanish-American War. Second Lieut. Tully McCrea (W. P.), retired, 1903, as brigadier general, U.S.A.

Second Artillery: First Lieut. Alex. C. M. Pennington (W. P.), brigadier general in the Spanish-American campaigns; retired October, 1899. Lieut. Carle A. Woodruff, retired as brigadier general 1903. Lieut. Edward B. Williston, retired July, 1900, brigadier general.

Third Artillery: Henry Carroll was first sergeant of Battery E at Gettysburg; won a commission in the cavalry service in 1864; and in 1898 was wounded in command of a brigade at Santiago; he died on the retired list as brigadier general in 1908.

ROSTER OF ARMY OF THE POTOMAC

Fifth Artillery: David H. Kinzie, first lieutenant in command of a battery at Gettysburg; rose to be colonel in the artillery corps of the army in 1901, and later was retired with rank of brigadier general.

First Cavalry: Camillo C. C. Carr was sergeant major of this regiment at Gettysburg; commissioned second lieutenant, October, 1863; after the war campaigned twenty years on the plains; retired by age, 1906, brigadier general, U.S.A.

Sixth Cavalry: Second Lieut. Louis H. Carpenter, a private in 1861; commissioned in 1862; made colonel 5th U.S.C.C., October, 1864; rose to be brigadier general in the war with Spain; commanded a division and a province; retired October 19, 1899. Second Lieut. Adna R. Chaffee won his first brevet—to first lieutenant—at Gettysburg. On the 22d of July, 1861, at the age of nineteen he enlisted in this regiment; he was sergeant, first sergeant, and then, on March 13, 1863, a lieutenant; and on February 1, 1906, he was retired as lieutenant general, after a career of extraordinary scope, in the Civil War, on the plains, in Cuba, in command of the China Relief Expedition, and in the Philippine Islands. First Lieut. James F. Wade (son of the famous Senator from Ohio, Benjamin F. Wade) was on Pleasanton's staff, and won five brevets in the Civil War; in the Spanish-American conflict he commanded the Third Army Corps; was at the head of the Cuban Evacuation Commission, and served for four years in the Philippine Islands—for half that time in chief command—and was retired in 1907 as major general.

These officers are not by any means the only ones among the young men at Gettysburg in the Regulars who deserve such recognition; we have of necessity drawn the line at those who won the post of a general officer. There were others who in their line of promotion stopped just short of that and were retired as colonels—a notable rank in the Regular Army. There were still others—such as Capts. T. F. Rodenbough and David Stuart Gordon—who had reached the retired list before the Spanish War broke out, and who were advanced to the rank of brigadier general at a later date. Were men of this class added to the brief list we have made up, it would deepen the impression produced upon those who study this magnificent array. Without amplifying the record it may suffice to say that the student of the history of our country, pondering this brief but thrilling record, may well heed the lesson involved, and say to himself: Surely the nation may be glad that in its time of trial and danger it was able to produce men of this character and caliber from its hosts of young soldiers who were able and willing to serve the Union in its hour of danger!

III

ROSTER OF THE ARMY OF NORTHERN VIR-
GINIA AT GETTYSBURG

COMMANDER IN CHIEF

Gen. Robert Edward Lee (W. P.).[1]

FIRST ARMY CORPS

Lieut. Gen. James Longstreet (W. P.).

McLAWS'S DIVISION

Maj. Gen. Lafayette McLaws (W. P.).

Kershaw's Brigade: Brig. Gen. Joseph Brevard Kershaw. Gen. Kershaw (1822–1894), born in Camden, N. C., was educated for the law, and practised that profession. He served as a lieutenant in the Mexican War, and as a member of the legislature four years. From the colonelcy of the 2d South Carolina he rose to be brigadier and then major general; after the war he was chosen to the State Senate and elected as its president. In 1877 he became judge of the Fifth Circuit Court of South Carolina. Early in 1894 he was appointed postmaster of Camden, but soon after, April 12th, he died.

2d South Carolina, Col. John D. Kennedy, wounded; followed by Lieut. Col. F. Gaillard. (Col. Kennedy was six times wounded during the war, and rose to be a brigadier general. In 1865 he was elected to Congress, but was not seated. Later he served as a member of the legislature, lieutenant governor, and presidential elector. From 1886 to 1889 he was U. S. consul general at Shanghai, China. He died in Camden, April, 1896.) Losses, 154.

3d South Carolina. Col. J. D. Nance, who had been wounded at Fredericksburg, was detained from the early part of the fight. On arrival, July 3d, he took his place; meanwhile Maj. R. C. Maffett was in command. Losses, 83.

7th South Carolina, Col. D. Wyatt Aiken. Losses, 110.

8th South Carolina, Col. J. W. Hengan. Losses, 100. Maj. D. McD. McLeod mortally wounded.

15th South Carolina. Col. W. D. Saussure (a capt. in the Palmetto regiment in the Mexican War, and a capt. in the 1st Cavalry, Regular Army, from March 3, 1855, till March 1, 1861) was killed; "an irreparable loss," reported Kershaw. Maj. Wm. M. Gist then took command. Losses, 137.

3d South Carolina Battalion, Lieut. Col. W. G. Rice. Losses, 46.

Barksdale's Brigade: Brig. Gen. William Barksdale. Gen. Barksdale, born in Tennessee in 1821, settled in Mississippi in youth, and became a lawyer with strong political proclivities and gifts. He served as a non-commissioned officer in the Mexican War in the 2d Mississippi regiment, and in 1853 he became a member of Congress, where he took rank as a representative of "State's Rights" Democracy. From the colonelcy of the 13th Mississippi he was promoted to be brigadier general. He was of fiery and ardent temperament, an orator of singular power, and an impetuous leader on the field. In the tremendous charge he led on Thursday afternoon he fell mortally wounded.

13th Mississippi, Col. J. W. Carter. Losses, 165.

17th Mississippi, commanded first by Col. W. D. Holder (disabled), and then by Lieut. Col. John C. Fiser. Losses, 200.

18th Mississippi, Col. T. M. Griffin (wounded) and Lieut. Col. W. H. Luse. Losses, 100.

21st Mississippi. Losses, 103. Col. B. G. Humphreys, when Barksdale fell, took the brigade; Lieut. Col. Brandon, who later became colonel and then brigadier general, succeeded in command of the regiment. Col. Humphreys, who was made a brigadier general in the autumn after the battle, had been in his youth for a time a cadet at West Point; after the war he served as governor of his State; he died at the age of seventy-four in 1882. Lowry, in his history of the State, says: "His name will long remain the synonym for knightly honor, for fidelity to every trust, for loyalty to every duty."

Semmes's Brigade: Brig. Gen. Paul J. Semmes entered service as colonel of the 2d Georgia, and was advanced to be brigadier general March 11, 1862. He shared creditably in the battles on the Peninsula, and in later campaigns up to Gettysburg, where he was fatally wounded near the Peach Orchard on the second day. He was taken back to Virginia, where he died July 10, 1863.

10th Georgia, Col. John B. Weems. Losses, 86, not counting captured or missing.

50th Georgia, Col. W. R. Manning. Losses, 87, and others missing.

51st Georgia, Col. E. Ball. Losses, 55, and others missing.

53d Georgia, Col. James P. Sims. Losses, 87, and others missing. No reports of the work of this brigade are in print. The mortal wounding of its commander early in the fight, and the severe losses of the command, with consequent confusion, help to account for the lack of data.

Wofford's Brigade: Brig. Gen. William T. Wofford. Gen. Wofford

GETTYSBURG

served with gallantry in the Mexican War as a captain, and later practised law, and was a member of the legislature of his native State of Georgia. He strove against secession, but yielded to the current sentiment and went to the front as colonel of the 18th Georgia. Before he was commissioned brigadier general he had already commanded a brigade. After the war he was sent to Congress, but was not seated. He was a member of the Georgia Constitutional Convention of 1877. (In addition to the losses assigned to the regiments there were 112 reported missing or captured from the brigade as a whole. No record is to be found giving names of officers slain. The "legions" called after Cobb and Phillips were made up in part of cavalry, and these under the same name are registered in Stuart's division.)

16th Georgia, Col. Goode Bryan (W. P.). Losses, 61.
18th Georgia, Lieut. Col. S. Z. Ruff. Losses, 19.
24th Georgia, Col. Robert McMillan. Losses, 36.
Cobb's Legion, Lieut. Col. Luther J. Glenn. Losses, 22.
Phillips's Legion, Lieut. Col. E. S. Barclay. Losses, 28.
Artillery Battalion: Col. Henry C. Cabell.

1st North Carolina Artillery, Battery A, Capt. B. C. Manly. Losses 7. (Private H. E. Thain, during the cannonade on Friday, seized a shell, the fuse of which had become accidentally ignited, and ran with it several yards away from the limber, meanwhile pulling out the burning fuse, and thereby preventing an explosion and loss of life in the battery.)

Pulaski Artillery (Ga.), Capt. J. C. Fraser (fatally wounded; Pendleton, Lee's chief of artillery, speaks of Fraser's "unflinching nerve and efficient energy." Lieut. W. J. F. Furlong succeeded him in command). Losses, 18.

Troup Artillery (Ga.), Capt. H. H. Carlton (wounded); Lieut. C. W. Motes. Losses, 7.

1st Richmond Howitzers, Capt. E. S. McCarthy. Losses, 5.

PICKETT'S DIVISION

Maj. Gen. George E. Pickett (W. P.).

Garnett's Brigade: Brig. Gen. Richard Brooke Garnett (W. P.). Maj. Chas. S. Peyton, of the 19th Virginia, as the only field-officer left in this brigade when the charge was broken, and Garnett and hundreds of other brave men were dead or dying or captured, took command of the remnant, and from his pen we have the graphic report of the dreadful occasion and its incidents (*Official Records*, 2:385).

8th Virginia, Col. Eppa Hunton. The killed and wounded in the official reports are put at 54, but this is evidently an inadequate list. The *Confederate Military History* says: "Nearly all of Hunton's men were killed, wounded, or captured, some of them inside the lines of the enemy." Hunton was wounded, and his horse was killed under him. Notes of his career will be found in the story of the charge in the narrative of the battle.

18th Virginia, Lieut. Col. H. A. Carrington, wounded. Losses, 87, with many captured.

19th Virginia, Col. Henry Gannt, wounded. Lieut. Col. John T. Ellis was killed before the charge in the cannonade—a leader singularly attractive as a man and a soldier. Losses, 44, and many missing.

28th Virginia, Col. Robert C. Allen, killed; Lieut. Col. Wm. Watts, wounded. Losses, 77, and scores captured.

56th Virginia, Col. W. D. Stuart, killed, and Lieut. Col. P. P. Slaughter, wounded. Losses, 62, and many missing. No regimental reports are available. In Maj. Peyton's report, alluded to above, he indicates 941 killed, wounded, and missing out of a total of 1,427 officers and men taken into the fight. The *Official Records* give 302 killed and wounded and 539 missing. It is clear that these latter figures fall far below the facts.

Kemper's Brigade: Brig. Gen. James Lawson Kemper. Gen. Kemper (1823–1895), a Virginian of the highest standing and character, after recovering from his dreadful wounds, was made a major general. His work is dealt with in connection with the account of the final charge. When he fell the brigade was led by Col. Joseph Mayo, Jr., of the 3d Virginia, who was also wounded.

1st Virginia, Col. Lewis B. Williams, killed; Lieut. Col. Fred. G. Skinner, wounded. Losses, 64 killed and wounded, and many missing.

3d Virginia, Col. Joseph Mayo, Jr., wounded; his successor in command, Lieut. Col. A. D. Calcote, was wounded also. Losses, 67, and many captured.

7th Virginia, Col. W. T. Patton, killed; Lieut. Col. C. C. Floweree, wounded. Losses, 94, and many missing.

11th Virginia, Maj. Kirkwood Otey, wounded. Losses, 109, and the missing.

24th Virginia, Col. William R. Terry. Losses, 128, and others missing. Col. Terry was severely wounded at the head of his men. The missing from the brigade, not assigned to the regiments, were 317. No other names of officers are on record, and no reports are in print.

Armistead's Brigade: Brig. Gen. Lewis Addison Armistead, killed.

9th Virginia, Maj. John C. Owens, killed. Losses, 81, and the missing.

14th Virginia, Col. James C. Hodges, killed. Lieut. Col. William White, wounded. Losses, 108, and others missing.

38th Virginia, Col. E. C. Edmonds, killed, and Lieut. Col. P. B. Whittle, wounded. Losses, 170, and the missing.

53d Virginia, Col. W. R. Aylett, wounded. Losses, 104, and the captured.

57th Virginia, Col. John Bowie Magruder, killed. Losses, 121, and the missing.   In addition to the above data there were in the brigade, as a whole, 643 missing, making a total loss of 1,191.   It would seem that during the years that have elapsed since the battle an accurate list, at least of the officers who perished in this part of the battle, might have been collated.

Artillery Battalion: Maj. James Dearing (a cadet at West Point after appointment from Virginia in 1858 until April 22, 1861, when he was drawn to vacate his cadetship and enter the Confederate service). The following organizations were all from Virginia:

Fauquier Battery, Capt. R. M. Stribling.   Losses, 3.
Hampden Battery, Capt. W. H. Caskie.   Losses, 3.
Richmond Fayette Battery, Capt. M. C. Macon.   Losses, 6.
Virginia Battery, Capt. Joseph G. Blount.   Losses, 5.

HOOD'S DIVISION

Maj. Gen. John B. Hood (W. P.).   Gen. Hood was wounded in the Peach Orchard on Thursday afternoon, soon after the opening of the attack on the Union left flank.   Brig. Gen. E. M. Law then took the division.   Gen. Law, born in South Carolina in 1836, was graduated from the Military Academy of that State in Charleston, and served as a college professor for some years, being admitted to the bar after the Civil War.   From the colonelcy of the 4th Alabama he became brigadier general and then major general.   For years in his home town of Bartow, Fla., he has been an editor, and also for a while superintendent of a military school.   Interesting war reminiscences from his pen have appeared in the *Century* and other periodicals.

Law's Brigade: When Gen. Law took the division Col. James M. Sheffield commanded the brigade; his regiment in turn was led by Capt. T. J. Eubanks, 48th Alabama.

4th Alabama, Lieut. Col. L. H. Scruggs.   Losses, 87, including Capt. W. W. Leftwich, killed.

15th Alabama.   Losses, 161, including among the killed Capts. J. H. Allison and H. C. Brainard; Capt. John C. Oates was mortally wounded.   Col. William C. Oates, when disabled for the time, was followed in command by Capt. B. A. Hill.   Col. Oates, born in Alabama, 1835, was wounded six times, and lost his right arm in battle. He practised law after the war; was a member of the State legislature, and from 1881 to 1895 a member of Congress, then for two years governor.   He was a brigadier general in the war with Spain, and wrote *The War Between the Union and the Confederacy.*

44th Alabama, Col. Wm. F. Perry.   Losses, 94, including Capts. John M. Teague and Wm. T. Dunklin, killed.   Col. Perry (1823–1901) became a brigadier general; his profession was teaching; he was the first superintendent of public instruction for Alabama, and the organizer of its first system of public schools in 1854. For a score of years after the war he was a college professor.

47th Alabama. Losses, 40. Capt. Joseph Johnson and three other officers were killed. Lieut. Col. M. J. Bulger, who two weeks after the battle became colonel, was severely wounded; then Maj. J. M. Campbell commanded. Col. James W. J. Jackson was at times with the regiment, but apparently not in battle.

48th Alabama. Col. Sheffield, as noted above, commanded the brigade; then after the wounding of Lieut. Col. W. H. Hardwicke and Maj. C. B. St. John, Capt. T. J. Eubanks had charge. Losses, 102.

Robertson's Brigade: Brig. Gen. Jerome B. Robertson. Gen. Robertson, born in Kentucky, went in his youth, in 1835, to Texas and served in the army of that inchoate Commonwealth for two years, winning a captaincy. Later he was a member of the Texas Senate. From a captaincy in the 5th Texas at the opening of the Civil War he rose to be colonel and brigadier general. His regiments at Gettysburg were:

3d Arkansas, Col. Van H. Manning, wounded; after the war a Congressman from Mississippi; he was followed in this fight by Lieut. Col. R. S. Taylor, assisted by Maj. J. W. Reedy. Losses, 142.

1st Texas, Lieut. Col. P. A. Work. Losses, 93, including Lieut. B. A. Campbell, killed.

4th Texas, Col. J. C. G. Key, disabled; Lieut. Col. B. F. Carter also; Maj. J. P. Bane then commanded. Losses, 87.

5th Texas. Col. R. M. Powell was mortally wounded and captured at the head of his force climbing Round Top. Lieut. Col. K. Bryan took the regiment, but was also wounded; Maj. J. C. Rogers then took command. Losses, 109. In the brigade as a whole there were reported 120 missing, in addition to the regimental data.

Anderson's Brigade: Brig. Gen. George T. Anderson. This officer was severely wounded in the attack which his force made on the Devil's Den. Lieut. Col. William Luffman then took command. Anderson, from the colonelcy of the 11th Georgia, was made brigadier general November 1, 1862; he had acquired ability and reputation as a captain in the Mexican War, and was reckoned a good brigade commander. After the war he engaged in railroad service in Georgia, and was for years chief of police in Atlanta.

7th Georgia, Col. W. W. White. Losses for the campaign, 26.

8th Georgia, Col. John R. Towers. Losses, 139.

9th Georgia. Losses, 189, including the commander, Lieut. Col. John C. Mounger, and Lieut. E. W. Bowen, killed; Maj. W. M. Jones, in command for an hour, was wounded. Capt. J. M. D. King, following, was wounded, and Capt. George Hillyer was left in charge.

11th Georgia. Losses, 204. Col. F. H. Mitchell was severely wounded; Lieut. Col. Luffman was summoned to take the brigade; Maj. Henry D. McDaniel, next in command, was wounded, and Capt.

GETTYSBURG

W. H. Mitchell was finally in charge. Capts. M. T. Nunnally and John W. Stokes and Lieut. W. H. Baskin were among the killed.

59th Georgia, Col. Jack Brown, wounded, followed by Capt. M. G. Bass. Losses, 116. These terrific losses indicate the severity of the engagement at the Devil's Den and at the base of Little Round Top, where these Georgians made their attacks.

Benning's Brigade: Brig. Gen. Henry L. Benning. Henry Lewis Benning, born in Georgia April 2, 1814, a graduate of the University of Georgia, a lawyer who had served four years in the Assembly and six years on the Supreme Bench, was promoted from the colonelcy of the 17th Georgia to be brigadier and then major general. He had legal ability, a generous spirit, a superb physique, and courage united with martial leadership.

2d Georgia, Lieut. Col. Wm. T. Harris, killed in assaulting Round Top; was followed by Maj. W. S. Shepherd. Losses (only in part reported), 91.

15th Georgia, Col. D. M. DuBose. Losses, 171. Col. DuBose, graduate of the University of Mississippi, son-in-law of Robert Toombs and after the war for one term in Congress, was made brigadier general in 1864. He died in 1883.

17th Georgia, Col. Wesley C. Hodges. Losses, 90.

20th Georgia, Col. John A. Jones, killed; was followed by Lieut. Col. J. D. Waddell. Losses, 121. Lieut. F. McCrimmon killed.

Artillery Battalion: Maj. Mathis W. Henry (W. P.).
Branch Artillery (N. C.), Capt. A. C. Latham.
German Artillery (S. C.), Capt. Wm. K. Bachman.
Palmetto Light Artillery (S. C.), Capt. Hugh R. Garden.
Rowan Artillery (N. C.), Capt. James Reilly. The battalion had a loss of 27 not assigned to the batteries.

ARTILLERY RESERVE
Col. J. B. Walton.
Alexander's Battalion: Col. E. P. Alexander (W. P.).
Ashland Artillery (Va.), Capt. P. Woolfolk, Jr., wounded; Lieut. James Woolfolk.
Bedford Artillery (Va.), Capt. T. C. Jordan.
Virginia Battery (Va.), Capt. W. W. Parker.
Virginia Battery (Va.), Capt. O. B. Taylor.
Brooks Artillery (S. C.), Lieut. S. C. Gilbert.
Madison Light Artillery (La.), Capt. George V. Moody. The loss for the battalion was 139. Alexander had charge of the preparations for the final cannonade on Friday for about half the line along Seminary Ridge.

Washington Artillery Battalion (La.): Maj. B. F. Eshleman.
1st Battery, Capt. C. W. Squires.
2d Battery, Capt. J. B. Richardson.

ARMY OF NORTHERN VIRGINIA

3d Battery, Capt. M. B. Miller.
4th Battery, Capt. Joe Norcom, wounded; Lieut. H. A. Battles.
Loss for the battalion (not reported in detail), 45.

SECOND ARMY CORPS

Lieut. Gen. Richard S. Ewell (W. P.).

EARLY'S DIVISION

Maj. Gen. Jubal A. Early (W. P.).

Hays's Brigade: Harry T. Hays, of New Orleans, was commissioned brigadier general July 25, 1862, from the colonelcy of the 7th Louisiana. Just before the war ended he was made a major general; his gallantry in battle was proverbial. He died in his New Orleans home, August 21, 1876. This command took part in the capture of Winchester on the way north, losing 14 killed and 78 wounded, including Lieut. V. P. Terry, of the 7th, and Capt. Albert Dejean, of the 8th, killed. At Gettysburg the following were the regiments:

5th Louisiana. Col. Henry Forno led at Winchester; Maj. Alexander Hart and Capt. T. H. Biscoe at Gettysburg. Losses, 49, including Capt. F. Richardson, killed.

6th Louisiana, Lieut. Col. Joseph Hanlon. Losses, 60, including Capt. A. Cormier, killed.

7th Louisiana, Col. D. B. Penn. Losses, 57, including Lieut. W. P. Talbot, killed.

8th Louisiana. Col. T. D. Lewis was killed, and also Capt. Victor St. Martin and Lieut. A. Randolph. Losses, 75. Lieut. Col. A. de Blanc and Maj. G. A. Lester at different times were in command.

9th Louisiana, Col. Leroy A. Stafford (brig. gen. October, 1863; mortally wounded in the Wilderness, May, 1864). Losses, 72. Lieut. R. T. Crawford killed. Hays mentions specially the gallantry and skill of Cols. Stafford and Penn.

Smith's Brigade: Brig. Gen. William Smith. This officer had been prominent in his State for thirty years before the war as lawyer, politician, State senator, governor, and financier. He was a notable character, brave in battle, opinionated, patriotic, fond of stump-speaking, and full of warlike ambitions—which often outran his military capacity, particularly in view of his years—he was sixty-five when he won his first commission as a general; still he was twice wounded, and became a major general before the war closed. He served as a member of the Confederate Congress while holding military rank, dividing his time between the camp and the Congress; from January 1, 1864, till the end he served once more as governor. By his service in Congress at Washington from 1853 till 1861 he had become known to the country at large. Three regiments were in his brigade in Lee's army:

431

GETTYSBURG

31st Virginia, Col. John S. Hoffman. Losses, 27.

49th Virginia, Lieut. Col. J. Catlett Gibson. Losses, 100, including Capt. B. S. Jacobs and Lieut. Goodrich Mitchell, killed.

52d Virginia, Lieut. Col. James H. Skinner. Losses, 15. In addition the brigade commander reports for the brigade 9 losses on the retreat, at Hagerstown, and 32 missing, to be added to the regimental reports.

Hoke's Brigade: Gen. R. F. Hoke, the usual leader of this body, was laid up with wounds received in the campaign of Chancellorsville in May, 1863, and the commander at Gettysburg, Col. Isaac E. Avery, 6th North Carolina, was killed. Col. A. C. Godwin, 57th North Carolina, then led the command.

6th North Carolina, Maj. S. McD. Tate. Losses, 172. Capt. J. H. Burns and Lieut. A. J. Cheek, killed.

21st North Carolina, Col. W. W. Kirkland (promoted brig. gen. a month after the battle). Losses, 111.

57th North Carolina, Col. Archibald C. Godwin (brig. gen. August 5, 1864; killed at Winchester six weeks later). Losses, 62, including among the killed Capt. S. W. Gray and Lieut. L. H. Roney.

Gordon's Brigade: Brig. Gen. John B. Gordon. John Brown Gordon (1832–1904), educated in the University of Georgia, his native State, was a lawyer; he raised a company, the "Raccoon Roughs," which he offered to his own governor; but there were no troops needed just then, and his men were accepted by Alabama; he rapidly rose to be colonel of the 6th Alabama, and then to be brigadier general, major general, and lieutenant general. He was perhaps the only officer in Lee's army who showed very high military gifts without having received in his earlier life either military schooling or experience. He was a singularly magnetic leader, and by his voice, his example, and his rousing power he proved to be a marvelous leader in battle. His wife, a woman of many personal charms, went with him on his campaigns, and several times when he was wounded her skill and care saved his life. After the war he served two terms in the United States Senate, and two terms in the governorship of Georgia, and for many years as commander in chief of the United Confederate Veterans. He was an orator of fine abilities, and his lecture "The Last Days of the Confederacy," heard by thousands in many parts of the country, helped to bring together the dissevered sections and to create a new spirit of patriotic unity. The same may be said, and even more, concerning his book, finished just before his death, *Reminiscences of the Civil War.* His brigade at Gettysburg was as follows:

13th Georgia, Col. James M. Smith. Losses, 103. Capt. V. T. Nunnelie and Lieut. R. W. Meachum killed.

26th Georgia, Col. E. N. Atkinson. Losses, 11.

31st Georgia, Col. Clement A. Evans. Losses, 43. Lieuts. T. J. Fergusson and W. B. Patterson killed.

432

ARMY OF NORTHERN VIRGINIA

38th Georgia, Capt. W. L. McLeod. Losses, 92. Capt. C. A. Hawkins was killed at Winchester, and the following at Gettysburg: Capt. W. L. McLeod, and Lieuts. John Oglesby and W. F. Goodwin.

60th Georgia, Capt. W. B. Jones. Losses, 38, including Capt. J. B. Colding.

61st Georgia, Col. John H. Lamar. Losses, 93. Maj. Peter Brenan and Lieut. S. H. Rice killed. Col. Clement A. Evans, named above at the head of the 31st Georgia, later became a division commander. Before the war he was widely known in his State as a lawyer, county judge, and member of the State Senate. His great work, in twelve massive volumes (Atlanta, 1899), *Confederate Military History*, written by himself and a score or more of co-operating contributors, is an achievement of lasting worth. He also compiled and edited the *Military History of Georgia*. He served as a pastor and presiding elder for twenty-five years in the Methodist Episcopal Church, South, and also, late in life, as commander in chief of the United Confederate Veterans.

Artillery: Lieut. Col. H. P. Jones.

Charlottesville (Va.) Artillery, Capt. James McD. Carrington.

Courtney (Va.) Artillery, Capt. W. A. Tanner.

Staunton (Va.) Artillery, Capt. A. W. Garber.

Louisiana Guard Artillery, Capt. C. A. Green.

Out of the conflicting reports and data it appears that the losses of the battalion at Gettysburg and at Winchester, where Capt. C. Thompson, of the Louisiana Guard Battery, was mortally wounded, aggregated 23.

JOHNSON'S DIVISION

Maj. Gen. Edward Johnson (W. P.).

Steuart's Brigade: Brig. Gen. George H. Steuart (W. P.).

1st Maryland Battalion (also called "2d Regiment"). Lieut. Col. J. R. Herbert and Maj. W. W. Goldsborough, in succession, were severely wounded; then Capt. J. P. Crane took command. The regiment went into the fight with 500 and lost 250, including Capt. W. H. Murray and Lieuts. W. C. Wrightson and W. J. Brightfoot among the killed.

1st North Carolina, Col. H. A. Brown. Losses: at Winchester, 17; at Gettysburg, 52, including Lieut. Green Martin, mortally wounded, and Capt. J. S. R. Miller, killed at Winchester.

3d North Carolina, Maj. W. M. Parsley. Losses, at Winchester, 14, and at Gettysburg, 156 out of 300 in the fight. The official State history of the regiment gives the loss at 223.

10th Virginia, Col. E. T. H. Warren. Losses, 21.

23d Virginia, Lieut. Col. S. T. Walton. Losses, 18.

37th Virginia, Maj. H. C. Wood. Losses, 54.

Stonewall Brigade: Brig. Gen. James A. Walker. Gen. Walker

433

(1832–1901), in his boyhood, almost at the end of his four years' course at the Virginia Military Institute, took offense at something said to him by Prof. T. J. Jackson—later known as "Stonewall"—and challenged the teacher to fight a duel. The high-strung lad was dismissed without his diploma—which, years later, because of distinguished service in the Confederacy, was granted to him. In his military service he commanded the confidence and love of Jackson, and at Gettysburg commanded Jackson's old "Stonewall" Brigade. After the war Walker was a lawyer, a member of the Virginia House of Delegates, lieutenant governor of the Commonwealth, and for two terms in Congress. He became in his public life a factor for the promotion of peace and good will between all sections. This was his brigade:

2d Virginia, Col. J. Q. A. Nadenbousch. Losses, 14.

4th Virginia, Maj. William Terry. Losses, 138.

5th Virginia, Col. J. H. S. Funk. Losses, 51, including Lieut. Jacob H. Keifer, killed.

27th Virginia, Lieut. Col. D. M. Shriver. Losses, 41.

33d Virginia, Capt. J. B. Golladay. Losses, 55. Capts. G. C. Eastman and George R. Bedinger killed. In addition there were 61 reported as missing or captured from the brigade as a whole. Maj. Ferry, of the 4th Virginia, a graduate of the University of Virginia, became a brigadier general in 1864. After the war he was successful as a lawyer, and served two terms in Congress. He was accidentally drowned, September 5, 1888.

Nicholls's Brigade: Col. J. M. Williams (2d La.). Gen. Francis T. Nicholls, detained by severe wounds from the command of his brigade, had a distinguished civic career, ending in 1912, as related elsewhere.

1st Louisiana. Col. M. Nolan was killed; then Capts. Thomas Rice and E. D. Willett followed in command. Losses, 39.

2d Louisiana, Lieut. Col. R. E. Burke. Losses: 11 at Winchester, and 62 at Gettysburg.

10th Louisiana, Maj. T. N. Powell. Losses: 3 at Winchester, and 91 at Gettysburg.

14th Louisiana, Lieut. Col. David Zable. Losses, 65.

15th Louisiana, Maj. Andrew Brady. Losses, 38. (No records are in print showing what officers were killed.)

Jones's Brigade: Brig. Gen. John M. Jones (W. P.). (Gen. Jones was wounded July 2d, and Lieut. Col. R. H. Dungan, 48th Virginia, took the brigade for a day. Then Brig. Gen. Bradley T. Johnson, a distinguished Marylander, arrived and took command. He was a Princeton graduate, and was trained in law at Harvard. He won the rank of brig. gen. in the Confederate service; after the war he settled in Richmond in legal practice, and served some years in the Virginia Senate. He removed to Baltimore in 1879, where he died in 1903.

He wrote a life of Washington, one of Gen. Joseph E. Johnston, and other works.)

21st Virginia, Capt. W. P. Mosely (later lieut. col.). Losses, 50. Capts. J. M. Vermillion and C. W. S. Harris killed.

25th Virginia, Col. J. C. Higginbotham, wounded; was followed by Lieut. Col. J. A. Robinson. Losses, 70.

42d Virginia, Lieut. Col. R. W. Withers, wounded; was followed by Capt. Jesse M. Richardson. Losses, 56.

44th Virginia, Maj. N. Cobb in charge till wounded; was followed by Capt. T. R. Buckner. Losses, 56.

48th Virginia. While Lieut. Col. R. H. Dungan was in charge of the brigade Maj. Oscar White had the regiment. Losses, 76.

50th Virginia, Lieut. Col. L. H. N. Salyer. Losses, 99.

Artillery Battalion: Maj. J. W. Latimer. When Latimer was fatally wounded, Thursday evening, Capt. C. I. Raine took the battalion.

1st Maryland Battery, Capt. Wm. F. Dement. Losses, 5.

Alleghany Artillery (Va.), Capt. J. C. Carpenter. Losses, 24.

Chesapeake Artillery (Md.), Capt. W. D. Brown (mortally wounded). Losses, 16.

Lee Battery (Va.), Capt. C. I. Raine, followed by Lieut. W. W. Hardwicke. Losses, 4. The battery as a whole suffered a loss also at Winchester of 17.

RODES'S DIVISION

Maj. Gen. R. E. Rodes.[1]

Daniel's Brigade: Brig. Gen. Junius Daniel (W. P.).

32d North Carolina, Col. E. C. Brabble, killed at Spottsylvania May, 1864. Losses, 142, besides captured and missing. No names of slain officers reported.

43d North Carolina, Col. Thomas S. Kenan, wounded; was followed by Lieut. Col. W. Gaston Lewis, later colonel and then brigadier general. Losses, 147, besides captured and missing. Officers killed: Capt. Wm. C. Ousby; Lieuts. Julius J. Alexander, Thomas W. Baker, and W. W. Boggan.

45th North Carolina. Lieut. Col. Samuel H. Boyd, Maj. John R. Winston, and Capt. A. H. Galloway, in turn, fell wounded; then Capt. J. A. Hopkins commanded. Losses, 219, besides the missing. Officers killed: Capt. Peter P. Scales; Lieuts. J. M. Benton, George F. Boyd, William E. Harris.

53d North Carolina, Col. W. A. Owens. Losses, 117, besides the missing. Officers killed: Capts. G. M. G. Albright and Wm. J. Miller; Lieuts. C. F. Hall, Thomas H. Hall, and P. W. Hatrick.

2d North Carolina Battalion. Lieut. Col. H. L. Andrews, killed at the head of his men, was followed by Capt. Van Brown. Losses, 153,

[1] A sketch of this officer has already been given in a preceding chapter in this volume.

besides the missing. Ewell declares, however, that 200 killed and wounded were lost out of 240 engaged. Officers killed: Lieut. Col. Andrews; Lieuts. Wm. A. Brady and Ralph Gorrell.

In this brigade there were 116 captured or missing in addition to those assigned to regiments as given above.

Doles's Brigade: Brig. Gen. George Pierce Doles. Gen. Doles, born in Milledgeville, Ga., in 1830, was captain of the Baldwin Blues, a militia company of his town, before the war. In May, 1861, he and his men went into the 4th Georgia Infantry, of which he was at once made colonel. In November, 1862, he was made a brigadier, and in that capacity did constant service in the battles through which the Army of Northern Virginia went, until his death in the engagement at Bethesda Church, June 2, 1864. His integrity, personal courage, military devotion, and sterling character are stressed by his various commanding officers in their reports. The *History of the Doles-Cook Brigade*, with portrait, 632 pages (Atlanta, 1903), was compiled by Henry W. Thomas, of the 12th Georgia.

4th Georgia. Lieut. Col. R. E. Winn, killed on the first day, was followed by Maj. W. H. Willis. Losses, 45. Lieut. J. H. Riviere was also killed.

12th Georgia. Col. Edward Willis, a cadet at West Point at the opening of the war, who resigned to enter the Confederate service, was at the head of this regiment. He was mortally wounded at the head of a brigade near Bethesda Church, May 30, 1864. Losses, 49.

21st Georgia, Col. John T. Mercer (W. P.). Losses, 17.

44th Georgia. Col. S. P. Lumpkin lost a leg, was captured, and died of his injuries, September 11, 1863. Maj. W. H. Peebles succeeded to the command. Losses, 68.

Iverson's Brigade: Brig. Gen. Alfred Iverson. Gen. Iverson, born in Georgia February 14, 1829, was trained at the military institute of Alabama, and at seventeen enlisted in a Georgia regiment and served in the Mexican War. In 1855 he was appointed a first lieutenant in the 1st U. S. Cavalry, and served, chiefly on the plains, for six years in the Regular Army, resigning his commission March 21, 1861, to enter the service of the Confederacy. He became colonel of the 20th North Carolina Infantry August 20, 1861, and was promoted to a brigadiership November 1, 1862. In the last year of the war he served with distinction as leader of a cavalry brigade under Wheeler.

5th North Carolina. Capts. Speight B. West and Benjamin Robinson, in succession, were in command and were wounded; the only other captains were also wounded: James M. R. Taylor and Thomas N. Jordan; Lieuts. Matthew J. Malone, W. A. Carr, and Charles C. Rawles were killed. Losses, 143, besides about 50 missing.

12th North Carolina, Lieut. Col. W. S. Davis. Losses, 56.

20th North Carolina. Losses, 122, besides a proportionate share of 200 prisoners and missing summed up in the brigade reports, but not assigned to the regiments. Lieut. Col. Nelson Slough, in command, was wounded in the afternoon of the first day; Maj. John S. Brooks fell at the same time; Capt. Lewis T. Hicks then took charge. Lieuts. J. L. Gore .and F. C. Wilson were killed.

23d North Carolina. Losses, 134, with many captured or missing. Col. D. H. Christie, in command, fell mortally hurt; then in succession Lieut. Col. R. D. Johnston, Maj. C. C. Blacknall, and Capt. Abner D. Peace were wounded, leaving Capt. Wm. H. Johnston in command, and he afterward was captured. Lieut. Col. Johnston was made a brigadier. Officers killed: Capt. G. T. Baskerville; Lieuts. C. W. Champion, Junius B. French (the adjutant), and Wm. M. Munday.

The above data, frightful enough, do not begin to tell the story of the losses incurred at Gettysburg by this brigade, which was by its commander misplaced in line so that it was almost surrounded, after having been enfiladed and greatly damaged. The historian of the 12th declares that out of the 1,470 officers and men present, June 30th, on the way, there were but 400 left after the battle, and that in the consternation and confusion the accurate data were never ascertained.

Ramseur's Brigade: Brig. Gen. Stephen D. Ramseur (W. P.).

2d North Carolina, Maj. D. W. Hurt, wounded; was followed by Capt. James T. Scales. Losses, 32.

4th North Carolina, Col. Bryan Grimes (maj. gen. February 15, 1865). Losses, 56, including Lieut John B. Stockton, killed.

14th North Carolina, Col. R. Tyler Bennett, who was wounded and followed in command by Maj. Joseph H. Lambeth. Losses, 44, including Lieuts. James A. Griffith and Frank M. Harney, killed.

30th North Carolina, Col. Francis M. Parker, wounded; was followed by Maj. W. W. Sillers. Losses, 45, including Lieut. Ira T. Connell, killed.

O'Neal's Brigade: Col. E. A. O'Neal. Col. Edward A. O'Neal (1818–1891) had been commissioned brigadier general June 6, 1863, but his commission had not reached him at the time of the battle. He was a graduate of La Grange College, and had secured a fine law practice before the war, to which he returned when the struggle ended. He was governor of Alabama, 1882–1886.

3d Alabama, Col. Cullen A. Battle. Losses, 91, besides scores captured or missing. Col. Battle won a brigadiership in the battle, and later became a major general. He was born in 1829 and died in 1905. He was a lawyer and journalist and political leader of standing for years. In reconstruction times he was elected to Congress, but was not seated.

5th Alabama, Col. J. M. Hall. Losses, 209, including Lieut. A. J. Wilcox, killed.

6th Alabama. After Col. J. N. Lightfoot and Maj. Isaac F. Culver were disabled Capt. M. L. Bowie took command. Losses, 162.

GETTYSBURG

12th Alabama, Col. S. B. Pickens. Losses, 83, including Capt. J. T. Davis and Lieuts. Jefferson Bridges and J. M. Fletcher, killed.

26th Alabama. (No field-officers belonging to this regiment were in the campaign, and Lieut. Col. J. C. Goodgame, of the 12th, was assigned to the command.) Losses, 130, including Lieuts. John Fowler and W. L. Branyon, killed.

Artillery Battalion: Lieut. Col. Thomas H. Carter.

Jeff Davis Artillery (Ala.), Capt. W. J. Reese.

King William Artillery (Va.), Capt. W. P. Carter.

Morris Artillery (Va.), Capt. R. C. M. Page.

Orange Artillery (Va.), Capt. C. W. Fry.

This battalion suffered a loss of 65, but they were not in the reports distributed to the batteries to which they belonged.

Artillery Reserve

Col. J. Thompson Brown.

First Virginia Artillery Battalion: Capt. Willis J. Dance.

2d Richmond Howitzers, Capt. David Watson.

3d Richmond Howitzers, Capt. B. H. Smith, Jr.

Powhatan Artillery, Lieut. John M. Cunningham.

Rockbridge Artillery, Capt. A. Graham.

Salem Artillery, Lieut. C. B. Griffin.

Nelson's Battalion: Lieut. Col. William Nelson.

Amherst Artillery, Capt. T. J. Kirkpatrick.

Fluvanna Artillery, Capt. J. L. Massie.

Georgia Battery, Capt. John Milledge, Jr.

The losses incurred by this whole command at Winchester and Gettysburg aggregated 210; they are not assigned to the individual batteries.

THIRD ARMY CORPS

Lieut. Gen. Ambrose P. Hill (W. P.).

Anderson's Division

Maj. Gen. Richard H. Anderson (W. P.).

Wilcox's Brigade: Brig. Gen. Cadmus M. Wilcox (W. P.).

8th Alabama, Lieut. Col. Hilary A. Herbert. Losses, 161, besides many missing. Col. Herbert was born in South Carolina, but removed with his parents when ten years of age to Alabama. His educational equipment was received at the Universities of Alabama and Virginia, and his profession was that of a lawyer. He was severely wounded twice. From 1877 till 1893 he was a member of Congress, and from 1893 till 1897 he was Secretary of the Navy. After that experience he settled in Washington in the practice of law.

9th Alabama, Capt. J. Horace King. Losses, 58, besides the missing.

10th Alabama, Col. William H. Forney, wounded and captured. Lieut. Col. James E. Shelley followed in command. Forney became a brigadier general in 1864, and after the war served in the State Senate. Losses, 104, and the missing.

11th Alabama. Col. John C. C. Sanders and Maj. R. T. Fletcher were wounded. Lieut. Col. George E. Taylor led the regiment when the colonel fell. Losses, 75, and the missing.

14th Alabama. Col. Lucius Pinckard was wounded, and followed in command by Lieut. Col. James A. Broome. Losses, 48, and the missing.

The missing from the brigade, in addition to the above figures of the regiments, aggregated 257.

Mahone's Brigade: Brig. Gen. William Mahone (1826–1895), born in Virginia, a graduate of the Virginia Military Institute, trained as a teacher, a civil engineer, and in railroad service as an executive, rose to be a major general. After the war he became a successful railroad manager, helped to restore peaceful conditions to his State, served as United States Senator, was defeated for the governorship, but retained an influential hold on political affairs in the Commonwealth and the nation.

6th Virginia, Col. George T. Rogers. Losses, 3.

12th Virginia, Col. Daniel A. Weisiger (who served in the Mexican War; rose to be commander of the Mahone Brigade; was made brigadier general, and was three times wounded). Losses, 14.

16th Virginia, Col. Joseph H. Ham. Losses, 9.

41st Virginia, Col. William A. Parham. Losses, 12.

61st Virginia, Col. V. D. Groner. Losses, 12.

Wright's Brigade: Brig. Gen. Ambrose Ransom Wright. Gen. Wright (1826–1872) was a successful lawyer and active in politics. He became colonel of the 3d Georgia in May, 1861, and rose to be major general. After the struggle he settled in Augusta, editing the *Chronicle and Sentinel;* in 1872 he was elected to Congress, but died a few weeks after his election, lamented by his State and hosts of friends outside of Georgia as a gifted and brave soul. The charge he made on Hancock's line on Thursday evening, July 2d, was one of the critical incidents of the battle.

3d Georgia, Col. E. J. Walker. The colonel reports 196 casualties at Gettysburg, and 75 more on the way back to the Rappahannock; but the brigade reports in the *Official Records* give the loss at 100.

22d Georgia, led first by Col. Joseph A. Wasden, killed, and then by Capt. B. C. McCurry. Losses, 96, and the missing.

48th Georgia, Col. William Gibson was wounded and captured. Capt. M. R. Hall succeeded in command. Losses, 212, including 18 commissioned officers. (See *Confederate Military History*.)

2d Georgia Battalion, Maj. George W. Ross, shot fatally in the climax of the charge on Thursday evening, and died next day in the hands of the Union soldiers. Capt. C. R. Redding killed. Capt. Charles J. Moffett took charge when Ross fell. Losses, 49, and many missing.

Perry's Brigade: Commanded by Col. David Lang, 8th Florida.

2d Florida, Maj. W. R. Moore. Losses, 81. Maj. Moore was wounded and captured. Capt. Ballantine was also wounded in command.

5th Florida, Capt. R. N. Gardner. Losses, 75, including Capt. John Frink and Lieuts. John Frink, J. A. Jenkins, and J. C. Blake, killed. Gardner lost an arm, and Capt. Hollyman took the regiment.

8th Florida, Lieut. Col. Baya, the colonel being at the head of the brigade. Losses, 94.

In addition to the losses above recorded there were 205 captured and missing from the brigade as a body, but not assigned to their respective regiments. The brigade took 700 into the fight, and lost a total of 455 out of that aggregate. It may be recalled that this brigade is called in the reports by the name of its regular commander, Brig. Gen. Edward A. Perry, who, several times wounded, was so disabled that he could not serve in the Gettysburg campaign. From 1884 to 1888 Perry was governor of Florida.

Posey's Brigade: Brig. Gen. Carnot Posey. The commander of this brigade, Gen. Posey, gained some valuable military experience and a disabling wound as first lieutenant in Col. Jefferson Davis's 1st Mississippi Rifles at the battle of Buena Vista in the Mexican War. In the Civil War he entered the Confederate service as colonel of the 16th Mississippi, and served in Lee's army with a skill which received recognition in November, 1862, when he was promoted to be a brigadier. On October 14th, after Gettysburg, he was wounded at Bristoe Station, and died of the injury at Charlottesville, Va., November 13, 1863. At Gettysburg his brigade was made up of the following bodies of infantry from his native State: .

12th Mississippi, Col. W. H. Taylor. Losses, 7.

16th Mississippi, Col. Samuel E. Baker. Losses, 19.

19th Mississippi, Col. N. H. Harris. Losses, 27.

48th Mississippi, Col. Joseph M. Jayne. Losses, 30. Col. Harris, of the 19th, became brigadier general January 20, 1864, succeeding to the command of the brigade vacated by the death of Gen. Posey.

Sumter Artillery Battalion: Maj. John Lane. These three batteries were from Georgia—"Eleventh Georgia Battalion."

Battery A, Capt. Hugh M. Ross.

Battery B, Capt. George M. Patterson.

Battery C, Capt. John T. Wingfield.

The combined losses for the campaign were 30.

HETH'S DIVISION

Maj. Gen. Henry Heth (W. P.). Heth was wounded on the first day; then Pettigrew took the division.

First Brigade: Brig. Gen. James Johnston Pettigrew. When Pettigrew was assigned the command of the division Col. J. K. Marshall, 52d North Carolina, commanded the brigade. Gen. Pettigrew (who led the division when it shared the glory and the disasters of the final charge on the last day, and who lost his life at Falling Waters in defending the rear of Lee's army at the time of the crossing back into Virginia, at the close of the campaign, when he was thirty-five years of age) was a graduate of the State University, class of 1847, a trained lawyer whose mind had been enriched by European travel, and who had served in the South Carolina Legislature during a residence in his younger manhood in that Commonwealth. One of his forebears was the first Protestant Episcopal bishop of North Carolina, and his father was a member of Congress from that State. He showed himself on the battle-field a skilful and gallant officer. The brigade was as follows:

11th North Carolina, Col. Collett Leventhorpe. This officer had been a captain in the British Army, and was reckoned a most accomplished field-officer. Later he became brigadier general. He was wounded in this battle. Losses, 209, besides the missing. Officers killed: Maj. Egbert A. Ross; Lieuts. Thomas W. Cooper, Edward A. Rhodes, George W. Kincaid, John H. McDade, J. B. Lowrie, John A. Burgin, and John W. Burgin. Company A crossed the Potomac with a hundred men; it came out of the last charge with a lieutenant and eight men. Company C lost in that charge 32 killed and wounded out of 37.

26th North Carolina, Col. Harry K. Burgwyn. Losses, 86 killed, 502 wounded, and 126 missing—a total of 714 out of 800 taken into the fight. Col. Burgwyn, not yet twenty-three years of age, a man of gallantry and gifts, a graduate of the Virginia Military Institute, was killed. In addition Capts. S. P. Wagg and William Wilson, and Lieuts. J. R. Emerson, W. W. Richardson, and J. B. Holloway were killed. Capt. Tuttle, of Company F, took 91 into the fight; every man, including himself, was either killed or wounded.

47th North Carolina. Losses, 161, besides the missing. Capt. C. T. Iredell was killed. Capt. Joseph J. Davis, wounded and captured, lived to be a member of Congress, and later a justice of the Supreme Court of the State. Col. George H. Faribault was wounded, also Lieut. Col. John A. Graves, who was captured and died of his wound.

52d North Carolina. Losses, 147, and many missing or captured. Col. James K. Marshall, a commanding and noble figure at the head of his men, led this regiment in the first day's fight, and fell leading the brigade in the final charge. Lieut. Col. Marcus A. Parks was severely wounded and captured. Maj. John G. Richardson and Capts. Julius C. Blackburn and George C. McCain were killed.

Brockenbrough's Brigade: Col. J. M. Brockenbrough, 40th Virginia.

GETTYSBURG

40th Virginia, commanded in succession by Capt. T. E. Betts and Capt. R. B. Davis. Losses, 42.

47th Virginia, Col. Robert M. Mayo. Losses, 48.

55th Virginia, Col. W. S. Christian. Losses, 34.

22d Virginia Battalion, Maj. John S. Bowles. Losses, 24.

No reports are on record from the commanders of the brigade or of the regiments, and no mention is made of the officers killed and wounded, either in the aggregate or by name.

Archer's Brigade: Brig. Gen. James J. Archer. Gen. Archer, born in Maryland, was a captain of infantry in the Mexican War, and won a brevet as major for gallantry in the battle of Chapultepec, September 13, 1847. He was appointed a captain in the Regular Army, 9th Infantry, March 3, 1855, and served in that rank till May 14, 1861, when he resigned to enter the Confederate service, in which he served as brigadier general until his death, October 24, 1864. It will be recalled that he and a part of his brigade were captured in the first day's fight. Then Col. Birkett D. Fry led the brigade; in the last charge he was desperately wounded and captured, but recovered to return later to his post as brigadier general. Fry had a varied equipment for his adventurous career, received at Washington College, at West Point for a while, and at the Virginia Military Institute; he served in the Mexican War, was a "Forty-niner" in California, and a colonel and general in Walker's famous and ill-fated Nicaragua Expedition.

5th Alabama Battalion, Maj. A. S. Van de Graaff. Losses, 100— these figures correct the report in the *Official Records*, which name but 26. The correction comes from the *Confederate Military History*, in the section devoted to Alabama.

13th Alabama, Col. Birkett D. Fry. Losses, 45, and many missing, probably captured.

1st Tennessee (Provisional Army), Maj. Felix G. Buchanan. Losses, 42. Lieut. Col. George was wounded and captured.

7th Tennessee, Lieut. Col. S. G. Shepard. Losses, 23, and others missing. Maj. Fite and Capt. W. H. Williams, later major, wounded and captured. The latter lost an arm.

14th Tennessee, Capt. B. L. Phillips. Losses, 27, and many missing.

The number reported missing in the whole brigade of five regiments was 517. There is no way to tell how to distribute them regimentally.

Davis's Brigade: Brig. Gen. Joseph R. Davis, a nephew of Jefferson Davis, served as lieutenant colonel and then as colonel of the 10th Mississippi Infantry, and in 1862 was made a brigadier general. He rendered service throughout the war, and after surrendering at Appomattox returned to his home in Biloxi, Miss., and engaged in the duties of his profession, the law. He died September 15, 1896.

2d Mississippi, Col. J. M. Stone, wounded. Losses, 232.

11th Mississippi, Col. F. M. Green. Losses, 202.

42d Mississippi, Col. H. R. Miller. Losses, 265.

55th North Carolina, Col. John Kerr Connally. Losses—corrected from the data of the regimental historian in the official *History of North Carolina Regiments*—killed, 64; wounded, 172; captured, 200— a total of 436, a total surpassing any regimental record on either side except that of the 26th North Carolina, already noted. Col. Connally was wounded while holding aloft the colors; when he fell Maj. Belo, afterward colonel, caught the flag and was also stricken down. Connally after the war became a noted preacher in Asheville, and Col. Belo for years edited the *Galveston News*.

Artillery Battalion: Lieut. Col. John J. Garnett.

Donaldson Artillery (Va.), Capt. V. Maurin.

Huger Artillery (Va.), Capt. Joseph D. Moore.

Lewis Artillery (Va.), Capt. John W. Lewis.

Norfolk Light Artillery Blues (Va.), Capt. C. R. Grandy.

Total loss for the battalion—not assigned to the component batteries—22.

PENDER'S DIVISION

Maj. Gen. William D. Pender (W. P.). Gen. Pender, a West Point graduate, has due notice elsewhere in this volume. When Pender was fatally wounded on Thursday afternoon Gen. Lane was put in charge of the division. Just before the final charge Lane was superseded by Maj. Gen. I. R. Trimble, who was wounded and captured within an hour afterward. Then Lane again took the division.

First Brigade: Col. Abner Perrin. Col. Perrin led this brigade in place of Gen. McGowan, the regular commander, who had been disabled by wounds at Chancellorsville. Perrin, born in South Carolina in 1827, entered the service as captain, and became colonel when McGowan was promoted to be brigadier general, a rank which Perrin also won in September, 1863. Perrin was shot dead while leading his brigade into the bloody angle at Spottsylvania in May, 1864, just after that whirlpool of destruction had been occupied by Hancock's men. At Gettysburg this command included:

1st South Carolina, Maj. C. W. McCreary (Provisional Army). Losses, 95. Capt. W. T. Haskell killed.

1st South Carolina Rifles, Capt. Wm. M. Hadden. Losses, 11.

12th South Carolina, Col. John M. Miller. Losses, 132.

13th South Carolina, Lieut. Col. B. T. Brockman. Losses, 130.

14th South Carolina, Lieut. Col. Joseph N. Brown. Losses, 209.

Lane's Brigade: Brig. Gen. James H. Lane. When this officer commanded the division Col. C. M. Avery, 33d North Carolina, led the brigade. Gen. Lane, a native of Virginia, and a graduate of the Virginia Military Institute, served in that institution for a time as assistant professor of tactics; at the outbreak of the war he was pro-

GETTYSBURG

fessor in the North Carolina Military Institute at Charlotte. He was major of the 1st North Carolina, of which Daniel H. Hill, afterward general, was colonel, and then became colonel of the 28th North Carolina Infantry. On November 1, 1862, as a reward for many months of fine service he was made brigadier general, when but twenty-seven years of age. At Gettysburg his horse was killed under him, and half his men were killed or wounded. After the war he made a long and creditable record as a college professor in three different States.

7th North Carolina. Maj. J. McLeod Turner, severely wounded and captured, was followed by Capt. James G. Harris. Losses, 142.

18th North Carolina, Col. John D. Barry (brig. gen. August 3, 1864). Losses, 45, and many missing.

28th North Carolina. Col. S. D. Lowe at first led this body; when he was wounded Lieut. Col. W. H. A. Speer took command. Losses, 104, besides the missing. The officers killed or wounded are not indicated in the reports.

33d North Carolina, Col. C. M. Avery. Losses, 63. Maj. Joseph H. Saunders, at the head of his men in the final charge, fell near the Union breastworks severely wounded. Lieuts. H. H. Baker and Thomas A. Cowan were killed.

37th North Carolina, Col. W. M. Barbour. Losses, 88, besides the missing or captured. Among the killed were Maj. Owen N. Brown, and Lieuts. Lewis Battle, W. N. Nichols, William Doherty, Iowa M. Royster, and John P. Elms.

Third Brigade: Brig. Gen. Edward Lloyd Thomas. Gen. Thomas, a graduate of Emory College, Ga., served as a private in a Georgia regiment in the Mexican War, won a commission as lieutenant, and also by an act of special gallantry a vote of recognition from the Legislature in 1848. He was a planter before the Civil War, when he became colonel of the 35th Georgia, and was then promoted to be brigadier general. After the war he returned to his plantation. Later, in 1885, he was appointed to a clerkship in the Land Department, and then in the Bureau of Indian Affairs in Washington, D. C., where he died March 10, 1898. His command at Gettysburg consisted of the following regiments:

14th Georgia. Losses, 32.
35th Georgia. Losses, 48.
45th Georgia. Losses, 35.
49th Georgia. Losses, 37. Col. S. T. Player.

Scales's Brigade: Brig. Gen. Alfred Moore Scales. Gen. Scales, born in North Carolina November 26, 1827, became a leading lawyer, a member of the State Legislature, and then, in 1858, a member of Congress. Enlisting as a private, he rose to be brigadier general; he was wounded at Gettysburg, but returned to his work in the field when his hurts were healed. After the war he achieved distinction

444

in law, spent ten years in Congress, and a term in the governorship of his native State. From 1888 till his death in 1892 he was president of a bank in Greensboro. When he was wounded at Gettysburg he was followed in brigade command first by Lieut. Col. G. T. Gordon, and then by Col. Wm. Lee J. Lowrance.

13th North Carolina. Col. J. H. Hyman, when wounded, was followed by Lieut. Col. H. A. Rogers. The *Official Records*, once more, do not afford an adequate list of casualties—126. The regimental records give the data as follows: The regiment entered the fight with 180, increased to 195 by those who were late getting to the field. Of these only ten were left as the tattered remnant to get back into Virginia.

16th North Carolina, Capt. L. W. Stowe. Losses, 66, besides the missing.

22d North Carolina, Col. James Connor. Losses, 89, and the missing.

34th North Carolina, Col. W. L. J. Lowrance (wounded), and Lieut. Col. G. T. Gordon. Maj. George M. Clark was killed. Total losses, 64, besides the missing.

38th North Carolina. Col. W. J. Hoke, Lieut. Col. John Ashford, and Capt. Thornburg, the successive commanders, were disabled by wounds. The record of the *Official Records* as to casualties is clearly not correct, as the regimental history issued by the State declares that the losses on the first day alone were 100, and that there were many killed and wounded during the last charge. There were others also captured. There are 110 set down as missing for the brigade, and at Falling Waters, in addition, nearly 200 were captured. We do not wonder that Col. Lowrance says in his report that after the first day, when he took charge of the force, he found it "depressed, dilapidated, and almost unorganized."

Artillery Battalion: Maj. William T. Poague.

Albermarle Artillery (Va.), Capt. James W. Wyatt.

Charlotte Artillery (N. C.), Capt. Joseph Graham.

Madison Light Artillery (Miss.), Capt. George Ward.

Virginia Battery, Capt. J. V. Brooke.

Losses for the battalion, 32.

ARTILLERY RESERVE

Col. Reuben Lindsay Walker, chief of this body, had risen from the command of a battery; was a graduate of the Virginia Military Institute, and had won distinction as a civil and railroad engineer before the war. He was made brigadier general early in 1865, and was recognized as one of the experts in his arm of the service. At Gettysburg he had the following Virginia organizations under him as the artillery reserve:

GETTYSBURG

McIntosh's Battalion: Maj. D. G. McIntosh.
Danville Artillery (Va.), Capt. R. S. Rice.
Hardaway Artillery (Ala.), Capt. W. B. Hurt.
2d Rockbridge Artillery (Va.), Lieut. Samuel Wallace.
Virginia Battery, Capt. M. Johnson.
The loss of this battalion was 32.
Pegram's Battalion: Commanded part of the time by Maj. W. J.
Pegram, and part of the time by Capt. E. B. Brunson.
Crenshaw Battery (Va.).
Fredericksburg Artillery (Va.), Capt. E. A. Marye.
Letcher Artillery (Va.), Capt. T. A. Brander.
Pee Dee Artillery (S. C.), Lieut. Wm. E. Zimmerman.
Purcell Artillery (Va.), Capt. Joseph McGraw.
Casualties for the battalion, 48.

STUART'S CAVALRY DIVISION [1]

Maj. Gen. J. E. B. Stuart (W. P.).
Hampton's Brigade: Brig. Gen. Wade Hampton. (A sketch of this
officer is given in the story of the fight at Beverly Ford in Part I.)
1st North Carolina, Col. Laurence S. Baker (W. P.). Losses, 85,
including Maj. John H. Whitaker and Capt. W. J. Houston among
the killed.
1st South Carolina. Col. John L. Black led this regiment in the early
part of the campaign, and was wounded. No other commander is
mentioned. Losses, 60.
2d South Carolina. Col. M. C. Butler led the regiment, and by a
severe wound lost a foot. His later career is given in connection with
the Brandy Station affair. Losses, 47, including Lieut. Col. Frank
Hampton, mortally hurt.
Cobb's Georgia Legion. Col. P. M. B. Young, who had from 1857
two or three years of training at West Point, led this regiment a part
of the time. Losses, 54.
Jeff Davis Legion (Miss.). No commander given. Losses, 56.
Phillips's Legion (Ga.). No commander given. Losses, 41.
Robertson's Brigade: Brig. Gen. Beverly H. Robertson (W. P.).
4th North Carolina, Col. Dennis D. Ferebee. Losses, 186.
5th North Carolina, Col. Peter G. Evans. Losses, 131. Col.
Evans was mortally wounded on the way north at Upperville.
Fitz Lee's Brigade: Brig. Gen. Fitzhugh Lee (W. P.).
1st Virginia, Col. James H. Drake, mortally wounded. Losses, 47.
2d Virginia, Col. Thomas T. Munford. Losses, 74. Col. Munford

---

[1] The names of commanding officers, the names of officers slain, and the losses
are for the whole campaign. The cavalry were fighting from June 9th till the last
of July, and the data we give are for that period, and not merely for the dates
July 1–3.

446

rose to be a brigadier general and commander of a cavalry division. Born in Richmond in 1832, he was graduated from the Virginia Military Institute in 1852, and was a planter till the war broke out. After the war until his death, in 1911, he developed large capacity as an iron manufacturer and bridge engineer.

3d Virginia, Col. Thomas H. Owen. Losses, 64.

4th Virginia. Losses, 64. Col. Williams Carter Wickham, of this command, was four times wounded during the war and rose to be brigadier general. He was a graduate of the University of Virginia, a lawyer of rank, and a member of the House of Delegates and of the State Senate. Although he had fought against secession, yet he yielded to the sentiment of the State and went into the war, during which he was chosen to the Confederate Congress. After the war he was a remarkable railroad organizer, and aided to rehabilitate the finances of the Commonwealth, and served in the State Senate. He died in 1888, at the age of sixty-eight.

5th Virginia, Col. Thomas Lafayette Rosser (promoted to be brig. gen. and maj. gen. later in the conflict, and recognized as a singularly skilful cavalry leader). Born in Virginia, he entered West Point in 1856, but when he was about to graduate he resigned and entered the Confederate Army. After the war he became a notable railroad engineer, and was identified with the Northern Pacific and the Canadian Pacific roads in very responsible posts. He was made a brigadier general in the war with Spain. His death occurred at his home in Charlottesville, Va., in 1910.

No full list of the officers of the brigade who were killed is on record; it is known, however, that Maj. John Eells and Lieut. John L. Ragsdale, of the 5th, and Lieuts. Pierre Gibson and John W. Murray, of the 4th, were slain.

Jenkins's Brigade: Brig. Gen. Alfred G. Jenkins (wounded on the second day and followed in command by Col. M. J. Ferguson, 16th Virginia). Gen. Alfred Gallatin Jenkins, born in Virginia, 1830, was educated at the Virginia Military Institute at Washington College, Pennsylvania, and in the course of law at Harvard. He served in Congress 1857–1861, and later was also a member of the Confederate Congress. He made a reputation by his audacious and vigorous raids, in one of which he was defeated by Crook, in West Virginia, May 9, 1864, receiving a wound which cost him first his arm and then his life. There are no reports from him or from any officer in his command, and no statement of losses. His command was thus made up:

14th Virginia.

16th Virginia, Col. M. J. Ferguson.

17th Virginia.

34th Virginia Battalion, Lieut. Col. V. A. Witcher.

36th Virginia Battalion.

Capt. Thomas E. Jackson's Virginia Battery.

GETTYSBURG

Jones's Brigade: Brig. Gen. William E. Jones (W. P.).

6th Virginia, Maj. C. E. Flournoy. Losses, 90, including Lieuts. C. B. Brown, J. T. Mann, and John Allen, killed.

7th Virginia, Lieut. Col. Thomas Marshall. Losses, 90. Lieuts. Walter W. Buck, J. G. Shoup, and Erasmus Rosenberger, killed.

11th Virginia, Col. Lunsford L. Lomax (W. P.); later promoted to brigadier and major general. Losses, 55. Lieut. William M. Hockman killed.

35th Virginia Battalion, Lieut. Col. E. V. White. This organization was detached from the brigade during the campaign to accompany Ewell's corps in its advance toward the Susquehanna, in Pennsylvania. The losses at Fleetwood were 90; no further report is given.

W. H. F. Lee's Brigade: Col. John R. Chambliss, Jr. (W. P.). Brig. Gen. W. H. F. Lee, second son of Robert E. Lee, the regular commander of this brigade, was wounded June 9th, in the fight near Fleetwood, and taken prisoner. He was not exchanged until March, 1864. Meanwhile the command was held by Col. John R. Chambliss, Jr., afterward a brigadier general, a West Point graduate, who was killed in battle August 16, 1864.

2d North Carolina, Col. Solomon Williams (W. P.), killed at Fleetwood, where Lieut. J. G. Blessington was mortally wounded. Lieut. Cole was killed at Upperville. Lieut. Col. W. H. Fitzhugh Payne, 4th Virginia Cavalry, in temporary command of this regiment, was badly wounded and captured at Hanover, June 30th. After his return from captivity he was made brigadier general. After the war he rendered service in the Virginia Legislature. Losses, 60.

9th Virginia, Col. Richard L. T. Beale (1819–1893), trained at Dickinson College, Pennsylvania, a lawyer, in Congress in 1847–1849, in the State Senate 1857, became brigadier general, and commanded this brigade after the death of Chambliss. Losses, 93.

10th Virginia, Col. J. Lucius Davis (W. P.). Losses, 56.

13th Virginia. No commander indicated. Losses, 115.

Stuart's Horse Artillery: Maj. R. F. Beckham (W. P.).

Breathed's Virginia Battery, Capt. James Breathed.

Chew's Virginia Battery, Capt. R. P. Chew.

McGregor's Virginia Battery, Capt. W. M. McGregor.

Moorman's Virginia Battery, Capt. M. M. Moorman.

Griffin's 2d Maryland Battery, or "Baltimore Light Artillery," Capt. W. H. Griffin.

Hart's South Carolina Battery.

The losses for the battalion were 65.

Imboden's Command: Brig. Gen. John D. Imboden. This officer raised and commanded a semi-independent body of mounted rangers chiefly for use in the valley of Virginia. In his brigade there were the following troops:

18th Virginia, Col. George W. Imboden.

ARMY OF NORTHERN VIRGINIA

62d Virginia Mounted Infantry, Col. George H. Smith.
Virginia Partisan Rangers, Capt. John H. McNeill.
Virginia Battery, Capt. J. H. McClanahan.
The losses are not on record. No reports from Gen. Imboden or from any of his officers are in print.

IV

THE SEVERAL STATES AT GETTYSBURG AS REPRESENTED IN THE THREE ARMS OF THE SERVICE

ARMY OF THE POTOMAC

STATE	BATTERIES OF ARTILLERY	CAVALRY REGIMENTS	INFANTRY ORGANIZATIONS
Connecticut [1]	1		5
Delaware			2
Illinois		2	1
Indiana		2	5
Maine	3	1	10
Maryland	1	2	3
Massachusetts [2]	4	1	18
Michigan	1	4	7
Minnesota [2]			1
New Hampshire	1		2
New Jersey	2	1	12
New York	19	7	68
Ohio	4	2	13
Pennsylvania	7	8	68
Rhode Island	5	1	1
Vermont		1	10
West Virginia	1	2	1
Wisconsin			6
United States Regulars	23	4	11

[1] Two batteries of heavy artillery, B and M, on the way, were held at Westminster.
[2] Also a company of sharp-shooters.

ARMY OF NORTHERN VIRGINIA

STATE	BATTERIES OF ARTILLERY	CAVALRY ORGANIZATIONS	INFANTRY ORGANIZATIONS
Alabama	2		17
Arkansas			1
Florida			3
Georgia	5	1	35
Louisiana	7		10
Maryland	3	1	1
Mississippi	1	1	11
North Carolina	4	4	43
South Carolina	5	2	11
Tennessee			3
Texas			3
Virginia	39	15	41

NOTE.—In the Confederate Army a few of the infantry and cavalry organizations were called "battalions," the others "regiments." We have not discriminated in this enumeration between the two terms, for essentially they were the same.

V

ITINERARY OF THE ARMY OF THE POTOMAC FROM THE CROSSING AT EDWARDS FERRY TO GETTYSBURG, JUNE 25 TO JULY 2, 1863

June 25th. The following commands crossed the pontoon bridges at Edwards Ferry and bivouacked at the points indicated: First Corps, Barnesville, Md. Third Corps, between the Ferry and the mouth of the Monocacy. Eleventh Corps, Jefferson, Md. Artillery Reserve, Poolesville, Md. Stahel's Cavalry Division crossed at Young's Island Ford and went into bivouac not far away.

June 26th. The following crossed at Edwards Ferry, and bivouacked as follows: Second Corps, north side of the river, near Edwards Ferry. Fifth Corps, near the mouth of the Monocacy. Twelfth Corps, the mouth of the Monocacy. The forces which had already crossed moved as follows: First Corps, to Jefferson, Md. Third Corps, to Point of Rocks, Md. Eleventh Corps, to Middletown, Md. Artillery Reserve tarried at Poolesville. Stahel's cavalry division marched toward Frederick, Md.

June 27th. Sixth Corps, after crossing at Edwards Ferry, camped at Poolesville. Buford's cavalry division crossed the Ferry and tarried at Jefferson, Md. Gregg's cavalry division, after crossing, headed for Frederick. First Corps, Jefferson to Middletown. Second Corps, to Barnesville. Third Corps, to Middletown. Fifth Corps, to Ballinger's Creek, near Frederick. Eleventh Corps, in bivouac at Middletown. Twelfth Corps, to Knoxville. Artillery Reserve, to Frederick. Stahel's cavalry division reached Frederick. Crawford's Pennsylvania Reserves, from the defenses of Washington, crossed at Edwards Ferry, and halted at the mouth of the Monocacy, en route to Frederick.

June 28th. First Corps, Middletown to Frederick. Second Corps, Barnesville to Monocacy Junction. Third Corps, Middletown to Woodsborough. Sixth Corps, to Hyattstown. Eleventh Corps, to Frederick. Twelfth Corps, to Frederick. Buford's cavalry division, from Jefferson to Middletown. Gregg's cavalry division passed through Frederick and took place at New Market and Ridgeville. Stahel's cavalry division, at Frederick, was assigned to Kilpatrick—two new brigade leaders, Farnsworth and Custer, taking respectively the First and the Second brigades. Crawford's Pennsylvania Reserves arrived at Frederick and joined the Fifth Corps. On this date Hooker was displaced by Meade, whose corps, the Fifth, is now led by Sykes.

June 29th. First and Eleventh, to Emmitsburg. Second, to Uniontown. Third, to Taneytown. Fifth, through Frederick, to Liberty. Sixth, *via* New Market and Ridgeville, to New Windsor. Twelfth, to Taneytown and Bruceville.

Cavalry: Brigades of Devin and Gamble (Buford's division), from Middletown, through Boonsboro', Cavetown, and Monterey Pass, to Fairfield, Pa. Merritt's brigade, same division, Middletown to Mechanicstown. Gregg's division, to New Windsor. Kilpatrick's division, to Littlestown, Pa. Artillery Reserve, from Frederick to Bruceville.

June 30th. First Corps, Emmitsburg to Marsh Run. Third Corps, Taneytown to Bridgeport. Fifth Corps, to Union Mills, Sixth Corps, to Manchester. Twelfth, to Littlestown. Artillery Reserve, to Taneytown.

Cavalry: Buford, with two brigades, Gamble's and Devin's, from Fairfield through Emmitsburg to Gettysburg. Gregg's division, to Manchester and then to Westminster, where the trains were centering. Kilpatrick's division, to Hanover.

On the night of the 30th Lee's army was thus scattered: Stuart, with his three brigades on their raid, was headed north, nearing York, Pa. Longstreet was near Chambersburg, with his First Corps. Ewell, with Rodes's and Early's divisions of his corps, was in bivouac not far from Heidlersburg, Pa., about a dozen miles north of Gettysburg, en route for Cashtown, where Hill's corps was located, while Johnson's division

ITINERARY

(of Ewell's corps) was bivouacked on its way from the Cumberland Valley to Gettysburg, a day's march distant.

July 1st. Buford's cavalry, at Gettysburg, began their skirmishing, to keep the advancing troops of Hill in check, at five in the morning; a little before ten Reynolds arrived from Marsh Creek with Doubleday's division of the First Corps, closely followed by Robinson's and Wadsworth's divisions; at half past ten Howard arrived with his staff, facing the news that Reynolds had been shot and that he, Howard, was now in command of the field; of his Eleventh Corps, Barlow's division and Schurz's were soon in hand, and Steinwehr's men arrived an hour or two later, it being afternoon before any of them could be posted on the northern front of the town.

Late in the afternoon parts of the Third Corps were hurried forward from Emmitsburg, Sickles with portions of his First Division arriving at 7 P.M., Humphreys at midnight, and a brigade early next morning.

The Second Corps arrived after nightfall from Taneytown; the Fifth was near the field at midnight; the Sixth was marching under dreadful pressure in haste from Manchester for Gettysburg; the Twelfth had marched from Littlestown to Two Taverns, five miles from the field, arriving at Gettysburg from the latter point at five or six o'clock in the evening; the Artillery Reserve arrived at Gettysburg; the cavalry was spread out in the rear and on the flanks, Gregg near Manchester and Kilpatrick near Berlin.

Stannard's Vermont brigade, after a long march from Washington, arrived at Gettysburg at nightfall and joined the First Corps.

July 2d. The Second Corps, having bivouacked not far from the field, took its position in line; delayed troops of the Third Corps arrived early in the morning; the Fifth Corps by daylight was nearly all on the field; the Sixth Corps, marching all through the night of July 1st, and until two in the afternoon of July 2d, arrived at various intervals in the afternoon from two o'clock on till four.

Lockwood's brigade from the defenses of Washington arrived and joined the Twelfth Corps.

Gregg, with two brigades of cavalry, and Kilpatrick's entire division, arrived on the field. At 4 P.M. the whole force of Meade was on the field, except the cavalry that guarded the rear.

ADDENDUM

Page 390

[1] Capt. Henry H. Bingham, long a noted Philadelphian (1841–1912), served for three years on staff duty at the headquarters of the Second Corps, rising to be major and judge advocate and brevet brigadier general, and winning the Congressional medal of honor. He was a graduate of Jefferson College, a member of the bar, postmaster and clerk of the courts in his native city, and from 1879 till his death a member of Congress—for the later period the oldest member—the "dean of the House." He was slightly wounded in this battle, and Hancock says "acted with great gallantry."

Page 424

[1] The assistant adjutant general of the Army of Northern Virginia, Col. Walter Herron Taylor, served with Lee in all his battles, either in the foregoing relation or as aide. He was born in Norfolk, Va., in 1838, and still (1913) is a bank president in that city. He was graduated from Virginia Military Institute, and wrote *Four Years with General Lee*, 1877, and also a biography of Lee.

INDEX

A

Alexander, Col. E. P., 32, 35, 148, 230, 251, 293, 300, 320, 381, 430.

Alger, Col. Russell A., 418.

Allen, Col. R. C., 319.

Ames, Brig. Gen. Adelbert, 101, 172, 193, 354, 409.

Amsberg, Col. George von, 75.

Anderson, Brig. Gen. George T., 249, 429.

Anderson, Maj. Gen. R. H., 169, 172, 203, 250, 255, 262, 263, 301, 307, 308, 372, 438.

Archer, Brig. Gen. James J., 183, 185, 442.

Armistead, Brig. Gen. L. A., 8, 303, 305, 317, 325, 326, 427.

Armistead, Gen. Walker Keith, 317.

Armstrong, Capt. Samuel C., 325, 395.

Avery, Col. C. M., 301, 304, 305, 443.

Avery, Col. Isaac T., 273, 274.

Ayres, Brig. Gen. Romeyn B., 69, 172, 402.

B

Baker, Col. L. S., 379.

Barksdale, Brig. Gen. William, 8, 256, 261, 263, 311, 425.

Barlow, Brig. Gen. Francis C., 68, 69, 172, 192, 193, 195, 200, 408.

Barlow, Lieut. John W., 11, 352, 421.

Barnes, Brig. Gen. James, 172, 233, 235, 354, 401.

Bartlett, Brig. Gen. Joseph J., 73, 405.

Battine, Capt. Cecil, 9, 25, 225.

Baxter, Brig. Gen. Henry, 186, 190, 387.

Beardsley, Maj. William E., 168n.

Beaver, Gen. James A., 43, 391.

Beck, Brig. Gen. Romeyn, 354.

Beckham, Maj. R. F., 87, 100, 103, 382, 448.

Benham, Brig. Gen. Henry W., 352, 384.

Benjamin, Sec. Judah P., 17.

Benning, Brig. Gen. Henry L., 249, 430.

Berdan, Col. Hiram, 222.

Beveridge, Maj. John L., 165n, 414, 415.

Biddle, Col. Chapman, 56, 57, 185, 190, 388.

Bigelow, Capt. John, 260, 261.

Bingham, Capt. Henry H., 454.

Birney, Maj. Gen. David B., 48, 172, 223, 254, 312, 396.

Brewster, Col. William R., 74, 399.

Brockenbrough, Col. J. M., 187, 304, 305, 441.

Brockway, Lieut. Charles B., 275.

Brooke, Col. John R., 11, 58, 59, 392.

Brown, Lieut. Col. H. A., 281.

Brown, Col. J. Thompson, 172, 438.

Brunson, Capt. E. B., 446.

INDEX

INDEX

INDEX

INDEX

THE END